This volume is one of a series on Japanese society published by the University of California Press under a special arrangement with the Social Science Research Council. Each volume is based upon a conference attended by Japanese and foreign scholars; the purpose of each conference was to increase scholarly knowledge of Japanese society by enabling Japanese and foreign scholars to collaborate and to criticize each other's work. The conferences were sponsored by the Joint Committee on Japanese Studies of the American Council of Learned Societies and the Social Science Research Council, with funds provided by the Ford Foundation.

MODERN JAPANESE ORGANIZATION AND DECISION-MAKING

Sponsored by
the Social Science Research Council.

MODERN JAPANESE ORGANIZATION AND DECISION-MAKING

Edited by

Ezra F. Vogel

UNIVERSITY OF CALIFORNIA PRESS

Berkeley • *Los Angeles* • *London*

University of California Press
Berkeley and Los Angeles, California

University of California Press, Ltd.
London, England

Copyright © 1975, by
The Regents of the University of California

ISBN 0-520-02857-0
Library of Congress Catalog Card Number: 74-16721
Printed in the United States of America

Contents

III. CULTURAL AND EDUCATIONAL ORGANIZATION

Acknowledgments

These conference proceedings are a product of Japanese-American scholarly cooperation. The initial impetus for the conference came from the Joint Committee on Japanese Studies (JCJS) of the American Council of Learned Societies and the Social Science Research Council; funds were provided by the Ford Foundation. The organizers of two other JCJS conferences in this series—Professors Hugh Patrick of Yale and Albert Craig of Harvard—were generous in their suggestions for this conference, which was held on Maui, Hawaii, January 5–10, 1973. Professors Edwin O. Reischauer of Harvard, Robert E. Ward of Stanford, and John W. Hall of Yale also offered wise counsel at critical stages in the planning. John Creighton Campbell participated in the conference not only as a contributor but as the staff representative of the Social Science Research Council. He performed superbly in this role, and I am very grateful to him. Anna Laura Strow Rosow handled the mass of administrative details in Cambridge; Rick Dyck both translated some of the papers from Japanese into English and served as rapporteur at the conference. Susan Biele Alitto did a superb job in assisting me to edit the papers.

In Japan, Professor Kazuo Noda, a sociologist, a professor of business administration at Rikkyo University, and the director of the Japan Research Institute, accepted the burdens of planning and administration. Professor Noda nominated the Japanese participants, and the Institute served as their administrative office and translation center. The Institute not only contributed staff; it also furnished funds for the simultaneous translation that was provided at the conference.

I am particularly grateful to the contributors for their papers and for their graceful response to my harassments. All of us profited from the discussants at the conference as well as from the contributions of participants whose papers could not be included in the present volume.

E. F. V.

Contributors

ALBERT M. CRAIG is Professor of History at Harvard University where he is also the Associate Director of the Japan Institute and the Chairman of the Committee on the Ph.D. in History and East Asian Languages. He is the author of *Choshu in the Meiji Restoration*, co-author with John K. Fairbank and Edwin O. Reischauer of *East Asia: Tradition and Transformation*, and co-editor with Donald Shively of *Personality in Japanese History*.

GERALD L. CURTIS is Associate Professor of Political Science and Director of the East Asian Institute, Columbia University. He is the author of *Election Campaigning Japanese Style* and editor of *Japanese-American Relations in the Seventies*.

JOHN CREIGHTON CAMPBELL is Assistant Professor of Political Science at the University of Michigan and author of the forthcoming volume, *Contemporary Japanese Budget Politics*. An earlier version of his article in this volume received the first John M. H. Lindbeck Prize of the East Asian Institute, Columbia University.

GEORGE A. DE VOS is a psychologist and an anthropologist who is currently Professor of Anthropology at the University of California, Berkeley. His publications include *Socialization for Achievement* and, with Hiroshi Wagatsuma, *Japan's Invisible Race* and the forthcoming two-volume publication *Heritage of Endurance*.

PETER F. DRUCKER is Clarke Professor of Social Science at Claremont Graduate School, California, and Distinguished University Lecturer at the Graduate Business School, New York University. He is the author of *The Age of Discontinuity* and other works on international business. His latest publication is *Management: Tasks; Responsibilities; Practices*.

IVAN P. HALL currently resides in Japan where he is a consultant for the Harvard-Yenching Institute and the Harvard Council on East Asian Studies. His publications include the biography *Mori Arinori*.

KAZUO NODA is Professor at Rikkyo University and Director of the Japan Research Institute in Tokyo. He is the author of *Nihon no jūyaku* and other works on Japanese business.

YOSHIHISA OJIMI is a former administrative vice-minister of the Japanese Ministry of International Trade and Industry.

HERBERT PASSIN is affiliated with the East Asian Institute and Chairman of the Department of Sociology at Columbia University. His publications include *Society and Education in Japan, The United States and Japan* (ed.) *In Search of Identity* (with John W. Bennett).

HUGH PATRICK is Professor of Far Eastern Economics and Chairman of the Council on East Asian Studies, Yale University. His publications include *Monetary Policy and Central Banking in Contemporary Japan.*

THOMAS P. ROHLEN is Assistant Professor of Anthropology at Cowell College, the University of California, Santa Cruz. He is the author of *For Harmony and Strength: Japanese White Collar Organization in Anthropological Perspective.*

TAISHIRO SHIRAI, Professor of Industrial Relations in the Faculty of Business Administration, Hosei University, is also a public member of the Central Labor Relations Commission in Japan. His publications include *Rōdō kumiai no zaisei, Rōdō kumiai kanbu ron,* and *Kigyo betsu kumiai.*

NATHANIEL B. THAYER is Associate Professor and Director of Asian Studies at the School of Advanced International Studies, Johns Hopkins University. He is the author of *How the Conservatives Rule Japan.*

EZRA F. VOGEL is Director of the East Asian Research Center and Professor of Sociology at Harvard University. His publications include *Japan's New Middle Class.*

M. Y. YOSHINO, currently on leave from the University of California, Los Angeles, is Visiting Professor at the Graduate School of Business Administration, Harvard University. His publications include *Japan's Managerial System: Tradition and Innovation, The Japanese Marketing System: Adaptation and Innovation,* and the forthcoming volume *Multinational Spread of Japanese Enterprises: Strategy and Structure.*

Frequently Used Abbreviations

LDP   Liberal Democratic Party
DSP   Democratic Socialist Party
JCP   Japanese Communist Party
JSP   Japanese Socialist Party
MITI   Ministry of International Trade and Industry
MOF   Ministry of Finance

Editor's Note: The Japanese terminology has been standardized according to Kenkyusha, but there is variation in the text on diacritical marks following each author's individual usage. The selection by Yoshihisa Ojimi is based on an oral presentation and some of the ensuing discussion, as adapted by the editor. The selection by Peter Drucker includes a comment by Hugh Patrick.

Introduction:
Toward More Accurate Concepts

EZRA F. VOGEL

Progress in an academic field may be viewed as a series of successively closer approximations to reality. Since World War II a number of compelling concepts have advanced our understanding of Japanese society, but as scholarship progresses these have been modified and the scope of their applicability more precisely delimited. For example, shortly after World War II the concepts of *giri* (duty) and *ninjō* (human feeling) called attention to a fundamental conflict in Japanese attitudes, and *oyabun-kobun* (parent status-child status) was a key concept for understanding many economic and social relationships outside the family. Later, as the concepts were modified and the scope of their applicability more clearly specified, new concepts were introduced to explain other aspects of Japanese society.

The papers selected for this volume include analyses of political, economic, cultural, and educational organizations. The conference for which these papers were written was designed to present an overview of modern Japanese organization and decision-making but, in passing, the papers and the ensuing discussion had to come to terms with a number of concepts which currently dominate Western work on Japanese organization. In this process, some of these concepts were criticized and modified whereas others were reinforced, extended, or applied to additional phenomena. Since Japan has been changing so rapidly, one might legitimately raise the issue as to whether our effort to refine our understanding of Japan merely reflects a changing Japan rather than a change of our understanding. This essay endeavors to call attention to what many scholars at our conference considered a refinement in our understanding, but before trying to describe these more accurate statements of enduring characteristics of modern Japanese organization, one must first consider which qualities are related to the particular stages of development since World War II.

CHANGES IN ORGANIZATION AND ORGANIZATIONAL CLIMATE

Although the Japanese economy has grown almost continuously since the Meiji Restoration, the growth rate since World War II has been unusually rapid. In the first quarter century after World War II, Japanese companies modernized their physical plant and basically closed the technological gap with advanced Western countries. This process involved the purchase of foreign technology, heavy investment in new facilities, rapid increases in productivity, and the transformation of almost one-half of Japan's population from agricultural to industrial and service occupations. In the course of this very rapid modernization, plants that were able to modernize and compete in international trade were sometimes spectacularly successful, whereas many companies that were unable to modernize or keep pace with the rate of change went bankrupt. During this period there was an extraordinarily high rate of saving and reinvestment and extensive bank loans to finance the growth. Wages, welfare, and public services tended to lag slightly behind economic development, but since the mid-1950s, after the economy had fully recovered from World War II, improvements in wages and living standards have virtually kept pace with economic growth.

In the early postwar period there was a considerable surplus of labor and enormous competition for the openings in the better educational institutions and the more successful companies. By the late 1960s, there was a considerable shortage of labor, especially of young workers, since most organizations preferred to recruit young employees, pay them low salaries, and train them within the company. Business strategies were geared to modernization, rapid expansion of facilities, and rapid growth. The ministries' policies were designed to build up a modern industrial capacity to compete in world markets, while ensuring an adequate supply of raw materials.

Japanese companies are still geared to rapid growth, but by the late 1960s they were moving from labor-intensive industries, where their competitive advantage had been low wages, into high technology fields, where their competitive advantage was a combination of technical superiority, efficient management, and motivated workers at wages still below other highly developed countries. With the closing of the technological gap between Japan and other advanced countries and the rising cost of borrowing technology, the Japanese government and Japanese firms began to invest heavily in research and development.

After World War II, the government bureaucracy lost some of its coercive powers and the aura of the imperial way, but it maintained its power in guiding the country and gave top priority to economic development. In the early years after World War II the Ministry of International Trade and Industry (MITI), which played the critical role in industrial development, maintained considerable leverage in getting companies to accept "administrative guidance" because of its capacity to make decisions about foreign exchange. Although MITI and the banks lost some leverage as companies accumulated their own capital and foreign exchange, the governmental bureaucracy found new ways to maintain its leverage. MITI, for example, is likely to maintain its leverage for administrative guidance by its capacity to decide whether companies meet acceptable standards of pollution control and consumer protection. In the future, new regulations concerning incentives for relocating industry, strongly supported by MITI, are likely to provide new bases for ensuring that companies remain responsive to MITI guidance. Currency controls and flexible tax incentives have also enabled the Ministry of Finance to maintain considerable leverage over the economic life of the country.

Although there have been many political disagreements in this postwar period and many conflicts between companies and between the companies and the government, there had been a fundamental national consensus about the importance of economic growth and of Japan achieving a favorable position in international trade. With this high sense of purposiveness various bureaucratic and business leaders had been willing to sacrifice for national goals. Now, in the 1970s, there is increased recognition that other goals, connected with social welfare and the quality of life, are also important. As a result, there is no longer such a clear purposiveness, such a high level of consensus about the desirable goal, nor such willingness to sacrifice for economic goals.

MODIFICATIONS OF PREVIOUS CONCEPTS

A number of concepts currently used to describe various features of Japanese organization have taken on exaggerated importance in Western scholarly literature. In part, the exaggeration occurs because observations at a particular time and place have been assumed to be general characteristics over a long period with applicability to a wide range of phenomena. In part it occurs because certain Japanese expressions are assumed to represent unique practices, which, upon closer examination, are not very different from practices in the United States or other Western countries. In part it occurs because Americans have dominated most Western analyses of Japan, and what is really unique may not be Japanese patterns but American patterns. Among the concepts currently popular in the Western literature on Japanese organization that need to be modified are the following:

1. *Japan, Incorporated.*—The notion that Japanese government and business work so closely together that Japan resembles one large corporation is a conception used differently by different authors. Sometimes it describes big-business domination of the government decision-making process. Sometimes it describes business docility in the face of government direction. Sometimes it describes collusion between the two. Recently, in some circles competitive with Japanese business, the concept has taken on pernicious overtones, implying that close cooperation between government and business is illicit.

There is no question that, in general, there is a closer working relationship between government and business in Japan than in the United States. Compared to their American counterparts, the major ministries supervising economic activities are more concerned with improving Japanese economic capacities to compete in international markets and less concerned with regulating business and preventing unfair monopolistic practices. The Bank of Japan, for example, stands firmly behind the city banks, which in turn lend money to the largest Japanese corporations, and it is ready to exert itself to prevent these companies from going bankrupt.

But, as Gerald Curtis points out in his article, the notion that Japan behaves like one large corporation vastly exaggerates the contact between governmental and business leaders and the identity of purpose between the Japanese government and specific companies. It understates the tension between certain companies and various branches of the government, especially when government decisions are not in keeping with their companies' interests. It incorrectly implies that the government only makes decisions that are in the interest of big business. In fact, to remain in power, the Liberal Democratic Party (LDP) has to respond to a variety of demands: rice price supports, pollution control, improved social security, and trade and capital liberalization.

Compared with their American counterparts, Japanese businessmen meet more frequently to discuss problems of economic policy for the nation as a whole as well as specific programs and policies which would potentially benefit businesses of a particular kind. They are thus in a much better position to aggregate their interests and represent them to the Japanese government than are comparable American businesses.

Nonetheless, as Curtis points out, it is hard to identify any tight organization of *zaikai* (literally, financial circles, but generally referring to the business community's central leadership). To the extent that there has been effective coordination in the business community representing business interests as a whole, it has been led by a number of senior citizens in these financial circles. Just as the Meiji *genrō*, the senior political leaders, began to lose their power and influence as they aged and political authority became diffused, so the *zaikai genrō,* the senior leaders of the financial community, are currently aging, and their authority has already been diffused. This gradual dissipation of the senior economic leaders' power accelerated during the tenure of Premier Sato, when the political leaders chose to confer on economic matters not only with a small number of senior representatives of the so-called *zaikai,* but with large numbers of business leaders whose interests were not identical with those of the *zaikai genrō.* In short, no small circle of business leaders can now effectively speak for the business community as a whole, and as the public consensus on the priority of economic growth breaks down, the LDP will increasingly find it necessary to compromise big-business interests to stay in power.

2. *Ringi Sei.*[1] *Ringi Sei*—the system whereby documents are drafted at lower levels of an organization and then circulated to various units for approval—is sometimes described as the unique Japanese process of decision-making. *Ringi sei* is sometimes interpreted to mean that the real power of decision rests at lower levels or that decision-making is a slow, clumsy process in which no one has clear authority. The practice of *ringi sei* is widespread in Japanese companies and government offices, but the concept has been overinterpreted and misinterpreted in the Western literature.

For one thing, as Yoshihisa Ojimi points out, this concept understates the authority and initiative of leaders in an organization. Especially among organizations with an able and forthright leadership, not only do initiatives come from the leaders, but they exert close supervision over the drafting of documents at lower levels. Even where leadership is less vigorous and consultation between levels less frequent, section members drafting a memorandum are aware of the purposes of the organization and the wishes of their superiors, and they draft documents within this context. To be sure, leaders uncertain of their own authority are influenced by the convictions of people at lower levels in the organization; but more commonly, those at the lower levels of the organization are given leeway to draft documents only when they have the confidence of their superiors. They are acting within the bounds of explicit or implicit trust placed in them by their superiors.

Some leaders are concerned about the potential erosion of their authority and make an effort to prevent the drafting of documents unless they have given explicit approval. The *ringi* system is often an *ato ringi* system, in which the leaders make the major decisions and then encourage lower levels to draft documents in line with the decision. Of course, as Yoshino points out, the *ringi sei* rests on homogeneity and consensus, and when there is widespread consensus at all levels of an organization,

---

[1] Some of the ideas in this section were presented by Bernard Silberman in a paper that was given at the conference but which is not included in this volume.

documents can be drafted without explicit approval. But if disagreements arise at the lower levels in the course of drafting a document, they are generally taken to higher levels to be resolved.

It should also be noted that the *ringi* system is not used for all kinds of issues, but only those which are relatively complex and require a high level of coordination. Some sensitive issues, like personnel issues, are not handled by the *ringi* system at all. General questions of strategy are more likely to be discussed in meetings, and documents may be drafted only when specific measures are required.

To some extent *ringi* is a system for preserving the right to consultation of various sections of an organization. Some sections may put their stamp on documents without closely examining them, but the system is not necessarily one without responsibility. Rather a section's approval of a document generally means that either the document is not so important or it does not infringe on the section's sphere. As such, *ringi sei* is often not qualitatively different from the clearance system in the U.S. government. Thus it is characteristic of a more mature bureaucratic organization rather than of a young, dynamic organization with a strong leader. In short, *ringi* is not as unique as sometimes argued nor an indication that leaders of Japanese organizations are lacking in authority and initiative.

3. Seniority and Permanent Employment Systems.—In large businesses and government bureaucracies, there is an expectation that a regular employee will remain with the organization until he retires and that his salary and title will continue to improve with length of service. It is also extremely rare for a regular employee to serve under a younger employee in the same general line of work. However, the concepts of "permanent employment" and "seniority system" have sometimes been used indiscriminately by Westerners to explain too much.

For one thing, permanent employment and the seniority system apply only to a minority of workers in Japan. They do not apply to farmers or to those employed in small commercial or industrial establishments. Nor do these concepts apply to the large groups of so-called temporary workers who are paid regular wages but are not given the same kind of assurance about permanent employment or the same rate of promotion as regular employees. For example, most young women in an organization are not permanent and are expected to retire when they marry or become pregnant with their first child. Most housewives who come back to work after children are in school are classified as temporary employees even if they remain within the same organization for many years. Other workers in large organizations such as salesmen, special technicians, or unskilled workers are also not necessarily treated as regular permanent employees under the seniority system.

The attention given to permanent employment and the seniority system also understates the degree of mobility from one firm to another. The number of small firms that go bankrupt has remained very high, and even in large firms it is no longer rare for an employee to move from one company to another company that is not directly competitive. It is also common for an employee to move from one company to another that is in some way related to the first. Thus, within a major company, a person may move from one "child company" to another, or from a "parent company" to a newly established "child company."

The concepts of permanent employment and seniority have sometimes been explained as traditional holdovers out of line with economic rationality. It has been argued that the firm, unable to discharge an employee until retirement, must retain and pay higher wages to an older employee who is no longer useful. Several qualifications need to be made. First, since retirement in most companies takes place by age fifty or fifty-five, the so-called lifetime employment is really only employment for about thirty years. A person past fifty may obtain work in an affiliate of his original company, but it is not guaranteed if he is not needed, and in any case, his salary may be lower. Second, the system of increasing salary with seniority tends to be concentrated in those areas where skill and usefulness to a company are related to length of experience. Third, a company which provides high wages to senior employees also can pay less for junior employees who can look forward to seniority. Finally, even when there is not a direct relation between increased salary and increased usefulness to the company, the high level of employee commitment with this system may be beneficial to the company as a whole. The combination of early retirement, the frequent use of temporary workers, and the use of subcontracting firms where employment is not guaranteed all reduce the financial risks that a company with seniority and permanent employment policies would experience at a time of recession.

Although salary and title increase with age, the task which a person actually performs in a company is not necessarily related to salary and title, and is determined more by a person's actual skills. As Kazuo Noda points out, a subordinate may in fact be given great responsibility in accordance with his abilities, regardless of his salary and title.

The system of permanent employment and seniority results not from traditional Japanese practices, but from a combination of labor-market conditions, management decisions, and pressures from labor unions. After World War I, because of the shortage of skilled labor, many Japanese companies undertook to provide specialized training and to set up a system to ensure that the best-trained workers would remain with their company over a long period. The same was true for many companies after World War II. The pressure from labor unions was in the same direction because, in the period immediately after World War II, when good employment was difficult to find, unions fought for a system that provided job security.

4. *Growth Without Profit.*—A number of Western analysts, observing Japanese corporate behavior in the 1950s and 1960s, concluded that

corporations were interested not in profit but in growth. In fact, very rapid modernization and expansion in the fifties and sixties was necessary for companies to achieve economies of scale and to remain competitive on international markets. As Hugh Patrick points out, the illusion of disinterest in profit ignores a number of considerations. For one thing, the extraordinary interest in growth and modernization is characteristic of a specific period. Second, Japanese companies generally have a longer time perspective than American companies. Some American executives feel pressure to keep a high rate of return during a particular term of office. In contrast, the Japanese company is interested in longer term growth and profit. Third, the cultural value system makes it difficult for Japanese businessmen to acknowledge publicly their interest in profit. Unlike the American business ethic, which sees a harmony between the individual pursuit of profit and the general betterment of society, the more common Japanese ethical code views the individual pursuit of profit as inconsistent with societal benefit. Japanese business executives, while concerned with profit, are less likely to make such declarations in public.

5. School Cliques.—Many observers of Japan have stressed the importance of alumni cliques both within an organization and between organizations. It is true that many senior leaders in the Japanese bureaucracy are graduates of Tokyo University and that some leading business and government leaders knew each other in high school or college. However, the importance of such ties has often been overestimated, and therefore needs qualification.

People within a given organization, and especially within business organizations, are unlikely to form friendships primarily on the basis of school ties. Having attended a good school is an advantage in entering a given company. However, as Thomas Rohlen says, once a person enters a company or a ministry, he forms close associations more on the basis of daily work relationships than on the basis of old school ties.

Even when people within a given company go through school friends to contact people in the government or in other businesses, they are doing so to better represent the interests of their organization. It would be highly unusual to advocate policies inimical to one's unit because of friends in other organizations. In short, old school and personal relationships can help cement ties when consistent with organizational objectives.

CONCEPTS REINFORCED AND EXTENDED

1. Groupism.—Western and Japanese observers have long noted the identification of a Japanese with his organization, and especially his work organization. A Japanese employee is more likely to identify with the organization where he works than with a professional or occupational specialty. In an earlier period, Western sociologists like Weber, Durkheim, and Parsons described professional and occupational groupings as the major source of group belongingness for industrial societies. The rapid pace of social change in postindustrial societies, however, has meant that a definition of an occupational specialty appropriate at one time is not necessarily appropriate for a later period. Therefore, one can argue that the Japanese identification with company is perhaps better suited to rapid social change than the occupational identification. With the assurance that an employee is likely to remain in its employ, a company can safely invest in retraining for up-to-date skills, and a declining occupational specialty does not need to protect itself with a feather-bedding strike.

Although many observers have already called attention to the importance of this kind of group identification in Japan, several considerations, sometimes neglected, should be added. For one thing, it is important to recognize the conscious management effort to maintain a sense of belonging within an organization. An example Rohlen points out is the companies' efforts to "capture" the recreational groups as affluence enables more company employees to engage in individual or family recreational activities. The companies themselves set up various kinds of activity and sport groups for their employees, often along the lines of college activity groups. They also consciously use such events as vacation trips, celebrations of employees' birthdays, entering and leaving the company, and year-end parties as ritual occasions to reinforce the solidarity of the group. Furthermore, as Noda has shown, in composing sections in a company or government bureau, an effort is made by the leaders to form a team that can work well together.

Second, the phenomenon of groupism applies not only to family and work units, but to political factions and to a large range of secondary groups that develop a much higher degree of solidarity than comparable groups in the United States. Thus, for example, the solidarity among people who entered the company or ministry in the same year or who work in the same section is much higher than in the United States. New ad hoc groups formed for specific purposes across organizational lines also have mechanisms for achieving solidarity very rapidly. Whether by recreation or drinking, or some other kind of ceremonial activity, they quickly develop a climate facilitating close interaction. A wide range of study groups, tour groups, special task forces, and other ad hoc groups mediate among different organizations.

Third, however, the group orientation should not be interpreted to mean that there are not tremendous rivalries and considerable room for politics and manipulation within an organization over questions relating to basic issues of policy and personnel. Indeed, it is partly a reflection of the deep involvement of individuals in the organization that these rivalries are so intense. This is in striking contrast to more anomic organizations where these issues can be handled with more detachment or impersonality.

One special case of groupism, which has received relatively little attention heretofore and which basically affects public understanding of public affairs, is the press club described by Nathaniel Thayer. A reporter, while loyal to his own newspaper company, also develops strong ties with those in the same press club—a club composed of reporters from all newspapers who cover the same ministry or branch of government. This solidarity is sufficiently strong that the prevailing club view leads to virtual unanimity of articles concerning that ministry. Although the phenomenon of an individual bound by the consensus in his group is prominent in all organizations, the press club situation may adversely affect expression of contrary opinions when a consensus is not in accord with the facts or the best interests of the public.

2. *Long-Range Goal Orientation.*—Japanese groups are very task oriented, and the solidarity of groups in economic and political organizations is related to the goals of their groups. The definition of a task by the group is generally long term, and group members are generally willing to subordinate short-term interests, whether personal or organizational, to long-range goals. At the psychological level, George De Vos shows how individuals are willing to endure long periods of adversity, including hard work at low wages, in order to achieve greater success in the long run. De Vos points to the optimism about what can be accomplished in the long run as intrinsic to the individual's capacity to endure.

As Peter Drucker points out, the long-range goal orientation of an organization is much more important than tradition. Although the change after World War II has been unusually rapid, the general capacity to work for a distant goal was characteristic of Japan before the war as well.

Because the integration of institutions depends less on rules and regulations and more on solid unity on long-range goals, there is considerable flexibility in devising means for implementing these goals. As Robert Ward pointed out in the discussion at the conference, for example, there is so much flexibility within the bureaucracy that officials in one ministry can be assigned tasks in another as needed.

To be sure, long-range plans are sometimes vague and often altered as a result of changes in mood. Yet what appears as excessive fluctuation or uncertainty may simply be a particular stage, which is seen by executives in a longer time perspective. Often executives are willing to undergo a very lengthy period of study, experimentation, ferment, and discussion before taking action. However, when the desirable course of action for the long run becomes clear, an organization has great capacity to mobilize its members toward the achievement of the organization's basic goals.

3. *Nemawashi*—(literally, "binding the roots of a plant before pulling it out," used to refer to the practice of broad consultation before taking action). What is perhaps more characteristic of Japanese organization than the *ringi* system is the frequency of consultation. There is almost continuous consultation among peers in an organization and between levels and between units. The consultation varies from mundane detail to broad general issues, and usually it takes place in a climate of great

mutual confidence and support. As a result, a great deal of time may often pass before a decision is arrived at. Usually the executives in an organization are reluctant to move until a consensus is reached, but if the issues are sharply drawn and the executives must make a choice, they try to gain widespread support before making these decisions. When a consensus is finally reached, there is a high degree of support among members of an organization for the decision and greater willingness to implement it.

Some Japanese executives have expressed surprise and amazement at the brilliant analytical discussions of possible options carried on at small group meetings of high-level American company management, and by the rational, analytic way in which American executives choose from several possible options at such a meeting. In contrast, the Japanese firm is inclined to talk an issue out among large numbers of people, thereby creating a much greater organizational involvement and commitment before a decision is made.

In general, the Japanese organization is less bound by legalistic interpretations or precise statements of rights, duties, and offices. There tends to be much more flexibility, depending on the current prevailing mood, and in general there are no legalistic rules or regulations which inhibit action once there is a consensus that a certain action is desirable.

4. *Fair Share.*—Group competition is intense at all levels in Japan, but within a clearly defined sphere, groups, in effect, constitute an informal league, with clearly defined rules about what is "fair play." When conflicts between the groups have to be resolved at higher levels, there is a strong notion that each group is entitled to its "fair share."

In many fields, there are myriads of rapidly changing companies, but among large companies competing in a given market, there is usually a finite league of competitors. Although they compete fiercely for an increase in market share, large competitors do not expect to drive each other into bankruptcy. There is recognition of the principle of equitable treatment when a government ministry like MITI has to rule on matters which affect the livelihood of companies in a given market. If one company is disadvantaged by a decision at one time, it is taken for granted that the ministry should make an effort to give assistance to that company at a later time.

John Campbell, in his study of the Japanese budget, illustrates the importance of the concept of "fair share" in allocations. In contrast to the U.S. Budget Bureau, which tries to reach rational overall decisions that affect the overall budget, the Japanese budget is generally based largely on the needs of the ministries. Ministry of Finance officials who oversee the budgeting process view themselves as expert mediators rather than as creators of national priorities. Thus there tends to be less drastic change in the portion of the national budget allocated to different fields than in the United States. Although ministries exert themselves to find worthy projects to increase their share of the national budget, in fact, the allocation to a ministry does not change greatly from year to year, and each ministry must then make the tough decision of how to allocate the share it receives to its various programs.

Similarly, the concept of fair share applies to expenses for different regions of the country, and the Local Autonomy Ministry attempts to redistribute funds to the various prefectures on the basis of need. There is also an effort to expend funds in the backward areas, thus reducing imbalances from one part of the country to another.

Within the LDP, the concept of fair share is also very strong among the factions. It is a major factor, for example, not only for allocating party funds, but for determining cabinet appointments. In short, when a league of competitors has been defined, there are certain informal rules that regulate the behavior of the various competitors.

5. *Bureaucratic Elitism.*—As Edwin Reischauer pointed out at the conference, unlike the United States but more like the European pattern, members of government ministries in Japan enjoy enormously high status. Admission to the ministries is intensely competitive and based largely on objective examinations. Ministries are thereby able to recruit extraordinarily talented young men committed to lifetime careers. Upper-level officials in a ministry, therefore, have tremendous dedication to their ministry. Despite criticism of the bureaucracy after World War II, as the bureaucracy lost some of the aura of serving the emperor, and the source for recruitment greatly expanded with the extension of higher education, bureaucrats nonetheless maintain widespread respect from the public.

Because the bureaucracy has talented people, who do careful staff work on a variety of problems, politicians and even business companies must rely on their judgments. When the steel companies expanded against the advice of MITI officials and it later turned out that the expansion was clearly unwise, some MITI officials were pleased that the companies had learned their lesson, that the rare experience of not following administrative guidance on an important issue had proved unwise.

Although Keidanren (Federation of Economic Organizations), the LDP, and some other business and political organizations have small research staffs, they do not compare in size and scope to the research staffs of the ministries, and they must rely upon the ministries for detailed work on any question. It is not surprising, therefore, that a very high proportion of the bills considered in the Diet orginate not with individual Diet members, but come from the ministries through the cabinet.

As Reischauer pointed out at the conference, because the bureaucrats are so unambiguously in elite positions, they have the confidence to express themselves much more forthrightly. The various ministries are, to a large extent, self-contained under the direction of the senior vice-minister. Outside political leaders, even including those who are appointed ministers, never have the degree of political leverage inside the ministries that American cabinet officers are expected to have over their departments. The American cabinet officer may bring to his department a number of his own aides and initiate a number of new policies in the hope of gaining the major role in directing the affairs of the department. His counterpart, the Japanese minister, does not expect to have the same degree of control over a ministry and must work through the vice-minister. Just as a high-level bureaucrat who has come up from the ranks of a ministry invariably directs the ministry as administrative vice-minister, so in the Foreign Ministry, no outside political appointees are made ambassador. Therefore, senior officers in the foreign service have more confidence about the probability of moving into senior ambassador positions than their American counterparts.

The high quality and integrity of the bureaucrat, the respect of the Japanese public, and the relatively self-contained nature of a ministry enables bureaucrats to be relatively free from political pressure and to work for what they consider the good of the country. As a result, the Japanese government has enjoyed high-quality leadership with considerable continuity and long-term perspective regardless of the rapid changes in political leaders.

6. *Cores of Business Leadership.*—Although leaders are bounded by the consensus within their organization, the leaders of most business firms, as in ministries, have worked together for many years and can make bold decisions considered in the long-range interest of the company. This core of executives in a given firm has been able to chart well-considered long-range policies for the firm. Japanese executives have shown an extraordinary willingness to send representatives all over the world to get ideas for major and minor improvements. With a high degree of organizational solidarity, they can guide issues through long periods of *nemawashi*, arrive at decisions in their interest, and mobilize personnel to achieve these goals. Buoyed by rapid growth rates and optimism about Japan's future, backed by the banks and in turn by the government, the leaders of the largest firms in Japan have been willing to stake out initiatives as bold and ambitious as any in the world.

PART ONE

Political Organization

Functional and Dysfunctional Aspects of Government Bureaucracy

ALBERT M. CRAIG

There is no language in the world in which the word "bureaucrat" means something good. In Japanese the word *kanryō* has exceedingly unpleasant overtones. It suggests pettiness, self-importance, narrowness, and formalism—attributes, in the Confucian phrase, of a "small man." Japanese historians tend to view the modern Japanese bureaucrat as the willing tool of all of the villains of history from the absolutist leaders of the early Meiji to the undemocratic party leaders of the Taisho, the militarists of the thirties, and the conservative party politicians of today. In the historical literature perhaps the only figure that rivals the bureaucrat as a subject of opprobrium is the "parasitic landlord." Some critics even suggest that the bureaucracy has dominated policy formation, bringing to heel the elected political leaders who are nominally in charge of policy.

One may object that both "bureaucrat" (*kanryō*) and "official" (*yakunin*) are pejorative terms. *Kanri*, which also may be rendered as "official," sounds much better. It has a dignified ring; it suggests capability, steadfastness of purpose, and trustworthiness. It was the term used in the Meiji constitution to speak of "the officials of the emperor." But it is not the term that enters the mind of the average Japanese when he thinks of Japanese officialdom.

Even more critical of bureaucracy than the writings of postwar historians is a second large literature written by ex-bureaucrats and newspaper reporters to expose the foibles, failings, formalism, and frustrations of bureaucratic life in Japan. This genre of books elucidates what is wrong with Japanese bureaucracy. It gives firsthand illustrations of the dysfunctions that can be found in government administration. If Japanese bureaucracy did not work, this literature would tell why.[1]

During the past few years I have been studying early Meiji government and bureaucracy. In connection with this study, hoping in some measure to triangulate back from the present, I have read most of this exposé literature, and I have also spent several months visiting Japanese government offices—at the local, prefectural, and national levels—and talking with government officials. This paper is an attempt to reconcile what I have read with what I have seen and heard.

I would stress in advance that I am not out to whitewash Japanese bureaucracy. It does have dysfunctions. Japanese officials all agree that they exist. There is some truth in the claim by Japanese scholars that Westerners, seeking to explain Japan's "economic miracle," sometimes adopt an overly rosy view of the Japanese ability to cooperate and work harmoniously for commonly held goals. Even so, in comparison with most bureaucracies in the world, Japanese bureaucracy does get things done. The question must be posed: given its dysfunctions, why does it work as well as it does?

AN ELITE BUREAUCRACY

Weber argued for the legal character of bureaucracy. His characterization fits Japan rather well. Whether in the Ministry of Labor or the Ministry of Finance, the top career bureaucrats tend to be law school graduates. Their life as officials is governed by regulations and ordinances, which they observe and obey. Their work consists of drafting laws, planning the projects that will be embodied in bills, and enforcing laws already passed.

But many other matters also affect how bureaucracy functions. One is the prestige that the official enjoys in his society and the way it helps or hinders recruitment. In the Tokugawa era (1600–1868) officials were ranking samurai, the elite within the military aristocracy. After the Restoration, government officials were, perhaps more than the army, the legitimate heirs of the samurai. For a time after the Restoration even local post-office officials wore swords. In 1876 one government leader wrote: "Carefully observing today's situation, the peasants, the merchants, the samurai, all under heaven are dissatisfied . . . only officials are pleased with their lot." [2] There was ample reason for their satisfaction: they were

---

[1] The best scholarly work on Japanese bureaucracy is Tsuji Kiyoaki, *Nihon kanryōsei no kenkyū* [A Study of the Japanese Bureaucratic System] (Tokyo, 1969). Representative works in the genre of exposé literature are Imai Kazuo, *Kanryō, sono seitai to uchimaku* [Bureaucracy, Its Mode of Life and Inner Workings] (Tokyo, 1953); Masuda Yoneji, *Oyakunin* [Honorable Official] (Tokyo, 1956); Mainichi shimbunsha, ed., *Kanryō Nippon* [Bureaucratic Japan] (Tokyo, 1956); Tokyo shimbunsha, ed., *Kanchō monogatari* [A Tale of Government Offices] (Tokyo, 1962); and Hori Makoto, *Oshoku* [Corruption] (Tokyo, 1957). Of the latter works, the volume by Imai is by far the best. He exaggerates so that his book will sell, but he writes with insight, humor, and wit.

[2] *Kido Kōin nikki* [The Kido Kōin Diaries] (Tokyo, 1933), III, 433.

the officials of the emperor and partook of his glory. Higher officials, from a slightly later period, had fancy uniforms with shiny buttons, braids, and swords to wear on ceremonial occasions. Their pay was high. Even a lower official (*hanninkan*), Ukai Nobushige has stated, could afford to visit geisha.[3] It was not until the 1920s that the salaries of company managers pulled ahead of those of government officials at the same educational level.

After World War II the pay of bureaucrats declined relative to other sectors of society. They were redefined in the 1947 constitution as "servants of the people" (*kokumin no kōboku*). They were stripped of their symbolic perquisites. Decorations, for example, were abolished for a time. And, reflecting the decline in their livelihood and morale, incidents of corruption or bribery, exceedingly rare before the war, began to be reported. Yet many of the best graduates of the Law Faculty of Tokyo University continued to enter the bureaucracy. Perhaps only in France and Germany did officials have a comparable sense of themselves as an academic elite.

Imai Kazuo, a former bureau chief in the Ministry of Finance, recounts an occasion when a student, armed with a letter of introduction, called on a bureau chief in a central ministry in the hope of obtaining a job. He was asked about his university record and then dismissed with: "You haven't got a chance with only that number of As. I had seventeen. The famous Professor So-and-so at the university had only fifteen, a considerably poorer record than mine." The student left in chagrin. When first told of this conversation, Imai remarked on how true to life it was.[4] The same consciousness is reflected in the more recent words of a ten-year MITI bureaucrat who asserted: "We [graduates] of the [Tokyo University] Law Faculty are the most Japanese of Japanese" since Japan is essentially an "examination society."[5]

Within the bureaucracy there was and is a sharp cleavage between the elite of career officials, who have passed the special higher examination, and lower-level bureaucrats. Distinguishing between these two levels enables one to resolve many contradictory statements about Japanese bureaucracy. I arrive at a bimodal view: of exceedingly able men directing the work of the central ministries, but much less able men in the offices of local government; of graduates from the two or three best universities versus those from lesser schools and, at a lower level yet, high school graduates; of generalists versus specialists, technicians, and clerks; of relative freedom in creative work versus mechanical, rote tasks; of the satisfaction of power versus the frustrations of a narrow routine. Of course, the bimodality is not simply between the central ministries and local government. Those who will reach the highest appointive positions in the

---

[3] Ukai Nobushige, personal communication. Imai makes the same point, *Kanryō*, p. 25.

[4] Imai, *Kanryō*, pp. 47–48.

[5] Kawamoto Tarō, "Sore demo Tōdai hōgakubu wa Nihon o ugokasu" [Even Then, It is the Law Faculty of Tokyo University that Moves Japan], *Bungei shunjū*, September 1972, p. 179.

central government will spend some time in prefectural-level offices. There are planning and executive posts at the prefectural level that are highly demanding, and many of the sections of the central ministries are filled with clerks, assistants, researchers, and temporary employees performing the most routine kind of work.

The elite bureaucrats move frequently from post to post and often occupy certain positions which are, as it were, on a special track, reserved for the most promising careerists. In the late Meiji period, a Tokyo University graduate might enter the Home Ministry, then become the assistant chief of police in a small city, move back to a different bureau in the ministry, then to a prefectural government post, and so on. Today, a Finance Ministry official may have a similar career pattern—moving from the ministry to a brief appointment in a prefectural tax office, then back to the ministry, then again to a prefectural office, and then back again to the ministry. Even after the Occupation separation—along American lines— of central and prefectural government, this type of transfer of officials from the central to the state level still continues.

The special aura of power that still surrounds the elite administrators can be explained partially in terms of their postcareer pattern. There is an unwritten rule in the bureaucracy that university graduates who entered in any given year cannot serve under men who entered at the same time or later. Since bureaucracy is pyramidal—the number of posts at each higher rank decreases—this rule means that those of each class passed over for promotion must be retired. This resembles the system in the armed forces of the United States. Some of those sloughed off in this fashion are kept in service for a while longer by postings to high positions in prefectural governments. But even the few who become bureau chiefs or vice-ministers, the highest posts in the system, are usually retired in their early or middle fifties. These men, the elite of the elite, often receive their rewards for loyal service after retirement. Some become the directors of corporations, receiving fees considerably greater than their former salaries. Some are appointed as members of semi-official advisory commissions (*shingikai*). A few begin a political career and make it to the Diet, and a handful achieve the eminence of a cabinet post. Because such postretirement careers are the pattern in Japan (some ministries are better situated for this than others), even the junior bureaucrat who has passed the higher examination is viewed as a possible future member of the select company that defines Japan's national goals.[6] This contributes to his status,

---

[6] In the *Kanchō monogatari*, the commissions and other *gaikaku dantai* are compared to Ubasuteyama, the folktale mountain where the old were abandoned when they could no longer contribute to the life of the community. See *Kanchō monogatari*, p. 45. Sometimes the financial power of the ministry is employed to assure a good reception for its retirees. In one instance the Education Faculty at a Japanese national university was asked by the Ministry of Education to take on as a professor an official of a certain rank who had been passed over for promotion in the ministry. The faculty council argued about the matter for some time. Eventually they accepted the official and gave him the appointment. As a trade-off they

even though his salary may be less than his opposite number in Mitsubishi.

Because of the variety of career patterns, even among the higher
officialdom, there is no unanimity about the merit of life in the
bureaucracy. One official of the prewar Home Ministry privately compared the life of the official to "soaking in lukewarm water." It lacks the
satisfaction of a good hot bath, yet "as long as one remains in it, one will
not catch cold. But if one loses his patience and jumps out, he will
invariably come down with a cold." [7] On the other extreme the editorialist
Akimoto Hideo once rode on the bullet train with a budget examiner, one
of the most powerful officials of the Finance Ministry. The official
suddenly told him to look out the window. "See that bridge over there? I
built it." A few minutes later he pointed out: "See that road? The wide
one. That's my work too." Then after a while he said again: "See that
windbreak forest over there? That was one of my most difficult jobs."
Akimoto noted the expression of consummate satisfaction on the face of
the official.[8] Between these two extremes are the observations of a young
career official in the Foreign Ministry:

We climb the hierarchy with exactly the same speed. The question is which post
one is assigned to. This is not an absolute indicator, as the Foreign Ministry has the
policy of assigning career officers alternately between good (Europe and the
United States) and not so desirable (Africa, some of the Asian countries, and South
America) posts. As we climb with the same speed, there is no real competition,
although almost all of us, having gone through a very competitive educational
system, are competitive in a good sense. That is, everybody is a genuinely hard
worker, disliking easy posts. Usually we are intelligent, but, surprisingly, some of us
are not so intelligent. Because we are given reasonably responsible and important

received a large, handsome new building. Imai writes of another instance in which a post as
section head opened up in a prefecture. A man, able, experienced, and first in line in the
prefectural officialdom, was chosen for the job. But when permission was asked of the
ministry concerned, the man was rejected. (The officials who handle the prefectural affairs of
the central ministries are appointed only with the approval of the ministry concerned.) The
governor took the unusual step of going to Tokyo and asking the ministry to let him have the
man he wanted. He was, however, turned down and had to accept a man sent out from the
ministry. The man from the ministry was older, less able, and less experienced. Imai writes
that for the ministry to send this official who was old, lacking in ability, but without glaring
failures in his record, to an honorable post in the countryside was a way of getting rid of
deadwood (funzumari o dakai suru) in the ministry. When he arrived to take up the post of
section head in the prefecture, he was not well received. The new appointee, however, was
exultant at having attained the post of section head, and immediately ordered his underlings
to procure a car for his personal use. There was no car in the budget, and his juniors reported
back that it was impossible. The new section head berated them as incompetents and said he
himself would get it from the ministry. His juniors felt that at a time of budgetary cuts the
frugal ministry would not waste money on such a sad figure of a section chief (chinpira kachō).
But he surprised them by coming back with an allocation, which he used to buy the car. This
established his reputation in the prefectural bureaucracy as a real somebody. Even though it
was a complete waste of money, having forced the prefecture to accept the man, the ministry
had to pay this price to get him established. Imai, Kanryō, pp. 188–190.

[7] Imai, Kanryō, pp. 36–37.

[8] Kawamoto, "Tōdai hōgakubu," p. 171.

jobs while in junior grade, the stupid ones become conspicuous at once. They are not, however, punished, at least in salary or grade. This kind of promotion continues until we become counselors. From then on it is luck.

We share the same interests both in personal matters and professionally. Over dinner or cocktails we talk a lot about foreign affairs and are quite willing to be critical of the government, though we aren't to people who might quote us. The atmosphere of the office, either in Tokyo or abroad, depends a great deal on the personality of the men, particularly of the chief. Generally speaking, discussion is free. We are invited to dissent. The level of discussion is usually high. For example, I am in charge of such and such a matter and am expected to know the facts about it. Facts are important. Treaty clauses, technical details of strategic thinking, dates, figures, etc., are considered more important than sheer speculation, although speculation, too, is expected of us. We often say that if an officer is incapable of becoming an expert in six months concerning the subject matter of his assignment, he shouldn't be taken seriously. The majority of the officers accomplish this mark with ease.[9]

When one talks with the higher officials of other ministries, the content of their work may vary, but the sense of competence and self-confidence they project is much the same. In this respect they are not unlike Japanese business leaders.

Is this elitist consciousness appropriate in a democratic polity? Many Japanese say that it is not, arguing that bureaucrats tend to look down on civilians from their position of superiority. This is summed up in the old maxim, "officials are honored and the people are despised" (kanson minpi). It is not that the populace distrusts the bureaucracy—though some on the left do. Most recognize its competence and give it a measure of respect. It is not too much to say, in fact, that many in the opposition parties dislike it because of its competence. But all complain of the arrogance of officials. The resentment against this arrogance may be the most seriously dysfunctional aspect of the whole system.

Masuda Yoneji, a onetime official in the Ministry of Labor, wrote that after he became section chief, visitors to the ministry would bow deeply and speak to him in exaggeratedly polite language as if he were "a member of a different race." When he went to inspect a textile mill in Aichi, he was made to feel a degree of superiority and satisfaction as never before in his life. He was met on the train platform by the section chief, a ten-year official, and his two aides from the local government office. They treated him politely, bowed, carried his briefcase to the waiting car, and escorted him to the local inn. After he bathed, he was visited by the works manager and section head in charge of labor affairs of the factory he was to inspect. They called in geisha, plied him with drinks, and in general treated him with such a combination of respect and deference (English does not do justice to the expressions used) that for the first time in his life he felt the "indescribable pleasure" of embodying in himself "the power of

---

[9] Personal communication. I have been asked not to cite the interviewee by name.

the state." [10] Imai, after describing instances of the same kind of obsequious behavior in even more loving detail, offers an analysis of it:

In the course of such experiences—like starting to smoke or taking up the habit of an evening drink—one at first feels a little ticklish, but before long it begins to feel good, and one feels that something is missing if he isn't treated in this way. Next one feels an inward dissatisfaction, and in the final stage, one advances to the symptom of indignation. It is exactly the same as addiction to a drug. . . . The more one is a petty, self-righteous type (*ki no chiisai zennin gata*), the more likely he is to fall prey to this disease of "bureaucratic mentality" and the worse will be its ravages. . . . And almost no one is entirely immune.[11]

Nor would it exaggerate to say that there are some who look forward to catching the disease. In 1972 a student who had passed the entrance examination for Tokyo University was interviewed on television and asked about his future. He replied, and his face was radiant as he spoke: "I've been accepted by the Law Faculty. In the future I'll pass the exam of the Ministry of Justice and become a judge. As a judge I'll be a god. I'll have the power of life and death over men. I'll be able to move society in any direction I please." [12] In this response there is an element of brashness and an element of black humor, together with a large measure of overoptimistic anticipation. Yet it is not wholly off the mark. The entering freshman in the Law Faculty of Tokyo University, if he perseveres, stands a good chance of becoming a judge. Judges in Japan are officials of a kind. The path to becoming a judge is separate but not different from that into the Ministry of Justice. The kind of authority exercised by a judge and the unassailable character of his position is, like that of other officials, based on a legal monopoly of certain powers. The potential of those officials who fell prey to the "disease of bureaucratic mentality" to act arrogantly stemmed from a system that, until recently, had few political checks on the use of this power.

Since Japanese officialdom is characterized by bimodality, its relations to the clientele it serves are also of two kinds. Higher officials deal mainly with other officials and politicians, or with corporations and other large organizations. They rarely come into contact with the average citizen. The attitude of the higher officials toward, say, corporations is determined by a combination of law, custom, and politics. As in most countries, most laws are not strictly enforced most of the time; they function as guidelines or limits. Bureaucrats could throw the economy into chaos if they began to implement strictly all of the laws for which they are responsible, just as police can start a crime wave by enforcing all of the laws in the criminal code. Of course they do not. Yet because of the unused discretionary power of the bureaucracy, companies large and small take great pains to avoid

---

[10] Masuda, *Oyakunin*, pp. 35–36.
[11] Imai, *Kanryō*, pp. 52–53.
[12] Kawamoto, "Tōdai hōgakubu," p. 171.

falling into its bad graces. Businessmen employ a precautionary politeness in dealing with officials. They assume an inferior status and treat even low-ranking officials with an exaggerated deference—as if they were ministers of cabinet rank. This has been brought to a high art. It is the safe way of manipulating officials. It is seen as a low price to pay for getting along with a bureaucracy that is largely honest and supportive toward business. But it is resented nonetheless, for businessmen feel that it is they and not the bureaucracy that are the propulsive force in today's Japan.

The attitude of the local bureaucracy toward its civilian clientele is perhaps the more serious problem. Whether a Japanese is going to the district office for a copy of his birth registration certificate or to the local tax office, he goes in some degree as a supplicant. If he does not act as one, he can, depending on the circumstances, be made to wait or told to come back another day. The official is doing him a favor. The official tends to see the power of the office as his personal power. The resentment engendered by this kind of treatment is widespread and affects the Japanese view of government. This is far from being as uniquely Japanese as the Japanese imagine. In good measure it is the behavior of the *petit fonctionnaire* anywhere.[13] It is especially characteristic of countries where democracy is recent and is predated by a bureaucratic tradition. Yet perhaps it is more visible in Japan where degrees of politeness can be precisely measured by the depth of bows and the incremental use of honorific language.

In Japanese society at present there are some trends that run counter to the tradition of bureaucratic arrogance. Local government in the early postwar years was predominantly in the hands of conservative politicians who, appealing to all of the voters, were not formally identified with a party. Recent local elections, however, especially those in the larger cities, have become politicized; the power of the conservatives has been challenged. To attract voters, many administrations have adopted a new service orientation toward the citizenry. "Progressive" politicians, such as the mayor of Kyoto, have established "citizen consultation offices" (*shimin sōdanshitsu*) to handle complaints about broken roads, garbage, or what-ever. Conservative mayors have reacted by setting up similar offices. The mayor of Matsudo in Chiba Prefecture called his the "do-it-right-away section" (*sugu yaru ka*). Through such small changes the attitudes of officials are being democratized little by little. The outbreak of "residents' movements" during the early seventies in protest against pollution is a parallel development. As these movements turn to the electoral process,

---

[13] Bureaucratic subordinates may suffer along with the public. Imai tells the story of an official who after thirty years became head of a small government office. He lined his staff up before New Year's and after lecturing them on the proper attitude toward their work said: "It is most regrettable that recently the number of officials who do not understand propriety have increased. At the end of last year there were even some who brought me year-end presents bought at a department store special sale." Imai, *Kanryō*, p. 61.

local government officials move further in the direction of accommodating public interests.

VERTICAL RELATIONSHIPS AND CLIQUES

Japanese officials are Japanese and bring with them into bureaucracy patterns of behavior characteristic of their society. If the laws, ordinances, and regulations constitute the formal system of the bureaucracy, then these patterns of social relations that affect official behavior may be called the informal system. Two aspects of the informal system are so important to the way Japanese government functions that they merit special comment. One is the vertical personal tie; the dysfunction associated with this is cliquism. The other is the solidarity of the office, which gives rise to interoffice jealousies and struggles over jurisdictions.

Japan's premodern society was organized about the vertical personal tie. Not only did this "feudal" bond define the relationship between lords and their samurai vassals, but it encompassed other relationships as well: that of master artisans and their apprentices, of merchants and their clerks, and so on. Within the domain governments, personal ties also formed between senior and junior officials. These became the basis for the political cliques which played a constant role in the politics of that age.

One view of government in premodern Japan holds that it was essentially feudal, however encrusted with laws and bureaucratic practices. If one follows this interpretation, then the transition to the more legalistic bureaucracy of the Meiji era becomes a sort of quantum jump. A second view argues that the late Tokugawa government was essentially bureaucratic, though with a great variety of lingering feudal survivals. This view permits a more evolutionary interpretation of the formation of the modern Japanese state. Yet even this second view must recognize that personal ties remained important after the opening of the modern era. When an early Meiji leader moved from one post to another, he took with him a number of his "men." By mid-Meiji this practice was discouraged as disruptive of order within the ministries of government. Yet as Roger Hackett has shown in his analysis of the "Yamagata machine," personal ties only slowly diminished in importance. Cliques were found in most ministries as well as in the services during the troubled years of the thirties, and, in some measure, still exist in most ministries today.

When a new class of university graduates enters a ministry, they do not join a clique immediately. Rather, they spend ten years or so in one or another post learning the work of the ministry. During this period they establish working relationships with their seniors. Seniors want able juniors. By the time a junior becomes a section chief, he will probably have established particularly good relationships with one or two senior officials. When the senior official becomes a bureau chief or vice-minister, he may recommend those juniors who are close to him for key positions. And after the senior official has retired, if he should enter the Diet or the cabinet, or join a government commission, these relationships may become even more important. Perhaps the essence of the personal clique is that it creates an unofficial link between the bureaucracy and the world of politics.

Viewed in qualitative terms, what is most striking about the personal tie is the easiness of the relationship between junior and senior. This easiness sustains an unimpeded two-way flow of communications. This is a critical consideration for Japanese bureaucracy and contrasts with the situation in some other countries. Michel Crozier's study of French bureaucracy, for example, found that egalitarian sentiments were so strong in France as to produce "strata isolation" and a breakdown of communications between different levels in its bureaucratic hierarchy.[14] In India the haughtiness or abruptness of senior officials often makes them unwilling to listen to what their juniors have to say—leading to a serious lack of feedback within the Indian bureaucracy. In Japan, however, the weakness of the sort of egalitarian sentiment that would require the self to hold those who are not equals at arm's length makes vertical communications less difficult. Language reflects the absence of barriers. Once their relationship is established, the senior will speak to the junior in familiar terms (calling him So-and-so *kun*). This suggests a paternalistic warmth and kindly concern for the future of the junior, his training, and his welfare in general. The junior accepts this, is respectful, and works hard. At moments he may even show a kind of *amae* (active dependency) toward his superior. Of course, the emotional content in such relationships is not usually apparent. There are circumstances when it can be expressed, but most call for businesslike formality and impersonality.

Another related factor contributing to the ease of the vertical personal relationship in Japan is the relatively easy acceptance of status distinctions. When I have suggested this explanation to Japanese friends, they have usually disagreed with me, arguing that they resent status distinctions as much as anyone. Yet I feel that what they find unacceptable is not status per se, but certain kinds of behavior by persons in high-status positions. To put this in a comparative context, there is a well-known study in which a sociologist compared human relations on a British ship and an American ship. He found that the American ship had a more elaborate set of rules regulating the behavior of the ship's personnel. His explanation was that the American sense of egalitarianism is such that more rules are required to produce the order that the British obtained with less effort due to their ingrained sense of class. In terms of this comparison the Japanese are more like the British—though in Japan it is distinctions of status, rather than class, that are recognized and respected. A Japanese ship, I would guess, would require even fewer rules regarding the proper

---

[14] Michel Crozier, *The Bureaucratic Phenomenon* (Chicago: University of Chicago Press, 1964), pp. 220–224.

behavior due seniors than the British ship. At the same time the Japanese ship would probably go beyond either the American or British ship in drawing up a uniform system of status rankings. The use of court ranks gave all Meiji officials fixed positions in a unified hierarchy of statuses from the late 1860s. When court ranks were dropped, a standardized nomenclature for positions was substituted. When this was discarded during the Occupation period, officials frequently complained of not knowing the meaning of the names of positions on the *meishi* (name cards) of other officials.[15]

Alongside the personal cliques within Japanese bureaucracy, overlapping them and often confused with them, is a second kind of grouping that is also called a clique in Japanese. I call these the official cliques. During the Meiji and Taisho eras there were the Satsuma and Chōshū domain cliques (*hanbatsu*), and from the middle of the Meiji era until the present there were school cliques (*gakubatsu*), particularly that of the Law Faculty of Tokyo University.

The essential distinction that I would draw between the official clique and the personal clique is that while the official clique may contain networks of personal ties, it has an objective base external to the bureaucracy. The personal clique does not. The balanced recruitment of officials from Satsuma and Chōshū was not solely a matter of balances between offices, but was part of a larger equilibrium on which the new state was built. It reflected the fact that these two domains had the balance of military strength in the country and controlled access to the emperor. Once in the government, Chōshū officials usually joined personal cliques under other officials from the same domain. But they also recruited able men from other domains into their own personal cliques. Ōkuma, for example, was first attached to the personal clique of Kido of Chōshū and then to that of Ōkubo of Satsuma. He had Chōshū men in his own personal following even while he was a follower of Ōkubo. Even in the early Meiji years personal cliques were not congruent with official cliques.

The distinction was even clearer in the case of school cliques. Tokyo University was established as the training ground for the bureaucracy. The "Tokyo University clique" was always more the name for a system of preferential recruitment than it was a functional bureaucratic clique. The

---

[15] Imai, *Kanryō*, p. 65. Vertical relationships are not always as lovely (or "old-fashioned") as I have described them. The superior may be arrogant or cold. He may be a whipcracker, feared by his subordinates, but unable to evoke their loyalty. See Masuda, *Oyakunin*, pp. 38–44, for examples. A superior may refuse to warm up to a junior who went to the wrong school or who lacks ability. Conversely, it may be the modern junior who rejects the assumptions of paternalism on the part of the senior, especially when the paternalism is used as a thin cover for exploitation. The polite language of such a junior may be devoid of any human feeling, or may merely conceal his contempt. Masuda also discusses officials who are liked, but ineffective (ibid., pp. 45–61) or are too brilliant to be effective (ibid., p. 61). On the latter point, Noda Kazuo has commented that leadership in Japan requires warmth rather than sharpness.

cliques in the Foreign Ministry, which during the 1930s stood in opposition to one another regarding government policy, were all, basically, Tokyo University cliques. Even today the distinction between personal and official cliques continues. Of course, it goes without saying that "old boy" ties did not hurt. A graduate of the Tokyo University Law Faculty entering a ministry was a *kōhai* (later graduate—junior) vis-à-vis *senpai* (former graduates—seniors) already established in the ministry. They had a common ground on which to build a relationship. There was a presumption that the junior would be talented, whereas an "outsider" would have to demonstrate his ability. If matters went poorly, a man not from Tokyo University might still feel himself an outsider ten years after entering the ministry.

Because of the historical resentment against the Sat-Chō cliques, because of the resentment against Tokyo University, because official cliques are confused with personal cliques and personal cliques are seen as running counter to the public interest, cliques are much talked about as an evil in Japan. Critics argue that cliques prevent the recognition of talent. They see the bureaucracy as a system in which preferential recruitment leads to preferential promotion and then to differential rewards. Others see in the ethic of personal loyalty a negative survival of Japan's feudal past. Matsumoto Seichō, a socialist and long-time critic of Japanese bureaucracy, could write a plausible detective novel about a government office in which the assistant section chief shoulders the blame to cover up a crime committed by his superiors.

Bureaucratic cliques, however, are not simply feudal survivals. They are tolerated because they have positive functions as well. One is to bypass an occasional blockage up-and-down the organization by forming a conduit for communications outside of channels. Another important function is lateral communication with a high level of trust. The coordination of work on a horizontal axis is often difficult within Japanese bureaucracy since vertical ties are so important that they always take precedence. But if the chief of one bureau was formerly the section chief in another bureau, he may well know its present section chief and will certainly know some of its permanent lower officials. This may enable him to reach them directly without going through the other bureau chief, especially if he is close to the present section chief. His effectiveness as a bureaucrat depends in some measure on the cultivation of such personal ties. (One of the arguments constantly heard within organizations in Japan against the recruitment of persons not fresh out of university is that they will not be able to function effectively since they will be strangers in the organization.)

Personal cliques are limited to the confines of a single ministry since officials are not transferred from one ministry to another. Consequently personal cliques are of no use in coordinating work between ministries. But personal friendships or the official clique are sometimes of use. If an acquaintance from the same class at Tokyo University is in another ministry, a short telephone call may accomplish what would take days or weeks if sent up, over, and down, through channels. Phone calls, of course, are made constantly even when personal ties are lacking, but jurisdictional sensitivities are so acute that they are often ineffective. Thus, when a bureau in, say, the Ministry of Agriculture and Forestry has business with a bureau in the Ministry of Finance, the bureau chief may ask his subordinates if they know anyone in that bureau. Or officials in different ministries who did not know each other in school may establish a working relationship on the ground of having attended the same school. In a variety of ways, the informal system within the bureaucracy complements and is necessary to the formal system.[16]

SOLIDARITY AND JURISDICTIONAL JEALOUSIES

A second major characteristic of Japanese social relations is work-group solidarity—the sense of common purpose, cohesion, and belonging that unites a section, bureau, or ministry. The dysfunction associated with this is a we-versus-them attitude toward other offices or ministries that often makes cooperation difficult. There are various terms in the literature which describe this; each involves a slightly different context and perspective. If the focus is on the powers of an office and the extent of its authority, then "the roped off area" (*nawabari*) or "the limit of authority" (*kengen*) may be used. If there is a struggle between two offices over a conflicting jurisdiction, then *kengen arasoi* may be used. If the autonomy of the ministries is under discussion, then the term is *kakkyosei* or "sectional independence," a term used in earlier times to refer to the independent power of regional feudal domains.

The keen awareness of jurisdictional limits is not new in Japan, and certainly not unique to Japan, though office solidarity may make it stronger in Japan than elsewhere. Even in the Edo period in the regulations of the bakufu exchequer (*kanjō bugyō*), great care was taken to spell out the specific functions and the limits of competence of its various suboffices. An English engineer working for the Ministry of Public Works during the early Meiji period described the same scrupulous concern for jurisdictions—almost as if they resembled the boundaries of fiefs—in the following words: "The Vice-Minister of Public Works was himself in no

---

[16] Another aspect of the society of bureaucrats, if not of bureaucratic society, is marriage. The wives of bureaucrats like the wives of businessmen are not supposed to intrude into the world of the office, and in fact they usually do not. Still, everyone is aware of marriage ties. The foreigner in Japan is always struck by how small and interconnected the Japanese establishment is. Businessmen and bankers went to the same universities as the higher officials. The majority of students at these universities are born outside of the magic circle of power, but after graduating and entering an office they tend to marry the daughters of the elite of the previous generation. The establishment almost appears to perpetuate itself by matrilineal adoption.

way connected with the project, owing to the curious mutual jealousy of departments and consequent duplication of administrative arrangements constantly to be remarked in Japan. . . ." [17] Even as the bureaucracy became more modern, these intraministry jealousies did not disappear. Before World War II an official in the Ministry of Finance was sent to another section of the same ministry to borrow some statistical materials, which that section had collected from all of the prefectures in Japan, but which it no longer was using. The request was turned down by the chief of the other section, whose last words were: "If the materials are so necessary, why doesn't your section notify the prefectures and collect them separately?" The conclusion of the official, albeit slightly overstated, was that the jurisdictions of Japanese offices are, like the person of the emperor, "sacred and inviolable" (*shinsei ni shite okasu bekarazu*).[18]

Between ministries, competition and jealousies are even more frequent. Ministries have varying levels of prestige, and the Finance Ministry is the most powerful and the most prestigious because of its authority to approve or disapprove of not only the general budgets of other ministries but also of their specific projects. Other ministries resent their dependence on it. When meetings must be held between officials of different ministries, the question of who should come to whom is exceedingly delicate. Also, the question of whose approval to get first is a touchy matter. If one office feels slighted or taken for granted, then it may make trouble. During World War II, Ayukawa Gisuke was put in charge of Manchurian heavy industry, taking it over with a "force that would stop a bird in flight." Yet when he came to Tokyo with his yearly plan, he had to repeat the same explanation over and over tens of times, visiting each of the ministries concerned. He also had to proceed in the proper order[19] and call on them according to the convenience of their bureau chiefs. When busy, they did not give him an appointment on the hour and day requested. The entire process required more than a month. That so powerful and dynamic a figure as Ayukawa was subjected to such treatment in wartime, one author writes, makes one realize how staunchly the splendid bureaucratic tradition of "protecting one's territory" is upheld.[20]

The exposé literature abounds with examples, such as those given above, of the dysfunctions inherent in jurisdictional jealousies. Yet even such prickly antagonism toward organizations other than one's own has a silver lining—the strong positive identification with one's own office and with its goals. When there is work to be done, Japanese officials work long hours; I have walked through the corridors of several ministries at six or seven in the evening and have been surprised at the number of officials still at their

---

[17] E. G. Holtham, *Eight Years in Japan* (London, 1883), p. 271.

[18] Imai, *Kanryō*, p. 142.

[19] Ministries were ranked in 1885, and those formed after that time were ranked in order of formation.

[20] Imai, *Kanryō*, pp. 161–162.

desks. They feel their work is important and are proud of it. They feel that they are a vital part of an enterprise. And their awareness of belonging to the little society of the office is reinforced, as Nakane Chie has described it, by drinking or playing mahjong together after hours, or by office outings to the sea or a hotspring once or twice a year.

How then is this office solidarity reconciled with cliques? The answer, first of all, is that the office in which junior officials, clerks, typists, and researchers work together—or even the section with much coming and going among several closely grouped rooms—is below the level of cliques. The section chief may be particularly close to one or another senior, but the personal clique stops with him. (The assistant section chief will also give a special kind of personal allegiance to his boss, but, because of his limited career mobility, he is not usually considered a clique member.) Among the higher posts in the ministry there is also a kind of solidarity or esprit de corps. Arising from the face-to-face contacts of the higher officials, their sense of mission, and their elite consciousness, this sense of solidarity is what binds the ministry together. Ministerial solidarity is always in a delicate balance with personal vertical ties. As the higher officials move about from post to post, they must work now with one man and then with another. Particular vertical ties are never permitted to become so strong that they interfere with work relations. To the extent such ties are seen as related to official cliques, they are criticized—as the intrusion of particularism where only merit should count. To the extent they are seen as personal cliques, they are more often interpreted positively as good senior-junior working relationships of the kind that contribute to the accomplishment of the ministry's task.

DECISION-MAKING

Much of the writing on decision-making in Japan has focused on the defects of the *ringi* system—the procedure by which papers are passed up and down the line, from section to section and bureau to bureau, until they have gathered the required number of seals of approval. In the paragraphs that follow I would like to suggest that this emphasis is more an obstacle than an aid to our understanding. It makes Japanese office procedures mysteriously different from our own. Before turning to the internal workings of bureaucracy, however, it is necessary to touch briefly on the political context of Japanese bureaucracy.

Weber said that above every bureaucracy is a political system that sets the goals. This is clearly true in both Japan and the United States: the Diet and Congress pass laws; the respective administrations see that the laws are carried out. Yet there are significant procedural differences. In the United States bills may be drafted by congressmen (Taft-Hartley, Burke-Hartke) or by the president's White House staff, as well as in the various departments of the federal government; in Japan the overwhelming majority of bills are drafted by bureaucrats in the ministries. If the drafting of bills is a political function, then in Weber's terms, part of the Japanese political system is found within the higher bureaucracy; if it is not, then a part of the American bureaucracy is located within the political system, above the departments of government. It is possible to resolve the two alternatives by saying that the Japanese bureaucracy performs staff functions for the political leaders of a kind not done by department bureaucrats in the United States. But "staff functions" is a vague term. If it means the actual drafting of laws, then does it not betoken at least a partial role in the setting of goals? In any case, it is clear that the central ministries of state in Japan are considerably more powerful than the equivalent American departments.

A second major difference is the degree of insulation from politics. The American department is open at the bottom, open at the middle to men with experience, and at the top it is infiltrated by political appointees down to the assistant secretary level (the equivalent, perhaps, of the Japanese bureau chief). In contrast, the Japanese ministry is a closed body. It recruits only at the bottom and takes only virgin labor—fresh out of school and plastic. At the top of each ministry there are three nonbureaucratic posts: the minister who is in the cabinet and two "political vice-ministers" from the Diet. These are powerful figures, yet by and large these men deal with the ministry through the bureaucratic vice-minister. They do not penetrate the ministry; the ministry maintains its insulated corporate unity beneath them; it is not politicized.

One reason for the weak politicization of the bureaucracy was its prewar tradition of neutrality; the laws that framed it were designed to keep it separate from politics. But perhaps more important was the fact that throughout the postwar period the Japanese bureaucracy has had a single master, which it has been able to serve with a rare singleness of mind. Had power alternated between parties with different programs, it would have been necessary to develop mechanisms within the bureaucracy to handle the shift of policy. Whatever form these might have taken, the conse-quence inevitably would have been the politicization of the upper levels of officials in the ministries. Since this has not been necessary, the result has been a bureaucracy that is both conservative and apolitical and that has worked in harmony with a series of conservative administrations.[21]

---

[21] The question of the influence of ideology on bureaucratic behavior, raised by Blau, is not easy to answer in the case of Japan. It is easier to prove homogeneity than conservatism, especially since the latter term has different meanings in Japan than in the United States. Imai (*Kanryō*, p. 96) writes that drafts are considered at innumerable *kaigi* and are revised over and over again, but the discussion of them never leaves a certain framework since everyone at the *kaigi* has the same education and background of experience. Kawamoto, ("Tōdai hōgakubu," p. 170) buttresses this contention with figures from Kubota Akira: 79 percent of Japan's postwar higher bureaucracy were from Tokyo University, 47.3 percent of England's from Oxford and Cambridge, 11.2 percent of America's from Harvard. Masuda (*Oyakunin*, pp. 153–154, 162–167), on the other hand, talks of the recruitment of radical

Japanese bureaucrats would agree with the description of the bureaucracy as apolitical. They emphasize that Japanese bureaucracy is not racked by the dissensions of party strife. They see themselves as operating above politics in the national interest. Occasionally a bureaucrat will suggest that the factions within the Liberal Democratic Party (LDP) are the equivalents of parties in other countries. After a shuffling of cabinet portfolios, a new minister may put in "his man" as vice-minister or as bureau chief in a key bureau. Yet his man will be a career official whom he knows, who can work with those already in the ministry, and who has the seniority and experience needed for the appointment. Such an appointment usually has few implications for policy. And often dramatic changes occur in the cabinet and in national policy without any corresponding shifts of personnel within the ministries. When Tanaka became prime minister, for example, Japan's China policy turned completely about. However, hard-line officials in the Foreign Ministry with ties to the Fukuda clique did not lose their positions. They continued to handle China policy. But the policy they made and the speeches they gave in defense of it were markedly different in content.

Bureaucrats, however, protest the label of "conservative," arguing that they have a sphere of autonomy and do not look simply to the LDP. In drafting a bill, for example, they often check with the socialists as well as with the LDP. Officials also point out that, from time to time, the bureaucracy is successful in opposing the policy directives of LDP organs. Even the socialists, bureaucrats argue, recognize their fairness and their concern for the national interest. I feel that the preceding points are not untrue, but need some qualification. Token coordination with opposition parties is a way of helping the LDP avoid the charge of "tyranny of the majority" on the floor of the Diet. Small changes in a bill that is not controversial may even enable the government to obtain socialist support for the measure. The socialists' recognition of the fairness of the bureaucracy—to the extent that this is recognized—is a recognition that the bureaucracy is as national or as impartial as they could expect *given LDP control of the government.* Bureaucratic opposition to LDP policies is, in fact, very small. Consider the case cited by one official in which the Ministry of Agriculture and Forestry resisted the demands of the Agricultural and Forestry Division (Nōrinbukai) of the LDP Policy Affairs Research Council (Seimu chōsakai) for higher prices for agricultural products. Such prices are a subsidy to farmers who vote conservative. The successful resistance by the ministry cannot be interpreted simply as bureaucratic independence of the LDP. It must be seen as a minor defeat for LDP farm interests in order to achieve a balance with growing LDP

---

graduates into the Ministry of Labor in the early postwar era, of his own position as a section chief of a reactionary government, and of how the radicals sobered up after some time in service.

urban interests. Too much pandering to the farmer, a declining percent-age of the population, would weaken the LDP in the cities.

Qualifications such as these suggest that it is not unfair to apply the label of conservative to the higher bureaucracy. Most, though not all, of its members make no bones in private about their support for the LDP. They see the LDP as the party closest to the national interest, and they are willing and efficient in carrying out its policies.

Can one, then, not go a step further and argue that the bureaucracy has been permitted to maintain its substantial autonomy and powers because of its willingness to act for the LDP? This question can be examined in terms of where the initiative comes from when a bill is drafted. Is it from the bureaucracy, from the party by way of the divisions of the Policy Affairs Research Council, or from the commissions made up of business-men, professors, Diet members, and retired bureaucrats? The answer varies. For a politically neutral matter—a law intended to aid the implementation of other laws—the initiative may come wholly from within the bureaucracy. For a political sensitive matter, such as the violence in the universities during the late sixties, the LDP will define the general sense of what is to be done, and the Central Educational Commission will provide specific policy guidelines. Since neither organiza-tion has an adequate staff, the Ministry of Education will draft the actual bill. In this situation the politicians feel that they are in control and are using the bureaucracy to handle the technical details. They are confident that the product will be what they desire. The bureaucrats feel that their input into party policy is greater than party influence on their drafts. Each side appears satisfied with the relationship. If there is delusion, it is on the side of the bureaucracy, which feels that its autonomy and powers are properly its own and the result of its ability.

Discussion of the decision-making process within the bureaucracy itself needs several prefatory remarks. First, most decisions in the bureaucracy are concerned with carrying out laws already passed. The actual enforcement or implementation of the provisions is often handled by prefectural governments. For example, agricultural extension services, which in the United States would be handled by local offices of the federal government, are in Japan "delegated" by the Ministry of Agriculture and Forestry to the prefectures. This was the Japanese prewar practice, and it continued even after the Occupation reforms. Central government control over prefectural expenditures permits a very tight rein on the way in which the delegated functions will be carried out. Decisions regarding the interpretation of laws, for example, are referred back to the concerned ministry.

Second, the majority of matters in Japanese organizations, as elsewhere, are settled by the single decision (*senketsu*) of the appropriate official or office. This is, after all, what bureaucracy is about: the division of a complex task into simpler parts and the assignment of specific functions or jobs to specific offices. Most decisions occur within parameters already defined. They clearly fall within the jurisdiction of a single office, and neither infringe upon the authority nor offend the sensibilities of other offices. It would be silly to refer such decisions to complicated procedures. At most the matter will be passed to the official's superior for an automatic stamp of approval.

Third, both in business and government in Japan the decision-making process is fairly formalized. There are tables of organization and instructions saying what office shall deal with what kinds of matters. There are charts or lists saying how far up in the organization different matters must be taken for final approval. At times this will be indicated by checks in the appropriate space at the top of a document. At times regulations even spell out what kind of decision-making process shall handle what kind of matter.[22]

Let us, however, consider a complex decision, the draft of a new law that has political ramifications and affects the work of other ministries. Once initiated from above, it may go through the following stages:

1. Drafting the bill—done in the section (*ka*) that has responsibility for the matter. It will involve informal discussions within the section, and may involve querying other offices about what would be acceptable to them.

2. Consultation and meetings—informal talks and formal meetings to revise the draft and to gather support and approval for it.

3. Circulation—passing the completed document up and down through the concerned offices for seals of approval by the office chiefs until the draft reaches the office of the vice-minister. This may overlap the previous stage.

4. Submission—giving the document to the minister for consideration by the cabinet or submission to the Diet.

In drafting the bill, the main difference between the United States and Japan has already been referred to: in Japan it is usually done in the bureaucracy, in the United States it may be done in a Senate committee or in the White House. Yet even when an American bill is drafted in a department, there is a second difference: the American bill may well be drafted by the staff of a high-level official, whereas in Japan the vice-minister will give the job to the bureau chief concerned, who will pass it to the appropriate section where younger career officers will do the drafting. The difference in the two procedures reflects a difference in

---

[22] At least in regard to formal procedures, there are striking similarities between government and company bureaucracies. Compare, for example, the corporation forms and rules for *ringi* contained in Nihon keiei seisaku gakkai, ed., *Keiei shiryōshū taisei* [Collected materials on management] (Tokyo, 1968), IV, with those for government offices given by Tsuji Kiyoaki in "Decision-Making in the Japanese Government: A Study of *Ringisei*," in Robert Ward, ed., *Political Development in Modern Japan* (Princeton: Princeton University Press, 1968). Also see chap. 9 in M. Y. Yoshino, *Japan's Managerial System* (Cambridge, Mass.: MIT Press, 1968), for an interesting discussion of the varieties of decision-making in Japanese corporations.

organizational structure. Japanese bureaucracy is by and large a line organization. It is a vertical command structure of offices beneath offices beneath offices. It has few staff officials—that is to say, few officials who are attached laterally to high offices and who themselves have no subordinates.

Some coordination with other offices may take place even during the preparation of the original draft of a bill. If the measure involves two sections or two bureaus, the junior officials preparing the draft may sound out their opposites in the other concerned office. Most consultations with other offices, however, occur after the draft is completed and approved by the section chief. There is no predetermined order of consultation; this varies with the measure. Nor is it absolutely fixed which consultations will be formal and which informal. Informal consultations are sometimes called *nemawashi*. The primary reference of this term is to the preparations made in advance of transplanting a large tree: digging a trench around it, cutting the thick lateral roots, and bending the smaller roots circularly around the earth clump that will be moved. As applied to bureaucratic practice, it refers to the "spadework" involved in gathering together backing for a measure. The other form of consultation is the meeting (*kaigi*). In preparing a measure for the Diet, the document may first be brought before the weekly meeting of section chiefs of the ministry. Next it may be cleared with the appropriate division of the LDP Policy Affairs Research Council. All drafts of laws must also be cleared by the legal bureau of the cabinet (Naikaku hōseikyoku), which checks the compatibility of the proposed law with existing laws. One official from each ministry serves in this bureau; officials consider this a good assignment. If the bill involves money, it must be approved by the Ministry of Finance; this requires another meeting. At some point the draft may be considered at a meeting of the vice-minister and bureau chiefs of the concerned ministry, or a meeting of the vice-ministers of all of the ministries.

If there is a difference between the process of consultation in Japan and that of the United States, it is one of emphasis. In the United States the tendency is to call a meeting of the concerned offices and thrash out any differences in the open. Face-to-face disagreements are not avoided. Open confrontation is the rule rather than the exception. This is not to say, of course, that a good deal of "buttonholing" (the American version of *nemawashi*) will not precede the meeting. In Japan, on the other hand, the tendency is to settle differences beforehand through informal talks. This avoids open confrontation. It avoids a situation in which one man wins and another, who has openly revealed his position, is marked as a loser when the decision goes against him. Organizational solidarity will not tolerate procedures that create winners and losers. At times the building of a consensus requires compromises that actually affect the decision reached. At times the compromises are merely token gestures to placate someone who otherwise would be seen as a loser and make it possible for him to join in a nominal consensus. In Japan as elsewhere there are many either-or situations. Consensus cannot miraculously do away with hard decisions. Whoever wins acceptance for his policy and gains the authority to implement the new policy is left in a strong position. In this respect Japan is not as different from other countries as some writers have suggested.

Because of the importance of informal discussions, and because open confrontation is usually avoided at meetings, the function of the meeting can be reduced to the formal approval of a settlement already reached during informal talks. In this connection Imai Kazuo tells the story of a Tokyo middle-school baseball team, which, each inning before taking up its position on the field, would huddle at the pitcher's mound, put their arms on each other's shoulders, and listen to words from their captain. A visiting team from the countryside was lost in admiration at this sophisticated custom and decided to imitate it. Before the last inning they formed a circle around the mound. But the captain of the team, having no strategic message to impart, merely said: "Let's all eat watermelon after the game." Imai continues: "I will probably be criticized for comparing the *kaigi* (meeting) in governmental offices with this watermelon *kaigi*. Yet such *kaigi* are not altogether lacking." [23]

Meetings of bureau chiefs or section chiefs are held with such frequency that many may lack issues to discuss, or they may deal chiefly with matters of jurisdictions. The potential for a drift toward formalism in any routine procedure is always strong. Yet even Imai's criticism stopped at "not altogether lacking." I would stress, based on conversations with officials, the centrality of the meeting in the decision-making process. Discussions at meetings are often substantial. Drafts are revised and rerevised. At times an office opposed to a measure will openly denounce it at the start of a meeting as a tactic to force others to compromise—since to override his objection would make him a loser. (Of course, such a tactic is used infrequently. Potential conflict situations are usually resolved beforehand.)

Nakane Chie has written that Japan is a land of interminable meetings, dragged out in the name of democracy—which in Japan really means harmony.[24] This may be true of faculty meetings in Japanese universities where ideological differences make informal agreements difficult. It is also true of Diet sessions where face-to-face confrontation is institutionalized and the opposition can use the value of harmony against the "tyranny of the majority." But it does not characterize meetings within the bureaucracy where differences are concerned with means, not ends.

There is also a difference between Japan and the United States in regard to stage three, the circulation of documents. In the United States the decision taken at the meeting, or after a series of consultations and

---

[23] Imai, *Kanryō*, pp. 105–106.

[24] Chie Nakane, *Japanese Society* (Berkeley and Los Angeles: University of California Press, 1970), p. 145.

meetings, is final. All that remains is to inform other concerned persons of
the outcome. But in Japan, though agreement may be reached at the
meeting, the final formal approval occurs when the document is passed
from office to office and stamped with the seals of the responsible officials.
Some writings have gone so far as to argue that this paper-passing process
(the *ringi* system) is *the* decision-making process in Japan. The reason for
this undue emphasis on one part of the total process is that, while informal
consultation is hard to see and meetings so ordinary that they are hardly
worth mentioning, the *ringi* process is highly visible and peculiarly
Japanese. It is also because, *for unimportant matters,* the draft may be
circulated for approval without prior consultation or meetings. But for
significant matters, the primary function of the *ringi* system is to circulate
information about decisions already taken. As such, it strongly resembles
H. A. Simon's "referral and clearance system."

Viewing then the entire process of decision-making, and bearing in
mind that reality is more variable than the paradigm offered above, one
can say that the functions that are handled by the "meeting" in the
United States are in Japan distributed over the informal consultation, the
formal meeting, and to a small extent the *ringi* system. These are
differences of emphasis arising from differences in bureaucratic organization and social behavior, but overall the process is less dissimilar than it is
usually made out to be.

STRENGTHS AND WEAKNESSES
IN THE DECISION-MAKING PROCESS

The Japanese pattern of line organization has one obvious advantage over
the American line-staff pattern: young officials are given important work
and vital experience almost from the time they enter the ministry. In
contrast, the American college graduate who has just entered the
bureaucracy may have to wait ten or fifteen years before he is promoted to
a level where meaningful work is done. Japanese officials take for granted
the correctness of their procedures. When queried, senior officials reply
that the young are energetic and innovative while older officials have the
wisdom needed to tone down the final product. This attitude is not new in
Japan. In *On Serving One's Lord* (*Jikun teikō*) written in the 1730s, Kani
Yōsai, discussing the division of labor between lower and upper officials,
argued that "rough drafts (*aragoshirae*) should be made by lower officials
and then polished by higher officials." Ishii Shirō commented that this is
what is meant today by giving young officials "something to live for"
(*ikigai o ataeru*).[25]

---

[25] Professor Ishii's comment occurred during a discussion of the passage quoted. Kani
Yōsai, "Jikun teikō" [On Serving the Lord], *Nihon keizai taiten* [Compendium of Japanese
economic writings] (Tokyo, 1928), XIV, 189.

The exposé literature on Japanese bureaucracy, however, often views the same phenomenon in a much less favorable light. It points out the undue influence of young or lower officials on policy decisions as one of the major dysfunctions of the system. Such an influence is termed "politics by subordinate officials" (*zokuryō seiji* or *zokkan seiji*). In an extreme instance, even the word used to describe the overthrow of lords by their vassals (*gekokujō*) in feudal times has been applied to it. As evidence of this phenomenon, two kinds of examples are cited.

The first is the influence exercised by subordinate officers on the decisions that led to the Pacific War. In approaching this question one should note first that the sections concerned—such as the Operations Sections of the Army General Staff, the Military Affairs Section of the Army Ministry, the First Section of the Naval Affairs Bureau—were the key sections in the services. They contained the elite of the service elites, men comparable in every way (except breadth of vision) with the higher bureaucracy of the nonservice ministries. It was their job to draft policy and strategy for the services; they did not usurp this function. Second, the "subordinate officers" were not that young. Lieutenants and captains in the sections were young, but the majors and colonels who served as section chiefs were in their middle or late thirties. Third, many of these men had been military attachés in Germany and favored a strong pro-German policy. This operated as an ideological factor setting them off to some extent from the senior officers. This degree of ideological difference is unusual in Japanese bureaucracy. Even in these anomalous circumstances the middle-level officers could make their influence felt only because the generals and admirals themselves were divided on questions of policy, and because of a political situation in which strategic decisions displaced political decisions as generals and admirals replaced political leaders in the cabinet.

A recent visitor to the United States who had been a junior officer (not a section chief) in the Japanese Supreme Command from 1939 to 1945 was asked whether he had encountered the phenomenon of the "inferior overpowering the superior." He appeared not to understand the question. The next day he was asked who drafted the plans for the General Staff, and he replied that it was done by the younger officers. He was then asked whether the generals always agreed with the plans. He replied that sometimes there were difficulties, but he was unwilling to use the label of *gekokujō*. He described a process of testing, discussion, and compromise, with the superiors capable at any one point, if not at all points, of having their own way against the proposals of their junior staff. He also stated that disagreements were the exception and not the rule.

In short, the kind of influence that "juniors" had during the late thirties came from line organization (even the General Staff had a kind of line organization) in which policy was drafted in the section. But this type of organization could have the baleful consequences it had only because of a combination of exceptional circumstances. And even then, the influence of juniors should not be overestimated.

A second kind of example cited to illustrate the power of lower officials often centers on the figure of the assistant section chief (*kachō hosa*). This official may be a careerist on his way up, but is more likely to be a clerk who has not passed the higher examination. He may have a fairly long tenure in the post while careerist section chiefs come and go. Masuda Yoneji describes an incident which occurred during his years in the Ministry of Labor:

After two or three years as a section head I gradually became accustomed to the life of an official and learned the mores of the office. So I began, according to my own lights, to make small changes on documents to which I had previously given a blind seal. At this the administrative assistant came in bearing the sets of ledgers pertaining to drafts of documents, overtime, etc., and said: "Section chief. From now on please handle all of these yourself. I can no longer bear the responsibility for handling the papers of the section." With these words he piled up a mountainous stack of ledgers on my desk. I was dumbfounded by this sudden *coup d'état* on the part of this man on whom I had so relied. "Now, now there, don't say that. Won't you please take care of them," I replied, making a total, unconditional surrender. Afterwards I again fell into the pattern of putting a blind seal on whatever documents he gave me. With that his loyalty to me became even stronger than it had been before.[26]

Masuda had earlier described how his assistant covered up for him when he was absent from the office on a late social lunch, protecting him from the anger of the bureau chief. Masuda also described his assistant, an older, prewar type of official, as "sitting upright in his chair" and "running the various affairs of the office with the authority and dignity of an elder (*karō*)." [27] Masuda continued:

Of course what must be taken into consideration is that from this time I became unable to examine carefully all of the documents that came through the office, which was my primary responsibility in the statistical investigation section. I came to understand from my later experience that this sort of maneuver was, for good or bad, a special characteristic of the lower officials (*zokkan*).[28]

Another example of the same phenomenon was the case of "Emperor So-and-so," a permanent lower official in MITI, who was said to have the power to block a request, even when the minister favored it.

I would not deny the existence of the kind of subordinate power that these examples illustrate. But I would argue that it is office power, not policy-planning power. It is the kind of power held in the United States by

---

[26] Masuda, *Oyakunin*, pp. 29–30. Imai (*Kanryō*, pp. 220–221) tells a similar story of a confrontation between a brilliant and experienced minister, who had reduced his ministry to abject submission, and a clever bureau chief, who got the best of him with a variation of the same stratagem.

[27] Masuda, *Oyakunin*, p. 26.

[28] Ibid., p. 30.

certain master sergeants on army bases, by certain lower officials in government offices, or by long-term secretaries in university department offices. It is based on a strategic position in the organization and a technical mastery of official forms and the petty details of administrative routine that higher officials do not want to be bothered with. When such a person retires, higher officials are momentarily pleased at the prospect of regaining control of the nether reaches of their own organization, and then they immediately set about finding the same type of person as a replacement.

Thus my conclusions are as follows. First, there is nothing uniquely Japanese about office power and not too much can be made of it. Second, young career officials in Japan do have a special kind of influence. Only a handful of such men are admitted to a given ministry each year.[29] The key sections in a ministry are few in number. From the time they enter, they are apprentice policy-makers, and the system intends that they function as such. They draft bills. There is a saying often quoted by Japanese officials that "the original draft is in a 70 percent position of strength" (gen'an wa shichi bu no tsuyomi).[30] This is an index of their influence. But this is far from saying that Japanese bureaucracy is run from below. If one asks junior officials whether they dictate policy, they laugh. The opposite contention, that superiors are sometimes tyrannical and that juniors show a slavish deference toward them (jidai konjō) is also heard. Ex-officials who served in the prewar years are particularly fond of describing office martinets—almost as if they were mourning the passing of the type: the section chief who would return a draft without saying what was wrong with it until his underlings produced one that met with his approval, the bureau chief so fearful that his subordinates wet their pants and came down sick when called on the carpet before him,[31] or the section chief who made small meaningless changes in a draft so as not to incur the displeasure of a bureau chief known to dislike an automatic seal of approval.[32]

A second major criticism of Japanese decision-making in the exposé literature is that the ringi system has several built-in weaknesses. First, the flow of documents through offices is so great that office chiefs must blindly

---

[29] In the prewar years about 2,000 took the higher examination each year; only about 250 were successful. The system was reformed during the Occupation. To become an official one must now pass the kokka kōmuin saiyō shiken. This has three levels for graduates of high school, junior college, and university. It is administered by the Jinjiin (National Personnel Authority). I have been told by officials that the university level exam, the jōkyū shiken, has many more takers than in the prewar era, but that the number accepted by the ministries is only slightly larger. See Kanchō monogatari, p. 126, for a description of the new examination system. See Robert M. Spaulding, Imperial Japan's Higher Civil Service Examinations (Princeton: Princeton University Press, 1967), for a detailed analysis of the prewar system.

[30] This is quoted by Dietmember Kawasaki in the course of a discussion with Tsuji, Imai, Sumimoto, and Ukai, printed in Jinji gyōsei [Personnel Administration], 4.10 (September 1953).

[31] Masuda, Oyakunin, p. 27.

[32] Imai, Kanryō, pp. 100–101.

put their seals on papers that they have not read and do not know the contents of. Second, the time required for the papers to pass across the desks of the concerned office chiefs is so great and the potential capacity of any official to sabotage or critically delay the decision by letting the document sit on his desk is such that the system is slow, clumsy, and inefficient. Third, since a measure is drafted at one level, approved at another, and signed at all levels in between, the locus of responsibility is vague.

No one disagrees with the charge that the volume of paper flowing through offices is excessive. Imai writes that as the head of a small local government office he once affixed his seal eight thousand times in a single day, that this was the record for the year, though he was not trying to set a record, and that it took all of his energies to keep on hitting the right spot.[33] Judging from the writings of ex-bureaucrats, there is even a kind of mystique built up above the seal. One official bragged that "a person's character is revealed in a single stamp of the seal" (*hanko hitotsu ni mo jinkaku ga deru*).[34] Another official who forgot his seal two days running was scolded by his chief: "The seal of an official is like the rifle of a soldier. Is there a soldier who would go to the battlefield two days in a row without his rifle." [35] On the other hand, most officials I have talked to say that the problem of the "blind seal" is exaggerated. A great volume of paper flows over the average desk. Most of it gets a blind seal. Sometimes an assistant does the actual stamping. Mistakes do occur. But important papers are picked out and read.

Regarding the problem of delays, the Japanese literature stresses the capacity of an official, who was not invited to the meeting where a draft was approved or who feels that the authority of his office has been slighted, to pigeonhole a document during the circulation (*ringi*) process. Such an official can hold up (*nigiri komu*) the draft bill by saying, "let me research it a bit" or "let me think about it some more," and when pressed can reply, "just now I'm very busy" or "a little more time." Imai compares the affixing of the seal to the procedure at a customs barrier or the authority to issue a visa: the greater the number of barriers controlled, "the greater the opportunities to inflict maliciously one's power on (*ijiwaru*) others." [36] My impression, however, is that the slowness of Japanese decision-making (if it is slower than in other countries) arises from the need for a measure of consensus in the process of consultation and meetings rather than from passive resistance during the circulation of the document. If an important matter has been resolved, if it has had a settlement (*matome*) at each level

---

[33] Ibid., pp. 127–128. Can we believe one stamp of the seal every 3.6 seconds with no time off for tea?

[34] Kaikō Ken, "Aru tochō shokuin no ichi nichi" [One Day in the Life of a City Official], *Shūkan asahi* [The weekly Asahi], September 16, 1964, p. 32.

[35] Imai, *Kanryō*, p. 126.

[36] Ibid., pp. 125–126.

up the hierarchy, it is extremely difficult to block. The necessary seals can
be obtained by orders from above, by energizing the personal clique, or the
responsible official can hand-carry the document around from desk to
desk, in each case bowing and waiting for the official to affix his seal. Few
officials can hold out under such pressure. Even Imai suggests that on
occasions an obstinate official can be "bowled over with adulation" (*ogami
taosareta*).[37]

The problem of responsibility or the lack of it in Japanese bureaucracy
is more complex. Only a portion of the problem is involved with the *ringi*
system. Imai writes that no one talks about responsibility as much as the
bureaucrat. It is a favorite word, yet what he really means by it is the
power of his office, not his duty.[38] Certainly in Japan the value of work
does not lie solely in the work itself. Rather, work validates one's
membership in the work group, work justifies office solidarity. Since any
bureaucracy is hierarchical, responsibility is heaviest at the top. But in
Japan the tendency to vest all responsibility in the head of the
organization is carried to an extreme that appears ridiculous in Western
eyes (and in some Japanese eyes as well). If a train crashes and lives are
lost, be it sabotage or the negligence of a switchman, the director of the
national railways may offer his resignation. When Ambassador Reischauer
was stabbed, the director-general of Public Safety offered to resign, though
this was an attempt at what the Japanese term an "instant assassination"
for which the director general had not the faintest responsibility by
Western standards. In part, this notion of responsibility was influenced by
German legal concepts adopted during the Meiji period, according to
which total responsibility was vested in each minister. But it also reflects
the fact that organizational solidarity in Japan is symbolized by loyalty to
its head. To justify this loyalty and maintain solidarity, the head assumes
responsibility for incidents highly visible to the outside society.

The same sweeping responsibility was accepted by Tanaka Kakuei
when he was appointed to head the Ministry of Finance. His words to the
assembled bureaucrats of that ministry were: "You are the elite of the
elite. No one can match your intelligence. Accordingly I will leave
the thinking to you. And I, Kakuei, am ready to bear full responsibility for
the consequences of your thought." [39] One of the Meiji leaders used almost
exactly the same words when he took over a ministry during the 1870s.
Tanaka's speech was calculated to elicit loyalty and hard work. Ex-
officials often criticize the don't-rock-the-boat (*kotonakare shugi*) mentality
of Japanese bureaucracy. Tanaka was telling his ministry that no one
would be punished for new initiatives and creativity. Perhaps he was also
telling them that, though not a graduate-bureaucrat himself, he knew how
to handle bureaucrats.

---

[37] Ibid., p. 150.
[38] Ibid., pp. 111–113.
[39] Kawamoto, "Tōdai hōgakubu," p. 180.

Within the ministry the same solidarity is reflected in the diffuseness or collective nature of responsibility. In the exposé literature the problem is viewed as a consequence of the separation of work and authority. The lower official feels only a limited responsibility since he is merely submitting a draft. Higher officials feel only a nominal responsibility since they receive a completed document already bearing a number of seals of "approval."

I do not disagree with the description, but it needs several qualifications. First, this problem is not unknown elsewhere; the United States, too, has the proverbial official who never signed what he wrote, or wrote what he signed. Japanese line organization merely increases the magnitude of the problem. Second, though some officials assert that responsibility is vague and collective responsibility is no responsibility, others protest that responsibility is not so vague. They contend that whoever may prepare the draft, it is the section chief who bears the primary responsibility and his bureau chief who takes a share of it. Seals by other offices only peripherally concerned with the matter mean the document has been seen and not objected to. Third, to the extent that responsibility is collective, it rests to that extent on the consensus formed during consultations and meetings. The final formal document with its collection of seals may symbolize the consensus, but it is subsequent to it. As long as consensus is seen as necessary, even doing away with the circulation of documents would not produce a different kind of decision-making.

CONCLUSION

It is not easy to evaluate the performance of a bureaucracy. In the case of a private company, the profits from the sale of its product provide a yardstick by which to measure the efficiency of its parts. But government bureaucracy has no production schedules, no sales, and no profits, and it is difficult even to define its product. Japan's postwar goal was economic growth. The bureaucracy effectively translated this goal into policies highly supportive toward business. And perhaps just as important for growth was that the bureaucracy interfered very little in the decentralized decision-making of private companies. Imai writes that officials know little of the real world and for them to draw up laws is "like a tailor making a suit without taking measurements." [40] The combination of supportive policies and noninterference created a maximal environment for growth. But a by-product of the policy was instances of chemical poisoning without a parallel in the world.

It is difficult, too, to compare one bureaucracy with another for they vary in their organizations, functions, and positions in their polities. It requires a formidable exercise of imagination to envision a Japanese

[40] Imai, *Kanryō*, p. 111.

Henry Kissinger usurping the policy-making functions of the Foreign Ministry. Japanese diplomats smile and dismiss the possibility. Yet the powers and the insulated, self-contained nature of the ministries in Japan, which Japanese officials take for granted, may have more to do with the Japanese pattern of one-party government than with the legal position of the bureaucracy or with its intrinsic quality. If Japan's parliamentary system continues in good health, and if parties or coalitions of parties should begin to alternate in power, then the present bureaucracy could change quite suddenly. A two-platoon system could develop within the top ranks of the central ministries, or the parties could develop within their organizations the equivalent of White House staffs as a countervailing force against the know-how of the ministries. The embryos of such staffs already exist. If such changes occurred, the bureaucracy might be much less efficient since it would no longer be carrying out policies that it had a hand in drafting. In any case, it is clear that much of the autonomy of the existing bureaucracy—which present-day Japanese officials see as an eternal verity—is in fact precariously dependent on political factors external to the bureaucracy itself.

Turning from the external situation to the internal workings of the bureaucracy, I would argue for a mixed analysis of the formal system and the informal patterns found in the larger society. The solidarity of the office, for example, forms almost spontaneously in response to the psychological need to belong to a warm, interdependent social group. It is a need that exists prior to the bureaucracy. The office group resembles the solidarity of nonbureaucratic groups in Japan. It arises wholly apart from the official purposes of the office organization. The particular character of vertical ties among Japanese bureaucrats can also be explained in terms of patterns of human relationships learned before they became officials. Yet once brought into the office, these general social proclivities—which can assume a variety of forms—are molded onto the formal structure and are adapted to serve the official ends of the organization. The personal clique becomes a vertical action group. The office community becomes a work team. The energies of the informal system are thus harnessed to the service of the official system.

Harnessing such energies, however, does not mean that they have been wholly converted into a positive force. The favoritism and discrimination associated with the personal clique remain dysfunctional. The office community uses the jurisdictional powers it is given by the official system to reinforce its natural animosities toward outgroups, producing frictions that interfere with the work of the organization as a whole.

This suggests that all bureaucracies are necessarily imperfect since the requirements of perfection are mutually contradictory. If vertical communication is easy, then horizontal communication is likely to be difficult. The ease of vertical relationships in Japan, in contrast to France or India, is a plus factor; yet it is just this ease that nurtures the personal ties that lead to the formation of cliques. To eliminate cliques would require a change in the nature of personal ties, which would doubtless lead to a new set of dysfunctions. Solidarity is good, but poor cooperation between offices is not. Rules are necessary if the workings of an office are to be rational and predictable, yet to the extent an office is bound by rules there is the opposite danger of formalism. Men of ability are necessary for good government, yet if men of great talents are recruited, elitism is hard to avoid.

I do not mean to imply that dysfunctions should be welcomed. Some dysfunctions such as corruption have an entirely negative input. In many countries the dysfunctions of bureaucracy are so severe that the tasks set by political leaders are not accomplished. But I would suggest that particular dysfunctions should be judged in the larger context of the end results produced by the bureaucracy. If the bureaucracy gets the job done, then some entropy in the system can be tolerated. Japanese bureaucracy is not the model of efficiency that some who talk of Japan, Incorporated, would have, nor is it the neutral body pursuing national interests that the bureaucrats themselves often describe. But neither is it the jumble of dysfunctions portrayed in the writings of its critics. Japanese officials work long hours when necessary; in terms of any comparative standard they are honest; and they accomplish most of the tasks set for them with a reasonable competence.

Big Business and Political Influence

GERALD L. CURTIS

INTRODUCTION [1]

Notwithstanding the lack of careful empirical studies of decision-making in Japan, a widely shared notion of the structure of power in Japanese society has taken strong hold. At the most vulgar level it is expressed as "Japan, Incorporated." At a somewhat, but not very much, more sophisticated level it is manifested in the thesis that Japan is run by a triumvirate of business, the bureaucracy, and the Liberal Democratic Party (LDP); that "organized business, the party government, and the administrative bureaucracy are the three legs of the tripod on which the Japanese political system rests. . . . The spectacle of Japanese politics is in

---

[1] The research for this paper was made possible by the cooperation of numerous businessmen, staff members of the major economic federations, journalists, and other observers of the business and political scene in Japan. I have cited only a few of them directly in this paper, but they have all contributed immensely to my work. Interviewing took place in Tokyo at various times during 1972. The following is a partial list of persons interviewed and the organizations with which they are affiliated: Fujii Heigo (Nippon Steel), Hakojima Shinichi (*Asahi Shinbun*), Hanamura Nihachiro (Keidanren), Iwasa Yoshizane (Fuji Bank), Ishikawa Shozo (NHK), Kikawada Kazutaka (Keizai Doyukai), Miyoshi Masaya (Keidanren), Mizukami Tatsuzo (Mitsui Bussan), Murakami Hiroshi (Kyodo Tsushin), Nakayama Sohei (Kogyo Ginko), Naruse Takeo (Nikkeiren), Nukazawa Kazuo (Keidanren), Sakurauchi Takeshi (Mitsui Bussan), Shimamoto Akinori (Keidanren), Shirai Hisaya (*Asahi Shinbun*), Suzuki Yukio (*Nihon Keizai Shinbun*), Takeyama Yasuo (*Nihon Keizai Shinbun*), Taki Takaaki (Nissho), Uemura Kogoro (Keidanren), Yamaguchi Hiroshi (*Zaikai*), Yamashita Seiichi (Keizai Doyukai), Yoshimura Kazuo (Nikkeiren), Shimanouchi Toshiro (Keidanren).

a sense a dramatic production, presented jointly by the business community, the ruling party, and the administrative bureaucracy." [2]

Any study of business influence on government and politics raises extremely difficult conceptual and methodological problems. It involves examination of widely held assumptions about the structure of power in Japanese society. It raises questions about "elitist" and "pluralist" approaches to politics that are at the heart of much of the controversy in political science. It becomes intertwined with problems of defining and distinguishing between such concepts as influence and power, unwieldy concepts to use with any kind of consistency and precision.

This paper does not attempt to develop any general theory of business-government interaction in Japan or to draw any definitive conclusions about big-business influence in Japanese politics. Our knowledge of Japanese governmental decision-making is too fragmentary to allow for such generalizations at this stage. Indeed, it has been the penchant of some observers for drawing overly broad generalizations that has created so many inappropriate stereotypes of Japanese practices.

This paper deals with just a few selected aspects of business-government relations. Career mobility, the informal interaction between leading businessmen and government officials, and the operations of Keidanren (the Federation of Economic Organization) and the other major economic organizations have been pointed to by many writers as accounting for what makes business-government interaction in Japan supposedly unique.

To say that the conservative party in Japan tries to serve the interests of businessmen is not to say anything that is not true of conservative parties in the United States and other capitalist economies. The attention that has focused on the business-government relationship in Japan, however, has involved questions of the mechanisms available to the big business community for the exercise of influence as well as questions of the degree to which the political system is responsive to big business interests.

To raise such questions is to reveal their extreme complexity. How does one measure influence? How does one trace the source of particular policies? What kinds of standards can be established that would allow for truly comparative analysis? Some mechanisms for exercising influence that are crucial in one country may be unimportant in another. In the United States, for instance, an extremely high rate of career mobility from business to government—in both elective and appointive offices—provides an important mechanism for facilitating business influence on government. In Japan, such mobility is virtually nonexistent. On the other hand, business organizations such as the National Association of Manufacturers or the Chamber of Commerce of the United States are relatively weak interest-group structures compared to their counterparts in Europe and

---

[2] Chitoshi Yanaga, *Big Business in Japanese Politics* (New Haven: Yale University Press, 1968), pp. 28–29.

Japan. Although it is usually assumed that government-business interaction is more intimate and the political influence of business is greater in Japan than in the United States, it would be extremely difficult to make a comparative study that could demonstrate that position. Depending on the criteria employed, it might be easier to make a convincing argument that big business's political influence is greater in the United States than in Japan—at least under the Nixon administration.

The problems of analyzing business influence in Japanese politics are complicated by the fact that much of the writing on the subject contains comparisons, implicit or explicit, with American business-government relations that are terribly distorted. There is a tendency to assume that the United States is still the country of the individual entrepreneur and strong antitrust policies and that the speed and direction of economic development is dependent on the unimpeded play of market forces. American businessmen in particular talk of "Japan, Incorporated" in comparison with an American economic system that may have existed in the time of their fathers or grandfathers, but hardly exists today.[3] If one looks at the late-twentieth-century Japanese economy from the perspective of the late-nineteenth-century American one, the degree of government-business interaction seems great indeed.

There is no question that the Ministry of International Trade and Industry (MITI) has had, in the past, an intimate relationship with Japanese business. It is also true that the history of Japanese government encouragement of capitalism in the Meiji period has had a continuing effect on the style of business-government interaction. But even the most ardent supporters of a theory of a cohesive ruling elite in Japan are forced to qualify their statements when faced with empirical evidence of Japanese practices.

The United States Department of Commerce study on government-business relations in Japan is a good example. The author of the volume concludes that "there is a special style and scope to interaction between government and business in Japan which makes it distinctive"; that " 'Japan Incorporated' is an Economic Fact of Life." [4] Close to half the volume, however, is devoted to a series of commissioned case studies. Based on these studies, the author was forced to so qualify the meaning of "Japan, Incorporated" as to render it largely meaningless. The author admits that the studies demonstrate that advance planning is neither as long range nor as far reaching as had been thought; that interaction between Keidanren and MITI varies considerably from case to case and suggests no single pattern; that industry operates on its own initiative and

[3] Such statements as "Japan's economic destiny has not been left to the free play of market forces," suggest a comparison with contemporary America that is untenable. Eugene J. Kaplan, *Japan, The Government-Business Relationship, A Guide for the American Businessman*, (Washington, D.C.: U.S. Department of Commerce, February 1972), p. 10

[4] Ibid., p. 70.

without governmental intervention to a greater extent than had been
assumed; and that there is often such considerable conflict between
ministries in the bureaucracy, that "Japanese ministries often appear to
operate a great deal more independently of the Prime Minister and each
other than would be the case in this country."[5] Finally, the author
concludes that on the basis of the empirical evidence available: "The
government cannot effectively interpose its judgments on the corporate
structure. It can encourage but not dictate mergers or formal combina-
tions. MITI has therefore sought, *generally with little success,* to stimulate
consolidation through its exercise of a variety of levers on industry."[6]

The main problem with much of the non-Marxist theory regarding a
Japanese power elite is that it has attempted to attribute to Japanese
culture as a whole behavior that is the consequence of a particular
combination of factors in a unique historical period. Marxist theory—as
skeptical as one may be of its rooting in empirical fact—is nonetheless
strong as theory since it places Japan in a universal and comparative
context: Japan is ruled by a particular power elite because it has a
capitalist economy. Non-Marxist defenders of a power-elite theory of
Japanese politics make comparative analysis impossible: Japan is ruled by
a power elite because of the unique characteristics of its people's
psychology and of its social institutions.

There is often a time lag between reality and generally shared
perceptions of that reality. In postwar Japan, the gap between image and
reality is particularly serious because of the extremely rapid pace of
change. Generalizations about the role of Japan's economic organizations
that would have been accurate ten years ago, for instance, are inaccurate
today. Data from the 1950s on the occupational backgrounds of Diet
members gives a picture of career mobility from business to government
that has little relevance to the Japan of the 1970s. The substance of the
relationship between business and government in the postwar period has
been the consequence of particular economic, social, and political
conditions. As these conditions change so does the nature of that
relationship.

Thus, this paper challenges some of the more widely accepted assumptions of how certain mechanisms facilitate business-government interaction
in Japan. Such an exercise is desirable for purposes both of refuting an
inaccurate stereotype of "Japan, Incorporated" and stimulating new
research into questions of the structure of political power in present day
Japan.

THE MYTH OF *ZAIKAI* OMNIPOTENCE

Zaikai, in literal translation, means the financial world, but it also means

---

[5] Ibid., p. 52.
[6] Ibid., p. 56. Italics added.

something much broader, and at the same time more specific. Although writers have had difficulty arriving at a generally agreed upon definition for it, the *zaikai* has been credited by many with unparalleled powers over Japanese politics.

In his acceptance speech after defeating Kono Ichiro in the 1965 LDP presidential election, former Prime Minister Sato Eisaku made a famous slip of the tongue. He started out by saying: "On this occasion *zaikai*'s . . . ," then stopped and rephrased it: "On this occasion the people's support . . ."[7] To many people, "*zaikai*'s power over the conservative party," as one group of Japanese commentators put it, "is absolute."[8] "In fact, Japan's politics and economy cannot move even one step if the wishes of *zaikai* are ignored. To put it another way, if *zaikai* decides it wants something, it can get practically anything."[9] In the view of Chitoshi Yanaga, "*zaikai*'s power of life and death over governments has been dramatically demonstrated time and again. Candidacy for the premiership is unthinkable without its tacit approval, and the prime minister's days are numbered if his policies or methods no longer meet with its approval."[10]

All of this suggests rather awesome power for *zaikai*. But Yanaga goes on to say that *zaikai* is really not a coherent group: "*Zaikai*, however, is by no means a monolithic structure. . . . The diversity of attitudes, motives, and interests that characterize *zaikai* has made the cooperation of the larger key organizations (Keidanren; Nikkeiren—Japanese Federation of Employers' Association; Keizai Doyukai—Japanese Committee for Economic Development; and Nissho—Japanese Chamber of Commerce and Industry) indispensable in achieving consensus and in presenting a united front on issues and problems."[11]

The United States Department of Commerce study of business-government relations in Japan makes a similar point about the role of these key organizations in harmonizing *zaikai* views. Unfortunately, it adds to the confusion by mistakenly referring to *zaikai* as a discrete group like the Industrial Problems Research Council (Sanken—the Sangyō Mondai Kenyūkai):

---

[7] Quoted in Editorial staff, "Shinshushō tanjō" [The making of a new prime minister], *Bungei shunjū*, special August 1972 ed., p. 92.

[8] Editorial staff, "Keidanren: Zaikai kenryoku no sōhonzan" [Keidanren: The headquarters of *zaikai* power], in "Nihon zaikai no genjō" [The present situation of Japan's *zaikai*], special issue of *Zaikai tenbō*, January 1, 1967, p. 23.

[9] Ibid., p. 22.

[10] Yanaga, *Big Business*, pp. 32–33. A similar view is expressed in a recent Japanese publication: "In the real meaning [of the term] the greatest, most powerful pressure group is *zaikai* whose desires it is taboo for the political world and the bureaucracy to reject. In legislation as well as in administration, *zaikai* demands, which might be thought totally unreasonable, are all accepted. Moreover, no matter what occurs, it does not give up any rights it has won." Yamamoto Masao, ed., *Keizai kanryō no jittai* [The real facts of the economic ministries] (Tokyo, 1972), p. 22.

[11] Yanaga, *Big Business*, p. 33.

In their fairly frequent informal discussion meetings Sanken and *zaikai* focus on the major issues confronting Japanese society, as well as Japan's economy. The many different points of view, motives, and interests of these business leaders tend to be harmonized within the councils of the Keidanren and the other major federations. . . . Moreover, the harmonization process, besides providing a national consensus for big business, helps Sanken and *zaikai* members transcend the narrower interests of the corporations, banks, and organizations with which they are affiliated for a more national perspective on these issues.[12]

As these quotations suggest, the meaning of *zaikai* is shrouded in considerable conceptual confusion. Part of the reason for the confusion is that the term has a number of meanings in Japanese. Although literally it means the financial world, it sometimes refers to the entire economic community or businessmen generally, as when people talk of *zaikai, seikai* (political world), or *gakkai* (academic world). But *zaikai,* as commonly used, refers to something more specific than the entire business community. According to one author, it refers to the relatively small number of leaders of the business world who "hold the line of communication to the political world";[13] in the words of another, to those business leaders who "engage in and control economic activities for the benefit of the capitalist system and political activities to maintain the present political structure. . . ." [14] The term is sometimes used to refer to individuals and at other times to the place where these individuals meet. Suzuki Yukio has suggested that *zaikai* is the place where business leaders function as a power elite.[15]

Translating *zaikai* as the business elite or the business world's power elite does not quite convey the Japanese flavor of the term. Other countries have business elites but only Japan has *zaikai*. At the base of the distinction seems to be the fact that the men who make up this elite in Japan spend an extraordinary amount of time in so-called *zaikai* activities (*zaikai katsudō*)—activities that are not directly related to their own companies, but which seek to represent the interests of the business community as a whole.

---

[12] Kaplan, *Japan, The Government-Business Relationship*, pp. 36–37.

[13] Yamaguchi Hiroshi, "Kakufuku sensō Ka Nihon zaikai" [Japan's *zaikai* in the Tanaka-Fukuda war], *Zaikai*, July 15, 1972, p. 117.

[14] Hirata Masami, "Zaikai no kenryoku keisei kō" [The structure of *zaikai* power], *Zaikai tenbō*, January 1, 1967, p. 14.

[15] Suzuki Yukio, *Seiji o ugokasu keieisha* [Businessmen who influence politics] (Tokyo, 1965), p. 28. Professor Yanaga defines *zaikai* rather dramatically, and I believe inaccurately, as follows: "In journalistic usage it more often than not refers to the leaders of big business, particularly to leaders who have the support of the powerful economic organizations—the closed circle of organization-based, power-wielding activists. . . . *Zaikai* also denotes the place where the craving for political power is openly expressed and gratified—that hypothetical arena in which big business influences the government, or even society as a whole. Most frequently identified with the term *zaikai* are the top executives of four big-business organizations . . . and executives of the Japan Industrial Club whose board of directors consists of the presidents of the key organizations and the elder statesmen of business, industry, and finance." See Yanaga, *Big Business*, p. 32.

Zaikai, as the term is commonly used, might be defined as the group of major industrial and financial leaders who spend a significant portion of their time in activities that relate to the economy in general and the society at large, generally through active participation in one or more of the four major economic organizations.

Not all leaders of large industry are considered *zaikai* members (*zaikaijin*). Many of the leaders of firms affiliated with the former *zaibatsu* are not active in *zaikai* and most of the postwar self-made men—like Matsushita, Honda and Idemitsu—are considered outside the *zaikai*. On the other hand, some of the leading *zaikai* members are not leaders of major industries. Uemura Kogoro, for instance, the president of Keidan-ren and the man referred to as the "prime minister of *zaikai*" is not even a businessman, but a former bureaucrat who has been with Keidanren since the founding of the organization.[16]

Virtually all those generally regarded as *zaikai* members are elderly men who have been in top leadership positions for almost the entire postwar period. The average age of the vice-presidents of Keidanren, for instance, is seventy-three, and President Uemara is seventy-nine. The *zaikai* can be characterized as the business community's group of elder statesmen, a group of extremely capable business managers[17] that has led Japan through reconstruction and high economic growth and has dominated her major economic organizations. When people talk of big business's influence in Japanese politics, they are largely talking of the influence of *zaikai,* the elder statesmen who seek to represent the interests of the business community vis-à-vis the government, the public, and in the international arena.

It is one thing to argue that *zaikai* has been a potent force in Japanese politics. It is another to argue, as so many do, that *zaikai* has "life and death" powers over the government. Such a position ignores those occasions when *zaikai* has been unable to have its way. Instances of *zaikai*'s inability to control the LDP presidential election, for instance, are as evident as instances where *zaikai* has allegedly manipulated the election. *Zaikai* was unsuccessful in forcing Hatoyama's resignation before he normalized relations with the Soviet Union; was unable to bring about a Kishi victory over Ishibashi upon Hatoyama's retirement; could not prevent Sato from running against Ikeda when Ikeda ran for a third term;[18] and most recently was unable to prevent Tanaka from winning

---

[16] For a brief description of Uemura's background and leadership style see my article, "Organizational Leadership in Japan's Economic Community," *Journal of International Affairs* 26.2(1972): 181–182.

[17] In Japan, as in the United States, there has developed in the postwar period a separation of management from ownership. The men in *zaikai* are not for the most part capitalists in the classic sense, but professional managers.

[18] Ikeda defeated Sato, but tremendous pressure was put on Sato not to make a contest. Information on this incident and other aspects of *zaikai* 's political activities were provided by Fujii Heigo, vice-president of the Nippon Steel Company in an interview on July 25, 1972.

over Fukuda in the 1972 LDP presidential race. *Zaikai* has been influential
in LDP politics, but this influence has varied with time and issue.

Tanaka's success in the LDP presidential election represents a particularly strong challenge to the thesis of *zaikai* omnipotence. Tanaka won the
election in spite of big business, and not because of it. Even if, by election
day, many *zaikai* members supported Tanaka, or more commonly,
adopted an attitude of "equal distance" (*tōkyori*)[19] from Tanaka and
Fukuda, this was because they had realized the futility of continued
support for Fukuda and not because they had changed their minds about
whom they would like to see succeed Prime Minister Sato.[20]

Nonetheless, believers in *zaikai* omnipotence cling to the notion that
zaikai was responsible for Tanaka's victory, or at least, that it could have
prevented the victory if it had been determined to do so. Some writers,
despite considerable evidence to the contrary, argue that the *zaikai* met
several months before the election and decided to shift its support from
Fukuda to Tanaka. Another commonly heard view was that *zaikai* had
conceived and brought about the alliance between the Tanaka and Ōhira
factions. In this way *zaikai* was able to use "reliable" former-bureaucrat
and Ikeda-disciple Ōhira to keep "unpredictable" Tanaka in line.
Similarly, it was *zaikai* that "dispatched" LDP-member Ishida Bakuei to
join the Miki Takeo faction as Miki's "chief of staff" to restrain Miki from
continuing his alleged one-sided position on the China-normalization
question.[21] Finally, since "the more than ten billion yen in hard cash that
flew around [the LDP presidential election] all came from *zaikai*, now it is
the turn for the new government to receive its 'bill' from *zaikai*." [22] All of

---

[19] This was a term that Fujii Heigo takes credit for having coined to express *zaikai*'s
neutrality in the last days of the "Tanaka-Fukuda war" (*Kakufuku sensō*) over the LDP
presidency.

[20] The resignation of Prime Minister Tanaka in December 1974, some observers have
argued, was due to *zaikai* pressure. But Tanaka never had the support of the *zaikai*. In 1972 he
was able to overcome *zaikai* opposition to his candidacy because he was widely regarded
within the LDP as being capable of restoring greater popular support to the party. If Fukuda
had instilled a similar confidence, it is hard to imagine that Tanaka would have been
successful no matter what tactics he may have employed in an effort to win the party
presidency. By the fall of 1974 it was clear that Tanaka had not been able to reverse the tide
of declining LDP support; that he had fallen in personal popularity to a point unprecedented
by any former Prime Minister; and that the excesses of the Tanaka led LDP Upper House
election campaign in the summer of 1974 and the aftermath of charges of unethical if not
illegal financial dealings had turned him into a major liability for the party. It then moved
with remarkable speed to remove him from office. Big business leaders may have played a
role in hastening his departure but they were able to do so by riding a tide of broad based,
popular opposition to Tanaka. It was the opposition parties, the press, and most importantly
the general public dissatisfaction with Tanaka that turned the LDP against him and brought
about his downfall.

[21] These arguments were made in an article by the editorial staff of *Bungei shunjū*, Japan's
most widely circulated monthly magazine. See "Shinshushō tanjō," pp. 92–106.

[22] Ibid., p. 97.

this makes interesting reading but is more in the realm of fantasy than political analysis.[23]

Among the advantages of the power-elite approach to the study of politics is that no amount of evidence can disprove the theory that an elite rules, and that even the lack of evidence can be used to support the theory. Evidence contradicting the model is dismissed either as related to issues with which the business elite is not really concerned,[24] or as further proof of big-business skill in concealing its infamous role—further substantiation that big business, indeed, is the invisible hand manipulating politicians and politics.

BUSINESS-IN-GOVERNMENT

One of the most salient features of contemporary Japanese politics is the limited lateral entry of businessmen into elective politics and appointive government office. This has been particularly true in recent years, but has been the clear trend since the unification of the conservative parties in 1955. It is crucial to distinguish between patterns prevalent in the pre-party-merger period and those that have since prevailed. Unfortunately, this distinction is often not made, and some recent publications have continued to present the erroneous view that big business is represented in considerable numbers in the Diet and in the government.[25] One recent study, based on data mainly from 1953 and 1954, maintains that "nearly one-third of the Japanese House of Representatives is made up of businessmen and former businessmen"[26] and that "big business is formally represented in the government by Cabinet Ministers of its choice."[27] Using more recent data, we discover that businessmen account for no more than 15 percent of lower-house members in the LDP. Businessmen rank only third in representation in the LDP Diet delegation, well behind former bureaucrats, who comprise about 30 percent of the Diet delegation, and professional politicians, who account for 24 percent.[28]

Furthermore, it is important to distinguish in the case of Japan between "nationally" oriented and "locality" oriented politicians.[29] The business-

---

[23] Furthermore, an important characteristic of this election was that much of the money used by Tanaka apparently came not from *zaikai* but from non-*zaikai* businessmen such as the president of Kokusai Kōgyōsha, Osano Kenji, and from Tanaka's own resources.

[24] This is a criticism often made of Robert Dahl's study of New Haven, *Who Governs?* (New Haven: Yale University Press, 1961). Typical of the criticism is that raised by Peter Bachrach and Morton Baratz, *Power and Poverty* (London: Oxford University Press, 1970), pp. 9–16.

[25] These include the Yanaga book, the U.S. Department of Commerce study, and the revised edition of Hugh Borton's *Japan's Modern Century* (New York: Ronald Press, 1970), pp. 504–505. The last two books rely on the Yanaga study for their data.

[26] Yanaga, *Big Business*, p. 27.

[27] Ibid., p. 70.

[28] Data compiled from Sugimori Yasuji, "Jimintō zengiin no keireki bunseki" (An analysis of the background of the LDP Diet member), *Jiyū*, May 1968, pp. 36–57.

[29] Gerald L. Curtis, *Election Campaigning Japanese Style* (New York: Columbia University Press, 1971), p. 3.

men who make up 15 percent of the LDP Diet contingent include representatives of big businesses and owners of small countryside stores. If a distinction is made between the nationally oriented representatives of big business and the locality oriented small businessmen, the number of *zaikai* representatives in politics becomes considerably smaller.

The lack of significant career mobility from business to politics is reflected also in the career backgrounds of the men who have become Japan's postwar prime ministers. No prime minister in postwar Japan comes with a career background in big business. Yoshida Shigeru was a former Foreign Ministry official; Hatoyama Ichiro was a prewar politician; Ishibashi Tanzan was a journalist; Kishi Nobusuke, Ikeda Hayato, and Sato Eisaku all were former bureaucrats. Tanaka Kakuei is typed in the Japanese classification scheme as a professional politician because of his more than twenty-five years in the Diet. Nonetheless, he is the first postwar prime minister to be independently wealthy, having amassed a personal fortune in the construction industry. He is not, however, from the nationally oriented big business establishment. The only such businessman to make a serious attempt at becoming prime minister has been Fujiyama Aiichiro, former president of the Japan Chamber of Commerce and Industry. Fujiyama was notably unsuccessful in his effort.

No LDP faction leader comes from a career in big business. A group of younger Diet members led by Kosaka Tokusaburo, himself a second-term member, is probably the only factionlike group in the LDP led by someone clearly from a *zaikai* background. Kosaka was president of the Shin'etsu Chemical Company and an active member of Nikkeiren, the Japan Federation of Employers' Associations.

If we look at the cabinet, businessmen do appear somewhat stronger in one regard. A prerequisite for appointment to the cabinet, as a rule, is success in five or six Diet elections. However, there are fewer cabinet posts than there are Diet members with the requisite seniority. An analysis of cabinet appointments shows that, within the group with equivalent seniority, former bureaucrats have the best chance for appointment, businessmen are second, and professional politicians rank third. This means that where businessmen are successful in being elected to the Diet, they are successful in eventually getting into the cabinet. But the number is small to begin with.

Under the Japanese constitution, the prime minister is required to appoint a majority of cabinet ministers from among members of the Diet. Since there are twenty-one people in the cabinet, the prime minister could appoint as many as ten people from the business world if he so wished. In fact, however, the prime minister almost never goes outside the Diet for his ministers. Again, Fujiyama Aiichiro is the only exception since the formation of the LDP in 1955. In 1957 Prime Minister Kishi appointed Fujiyama as foreign minister. It was after his appointment that Fujiyama ran for and was elected to the Diet. The dynamics of factional politics within the LDP leave little room for the appointment of outsiders to these coveted cabinet posts.

A similar pattern prevails in the recruitment of businessmen into other appointive government positions. Here again there is a marked difference between the pre- and post-party-merger periods. Before the party merger, businessmen were often appointed ambassadors, for instance, to undertake specific missions for the government. This trend reached its height in the fifties when numerous businessmen were recruited by the government to negotiate reparation agreements with Southeast Asian countries. Businessmen were also sent abroad in considerable numbers on official economic missions. Such practices have diminished in more recent years. Furthermore, unlike the United States, every regular ambassadorial appointment is made from among career foreign ministry officials. There is no system of rewarding the large financial contributor to the LDP with an ambassadorship. In fact, virtually all posts in the bureaucracy, except for those of the cabinet ministers themselves, are filled by persons recruited from within the career service. This is a very different situation from that prevailing in the United States where political appointments often reach down several levels in the bureaucratic hierarchy.

Businessmen appointed to other governmental positions are also notable for being small in number. Commentators often point to Usami Makoto, former president of the Mitsubishi Bank, who served as president of the Bank of Japan from 1964 to 1969. But Usami is the exception that proves the rule. His successor, Sasaki Tadashi, reestablishes the more common pattern: he was a career bureaucrat in the Bank of Japan.

Business participation on governmental advisory commissions does not represent career mobility in the strict sense, but can be considered under this rubric of business-in-government broadly defined. Each ministry as well as the prime minister's office has numerous advisory commissions (*shingikai*). The system was first introduced during the American Occupation and became so popular that at one point there were over 250 of these commissions in operation. Since 1960, the government has been making an effort to cut down on their number, but the advisory commission has now become an integral part of the governmental structure.[30] In 1971 important leaders of the business community served on a variety of government committees including the Consultative Committee on Foreign Ministry Personnel, the Economic Consultative Council attached to the prime minister's office, the Finance Ministry's Consultative Council on Finance, and the Education Ministry's Central Consultative Council on Education.

There is no question but that such commissions can provide a

---

[30] Kazuo Nukazawa, "Government-Business Relations in Japan," mimeo (1971), p. 7. Despite attempts to cut down on the number, government figures indicate that in 1972 there were 236 *shingikai* in existence. Figures cited in Yamamoto, *Keizai kanryō*, p. 47.

mechanism for the exercise of influence. But it is important not to exaggerate their importance. For one thing they are for the most part consultative, not decision-making or administrative organs. Second, businessmen share membership on them with scholars and other groups and thus are not in a position simply to manipulate them at will. Third, selection of commission members is made by the relevant ministry. As a result, there may be as much difference of opinion among the businessmen on the commission as between business and other commission members. Moreover, those businessmen whose views appear most congenial to the bureaucrats responsible for deciding commission membership are those likely to be selected. Finally, there are no simple answers to the question of how advisory commissions affect public policy. In some cases influence is probably very great; in others minimal. There are some instances where the advisory commissions help push government policy in new directions; it is more likely, however, that in many cases, advisory commissions probably provide the government an opportunity to co-opt support for policies that the bureaucracy has already determined.[31]

Career mobility between government and business in Japan is a one-way street. The only significant movement is from government into business, a pattern Japanese refer to as *amakudari*.[32] Such a pattern is also prevalent in Western countries, but there are elements to the Japanese case that are particularly notable.

Because of the early retirement characteristic of most Japanese ministries, bureaucratic entry into business takes place at a relatively young age. Furthermore, bureaucrats as a rule enter businesses that have close working relations with their ministry. Thus, finance ministry bureaucrats tend to go to banks and other financial institutions, MITI officials to large industry, construction ministry officials to construction companies. Legally, bureaucrats are prohibited for two years after retirement from going to work for a firm with which they have had official dealings within the five years preceding retirement. But this rule has little practical impact. A company looks for a retiring bureaucrat who has the right personal connections within the appropriate ministries, although this need not be someone with whom the firm has had personal dealings.

Dramatic examples of *amakudari* abound. In the steel industry, for example, the Nippon Steel Company lists three former vice-ministers of MITI among its executives, Kawasaki Steel has a former vice-minister of the Economic Planning Agency, and Kobe Steel has another former high

---

[31] One Keidanren staff member has argued: "More often than not, these *shingikai* become spokesmen for bureaucratic interests. The government chooses the committee members and presses for acceptance of its views as the consensus of the *shingikai*." Nukazawa, "Government-Business Relations," p. 7.

[32] Literally "descending from heaven." It has been suggested in jest recently that in light of the greater affluence found in business than in the bureaucracy and the alleged declining prestige of the bureaucracy in Japan, bureaucrats who move into business should be referred to as *amaagari*, "ascending to heaven."

official from MITI. The Tokyo, Kansai, and Hokkaido Electric and Power Companies each has a former MITI vice-minister on its executive board. The presidents of four of the fourteen city banks are former Finance Ministry officials.

Undoubtedly, *amakudari* plays a role in facilitating business-government communication, if not coordination. But here too the situation is not free of ambiguity. For one thing, some of the recruitment of bureaucrats into private business is not due to business initiative. Early retirement, particularly in the economic ministries, and poor retirement benefits, leave men in their early fifties with many productive years ahead of them and without employment. Ministries have increasingly sought to prevail upon industry to hire such bureaucrats; thus, helping retiring bureaucrats find jobs is often viewed as a moral obligation, if not a legal one. Furthermore, finding a job in industry for a bureaucrat is a way to reduce the number of people competing for promotion as the channel of advancement narrows sharply at the upper reaches of the bureaucratic hierarchy. In short, some degree of career mobility from government to business is the consequence not of business-government collusion or of business efforts to penetrate governmental decision-making structures, but of the internal dynamics of the Japanese bureaucratic system.

Bureaucrats are not always hired by business primarily because of their governmental connections. Often they are hired for their technical skills. Accordingly, entry into business does not in itself demonstrate anything conclusive about a former bureaucrat's role in a particular business firm.

Despite these qualifying remarks, the consequences for business-government relations of the bureaucrat-turned-businessman pattern is an important subject, which deserves further study. I would only suggest that, until the evidence is in, one resist the temptation to draw easy conclusions.

On the other hand, insofar as patterns of businessmen's participation in electoral politics and in government is concerned, I would hope that the preceding discussion has made it clear that business-in-government is a comparatively insignificant mechanism for facilitating business influence over government. Advisory commissions surely do provide opportunities for businessmen to have access to important information, to develop close personal contacts with important bureaucrats, and at least to be a part of the input structure in the decision-making process. In terms of affecting the decision-making process itself, however, such commission participation is no equal to the career mobility from business to government in the United States. Influence in this context is no substitute for power.

INFORMAL ELITE COORDINATION

Important in power elite theory, particularly as developed by C. Wright Mills, is the assumption that informal, social ties among elite groups reinforce a common value consensus, provide opportunities for arriving at policy agreements, and account for the ease with which certain groups can walk through the corridors of power.[33] When this elitist approach is applied to Japan, the result is a picture of an intimate, conflict-free family of politicians, bureaucrats, and businessmen working together to steer the course of government policies. Geisha houses in Akasaka and Shimbashi become the power centers where an elite meets over sake to determine Japan's future. School and marriage ties become the glue that holds members of the ruling class together. Particular cultural traits become the key for explaining why informal communication is so particularly significant in Japan.

Informal contact between top political and business leaders obviously plays a part in structuring business-government communication, but available evidence does not suggest that informal elite coordination is as crucial a mechanism for enabling business to exercise a major political role as many writers contend.

A comparative perspective is necessary in one basic regard. American observers who express surprise at the degree of informal contact between business and the political leadership are reflecting not so much the exotic nature of Japanese social intercourse as the uniqueness of the American geographical dispersion of elite groups. The fact that, unlike Washington, Tokyo is the center for almost everything is basic to understanding why there is such apparent elite contact in Japan. Similar patterns probably exist in London or Paris. Indeed, the importance of physical proximity is reflected in the increasing involvement of Osaka businessmen in Tokyo *zaikai* activities. Osaka businessmen have traditionally stayed aloof from the Tokyo business establishment and government. This attitude has been breaking down in recent years for a number of reasons, one of which is simply the development of the "bullet" trains. The increase in Osaka business involvement in Keidanren, on governmental advisory boards, and in the informal groups that meet with the political leadership seems directly related to improvements in the transportation system.

Some observers place great emphasis on the importance of school and marriage ties in binding together Japan's alleged power elite. While the importance Japanese attach to school ties is obvious, their impact on political life is not easily determined and their integrating role should not be oversimplified. Many classmates are political enemies and not all businessmen and politicians who graduated from the same class at Todai become bosom friends. The following kind of exaggeration is anything but helpful to an understanding of how school loyalties get translated into political behavior: "At the peak of his [a well-known businessman named Kato Takeo] career, he was the elder statesman and *oyabun* of all Keio University graduates, many of whom occupied powerful positions in business and finance." [34]

---

[33] C. Wright Mills, *The Power Elite* (New York: Oxford University Press, 1959).

[34] Yanaga, *Big Business*, p. 17.

The study of *keibatsu* (marriage ties) is very popular in Japan; one can easily find a genealogy chart on virtually every businessman and politician. But modern Japan has not had a strong tradition of a closed ruling class. Nepotism is of minor importance. Almost all executives of large corporations are salaried employees, not business owners, with no ability to pass on their businesses to their offspring. In politics, "second generation" Diet members, the sons of deceased or retired politicians, are often successful in the election immediately following the death of the incumbent and unsuccessful in staying in office beyond that. All the efforts supposedly being made to knit Japan's ruling elite together are somewhat in vain if the progeny of the alliances cannot inherit positions of power. Finally, the fact that people are third cousins does not necessarily say anything about their political behavior. Sato Eisaku and Miki Takeo are relatives, but one would have a difficult time explaining why that is politically important.

Although there is a tendency, in my view, to exaggerate the uniqueness and intensity of informal business-government contact in Japan, it is clear that Japan does have some unique mechanisms for facilitating informal elite contacts. Most conspicuous are the clubs of the prime minister and other top political leaders where they join with business leaders on a regular basis for informal discussion.

Since these clubs generally have meetings that are private and off the record (and usually held in the exotic setting of an Akasaka geisha house), they allow the observer to engage the full potential of his imagination in deciding what goes on at them. Some participants suggest that they are important in ensuring that the political leadership does not do anything "rash" against big-business interests. Others imply that they have a more positive function in building a consensus on important issues and in coordinating public statements of business and political leaders. Still others suggest that they have only minor importance. The observer need only choose his informants carefully to substantiate his preconceptions.

There is some evidence that helps put the role of these clubs in perspective. Most important is the trend for the clubs to become institutionalized. This was particularly true during Sato's long tenure. Clubs were once truly informal groupings of politicians and close business supporters. Today they are organizations. To be a member of one of the prime minister's clubs is to be recognized as a member of the establishment. The easy informality and intimacy that previously characterized relations between Japan's political and business leadership has gradually given way to a more formal kind of relationship. As informality has declined, the old clubs have become more structured, less intimate, and larger institutions.

The Ikeda era represented the culmination of an era of intimate personal ties between business and political leaders that dates from the time of the Yoshida administration. Ikeda was made Yoshida's finance minister while still a first-term member of the Diet. He was recommended for that post by Miyajima Seijiro, former president of the Japan Industrial Club and Yoshida's closest business associate. This Yoshida-Miyajima relationship was mirrored years later by the close personal relationship between Ikeda and the group of businessmen called the Kobachū group because it was led by Kobayashi Ataru (Chū), former president of the Japan Development Bank and a close colleague of Miyajima. Members in this group included, among others, Sakurada Takeshi of Nisshinbo, Nagano Shigeo of Fuji (now Nippon) Steel, the late Mizuno Shigeo of *Sankei Shinbun*, Imazato Hiroki of Nihon Seikō, and Shikanai Nobutaka of Fuji Television. Two characteristics of this group are particularly important. First, its members were (and several still are) active leaders in Nikkeiren and Keizai Doyukai and not in Keidanren. Second, they are not, with the exception of Nagano, representatives of "big" business. During the Ikeda period this group, particularly Kobayashi, Nagano, Mizuno, and Sakurada (who were referred to as the "*zaikai* four emperors"), was an active political force, channeling political funds to the LDP and maintaining the most intimate contact with the political leadership.

Sato's long tenure broke down these personal ties and reduced the importance of the clubs that had been established to bring the prime minister and the business leaders together. For one thing, Sato's personal style was quite different from Ikeda's. Business leaders commonly contrast Ikeda's outgoing, informal, argumentative approach with Sato's officious, bureaucratic, noncommittal style. Whether it made any difference in policy or not is an open question, but businessmen at least felt that with Ikeda they had an opportunity to fully discuss issues and bring him around to their view. With Sato they could never be sure their view was understood or what Sato's position was.

Furthermore, Sato made a concerted effort to expand his business ties beyond the relatively small group of business leaders that had been close to Ikeda. Sato set up an unprecedented number of clubs to expand his contacts. This led one contemporary observer to remark that the "Sato administration is in danger of opening up too many separate, multiple routes to the business community, and without any structure or order it runs the danger of losing its close *zaikai* ties." [35] This is precisely what did happen and is part of the reason for Sato's long tenure and *zaikai*'s declining influence. Imazato Hiroki remarked at the beginning of the Sato period: "Our era has for all practical purposes ended with the establishment of the Sato regime." [36] This view was echoed after Sato left the prime ministership by Nagano Shigeo in his remark: "The Sato era was different from the Ikeda era. The so-called *zaikai* four emperors didn't exist under Sato." [37]

---

[35] Suzuki, *Seiji o ugokasu keieisha*, p. 184.

[36] Quoted in ibid., p. 114.

[37] Quoted in Yamaguchi Hiroshi and Yuasa Masami, "Tanaka shinseiken de uō saō shita zaikaijintachi" [The Confusion of *Zaikai* leaders and the new Tanaka regime], *Zaikai*, August 1, 1972, p. 22.

If the close personal ties between political and business leaders were eroded during the Sato administration, they probably will be weakened even further during the Tanaka administration. Tanaka does, of course, have close relations with many business leaders. During the years he served as secretary general of the LDP, he was responsible for the Party's fund raising, and during the periods he served as finance minister and MITI minister, he was in constant and close contact with the business leadership. Shortly before his election as prime minister, the Getsuyōkai (the Monday Club) was established to bring Tanaka together with business leaders for periodic discussions.[38] But Tanaka has not had intimate personal ties with Japan's leading businessmen, and he has not had to depend on them for his own political funds. He has not given as much attention as many other LDP leaders to building his *zaikai* ties. He has been more solicitous than any former prime minister of the newly wealthy businessmen outside the business establishment that *zaikai* represents. Tanaka's personal style suggests a further decline in the importance of the prime minister's clubs as a mechanism for facilitating informal elite coordination.

Leaving aside the weakening personal ties, there is something essentially fanciful in the view that informal clubs play an important decision-making role, or more generally, that informal elite coordination is a crucially important feature of Japanese politics. Most decisions in complex societies, after all, are bureaucratic decisions and are handled through formal bureaucratic institutions. To assume that political and business leaders informally make decisions on issues is to deny the bureaucratization and complexity of the decision-making process. Furthermore, issues that are so controversial as to require a top-level political decision also are likely to arouse the active interest of numerous groups in the society. That clubs and other informal contacts give business leadership an opportunity to express views directly to the top political leadership is important, but when the political leadership has to make a decision, it has to take into consideration many other pressures besides those coming from big business.

In realistic terms, the prime minister's clubs are important to the extent that they give business leaders an access to the prime minister that is not available to other groups. But the degree to which such access has practical consequences for policy depends on such other factors as the issue involved, the degree of unanimity or dissension within the business leadership on that issue, and the strength of other forces in the society. There is no simple equation between access and influence. Demands can be communicated to the political leadership in a variety of ways. A

---

[38] The Getsuyōkai was organized by Mizukami Tatsuzo, adviser to Mitsui Bussan, and included at its first meeting after Tanaka's victory: Nagano and Inayama (Nippon Steel), Komai (Hitachi), Toyoda (Toyota), Doko (Toshiba), Fujino (Mitsubishi), Imazato (Nihon Seiko), Iwasa (Fuji), Tajitsu (Mitsubishi), and Nakayama (Industrial Bank). Information on the activities of the Getsuyōkai from Mizukami Tatsuzo interview, July 24, 1972.

private dinner party is one; a massive strike by organized labor is another.

In addition to all that has been said here, big business's access to the prime minister is not as great as is often assumed. It is, of course, impossible to get complete and accurate information on top-level informal interaction between big business and the prime minister. Meetings can be held in secret, understandings can be reached over the telephone, agreements can be made on the golf course. Nonetheless, the evidence available on the prime minister's activities does not suggest as intimate a relationship as is generally assumed.

The *Asahi Shinbun* publishes a column every morning describing the prime minister's schedule for the preceding day. While the reporters surely miss some things, they do a credible job of accounting for almost all the prime minister's time from early morning until his return home in the evening. An analysis of Prime Minister Sato's schedule as reported in the *Asahi* for a one-year period from July 1, 1971 to June 30, 1972, presents an interesting picture. The overwhelming proportion of his working day throughout this year was spent with top LDP politicians including his cabinet ministers. The second most time-consuming activity involved meetings with foreign dignitaries. This left little time for the business leadership, and almost all of that was at club meetings. Sato met with a *zaikai* group called the Itsukakai (Fifth Day of the Month Club)·once a month except for one month when there was no meeting. He met with the Chōeikai, another grouping of Tokyo's business leadership, six times, and with a group of Osaka-based businessmen in a club called the Kitchōkai nine times. He also met nine times with the Sansuikai, the members of which included former Prime Minister Kishi and Kishi's close associates in the business community, and had four meetings with the Kamomekai, a club of shipping industry leaders. There were five meetings with another *zaikai* group called the Akebonokai. In short, the prime minister met with different leaders of the business community according to a regular pattern of monthly or bimonthly meetings. There was only one group of businessmen that got to see him more than once a month. This was the Tsukiichikai, a group of businessmen from Yamaguchi prefecture where Sato is elected to the Diet. Sato is reported to have met with this group twenty-three times in twelve months. The privileged access of this group to the prime minister suggests that he may have been giving more attention to looking after his constituency than to seeking the advice of big businessmen on running the nation's affairs.

In addition to these group meetings there were nine meetings during the year with the leaders of the four economic organizations.[39] No more than

---

[39] The term *keizai dantai*—economic organizations—can refer to a vast array of trade and industrial associations, local merchant associations, and nationwide groups, but as used in this paper its meaning is restricted to what the Japanese call *zenkoku sōgōteki keizai dantai*, translated here as nationwide comprehensive economic organizations, economic federations, or, where there is no danger of confusion, simply economic organizations.

twenty additional meetings with businessmen were reported in the *Asahi* accounts for the entire period.

This public schedule, of course, is not complete, but it probably does give an accurate indication of the prime minister's division of time in a general sense. To assume that the prime minister spends a great deal of time with leaders of big business is to be unrealistic about his responsibilities. Almost all of his time is spent as president of his party in dealing with political issues, as head of his cabinet in dealing with governmental issues, and as head of state in dealing with matters of foreign relations. The schedule confirms that big business gets regular, institutionalized access to the prime minister. It does not support the view that the business leadership is intimately involved in the process of government.

POLITICAL FUNDS AND POLITICAL INFLUENCE [40]

One of the most striking features of the LDP is the extent of its dependence on big business contributions for its financial support and the degree to which the sources and amount of that support are hidden from public view. In a society that traditionally has been relatively free of corruption, it is noteworthy the extent to which extensive illegal financing of the political activities of politicians and political parties has become an integral part of the political system. But revelations in the seventies about corruption in the financing of American election campaigns should be a reminder that this is a universal and not a particularly Japanese problem. This point is important because writings on political funding in Japan tend to reflect the tendency of many Japanese to judge their own political behavior against extremely high standards of supposed "democratic" behavior, and thereby, to paint a particularly critical picture.

There is no doubt that money can buy political influence in Japan as it does elsewhere. But lest one succumb to the temptation of drawing overly broad conclusions about the extent to which political funding is the source of political influence for the Japanese big business community, mention should be made of a few factors that serve to inhibit the exercise of such influence.

First of all, the lack of a moderate opposition party with the potential for taking over power serves to weaken the credibility of any business threat to withhold funds from the LDP. It is often argued that the creation of a second moderate political party is necessary if Japan is to develop a "mature" democratic system. But ironically the development of a strong nonideological opposition party may serve to increase big business's political influence by making credible a threat to withdraw financial support from the LDP if certain polities are not adopted.

---

[40] This section is necessarily abbreviated because of space limitations. It is intended primarily to suggest some issues that need to be considered in any full length treatment of political funding in Japan.

Second, the financing of individual Diet-candidate campaigns on the local level is only indirectly provided by the big business community. LDP candidates tend to depend on local support and the backing of their faction leader. The latter is dependent on business contributions, but the ties between the business establishment and the LDP backbenchers is indirect.

Furthermore, a characteristic of political funding in present day Japan is the new role being played by wealthy businessmen who are not part of the big business establishment. Men who have made fortunes in recent years in real estate, construction and land development today comprise a powerful political force. They are not active in Keidanren or accepted as part of the big business community but many of them have intimate ties with LDP politicians and appear to be the source of a great deal of "under the table" money that allegedly passes hands between businessmen and politicians. One can hypothesize that the increasing importance of this group in funding LDP politicians, combined with a dramatic increase in the costs involved in professional political life, are resulting in an increase in political corruption. Such a development does not, however, strengthen the influence of the big business establishment over the LDP.

In the case of big business' political contributions, there is an apparent trend away from efforts to coordinate business contributions[41] and an increase in the development of ties between individual factions and particular business conglomerates. Rather than reinforcing an image of Japan, Incorporated such a trend threatens to revive in a new form a prewar funding pattern in which conservative political parties (instead of the large party factions today) received support from different large business enterprises.

The issue of political financing is complex and I would only suggest that a serious study of this question needs to take account of the factors mentioned above. Also to be meaningful, any analysis of business influence over the LDP needs to have a comparative perspective. Does big business exert more political influence through political contributions in Japan than it does in the United States or in France for example? One cannot, I believe, answer that question by arguing that the big business community coordinates its funding or maximizes its influence over the LDP through the machinations of the *zaikai* or through some other unique mechanism.

THE ORGANIZATION
OF BIG-BUSINESS INTERESTS

There are organizations in the United States—the Chamber of Commerce of the United States and the National Association of Manufacturers—that are comparable in name to Japan's major economic federations, but they

---

[41] In August 1974, Keidanren announced that it would no longer serve as a channel for political contributions by big business to the LDP.

do not perform the same functions. Japan's economic organizations are more comparable to several European organizations. They have historically provided an important mechanism for the representation of Japanese business interests and an organizational focus for *zaikai* activities.

The historical development of economic organizations in Japan is similar to that in Western countries.[42] By the end of the nineteenth century all of these countries had established Chambers of Commerce. With the First World War, each established a specifically industrialist organization, and after the war there was a general restructuring of economic organizations in Japan, Germany, Italy, and France.[43]

One difference between Japan and European countries is that Japan was some twenty years behind Europe in the development of an organization of businessmen to deal specifically with labor problems. Another difference is that there traditionally has been, and still is, a rather clear separation between Japanese economic organizations that represent big business and those that represent small and medium-sized enterprises. This is in part a reflection of the dual structure of the Japanese economy, and is in contrast to the situation in many European countries where economic organizations represent all industry. A further difference is that whereas European economic organizations have strong and active local branches, the most powerful economic organizations in Japan have little or no organization on the local level.

Government sponsorship of capitalism in the Meiji period was mirrored in the history of the development of Japan's first economic organizations. The first Japanese businessmen's organization, the Chamber of Commerce, was formed at government request and with government financial assistance; it was given legal status and served as a government advisory council.[44] This history is not as unique as it may seem; in Germany and other continental European states, early Chambers of Commerce served to some extent as semigovernmental organs. In the United States, even though the Chambers were originally local, purely private organizations of businessmen, the creation of the nationwide Chamber of Commerce was

---

[42] For a concise comparison of Japan's economic organizations with European and American ones, see Keidanren, *Keizai dantai rengōkai zenshi* [Comprehensive history of the Federation of Economic Organizations] (Tokyo, 1962), p. 323.

[43] The first industrialist organizations in western Europe, the United States, and Japan were all created within a ten-year period from just before the outbreak of World War I: The Italian CGII (Confederazione Generale dell'Industria Italiana) was founded in 1910; the American Chamber of Commerce of the United States (which despite its name represented industrialists as well as merchants) was created in 1912; the British FBI (Federation of British Industries) in 1916; the Japan Industrial Club in 1917; and the German BDI (Bundesverband der Deutschen Industrialler) in 1919.

[44] For an excellent study of the emergence and development of the Chamber of Commerce in Japan, see Nagata Masaomi, *Keizai dantai hatten shi* [History of the development of economic organizations] (Tokyo, 1956). Important documentary material on the origins of the Chamber are included in Nihon Shōkō Kaigisho, *Meiji hyakunen to shōkō kaigisho 90 nen no ayumi* [One hundred years from the Meiji Restoration and ninety years of the Chamber of Commerce and Industry] (Tokyo, 1968).

promoted largely by President Taft, and invitations to the first meeting of
the CCUS went out with President Taft's signature.[45] Furthermore,
although the Japan Chamber of Commerce was founded with considerable government intervention, the Japan Industrial Club in 1917 and the
Economic Federation in 1923 were founded on the initiative of the
business community without government participation. Government involvement in the establishment of the Chamber of Commerce was
important, however, because it did set a pattern for Japanese economic
organizations to serve an advisory role to government. That pattern was
adopted by later organizations and established itself in the activities of
postwar organizations as well.

The history of development of economic organizations in Japan is first
of all a history of the inability, despite the effort, to create one
comprehensive economic organization. In a rather ironic comment on the
view that the Japanese economic community is a united force, the authors
of Keidanren's history of economic organizations in Japan asked in
dismay, "Is the constant cycle of splintering and reunification and
splintering again the inescapable fate of Japan's economic organizations?" [46] Indeed, the history of these organizations is the history of a
constant shifting of power from one organization to another and the
creation of several, somewhat competitive, so-called comprehensive organizations. There is no organization that represents the business community;
there are several organizations that represent different elements within it.

A second factor in the history is the formation of a separate organization
to handle labor problems. The first such organization was Zensanren
(*Zenkoku sangyō dantai rengōkai*), founded in 1931. Its present-day successor is
Nikkeiren. Keidanren does not deal with labor problems.

A third important factor in the historical development of Japan's
economic organizations is that the postwar reorganization of prewar
institutions was undertaken in a period when the country was in a state of
physical collapse, economic chaos, and a social revolution being guided by
an alien occupation force. The structure and the purposes of the newly
created economic organizations were profoundly influenced by and were
in response to a unique and temporary situation. Japan's postwar
economic organizations have had to adapt to, or be rendered irrelevant by,
the dramatic changes that have affected Japan's society and economy in
the quarter century that has passed since their creation.

The organizations Japanese refer to as the *keizai yon dantai,* the four
organizations of the economic community, are Keidanren, Nikkeiren,
Keizai Doyukai and Nissho (the national Chamber of Commerce and
Industry of Japan). These organizations comprise the major institutions
for the representation of Japanese business interests. Among them,
Keidanren is the most powerful and prestigious.

---

[45] Keidanren, *Zenshi*, p. 9.
[46] Cited in *Zaikai tenbō*, p. 12.

Keidanren was originally founded as a comprehensive economic organization with a mandate—largely at the insistence of the American Occupation—to pay special attention to the interests of small- and medium-sized enterprises.[47] However, by 1952 Keidanren had become a spokesman for big business interests, and the constituent organizations representing small business, led by Fujiyama Aiichirō, bolted the organization. Since that time, Keidanren has developed an impressive organizational structure to serve the interests of its membership of 110 industrial, commercial, and financial associations and 739 leading corporations encompassing virtually all the major businesses in the country.

Keidanren strives to mobilize consensus within the business community and influence the government to adopt policies that are responsive to industry's wishes. To accomplish this, it has established an elaborate structure of committees to examine questions of concern to the business community and has created a number of mechanisms for ensuring that business views get fully represented to government.

Keidanren's thirty-seven committees cover the entire span of economic issues, both domestic and foreign, and are chaired by leading businessmen. The committee staffs stay in constant contact with lower- and middle-level bureaucrats in relevant government ministries.[48] In the case of Keidanren, this means primarily MITI. There is constant communication, exchange of documents, and meetings between Keidanren staff members and MITI bureaucrats. There are also regular meetings of Keidanren's leadership with top-level bureaucrats and cabinet ministers. Between August 1971 and May 1972, for instance, there were twenty meetings with top-level bureaucrats: four from the Finance Ministry (MOF), five from MITI, four from the Foreign Ministry, two from the Self-Defense Agency, one from the Construction Ministry, three from the Justice Ministry, and one from the Agriculture Ministry. Between July 1971 and May 1972, there were fifteen meetings with cabinet ministers: three with the prime minister, four with the finance minister, three with the MITI minister, two with the head of the Self-Defense Agency, one with the head of the Science and Technology Agency, one with the minister of transportation, and one with the construction minister. Between August and December 1971, there were also seven meetings with LDP party leaders which dealt exclusively with discussions of the tax sections in the draft of the following year's annual budget. There were no meetings with LDP leaders recorded in the schedule for the period from January to July of 1972.[49]

---

[47] For the early postwar history of Keidanren, see Keidanren, *Keidanren no 20 nen* [Keidanren's twenty years] (Tokyo, 1969) and Keidanren, *Zenshi*, pp. 490–505, 765–785.

[48] For an English-language description of Keidanren's organization and activities, see the pamphlet published by Keidanren, *Keidanren, Japan Federation of Economic Organizations* (Tokyo, 1972). In Japanese, see Keidanren, *20 nen*; Akimoto Hideo, *Keidanren* (Tokyo, 1969); and Yomiuri Shinbunsha, *Zaikai* (Tokyo, 1972), pp. 51–94.

[49] Compiled from the monthly reports of Keidanren activities contained in *Keidanren geppō*, July 1971–July 1972. "Top-level" bureaucrats, as used here, refers to people at the bureau-chief level and above. Another writer giving figures for the period from July 1970 to

Most of Keidanren's activities relate to economic issues of direct and immediate concern to the business community. The representations it makes to the government are concerned almost exclusively with concrete economic issues such as tax rates, international monetary policy, and liberalization policy.

Keidanren regularly issues various proposals, "requests," and "demands" to the government. Since 1954, as indicated in the accompanying table, Keidanren has issued about twenty such resolutions a year.[50] Changes in emphasis over the years reflect both changes in the economy and in Keidanren's organization. The absence of resolutions on labor policy or reconstruction after 1950, for example, reflects the division of responsibility between Keidanren and Nikkeiren from that time and the boon to Japanese industry brought about by the Korean War. The fact that resolutions concerning liberalization did not appear until 1959, and those concerning pollution until 1965, mirror patterns of postwar economic development in Japan. Needless to say, the fact that there were as many resolutions concerning the international monetary system in 1971 as there were in all the years up to 1967 is a fitting comment on the big-business community's concerns in the early 1970s.

The categories most often represented in the resolutions give an idea of the kinds of issues about which consensus within Keidanren is most successfully achieved. There are six categories in which Keidanren has issued more than thirty resolutions in its history (leaving aside the miscellaneous category). One of these categories is the economy in general, which refers mainly to such matters as forecasts concerning economic growth and the rate of inflation. Another is finance, which includes comments on government fiscal policies and the opinions Keidanren submits to the minister of finance each year on the new government budget. The Confederation of British Industries and other comparable European economic organizations also engage in the latter practice vis-à-vis their governments. The other well-represented categories relate to taxation, foreign trade, energy resources, and defense production. The largest number of defense-related resolutions in 1953 was in response to the establishment of the defense agency and the new emphasis on domestic weapons production.

June 1972 suggests that the number of top-level government officials was somewhat greater than the data in *Keidanren geppō* revealed. According to his figures, the source of which is not indicated, top-level government officials (including cabinet ministers) were invited to Keidanren seventy times. MITI officials were the most numerous, visiting twenty-three times; Foreign Ministry officials were next at thirteen visits; and Finance Ministry officials made twelve visits. The rest were from the Economic Planning Agency, Ministry of Transportation, Science and Technology Agency, Ministry of Agriculture, Ministry of Construction, and the Ministry of Justice. See Yamamoto, *Keizai kanryō*, p. 70.

[50] Data compiled from information contained in Keidanren, *20 nen*, for the period up to 1968, and in *Keidanren geppō* for the period from 1968 to 1972.

Table 1

Keidanren Resolutions 1945–1971

Year	45	46	47	48	49	50	51	52	53	54	55	56	57	58	59	60	61	62	63	64	65	66	67	68	69	70	71	Total
General Economy	0	4	1	3	8	3	2	2	1	2	0	1	2	2	0	2	1	3	3	3	3	2	2	2	3	3	2	60
Finance	0	0	2	5	6	7	3	3	3	1	3	0	0	1	1	0	1	0	1	1	1	1	1	1	1	1	0	42
Taxation	0	1	2	2	7	3	4	4	3	1	1	2	2	2	3	1	1	1	3	2	2	1	1	2	1	1	1	53
Capital	0	0	1	0	3	1	0	0	0	0	1	2	2	0	0	1	1	1	1	1	1	1	0	0	0	0	0	11
Customs Duties	0	0	0	0	1	1	0	1	1	0	0	0	0	0	1	0	0	1	0	0	0	1	0	0	0	0	0	8
Prices-Labor	1	1	2	7	4	2	0	1	0	0	0	0	0	0	0	0	0	0	0	0	0	0	0	0	0	0	0	17
International Relations	0	0	0	0	0	1	1	0	0	1	0	0	0	0	1	0	0	0	0	0	1	0	0	1	0	0	0	7
Foreign Trade	0	0	0	1	3	5	4	2	3	3	2	3	5	1	2	0	0	0	3	1	1	1	0	0	0	0	1	42
Economic Cooperation	0	0	0	1	0	1	1	0	0	0	1	1	0	1	2	1	2	1	2	2	1	2	1	0	1	0	0	18
U.S.-Japan Economic Relations	0	0	0	0	0	0	2	6	0	0	1	0	0	0	0	0	0	0	0	2	0	0	0	1	0	0	0	15
International Monetary System	0	0	0	0	0	0	1	0	0	0	0	0	0	1	1	0	2	1	0	0	0	1	0	0	0	0	4	10
Foreign Capital	0	0	0	0	0	0	0	1	2	0	0	1	0	0	0	0	0	0	0	0	0	0	0	0	1	0	0	6
Industrial Policy	0	5	1	2	2	2	0	3	0	0	0	0	0	0	0	0	3	0	0	0	0	0	0	1	0	0	0	21
Liberalization	0	0	0	0	0	0	0	0	0	0	0	1	0	2	0	2	0	1	0	0	0	0	2	0	0	0	0	6
Reconstruction of Industry	0	2	3	2	0	0	0	0	0	0	2	2	0	0	2	0	0	0	0	0	1	0	0	0	0	0	0	12
Industrial Technology	0	0	0	0	0	0	0	0	1	1	0	0	1	0	0	1	0	0	0	0	0	1	0	0	0	0	0	7
Pollution	0	0	0	0	0	0	0	0	0	0	2	1	0	1	0	0	1	2	0	1	1	0	0	0	0	1	0	8
Energy Resources	0	1	2	2	5	6	7	1	0	0	2	0	0	3	1	0	0	2	1	0	0	2	0	1	1	0	1	38
Transportation	0	0	0	0	1	1	2	1	1	0	0	1	1	2	3	3	3	1	0	1	0	0	1	0	0	0	0	24
Agriculture	1	0	0	0	1	1	3	1	1	0	1	0	1	3	0	1	1	1	1	1	1	1	1	0	0	0	0	19
Other Industries	1	1	0	0	0	2	0	0	0	1	0	0	0	0	0	0	0	0	0	0	0	0	0	0	0	0	0	5
Economy-Related Laws	0	0	0	2	2	2	2	0	0	1	1	0	0	2	1	2	0	1	2	0	2	4	1	0	2	1	0	28
Management	0	0	0	0	0	0	2	1	0	0	0	0	1	0	0	1	1	1	1	1	1	1	1	2	2	1	0	15
Small- and Medium-Sized Enterprises	0	0	0	0	0	2	2	1	0	0	0	0	3	0	0	0	0	0	0	0	0	1	1	0	0	0	0	6
Administrative Reform	0	0	1	0	0	1	0	1	0	0	0	0	0	3	1	0	1	1	3	2	1	0	0	0	0	0	0	8
Defense Production	0	0	0	0	0	3	0	0	15	5	4	1	3	3	0	2	0	3	1	6	0	1	0	0	0	0	0	46
Miscellaneous	3	2	3	3	4	3	2	4	3	1	2	1	0	0	1	1	1	1	1	0	0	0	1	0	0	0	0	36
TOTAL	6	17	18	28	50	43	34	34	37	17	19	18	23	21	17	16	21	19	22	19	14	18	12	15	11	10	9	568

At several points in the postwar period, Keidanren has joined together with other economic organizations to issue joint resolutions intended to bring the full influence of a united business community to bear on the government and political parties on essentially noneconomic issues. Among the resolutions listed in the miscellaneous category are eight that deal with political issues, six of which were issued jointly by the four economic organizations. However, seven of these either preceded or came at the time of the conservative party merger and were calls on the political leadership to establish political stability. The eighth was issued during the security treaty crisis in June 1960 and was a call for the protection of parliamentary democracy and the re-establishment of international trust.

The four organizations have joined together on other occasions as well to try to influence the course of political developments. The most famous incident perhaps was the demand by the four organizations' leaders in September 1956 that Prime Minister Hatoyama resign before going to the Soviet Union to sign the normalization agreement. Hatoyama did not take their advice.

The most recent example of a *zaikai* effort occurred one day after Tanaka became prime minister. On July 6, Kikawada, Uemura, Nagano, Sakurada, Doko, and Imazato called on Tanaka and presented a "request" (*yōbōsho*) of five articles.[51] The five articles called for the establishment of a political posture that would regain the people's faith, the establishment of strong political leadership, recognition and acceptance of Japan's international responsibilities, and creation of national solidarity. The fifth article called for a strong party structure. This meant overcoming factionalism and the deep split in the party caused by the Tanaka-Fukuda fight for the party presidency. "All efforts should be expended to discard small differences and in union improve the party and overcome the crisis" is the group's explanation of the meaning of the five articles.[52] As Nagano put it, "We are hoping for dynamic politics based on party unanimity."[53]

Such a representation by the leaders of the business community has no parallel in American society. For the business leadership to make demands on the political posture of the new prime minister, even before he had completed the formation of his cabinet, surely seems excessive, at least to an outside observer. But the meaning of the representation in terms of the exercise of political influence is not easy to discern. Obviously, if *zaikai* had been as powerful as sometimes alleged, Mr. Tanaka would not have

---

[51] Discussed in Saji Toshihiko, "Zaikai wa dō hyōka suru ka" [How we should evaluate the *zaikai*], *Chūō kōron*, September 1972, p. 116. Kikawada, Uemura, Nagano, and Sakurada are the heads respectively of Keizai Doyukai, Keidanren, Nissho, and Nikkeiren. Doko is chairman of the board of Toshiba and Imazato is president of Nihon Seiko. Both are active leaders in Keidanran.

[52] Saji, "Zaikai wa dō hyōka suru ka," p. 127.

[53] Ibid., p. 122.

become prime minister and the representation would not have been made in the first place.

The evidence available suggests a number of things about the operation of Keidanren. First of all, Keidanren is an organization concerned with economic matters of general interest to the business community. It is much more vital a meeting ground for Japanese business than is either the National Association of Manufacturers or the Chamber of Commerce for American businessmen. But in its organization and activities it is not unlike economic organizations in Europe. What distinguishes Keidanren from these European organizations is not the nature of its activities but the thoroughness with which it engages in them. Committee meetings involving the leaders of big business, study groups, lectures, speeches by government officials, meetings of trade and industrial associations, parties for visiting dignitaries, and the like occur on a daily basis.

Second, Keidanren's power as a consensus-mobilizing mechanism is exercised within a relatively limited issue area. It is able to mobilize a consensus of the entire business community, to "harmonize" the views of business leaders on the relatively small number of issues that do not involve conflicts within the business community itself. Keidanren has no magic formula for mobilizing a community consensus on issues about which the business community disagrees. Furthermore, the number of resolutions that Keidanren is able to generate each year conveys an exaggerated sense of consensus. Many of its resolutions are the product of such broad compromise that they emerge at a level of generality that largely undercuts their possible influence on government policy.

It is also true that consensus within Keidanren does not necessarily represent consensus within the big-business community. In discussing Keizai Doyukai's role, Keidanren's president Uemura remarked: "Sometimes they cause us trouble because after we go through the painstaking task of building a consensus, Doyukai leadership makes a pronouncement that reflects a different position and succeeds only in confusing the issue. Sometimes I wish they would think a little more carefully about what they say." [54]

Keidanren is an important source of funds for the LDP. It assesses each constituent trade or industrial association a defined amount for transmission to the Kokumin Kyōkai (National Association), an organization established to channel funds to the LDP. But Keidanren does not raise funds for individual factions or individual politicians. Businessmen use political contributions as a source of political influence, but they do so in direct association with LDP members. Keidanren does not provide a mechanism for the exercise of such influence.

Keidanren's structure and activities allow businessmen an opportunity to discuss issues with other businessmen as well as with government

---

[54] Uemura interview, January 1972.

officials and to gain access to information they might not otherwise have. But Keidanren's role as a pressure group in Japan's political system seems to be overestimated. For a variety of reasons Keidanren and the other economic organizations seem to be playing a decreasing interest- or pressure-group role.

Several factors account for this decline. Before 1955 the political party system was unstable, and there were no set patterns for recruitment of political leadership. In this period businessmen were most directly active in politics. Since 1955, clear patterns of political recruitment have been created, established parties have become increasingly institutionalized, patterns of bureaucratic recruitment and advancement are clearly defined, and businessmen have increasingly been excluded from leading political and governmental positions. Policy-making has become increasingly complex and bureaucratized, and this has reduced the opportunities for businessmen, acting through organizations such as Keidanren, to significantly affect the policy-making process.

Viewed from the business side, the growth of the economy and the new strength of Japanese enterprises make Japanese industry much less dependent on organizations such as Keidanren than they were in earlier years. One of the central reasons for creating Keidanren was to gain influence for business interests by combining the strength of over a thousand individual industries which had been weakened by the general economic collapse and the policies of the Occupation authorities. As industry regained its strength, the need to rely on Keidanren to champion industry's cause declined. With economic reconstruction, business became less dependent on government assistance. If anything, many businesses now are more concerned with guarding their independence from encroachments by MITI than seeking government support.

This trend has been strengthened by the gradual reconcentration of Japanese industry. Although the regrouped combines are not structured along the lines of the prewar *zaibatsu,* they are, like their namesakes, capable of protecting their own interests without reliance on Keidanren. Mitsubishi, Mitsui, Sumitomo, Fuji, and other conglomerates do not need Keidanren to the degree that any one element of these groups needed it in 1948. The large conglomerates have their own channels to government and political leaders, provide political funds to LDP politicians, and have their own research staffs. All of this lessens the importance of Keidanren in the total picture of business-government interaction.

With the expansion and the internationalization of the economy, the business community itself has become increasingly pluralistic. There are conflicts of interest within the big-business community that neither Keidanren nor any other organization can effectively mediate. Differences of opinion on the issue of voluntary export controls on textiles and on the rapid liberalization of the computer industry are just two recent examples of the kinds of issues that are increasingly dividing the business community. The consequences on the ability of Keidanren to perform a consensus-mobilizing function are obvious.

Furthermore, the increasing liberalization of the economy, with the consequent rise in foreign investment in Japan, coupled with the rise of a new group of Japanese business leaders have greatly disturbed the social cohesiveness of the Japanese business establishment. Keidanren, for example, has not only moved toward involving leaders of business traditionally considered outside the establishment (such as the automobile industry) in its highest executive positions, but has also begun to open its doors to membership by foreign-owned enterprises in Japan. All of this contributes to further breaking down the "club" atmosphere that had dominated Japan's economic organizations.

This trend is reinforced by the routinization of the mechanisms of business-government interaction themselves. Speeches by cabinet ministers at Keidanren are institutionalized; "informal" clubs bringing together political and business leaders are formalized; and much of what in an earlier age may have been a mechanism for exerting significant influence has now become ritual.

The clublike atmosphere at Keidanren and the intimate personal relationships between business and government leaders have also been affected by a number of developments in regard to the personalities active in *zaikai*. First, some of the most important personalities, commanding enormous respect within the business community and the deepest confidence of the political leadership—such as Miyajima Seijiro, Mizuno Shigeo, Kobayashi Ataru, and Ishizaka Taizo—have either retired or died. Similarly, the men with whom they were closest in the political world, namely Yoshida, Ikeda, and Sato, have also left the center of the stage.

Second, the men who control the leadership positions in the economic organizations and make up the so-called *zaikai* are almost all elderly and in positions of leadership virtually since the forming of these organizations a quarter of a century ago. There is a question whether their position today reflects their influence within the community and vis-à-vis the government, or whether their continued domination is little more than the phenomenon of a firmly entrenched and not particularly representative oligarchy. Several of the leading personalities in the business leadership are not active executives of their companies but devote practically all their time to *zaikai* activities.

Partly due to the domination of leadership positions by this group, many of the executives who are beginning to take over the top positions in Japanese industry have neither the personal ties with the political leadership nor command the respect within the business community of the present leadership group. Neither do they have the close ties among themselves that the older group has.

The editor-in-chief of the *Nikkei Shinbun* once remarked to me that "*zaikai* died with Ikeda," and that, ironically, it was a casualty of the success of the high economic growth policy.[55] *Zaikai,* as an institution, seems to be destined to a fate similar to that of the *genrō* in Meiji Japan—unable to survive the first generation in any meaningful sense. The conditions that gave rise to *zaikai* and lent it authority have been largely erased. The renewed strength of Japanese business, the pluralism within the business community, the internationalization of the economy, the emergence of a new, less cohesive generation of business and political leaders, and other factors suggest that while attempts to perpetuate it are likely, *zaikai* as a dynamic integrating institution in Japan's business community is unlikely to survive the generation of men who created it. This decline of *zaikai* in turn is likely to further encourage the trend toward pluralism presently evident.

The creation and development of the Industrial Problems Research Council perhaps can be best understood as a response by the business elite to these developments. The council was formed to be the new consensus-mobilizing mechanism, the "*zaikai* policy board" as the newspapers like to term it, the new structure for mediating intracommunity disputes and effectively representing business interests to the outside. It was founded in 1966 at the initiative of the head of the Keizai Doyukai, Kikawada Kazutaka, and gradually expanded in size from an original membership of seven to a membership today of twenty-three men representing the largest and most powerful of Japanese industry and finance.[56] It was founded partly to serve as an advisory group to Kikawada after he had been appointed chairman of the prime minister's economic advisory council. However, the main motivation for its founding apparently was the desire to have a small group of leading executives come together to discuss ways to deal with the challenges being created for Japanese industry by the increasing liberalization of the economy. One achievement of Sanken was to play a role in fostering the merger of the Fuji and Yahata steel companies.

Sanken has been regarded as Japan's "most prestigious business policy group" [57] and characterized as a "power above government." [58] It has in fact been rather ineffective. It relies on the staff of Keizai Doyukai and is limited in its activities. Its monthly luncheon meetings are usually attended, according to newspaper reporters, by less than half the membership. It is still regarded in some quarters as "Kikawada's group," and it was partly to overcome that impression and the impression that Sanken was intended to weaken Keidanren by usurping its consensus mobilizing function that the membership was increased.

---

[55] Takeyama Yasuo in a conversation in August 1972.

[56] A list of Sanken members can be found in Yomiuri Shinbunsha, *Zaikai,* p. 158.

[57] Kaplan, *Japan, The Government-Business Relationship,* p. 148.

[58] Hidetoshi Kato, "Sanken: A Power Above Government," *Japan Interpreter* 7:1 (Winter 1971): 36–42.

Sanken, in my view, emerged as an attempt by the business leadership to compensate for the inability of any other existing institution to mobilize and represent a community consensus. Since this inability is not due to the particular organizational structure of Keidanren, but is a consequence of developments in Japan's economic, social and political structures, I would hazard to guess that Sanken is destined to be unsuccessful in performing any major coordinating function.

Many business leaders still talk of the need for *kanmin kyōchō* (government-business harmony) and for *chōsei* (best translated in this context perhaps as government-business coordination). But one gets the feeling that the more *zaikai* leaders talk in these terms, the more they are reflecting the breakdown of postwar patterns of organization and interaction.

THE FUTURE OF JAPAN'S ECONOMIC ORGANIZATIONS

Any organization that exists over a considerable period of time faces the challenge of adapting to a changed environment. Keidanren, Keizai Doyukai, and Nikkeiren were founded over a quarter of a century ago in response to conditions that no longer exist. Keidanren was to mobilize the strength of a weakened and fractionalized Japanese business community; Keizai Doyukai was to give young executives an organizational base for contemplating the long-term reconstruction of the economy and the building of a "revised" capitalist system; "fighting" Nikkeiren was to coordinate management's efforts in battling a politically oriented labor movement. Today each of these organizations is in search of a new role.

It often happens, of course, that organizations do not adapt but either go out of existence or become increasingly irrelevant. It is sometimes suggested, for instance, that there is little to justify Nikkeiren's continued independent existence, that it should be disbanded and have its relevant functions absorbed by Keidanren. Uemura himself has suggested that this would be a sensible development, but an unlikely one.[59] Persons long involved in an organization develop a loyalty that need have little to do with the organization's functions. Employment for considerable numbers of people and impressive titles and honor for the organization's leadership combine to create vested interests in the organization's continued existence. Nikkeiren, as is true for the other organizations, is determined to find a new role—one, in this case, that will enable it to respond to the criticism that it is in fact nothing more than "the labor committee of Keidanren."

The present is a transitional period for these organizations, but the directions in which they are moving seem clear. Keidanren, perhaps most importantly, has had rapid growth in its international operations. It has a

---

[59] Uemura interview, January 1972.

skilled professional staff in its international economic affairs department
and has greatly expanded its activities as liaison between Japanese and
foreign business groups and in helping organize large-scale Japanese
investment programs in Iran, Brazil, and elsewhere around the globe. It
either conducts or sponsors businessmen's conferences with virtually all
European countries, the United States, Canada, and Australia. It has
committees on relations with Southeast Asian countries and increasingly
with Latin America. In 1970 it established a committee on cooperation
with Africa.

Its leaders are spending increasing amounts of time abroad. In a
one-year period from October 1970, President Uemura made five overseas
trips. Significantly, three of them were to the United States. He visited the
United States in October 1970 to discuss the textile issue; led an economic
mission to Iran in April 1971; went to Washington for the Eighth Annual
U.S.-Japan Businessmen's Conference in June; returned to the United
States in September to attend the dedication of the new Japan House in
New York, to which Keidanren makes a substantial annual contribution;
and then led a delegation to the European common market countries in
October.[60]

Keidanren has also expanded its research on pollution, oceanography,
and other such questions that can be effectively researched by a
comprehensive economic organization. These new directions also, of
course, reflect broader changes in the society. As pollution control,
consumer protection, and energy resources have become more central
issues of concern in Japan, Keidanren has moved quickly to establish new
staff sections and new committees to help formulate business positions for
dealing with them.

Keidanren has been moving away from trying to represent a unified
business community on specific issues and has been putting a greater
emphasis on considering broad questions of the long-range future of the
Japanese economy. This trend, as well as the element of competitiveness
that marks the relationship between Keidanren and Keizai Doyukai, were
reflected in Doyukai president Kikawada's remark: "Keidanren's role as a
petitioner for business is declining . . . and it is moving in the direction of
thinking of the total economic structure rather than solely of the benefits
for its member firms. It's improving." [61]

Many long-time domestic observers of Keidanren agree with these
observations of Keidanren's changing role. But foreign observers, who
have only recently discovered Keidanren, tend to see it as a remarkably
cohesive power center of Japanese business, a view that is more appropriate to the Keidanren of the late 1950s. This time lag in perception has

---

[60] Information on President Uemura's activities provided by former Ambassador Toshiro
Shimanouchi, counsellor to the president.

[61] Kikawada interview, January 1972. The president of the Fuji Bank, Iwasa Yoshizane,
made a similar point about Keidanren's development. Iwasa interview, January 1972.

created misconceptions in many a foreign businessman's mind of the organizational unity of the Japanese business community and the ability of a small leadership group to rally a consensus on any particular issue. Depending on the issue, it has led to unwarranted expectations that the business leadership would "do something," or unjustified suspicion that this leadership was indeed coordinating some strategy worked out in the councils of Keidanren.

Keidanren's increasing involvement in questions of long-term economic growth has done much to break down the clear distinction between Keidanren and Keizai Doyukai that once existed. This breakdown has been furthered by the increasing participation in Keidanren by Doyukai activists. Until rather recently most *zaikai* members tended to concentrate their activities in one or the other of the organizations. Today there is a considerable overlap of membership. Two of Doyukai's past presidents, for example, Iwasa Yoshizane and Mizukami Tatsuzo, are among the most active Keidanren leaders.

As a consequence, Doyukai's role has undergone a subtle change. Doyukai was founded by young executives and represented a different constituency than the more established Keidanren with its ties to the prewar Economic Federation. However, Keidanren, in its official twenty-year history, explains the reason for Doyukai's existence as follows:

The representatives of enterprises or associations in Keidanren are in principle limited to one person each, and these people gather and exchange views at Keidanren from a position of representing an association or enterprise. . . . Thus statements representing the association or enterprise are made at Keidanren, but these same people and other managers have the desire to organize a group as individuals. Keizai Doyukai is organized to meet that desire and wish.[62]

Doyukai is now defined as an organization to give Keidanren members (and others) an opportunity to discuss issues from a more individual position.

Keizai Doyukai, however, is intent on expanding its functions and proving its usefulness as an independent organization. It has developed, paralleling a similar trend in Keidanren, a role as a kind of de facto philanthropic organization in Japan. It sponsors a variety of activities, usually supported by foundations in the United States, from support for English language teaching programs to joint research programs with a number of American organizations. Doyukai's changing functions are best described by the organization itself:

As Japan has achieved a remarkable economic development, Keizai Doyukai has diversified its activities and has undertaken not only the problems of the Japanese economy as a whole, but also such other issues as area development and urban

---

[62] Keidanren, *20 nen*, p. 8.

renewal, small- and medium-sized enterprises, agriculture, research and development, and education.[63]

Like Keidanren, Nikkeiren also has greatly expanded its international role, largely because of its position as the representative of Japanese employers in the International Labor Organization. Internationalization of the economy has also lead it to develop new activities in the area of labor-management relations. It has been sponsoring for the last few years, for instance, an annual cruising seminar for people at the foreman level on labor-management relations, giving them a tour of parts of southeast Asia as well as an onboard education. It recently has established a management training center at the foot of Mount Fuji.

Nikkeiren was founded with the slogan: "Employers, be righteous and strong!" and took great pride in the fact that "at the time of the 'Red Purge' in 1950, [it] assisted in expelling well over ten thousand communists from enterprises, thus finally realizing industrial stabilization."[64] It was to business what Sōhyō (the General Council of Trade Unions of Japan) was to labor in the 1950s, and the bitter confrontation between the two organizations forms an important part of the history of the labor-union movement and labor-management relations in the postwar period. In the light of that history it is all the more remarkable to hear Nikkeiren's managing director say at the organization's annual conference in 1964: "I and others want to call on Sōhyō also to work harmoniously on labor problems. Sōhyō members as Japanese want to work for the development of the Japanese economy. Shouldn't we persevere and keep on trying to move near a harmonious relationship with Sōhyō and not attack it as an enemy in [labor] struggles?"[65]

Speaking in 1972, the president of Nikkeiren, Sakurada Takeshi, accented the organization's new posture with the following remarks in regard to that year's coming spring labor offensive:

There would be no other way for employers than to tackle this spring offensive with modesty and seriousness, and to conduct the labor-management negotiations with sincerity, regarding this as a place to educate and be educated. . . . Even when the negotiations fail and dispute [strike?] action is started, the private enterprises must stick to the stand that the "disputes are also the means for education" and wait for the restoration of peace without losing the attitude that both labor and management mutually educate and are educated through the disputes.[66]

Nikkeiren still spends much of its energy in giving assistance to industrial associations and enterprises in their bargaining with labor during the spring struggles, and it still serves as an important organization

---

[63] Keizai Doyukai, *Keizai Doyukai, Japan Committee for Economic Development* (Tokyo, 1971).

[64] Nikkeiren, "An Outline of the Japan Federation of Employers' Associations," pamphlet (Tokyo, November 1971).

[65] Quoted in *Zaikai tenbō*, p. 29.

[66] Quoted in *Nikkeiren News*, no. 48 (June 1972): 1.

in management's dealings with the labor union movement. But as labor has become increasingly concerned with actions to maximize its benefits under the present economic system and less concerned with political action to change that system, the "fighting" nature of Nikkeiren with the emphasis on political confrontation that the term implied in the 1950s has given way to a greater emphasis on research and management-training functions. It has for several years now argued for replacing the seniority and lifetime employment system with "a personnel management system which values individual employee's ability and competence in order to overcome labor shortage and to make Japanese enterprises more competitive in the international market." [67] It has an active research program dealing with issues of wages, promotion and retirement systems, social security and other welfare programs. It has established an Institute of Labor Economy, which does research in such areas as productivity and international wage comparisons, and periodically issues statistics on labor questions.

As big industry regained its strength and grew and set up its own research organs, Nikkeiren found itself playing an increasingly important role for small- and medium-sized enterprises in providing expertise on questions of labor-management relations. Nikkeiren, unlike Keidanren and Keizai Doyukai, has a network of active local branches. While the organization's role as the representative of big business in political struggles with the labor movement is declining, its function as a source of information and advice in dealing with problems of labor relations on the part of smaller firms appears to be increasing significantly.

The official twenty-year history of Nikkeiren provides perhaps the best expression of the organizational adaptation as well as its specific direction of change:

Seen only in terms of [management's] strategy against the labor unions, Nikkeiren may look as though it is becoming just the labor section of Keidanren. But this is nothing more than a one-sided view. It is very clear that now the main focus for Nikkeiren's overall activities is shifting from strategies for opposing the spring struggles and the labor unions to areas of much broader labor-management relations and the development of individual capabilities through its activities in job analysis (*shokumu bunseki*), educational development, mutual understanding (*ishi sotsū*), and the like.[68]

There are commonalities in the direction of change of all three economic organizations. They all are becoming increasingly involved in international affairs and are expanding research functions in areas where no one enterprise or industrial group performs. Keidanren and Nikkeiren are less involved in the day-to-day representation of Japanese business and employer interests and more active than in the past in the analysis of

---

[67] Nikkeiren, *An Outline*, p. 5.
[68] Nikkeiren, *20 nen* [A twenty-year history] (Tokyo, 1968), p. 12.

long-term trends and in research on problems of concern to the business community in general. In performing such functions Japan's economic organizations are acting in much the same way as comparable European organizations. Keidanren and the other economic organizations are likely to continue to perform important roles for the Japanese business community, but they will not be the consensus-mobilizing and representative roles that were so important earlier in the postwar period. Important as these organizations are, they no longer appear to play the role attributed to them of being "indispensable in achieving consensus and in presenting a united front on issues and problems." [69]

IN SUMMATION

There is minimal career mobility for businessmen into politics and government service. Informal elite coordination has largely broken down with the routinization of the mechanisms created to facilitate such coordination and the weakening of the close personal ties between business and political leaders. Economic organizations do not serve effectively as consensus-mobilizing mechanisms and are increasingly involved in consideration of long-term and general business problems rather than in the representation of business interests on specific issues. Big business can exert considerable influence through political contributions, but such efforts have taken place in an environment in which business has not perceived an acceptable alternative to the LDP and in which LDP leaders have been able to expand their sources of funds beyond the big business establishment.

The ruling elite model of Japanese politics has had to make a number of false assumptions about the organizational unity of the business community, its unanimity of views on specific issues, and its involvement in a broad range of governmental decisions. There are few case studies of decision-making in contemporary Japan, but it may be hypothesized that such studies would show what they have shown in the United States: that different groups participate in the decision-making process depending on the issue involved. [70]

Pluralist theory, on the other hand, has its own weaknesses. By focusing on the participants in the decision-making process, it runs the danger of underestimating or totally ignoring the extent to which certain participants share the values and represent the interests of groups not directly involved in the decision-making process. It can be argued that businessmen have not had to participate in the process directly because the

---

[69] Yanaga, *Big Business*, p. 33.

[70] One recent study of the budget-making process in Japan, for instance, argues that the business community exercises no significant role in determining how the financial resources of the government are allocated. See John Campbell, "Contemporary Japanese Budget Politics" (Ph.D. dissertation, Columbia University, 1973).

political leadership and the bureaucracy have shared a common perception of issues and have worked to serve business interests. The contribution of Marxist writings to an understanding of postwar Japanese politics, it seems to me, has been to emphasize this point.

It can be argued that the changes affecting Japan today make elitist theory less relevant and pluralist theory more relevant in the analysis of power and influence in Japanese politics. There was, until recently, a value consensus widely shared in Japan that emphasized rapid economic growth and industrial expansion. While there was an articulate body of opinion on the left that did not share this consensus, rapid growth was a goal to which the Japanese public at large, and not just the business sector, subscribed—a goal that often got translated into practice as what is good for big business is good for Japan.

That consensus is now breaking down. The position as the world's third largest economic power in terms of GNP has created enormous pressures on the government that conflict with business interests. International pressures for greater and faster liberalization and for "orderly marketing," and domestic pressures for improving the quality of life rather than simply expanding the size of the economy are testing, for the first time in a sense, the capacity of the Japanese political and administrative system to respond effectively to conflicting demands. The LDP's continued control of the government depends on its capacity to respond to new demands for a change in government priorities.

It is possible that the LDP will fail to respond to these pressures. Recent election results reflect widespread discontent with its policies. But if the history of the past twenty years is any guide, the LDP will strive to remain a "catchall" political party. Part of the LDP success in staying in power has been its ability to provide minimal satisfactions for all sectors supporting it: farmers, a sizable portion of the working class, in addition to big business, and other groups:

The diversity of interests in the circles from which the Conservative Party draws its money, and with which its leaders have close personal connections, gives the leaders considerable freedom of action. So does the existence of the mass electorate. To win a general election the Conservative Party must be supported by the great majority of middle class electors, and about half its vote must come from the working class. Rational policy requires concessions, and habit has taught the privileged classes reason.[71]

These words about the British Conservative Party are equally applicable to the Japanese conservative party over the past twenty years. It may be impossible for any party in an environment of relatively low economic growth to obtain the kind of broad based support in the future that the LDP has received in the past. But the imperatives of electoral politics

---

[71] Allen Potter, "Great Britain: Opposition with a Capital 'O'," in Robert A. Dahl, ed., *Political Oppositions in Western Democracies* (New Haven: Yale University Press, 1966), p. 31.

encourages the LDP to seek such support and to avoid becoming the political arm of any one particular interest group.

One might argue that as long as interests in conflict with those of big business remain unorganized, "latent" rather than "manifest" in Dahrendorf's terms,[72] a conservative party in a capitalist society will be responsive to business interests. The late development of interest groups in Japan and their sometimes unique relationships with the government ministries with which they have most contact may suggest that the LDP has been freer to represent big-business interests than the nature of its support base would imply. But this freedom is being increasingly curtailed as the era of one-party dominance comes to an end.

This article has had the limited objective of challenging assumptions on the effectiveness of some of the mechanisms the big-business community uses to exert political influence. I would not deny that businessmen in Japan, as in every capitalist society, can exercise influence over political leaders in ways that are not available to the average citizen. I do argue that the mechanisms considered most important for facilitating the exercise of business influence over government do not do what they are alleged to do.

We know little about the structure of power and influence in contemporary Japan. Nonetheless, images of that structure, reduced to easily remembered and inaccurate stereotypes, have been widely accepted both in Japan and abroad and do not aid understanding of the structure of power in Japanese society. I have tried to challenge some of the notions of how business-government relations exert influence in Japanese politics in the belief that this is a necessary step in building a more accurate understanding of the relationship between big business and political influence in Japan.

---

[72] Ralf Dahrendorf, *Class and Class Conflict in Industrial Society* (Palo Alto: Stanford University Press, 1959), p. 173.

Japanese Budget Baransu

JOHN CREIGHTON CAMPBELL

All countries draw up budgets to allocate governmental resources among national needs. Since needs always exceed resources, within every government conflict will occur between spending agencies and the organization assigned responsibility for enforcing restraint. Moreover, certain characteristic budgeting behaviors appear to be common everywhere, at least among the richer countries. Aaron Wildavsky, in his *The Politics of the Budgetary Process*, calls these behaviors "incrementalism"; he sees American budgeting as historical, specialized and fragmented, nonprogrammatic, sequential and repetitive, and conflict minimizing. More recent research confirms that these observations are valid elsewhere.[1]

Still, even if the broad outlines and procedures of budgetary systems are similar, it would be surprising if they turned out to be identical in detail. Budgeting, after all, plays a major part in "the authoritative allocation of values for a society," and so lies at the heart of a nation's political process. As politics among rich countries differ so must their budgetary systems. What might be the critical determinants of differences among budgetary systems? Those which immediately suggest themselves are differences in national economic conditions, formal or informal political structures, and political culture, particularly elite political culture.[2]

---

[1] Aaron Wildavsky, *The Politics of the Budgetary Process* (Boston: Little Brown, 1964). For other systems, see Thomas J. Anton, *The Politics of State Expenditure in Illinois* (Urbana: University of Illinois Press, 1966); Guy Lord, *The French Budgetary Process* (Berkeley and Los Angeles: University of California Press, 1973); and (on Great Britain) Hugh Heclo and Aaron Wildavsky, *The Private Government of Public Money* (London: Macmillan; Berkeley and Los Angeles: University of California Press, 1974).

[2] The list is suggested in Aaron Wildavsky, *Budgeting* (Boston: Little, Brown, forthcoming), chap. 1, "Toward a Comparative Theory of Budgetary Processes."

In the course of interviewing Japanese budget participants for a forthcoming study,[3] I became aware of a notion often expressed by the word *baransu*, a Japanese transliteration of the English word "balance." The word did not refer to equalizing governmental revenues and expenditures, as in American budget terminology; it seemed to mean evenhandedness, or equitable treatment. I also had occasion to examine Japanese budgetary statistics and found that (in comparison with similar American data) these indicated a very balanced pattern of allocations over time. That is, compared with the United States budget, the shares of the budget commanded by each ministry did not vary much from year to year.

These differences between Japan and the United States are expressed in Table 1, which shows average deviations of agency budget growth in one year from the growth of the total budget in that year. A zero would mean that in every year the agency's budget grew at precisely the same rate as the total budget. Institutional arrangements and budgetary classifications are different in the two countries, so this table must be used with caution, but it does seem to demonstrate that Japanese budget allocations do not fluctuate very much. It is as if the new revenues that become available each year are shared out more or less evenly so that each ministry gets about the same proportion of the new as it had of the old. The equilibrium of the previous year is maintained; no "unbalance" is introduced.

This paper is primarily an effort to relate this balanced pattern of budgetary outputs with the norm of *baransu* or evenhandedness observed among those who draw up the Japanese budget. I will first introduce the Japanese budgetary process, and discuss the meaning of the *baransu* concept, and then demonstrate how balance is manifest in the budgeting behavior of the three major participants in the process. The conclusions will offer some explanations of why balance ideas are so strong in Japan and suggest some possible effects of this behavior. However, it should be understood throughout that the Japanese budgetary system is still quite similar in many (perhaps most) respects to that of the United States and elsewhere. I have chosen to emphasize differences rather than similarities because they are more interesting. Among the several differences, including Japan's extraordinary economic growth and the unique role of the majority political party in budgeting, balance as an element of elite political culture is given special attention here for two reasons. First, since it shows up throughout the process, tracing balance offers an opportunity to survey many other important aspects of Japanese budget politics conveniently. Second, it seems likely that budget balancing is closely related to similar traits in other forms of Japanese organizational behavior.

[3] John C. Campbell, *Contemporary Japanese Budget Politics* (Berkeley and Los Angeles: University of California Press, forthcoming). This paper is based on the same research, which was supported by the Foreign Area Fellowship Program, and it was partly written under a Travel and Study Grant from the Ford Foundation. The conclusions, opinions, and other statements in this study are those of the author and not necessarily those of either agency.

Table 1* Average Yearly Deviations of Agencies from Total Growth of Budget

	Japan, 1961–1970				United States, 1959–1968		
Agency	Average Deviation (1)	Average Deviation (highest excluded) (2)	Share (1970) (3)	Agency	Average Deviation (4)	Average Deviation (highest excluded) (5)	Share (1968) (6)
A. The Twelve Agencies with Lowest Deviations							
1. Transport	2.32	1.83	2.30	1. Defense (military)	3.08	2.52	53.54
2. Education	2.54	2.27	10.64	2. Commerce	4.85	3.87	1.25
3. Prime Minister's Office[a]	2.91	1.89	15.36	3. Justice	5.53	5.12	0.32
4. Home Affairs[a]	3.00	2.62	21.22	4. Treasury	5.88	5.10	11.19
5. Courts	4.12	3.29	0.62	5. Veterans Administration	6.27	5.79	4.53
6. Health and Welfare	4.21	3.44	11.18	6. Judiciary	6.41	4.74	0.07
7. Construction	4.29	3.13	11.18	7. Atomic Energy Commission	7.04	5.63	1.72
8. Justice	4.58	3.93	1.19	8. Legislative	7.53	6.53	0.20
9. Foreign Affairs	4.61	4.03	0.57	9. General Services Administration	7.86	4.43	0.53
10. Post and Telecommunications	5.02	4.44	0.08	10. Defense (civilian)	8.23	6.69	1.05
11. Diet	6.17	5.43	0.24	11. Agriculture	9.18	8.04	4.48
12. Labor	6.83	6.20	1.49	12. Health, Education, and Welfare	9.80	7.58	8.69
B. The Six Largest Agencies							
1. Home Affairs[a]	3.00	2.62	21.22	1. Defense (military)	3.08	2.52	53.54
2. Prime Minister's Office	2.91	1.89	15.36	2. Treasury	5.88	5.10	11.19
3. Health and Welfare	4.21	3.44	13.38	3. HEW	9.80	7.22	8.69
4. Construction	4.29	3.13	11.18	4. Veterans Administration	6.27	5.79	4.53
5. Agriculture and Forestry	8.80	7.82	10.73	5. Agriculture	9.18	8.04	4.48
6. Education	2.54	2.27	10.64	6. National Aeronautics and Space Administration[b]	46.44	33.74	3.92

SOURCE: For Japan, unpublished MOF tables for initial budgets. For the United States, U.S. Bureau of the Budget, *The Budget of the United States Government*, Fiscal Years 1958–1963; and U.S. Bureau of the Budget or Office of Management and Budgeting, *The Budget in Brief*, Fiscal Years 1964–1968.

* If an item's budget in a given year is a and in the following year b, and the total budgets for those years A and B, then the item's budget shares will be a/A and b/B, and its "change in share" will be b/B divided by a/A or bA/aB. This figure is then multiplied by 100 to put it in percentage terms. Its deviation is its amount either above or below 100, which represents the growth of the total. The deviations for each item are then averaged over time. Columns 2 and 5 leave out the year of greatest deviation for each item to lessen the possibility of one extraordinary occurrence (such as the gain or loss of a bureau) distorting the average.

Both sets of figures represent the "executive budget" before it is sent to the legislature, not actual expenditures. Accounting principles differ, particularly in recording governmental receipts and intragovernmental expenditures. Therefore, the two sets are not strictly comparable. The time periods differ because of the availability of statistics. Although these qualifications do not invalidate the points made in the text, this table must not be used for other purposes, such as comparisons of expenditures in particular sectors.

[a] 1962–1970.   [b] 1961–1968.

THE JAPANESE BUDGETARY PROCESS

Under the constitution, the annual budget is to be prepared and sent to the Diet by the cabinet, but provisions of the Finance Law assign the responsibility of actual preparation to the Ministry of Finance (MOF) and its budget bureau (Shukeikyoku).

The Japanese fiscal year begins on April 1, so fiscal-year 1970 ran from April 1, 1970, through March 31, 1971. The process begins shortly after the beginning of each fiscal year, when the various ministries and other agencies (henceforth referred to as "the ministries") begin formulating their budget requests for the following fiscal year's budget. In recent years, MOF regulations have required each ministry to limit its request to 125 percent of the budget granted in the current year. To fit the demands of its own sections and bureaus within this limitation, each ministry undergoes a mini-budget process of its own in the summer months. The ministry requests, which usually amount to nearly the maximum permitted, are submitted to the MOF about August 31, after brief hearings that secure the general agreement of the appropriate Liberal Democratic Party (LDP) Policy Affairs Research Council (Seimu chōsakai, or Seichōkai) divisions (*bukai*).

During the month of September, ministry officials appear at the Budget Bureau to explain these requests to the budget examiners (*shukeikan*), who ask questions about program details but do not actually negotiate over budget figures at this stage. In October and November, the grinding work of budgeting is performed within the Budget Bureau as examiners and their staffs go over the requests in detail, discussing possible options with the responsible vice-director (there are three), the director, and other bureau officials.

At the same time, the Budget and Tax Bureau directors, ministry-level staff specialists, the administrative vice-minister, and other MOF officials discuss the total budget figure and other "macrobudgeting" questions. These deliberations are based primarily on an estimate of tax revenues and considerations of fiscal policy in regulation of the economy. Although final decisions do not come until mid-December, rough estimates of the funds available are in the Budget Bureau director's mind as he formulates the bureau's posture toward expenditure requests.

For about two weeks in early December, the MOF Ministerial Budget Conference meets to ratify, and sometimes modify, the draft budget prepared within the Budget Bureau, which is then called the "Finance Ministry draft." This series of meetings encompasses the entire chain of command from minister to examiner (and sometimes his assistants), along with other MOF bureau directors and staff. At the same time, the Budget Compilation Policy (Yosan hensei hōshin) is drawn up within the Budget Bureau and ratified at the ministry level. This brief and highly abstract statement sets forth the basic principles of the budget, and is passed by the cabinet at about the same time the MOF draft of the budget is released—despite the fact that, in theory, it is supposed to be the major cabinet-set policy to guide the MOF in compiling the budget.

During October and November, the regular organs of the LDP do not intervene in the compilation process going on within the Budget Bureau, although individual Dietmen will often let their preferences be known (for example, by accompanying groups of petitioners to the Finance Ministry). In December the Policy Affairs Research Council's Deliberation Commission (Seisaku shingikai or Seichō shingikai) draws up the annual LDP Budget Compilation Program (Yosan hensei taikō). This program is then passed by the Party Executive Council (Sōmukai) and referred to the cabinet and the MOF shortly before the release of the MOF draft.

The release of the MOF draft—scheduled for mid-December, though in recent years it has often been postponed until after the New Year holiday—begins the "revival negotiations" (*fukkatsu sesshō*) period of (since 1962) about a week. It appears that 3 to 5 percent of the total General Account[4] is allocated at this time in response to ministry appeals on MOF cuts and the final demands of the LDP. The latter, called political demands, are formulated in a brief process of LDP Research Council division hearings and recommendations, which are reviewed and adjusted by the Research Council Deliberation Commission and the Executive Council, and then implemented by the leadership through participation in the penultimate cabinet-minister-level negotiations and a final session between party and government top officials.

The budget, as modified, is called the "government draft." It is ratified by a cabinet meeting called immediately after the negotiations with the party and then sent up to the Diet. The opposition parties use the legislative budget deliberations as an opportunity for criticism and questions about government policies, but the budget itself is not amended. After passage, the MOF oversees the execution of the budget, and at the end of the fiscal year, there is a budget settlement and an independent audit by the Board of Audit. This study, however, is limited to the period that ends with the cabinet passage of the government draft.

BALANCE

We may approach the somewhat amorphous idea of balance through examining its formal usage. Kōno Kazuyuki, a former vice-minister of finance, said that balance—meaning the comparative balance (*hikaku kinkō*) among expenditures—is one of the two criteria used by the Budget Bureau in reviewing budgets.[5] Expenditures in the same category, or

---

[4] This figure, applicable particularly to the 1961–1967 period, was estimated by the author through comparing the MOF and government draft budgets for each year.

[5] The other criterion is "timing." See "Wagakuni ni okeru yosan hensei no kōzō to katei" [The structure and process of budget compilation in Japan] in *Gyōsei kanri no dōkō* [Trends in

similar items, should particularly be balanced, but the balance criterion should also be applied more widely. Similarly the economist Kotake Toyoji identified five criteria for budget review; "balance" meant relating expenditure levels to those of similar or related items.[6] Such explanations indicate the importance of the concept, but do not impart much of its content. When asked to define balance, a high Budget Bureau official said it means a round budget (marui yosan), one without "bulges" of too much money given to any one program, policy area, or agency.[7]

To balance a budget item one compares it with other items; it is in balance when it is not receiving too much, or too little, relative to other items. A similar idea in American budgeting is "fair share," a "convergence of expectations on roughly how much the agency is to receive in comparison to others" when the total budget is increased.[8] What balance is emerges more clearly by considering what balance is not: it is not setting an expenditure level by assessing how important a program is to national priorities; how effective it has been in the past; or even how much political support it has attracted. In particular, it is not a comparison of two similar or otherwise related programs to see which is better—which produces "more bang for the buck" in a cost-benefit analysis. Quite the opposite—balancing represents avoidance of comparisons among programs and their merits by implying that simply because they are similar they should receive the same or equivalent budgets.

What determines whether two items are similar and require balance? Kōno gives three examples. The simplest is that levels of benefits among the various government-supported health insurance systems should be balanced. Second, health insurance in general should be balanced against other social welfare programs like unemployment insurance and public assistance. Finally, compensation in the "postwar settlement" to groups like veterans, war-bereaved families, or those who lost their homes or overseas property should be equitable.[9] Of course, the question of what should be balanced—for example, individual benefits to members of these groups or the budget allocation for the group as a whole—is left open. From an administrative point of view, routine expenses will nearly always be balanced throughout the government, so a ministry will be assigned automobiles by its number of employees or maintenance expenses by square feet of office space. At the opposite extreme, some people hold that entire policy areas, such as social welfare and defense, require balance.

---

administrative management], ed. Nihon Gyōsei Gakkai (Tokyo: Keisō Shobō, 1957), pp. 70–71.

[6] The other criteria were reasonableness, limitations on resources, timing, and accuracy of calculations. Endō Shōkichi, ed., Yosan [Budget] (Tokyo: Yūhikaku, 1959), pp. 40–45.

[7] Interview with the author during his research in Japan, 1969–1970. To encourage frankness, most interviewees were promised anonymity and therefore are identified only in general terms by their positions.

[8] Wildavsky, Politics, p. 17.

[9] Kōno, "Kōzō to katei," p. 71.

Since each of these expenditure items is assigned to a particular administrative organ, balance may also be seen as equitable sharing among real organizations, whether sections or ministries.

Clearly, balance is not a tightly defined administrative rule. It is best understood in the first place as a value widely shared within the Japanese elite political culture, one that is well understood in principle even if argued about in application. Balance in this sense is an end, not a means. We might say that budget participants simply feel more comfortable when the budget seems to be balanced. However, the strength of this value also gives it two important instrumental functions: in Wildavsky's terms, it is a helpful "aid to calculation" which eases the massive decision-making burden on budgetary participants;[10] and it becomes a major strategic resource for all participants. Finally, the relative strength of this balance value means that other values—efficiency, responsiveness, perhaps even effectiveness—must be relatively weak. Thus, when the Japanese budget system is evaluated in terms of these other values, balance will be found to have dysfunctional aspects.

BALANCE FOR THE MINISTRIES

The ministries (plus some agencies) are the most salient level of administration in Japan; bureaus may be powerful but lack the coherence and independence typical in the United States. Ministries are large and complicated enough that even internal balance considerations are significant. They appear particularly when budget requests are decided. Since the request for each ministry must not exceed 125 percent of the budget actually received in the previous year, constituent bureaus cannot be permitted simply to ask what they wish. Either a similar percentage limitation must be imposed on each bureau within a ministry, or a miniature budget review process of cutting down bureau requests will be required. Although one informant said that the Ministry of Education followed the first practice (an extreme of balancing, and very stable), the latter is more common; most ministries impose either a softer limitation or none at all.

However, even under the latter pattern, the ministry-level accounting section (*kaikeika*) responsible for budgeting will often go to great lengths to maintain balanced treatment of bureaus. For example, a study of the Ministry of Agriculture and Forestry budget process in the early 1960s turned up the following set of guidelines for compilation:

Except for disaster reclamation projects, each public works item is adjusted so that the budgets of the Agricultural Land Bureau, the Forestry Agency and the Fisheries Agency have equivalent growth rates from the initial budgets of the

---

[10] See Wildavsky, *Politics*, chap. 2.

previous year. Disaster reclamation projects are adjusted restrictively so that the same rate of progress will apply to all.[11]

A mechanical formula like this obviates the need for the ministry's central staff to make value choices among programs, and therefore tends to dampen conflict among the bureaus. Agriculture is a ministry with relatively powerful bureaus. In others, the ministry-level staff (particularly the administrative vice-minister and deputy vice-minister) may have more influence over the bureaus and impose its own priorities on budget requests. Proportionally larger budgets may be requested for those programs that the ministry leadership thinks are most important or will look most attractive to the MOF.[12] The composition of budget requests from such ministries may therefore fluctuate more from year to year than those of more balanced ministries where the bureaus are more powerful.

Once the requests have been settled internally, the ministries turn to the task of obtaining as many funds as possible from the MOF.[13] Over the years they have developed many strategies for this. In the main, perhaps to a surprising extent, the repertoire of Japanese ministerial budgeting strategies closely resembles what is found in the United States and elsewhere; included are tactics using clientele groups, "camel's nose" techniques, substitutions and intricate accounting devices, the occasional lucky "crisis," and so forth.[14] Notable, however, is the extent to which the ministerial budgeter relies on the value of balance in arguing before the MOF. That is, rather than justifying a program or policy in terms of intrinsic merit or national need, he will claim that their item is entitled to the "same" level of effort as some other item.

On the most straightforward level, programs that are very similar in objectives and target groups will be balanced almost automatically. When benefits for one of the government-financed health insurance plans are raised, the Ministry of Health and Welfare will not have a difficult time in appealing for increases in the others. Similarly, increased support for national universities will occasion an appeal to the MOF to raise the government's contribution to private universities. When extended further, the demand for balance becomes a little more tenuous; an increase in college-level funds brings arguments for raising secondary-school support (or vice versa).[15]

---

[11] Katō Yoshitarō, "Yosan hensei ni tsuite: Nōrinshō no jirei" (Concerning the budget process: the case of the Ministry of Agriculture), *Keizai to keizaigaku*, nos. 23–24 (August 1968): 231–248.

[12] Another consideration that ministry budgeters must keep in mind is how budget requests will be received by clientele groups. Strong protests may be expected from beneficiaries of a program for which the ministry's request was relatively small or weak.

[13] There may also be other objectives, such as obtaining ministry (as opposed to LDP or interest-group) policy preferences, but the goal of maximizing income underlies most ministry budgeting behavior.

[14] For a detailed treatment, see Campbell, *Budget Politics*. Strategies in other countries are detailed in Wildavsky, *Budgeting*, chap. 10.

[15] Also note another usage, more limited and technical, referring to programs that are functionally related: they are "balanced" when the load imposed on one item by increasing

If the ministry hopes to receive more funds than can be justified by balancing with current expenditure levels of similar programs, it will have to go farther afield. For example, a Ministry of Education official, commenting on the budget for per-student allocations to private universities, said: "The MOF is usually tough on this item and wants to give us just an increase of 5 percent or so to cover cost increases. Therefore, we usually compare the proportions of the aid given today with *prewar* figures [for the same program] to show that this is much lower now."

Rather more common than citing prewar figures is the "keeping up with the Joneses" ploy—low Japanese expenditures in a given field are compared with those overseas. The references chosen vary with the program being emphasized: scientists seeking more research funds look toward American government-financed research and development programs; the Ministry of Health and Welfare points out the higher levels of social security payments in England and Scandinavia; the Ministry of Agriculture and Forestry defends its rice-price support system by noting that all industrialized countries subsidize agriculture.[16] Here, rather than seeking balance among specific programs, policy areas, or organizations, the appeal is to a fundamental sense that Japan as a nation should be in balance with its industrialized peers. Undoubtedly, the effectiveness of such arguments is due in large measure to Japan's century-old tendency toward using Western nations as both sources of innovation and bench marks of achievement.

When dealing with broader policy areas, appeals to balance are not as inherently plausible as they are for smaller programs with near-equivalent counterparts. Attempts by the Ministry of Health and Welfare to defend its budget provide an example. In the mid-1950s, it held that giving larger increases to defense than to social welfare would constitute "remilitarization," but when the defense growth rate slowed enough to make this argument unprofitable, welfare spokesmen began, instead, to compare their programs with the public works sector (on the general grounds that people are more important than things). It is interesting that the MOF did not respond to this ingenious rationale by arguing that public works and welfare are apples and oranges, essentially impossible to compare; rather, in 1961, the MOF manipulated its budget categories, adding enough programs usually counted as public works into the welfare total to balance the two sectors, at least rhetorically.[17]

---

the budget of another is fully covered. For example, an increase in medical insurance benefits to allow longer hospital stays requires increases in hospital subsidies to allow more beds and nurses; if a new harbor is built, the highway budget must be increased to provide connecting roads. See Endō, *Yosan*, pp. 44–45.

[16] For one such argument, see the "White Paper on Health and Welfare," trans. in *White Papers of Japan: 1969–1970* (Tokyo: Japan Institute of International Affairs, 1971), pp. 183–184.

[17] *Mainichi*, January 6, 1954; *Asahi*, January 6, 1961.

If a ministry cannot make a strong case for a balance in spending for its own policy area with that in another specific field, it invokes the more general notion of budget "share." Unless it can be proved that an activity has declined in importance during the preceding year—and the MOF is rarely venturesome enough to make such statements publicly—the ministry will argue that there is no reason it should not receive the same share of the budget (or perhaps of GNP) that it had previously. In other words, the item should have the same growth rate as the total budget. Such appeals are obviously not useful to ministries like welfare, which are trying to enlarge their budget shares, but for a ministry whose programs are under attack, "fair share" offers an attractive defense.

The most obvious example is the Ministry of Agriculture and Forestry, which despite strong support from the LDP has had to face a long-term decline in the importance of agriculture in Japan's economy. In the mid-1950s, when the total budget ceiling was held constant, this ministry's budget allocation was actually cut for three consecutive years. When growth resumed, ministry spokesmen tried to maintain the "10 percent principle"—that one-tenth of the budget should go to agriculture. Ikeda Hayato, newly installed as prime minister in time for the 1961 budget process, tried to initiate a gradual cutback in the proportion of national resources going to agriculture, but met with vehement protests from the agricultural ministry and its supporters in the LDP; in the end, an enormous grant to the rice-price control system had to be made during the appeals negotiations.[18] The growth rate in agricultural spending again dropped slightly below that of the budget as a whole in the 1965 MOF draft, and the protest from the same quarters was immediate.[19] Such "share-consciousness" gave agriculture and its supporters a reputation for caring little about programs, for desiring only to grab as much of the budget as they could regardless of how the money would be spent.[20] Rather similar was the response of the Ministry of Home Affairs to a cut in local taxes scheduled for 1960 (a time when the financial position of local governments, which this ministry represents, was relatively strong): "Losing this tax revenue was like a man getting hit by a car. Even if the victim is wealthy, he still deserves a solatium." [21]

The Defense Agency might provide a good case study of the helpfulness of balance ideas in a ministry's budget strategy. This agency finds it difficult to formulate objectively convincing budget proposals because it seems unlikely that the self-defense forces will be at war in the near future, and in any case they are limited to defending the Japanese main islands against conventional attack.[22] The military requirements for this task do

---

[18] *Nihon keizai*, September 10, 1960; *Asahi*, December 19, 1960, and January 8, 1961.

[19] *Nihon keizai*, December 24, 1964.

[20] Cf. "Yosan to atsuryoku" [Budget and pressure], no. 5, *Yomiuri*, December 5, 1965.

[21] *Nihon keizai*, January 1, 1960.

[22] See Martin E. Weinstein, *Japan's Postwar Defense Policy* (New York: Columbia University Press, 1971), pp. 122–127.

not rise very rapidly. Furthermore, political pressures prevent the agency from postulating even a hypothetical enemy, so its planning must be vague, and officials cannot use the familiar Pentagon ploy of racing to keep ahead of real or imagined Soviet military advances. Therefore, rather than basing budget demands on some measure of the exterior threat to the nation, supporters of more defense spending turn attention to the proportion of the national budget or GNP going to their sector. Stressing the point that this percentage has declined over time (until 1969) helps to obscure the rapid rise of the defense budget in absolute terms—because of high GNP growth, it has doubled about every six years.

This "fair share" concept is useful for keeping the defense budget growing at about the same rate as the national budget, but it does not provide an argument for major increases. Hence, defense industrialists and others seeking a large increase in military spending use another balance technique: the proportion of GNP going to defense in Japan compared with the much higher figure for the United States and other advanced countries. Such appeals—to raise Japan's defense GNP share from around 1 percent to 2 percent—are heard far more often than, say, arguments that a new weapons system is vital or that the mission of the forces should be extended.[23] After an interview in which this percentage of GNP criterion had been mentioned several times, a Defense Agency official was asked why—he conceded that it had little real meaning but "is the only objective indicator available."

The Defense Agency example displays all three functions of balance. Deciding a "proper" level for defense expenditures through more "objective" indicators would be most difficult, and so balancing (as a share of the budget, or as a comparison with other countries) offers a far simpler means of calculating budget requests. Just as important, however, is the underlying agreement within the budget system that balance is an important value in itself. Appealing to this norm thus became a helpful budget strategy for the agency.

BALANCE FOR THE LIBERAL DEMOCRATIC PARTY

Japan is probably unique, at least among capitalist nations, in the degree to which a political party organization directly penetrates the budget process. One or another segment of the LDP structure plays a part in nearly all budgetary decisions from the lowest to the highest levels. Still, the Party's real influence (in the sense of actually modifying budget outcomes) is not as extensive as might be imagined. This is largely because

---

[23] The MOF has often responded that the proper balance should be with pre-World War II American defense spending percentages. Material of great interest on this debate will be found in the special issue on "economic remilitarization" of *Ekonomisuto*, 47.47 (October 25, 1969): 56–63 esp.

the LDP's internal processes are so influenced by balance considerations.

Though many have viewed the LDP as "a loose coalition of factions," [24] it may also be seen as a coalition of many other groupings, which might be regional, interest based, or policy oriented. The devices that maintain the coalition vary depending on the salient issues of the moment, but many of them boil down to the principle enunciated by Dietman Fukunaga Kenji with respect to geographical balance in the Executive Council: "If all regions are represented, then no regions are overlooked." [25] To the extent the Party adheres to this principle, its capacity to favor one region or interest over another is inhibited; choosing among competing alternatives becomes more difficult. Such choices are the essence of budgeting.

There are a number of points for LDP entry into the budget process: individual dietmen seek projects on behalf of constituents; members band together in interest-group-sponsored "Dietmen's Leagues"; influential politicians obtain favors through personal or factional connections; and Party leaders participate in informal high-level discussion on top macro-budgeting issues like the size of the total budget. An important influence, though one hard to measure, is the review of ministerial requests by the divisions of the party's Policy Affairs Research Council in late summer. Although the requests themselves are not often modified significantly after these sessions, the fact that they are discussed, and in effect approved, by the division must be on the minds of the ministry officials who draw them up. Divisional views are also passed along to budget examiners by ministry officials. These and other fragmented interventions may be influential in one segment of the budget, but none has the potential for becoming a comprehensive, fully considered, official, and "rational" party plan. Our attention, therefore, focuses on formal intraparty budget processes, since these are (or at least once were) designed to impose the LDP's will on the budget as a whole.

There is an ideal view of how the party should participate in budgeting, endorsed by many politicians, officials, analysts, and newspaper editorial writers. They agree that although democracy allows an important voice for a majority party in budgeting, it should not intervene in the petty details of administration. The LDP should decide broad priorities for the budget each year, and identify policy innovations and new opportunities for governmental action. Procedurally, this ideal might mean that each division should critically examine detailed programs and plans, recommending which should be initiated or increased and which should be cut

---

[24] Robert E. Ward, *Japan's Political System* (Englewood Cliffs, N.J.: Prentice-Hall, 1967), p. 65.

[25] Nathaniel B. Thayer, *How the Conservatives Rule Japan* (Princeton, N.J.: Princeton University Press, 1969), pp. 122–127. On the LDP, also see Haruhiro Fukui, *Party in Power* (Berkeley and Los Angeles: University of California Press, 1970), esp. pp. 83–89; and Masumi Junnosuke, "Jiyū minshutō no soshiki to kinō" [The organization and functions of the Liberal Democratic Party] in *Nihon seiji gakkai nenpō* [The Annals of the Japanese Political Science Association] (Tokyo: Iwanami Shoten, 1967), pp. 34–77.

back or abolished. These divisional recommendations should be discussed objectively and from a "national" point of view by the Research Council's Deliberation Commission and the Executive Council. Their report on the highest priorities for the year would then be sent to the cabinet and the MOF early enough to guide the process of budget compilation.

At the creation of the LDP in 1955, many thought that this ideal of party participation in budgeting would be implemented. Business leaders hoped that party unification would bring a strong administration, able to restrain the mongering of popular programs typical of the earlier multi-party system; even some MOF officials predicted that more rational and priority-based policies would replace logrolling of politically favored items through Diet amendments.[26] However, participants were uncertain about what relationship of party to budget would emerge. Guesses ranged from a party takeover of the entire process to complete MOF independence, and even included a proposal to move the Budget Bureau from MOF to cabinet control. The first budget made up under the new party—that for 1956—proceeded through close consultations and cooperation between LDP and MOF leaders, and the Research Council's Deliberation Commission passed a very specific, yet rational and responsible set of budget recommendations. However, this cooperation broke down because pressure from rank-and-file Dietmen, demanding a few more yen for favored projects, could not be controlled by the party leadership. In the end, the leadership was forced to demand additional budgetary "intra-party adjustment expenses" to quiet down their followers, thereby violating earlier promises to the MOF and severely damaging the credibility of the LDP as a budgeting agency.

Budgeting means cutting; requests always add up to more than the resources available, and the purpose of budgetary mechanisms is to reduce these requests to manageable size. Because it controls the cabinet and the Diet, if the LDP within itself could have drawn up an implementable budget plan, it would have absolutely dominated the budget process. Alternatively, even granting that the enormous informational requirements and decision costs of item-by-item budgeting might make LDP production of a fully detailed draft impossible, concrete statements of priorities plus a realistic selection of new programs were well within the party's technical capabilities. Such a program was attempted in 1956 (and a few times afterwards), but floundered on the party's inability to control itself. In 1956 and repeatedly thereafter, the LDP demonstrated that it could not aggregate the interests and opinions of its constituent parts effectively and then enforce its final decisions. This fundamental problem is seen clearly in the LDP budget process as it appeared toward the end of the 1960s.

The building blocks of the party's official Budget Compilation Program

---

[26] *Tokyo shinbun*, September 17 and November 11, 1955; *Mainichi*, September 20, 1955.

are the reports of the Research Council's fifteen divisions. These divisions correspond generally to the ministries, and range in size from 44 members in the foreign relations division to 155 in agriculture and forestry.[27] Many members serve at their own request. Division-ministry relations are usually very close because of a number of factors: the many ministry ex-officials influential in the divisions; the ability of officials to implement a Dietman's policy ideas and aid his constituents; the importance of LDP contacts for an official's future career both inside and outside his ministry; and simply the ties that grow naturally from long association.

It is sometimes fruitful to regard the LDP organization as the real legislature of Japan; from this point of view, the Research Council divisions are equivalent to American legislative (not appropriations) committees. They are intimately concerned with the affairs of their corresponding ministries and ordinarily support their interests, inside and outside the party, against the competing claims of other agencies. According to ministry and party informants, divisions seldom oppose any portion of a budget request, and independent new suggestions from them are also rare. They commonly wish to see even more spent than the ministry has requested (though the 125 percent limitation normally prevents these desires from being included in requests), particularly for items with great local-constituency, interest-group, or popular appeal. During the budget process, divisions will often help coordinate tactics among interest group representatives, supporting Dietmen and ministry officials, and generally act as "cheering sections" for their ministries.

There are exceptions to this pattern. Divisions have been known to disagree sharply with their ministries on small or large points. Still, even in these cases, all divisions always call for more expenditures within their policy sectors. Statements such as "our policies x are important, but expenditures here should be deferred this year because policies y are still more critical" are never encountered. Therefore, if a comprehensive plan is to be prepared, the ministry-by-ministry reports must be aggregated by an upper-level body in the LDP—the Research Council's Deliberation Commission. This commission is made up of fifteen to twenty members with "impressive credentials";[28] it meets several times in early December to evaluate written and oral divisional recommendations and to draw up a draft of the Party's Budget Compilation Program. This program is then ratified—sometimes after a few deletions, additions, and changes—by the Executive Council.

An examination of the Budget Compilation Program for the 1970 budget will give an idea of the character of these documents. It is divided

---

[27] As of 1969. Jiyū Minshutō, *Seimu chōsakai meibō* [List of Policy Affairs Research Council members], June 21, 1969. There are also many special committees and investigatory commissions within the Research Council; with some exceptions, their budget roles are either minor or overlap with the divisions.

[28] Thayer, *Conservatives*, p. 217.

into two unequal parts; the first, called "basic policy" (*kihon hōshin*), has seven items.[29] Six are unexceptional slogans calling for growth without overstimulation, tax cuts, elimination of supplementary budgets, slowing inflation, administrative savings, and healthy local administration. Number 6 lists expenditure priorities: "emphasis" on social capital, comprehensive agricultural policies, promotion of small business, environmental problems and traffic safety, and reductions in nonessential items. The second part, "important policies" (*jūten jisaku*), is over ten times the length of the first part and has fourteen major headings (for example, "The Renovation of Education and the Promotion of Science and Technology"). Each is followed by several items, which in turn have subitems; the total number of entries not further subdivided is 116. The translation of one will give the flavor of this document. Under the heading "Promotion of Agriculture, Forestry, and Fishing," one of the three subitems under item 3, "Promotion of Fishing," reads:

Along with accelerating fishing-harbor construction, seashore-preservation works, and repair and construction of roads to fishing harbors, the establishment of large-scale underwater rocky areas for fishing, the development of new fishing grounds and structural reform works for coastal fishing will be systematically promoted.

Not all are quite this broad, but it will be appreciated that the 116 entries can cover a lot of ground. Indeed, most governmental programs are included somewhere in this document.

Thus the Budget Compilation Program is comprehensive, and because it is the product of detailed hearings followed by due deliberation and ratification by official party bodies, it may also be called exhaustive and authoritative. On the other hand, is it practical and influential? No, for at least three reasons: (1) No monetary figures are attached to the recommendations. For the most part, the document simply urges that each program be "stressed," "completed," or "strengthened." (2) Final passage of the program comes only two to four days before the MOF draft budget is released, too late to guide the compilers.[30] (3) There is virtually no indication of priority among the programs recommended. The fourteen headings under "important policies" provide a shopping list in almost arbitrary order. It is true that six expenditure programs are singled out for attention in item 6 of the "basic policy" section, but this is not at all a plausible list of the party's priorities for the 1970 budget, since other evidence indicates that no unusual attention was given to social capital or small business that year, and the themes of pollution and traffic safety

---

[29] The full text will be found in Zaisei Chōsakai, ed., *Kuni no yosan* [The nation's budget] (Tokyo: Dōyū Shobō, 1970), pp. 888–892.

[30] Since 1964, with the exception of the three cases when the budget process was extended over the New Year. Here, the program was released just before the holiday break, and the MOF draft just afterward.

were hardly mentioned again by LDP budget participants (agriculture did get extra attention in 1970, but this item is included in the "basic policy" list every year). And needless to say, the Party made no efforts toward reducing expenditures on nonessential items; quite the opposite.

If it is true that the LDP potentially could control the budget process through this program, why has it not done so? And if the document has no real effect, why is it still produced so laboriously? The answers to both questions have to do with "balance." Everything is included in the Compilation Program simply because then nothing need be left out, and each division's desires are represented. The policies are not listed by priority because this would represent a judgment by the Deliberation Commission or Executive Council that one division's recommendations are inferior to another's. Money figures are not included partly because, if they were cut, there would be opposition from the divisions, and if they were not cut the total would be embarrassingly large, well beyond any possible budget. (It should also be noted here that the LDP does not have the staff capability to prepare a specific "alternate budget," and that the MOF has pursued a consistent strategy of inhibiting other participants from discussing actual amounts of allocations.) Commission and council members, and LDP Dietmen generally, realize that the practice of making the program vague, all-encompassing, and late prevents it from having any influence, but have implicitly decided (after several attempts) that trying to reform the process is useless.

However, survival of the Budget Compilation Program should not be regarded as merely vestigial. It does have real functions. One is public relations: the document is given wide circulation and is designed to show both the general public (note the pollution and traffic safety items) and specific interest groups (agriculture, small business, local governments, and almost all others) that the party has their interests at heart. Perhaps more importantly, many Dietmen actively participate in this process and have their views taken into account in the final document. Finally, blame for omission of any recommendation in the final budget can be laid to the MOF, not the party, thereby mitigating resentment against the leadership. The "balance" of this symbolic output therefore functions to maintain satisfaction among party members and clientele.

However, not all products of formal LDP processes are merely symbolic in impact. At the later "revival negotiations" stage, under much more hurried conditions and without gestures toward public opinion, a truly influential set of recommendations is brought forth. This process begins shortly after the release of the MOF draft budget, when divisional members talk over the MOF cuts and possible responses with ministry officials. The divisions also receive copies of ministerial request forms, which they label with A, B, or C to indicate priority. Then, in a hectic, one-day series of hearings, the Research Council's Deliberation Commission listens to spokesmen of all the divisions (plus many related special committees and investigatory commissions) and marks these forms with its own symbols. For the most part, divisional recommendations are marked with equivalent symbols by the commission, preserving balance. However, some are marked with the *marusei* (a circle containing the character *sei,* which participants say refers to either *seiji,* politics, or *seisaku,* policy). This symbol indicates an item of party concern that should be taken up at the political level—either the cabinet minister negotiations (at which the Policy Affairs Research Council chairman is present) or the final top-level LDP-MOF talks. In 1970, about one-fifth of the items marked "A" by the divisions also received the *marusei* label. They represent real choices, true budgeting behavior, rather than the more usual evenhanded sharing out of benefits.

To support this point we may examine the contents of the thirty-nine *marusei* recommendations for 1970.[31] Their distribution by ministry was very uneven: twelve went to the Ministry of Agriculture and Forestry, nine to the Transport Ministry, and although the Ministry of Construction received only four, they covered 80 percent of its budget. The remainder was scattered much more thinly among the other ministries. Over half were for various types of public works. This pattern reflects the LDP's interest in programs with great appeal to local constituencies, particularly in rural areas. Notably absent were programs that drew much broader, but more diffuse, public interest—for example, pollution and traffic safety, emphasized so strongly in the earlier Budget Compilation Program, were completely ignored.

Indeed, these revival negotiations recommendations are not publicized by the Party and are written in a budget shorthand nearly unintelligible to outsiders. Few in number and quite specific, the *marusei* items are taken seriously by the ministries, both the rank-and-file leaders of the Party, and MOF budgeters. The LDP here sacrifices balance for effectiveness, symbolic image-creation for a real role in budgetary decision-making. Not that balance is completely neglected: virtually all divisional recommendations are formally endorsed somewhere in the Deliberation Commission's report, and when two divisions propose contradictory items, as commonly occurs when ministries battle over which will control a new activity, the commission may well grant the *marusei* impartially to both. At least eight of the thirty-nine *marusei* items for 1970 represented such overlaps, and two remained even after the report had been tidied up by the Executive Council on the following day.

The last point reflects on a claim often put forward by defenders of the

[31] Calculated from Jiyū Minshutō, Seisaku Chōsakai, "Kaku bukai fukkatsu yōkyū shiryō" [Materials on the revival requests of the various divisions] (Tokyo, January 27, 1970), an unpublished document of about 75 pages obtained by the author. Because the materials are incomplete, it is possible that one or two additional *marusei* grades had been awarded, but other evidence indicates this is unlikely. A more exhaustive discussion will be found in Campbell, *Budget Politics,* chap. 5.

LDP's role in the Japanese policy process, that the Party can effectively intervene when two ministries are at loggerheads, or on behalf of new activities that fall between the jurisdictions of two or more ministries. At least in the budget process, which is the major stream of domestic policy-making, such conflict resolution seems to occur rather rarely. Much more commonly, divisions back up their ministries, and the two aggregating bodies will lack the capacity to violate balance by choosing one over the other or by imposing an independent solution.[32]

More generally, party spokesmen often talk of party "dynamism" and flexibility, contrasted to the stodgy conservatism of the bureaucracy. This comment by an LDP leader's staff director in an interview is typical:

Bureaucrats are awfully good at riding along on an old policy, like a locomotive driver, but they can't change direction. This is because of organization . . . because of organizational ties, they can't start something new. The party, on the other hand, doesn't have to worry about the organizations fastened to [old programs] and instead can ask, what is the problem for the people? What did they ask for in the last election? So the party can become the engine to change policy.

Such statements are not devoid of insight; the party can sometimes free itself from the domination of pressures from below. However, its ideas usually originate in the ministries, and it rarely presses for programs against ministry interests. Its strongest positions are taken on those programs with the closest ties to the votes of specific groups (farmers, pensioners, local officials) and do not change very much over time.

Furthermore, the negative and inhibiting effects of party influence in budgeting must not be ignored. From the MOF point of view, it is party support for wasteful or "backward-looking" programs—such as agricultural price supports and deficit-ridden local railway lines—that prevents a shift of resources into newer and more pressing fields. In its 1968 "break fiscal rigidity movement" (*dakai zaisei kōchokuka undō*), the MOF singled out LDP protectionism as a major contributor to budget inflexibility. As long as the leadership of the LDP remains responsive to its lower level organs, and they, in turn, are so closely tied to ministries and other clientele groups, intervention by the party will not disturb the long-term balance of Japanese allocation patterns.

BALANCE FOR THE MINISTRY OF FINANCE

The Ministry of Finance stands at the center of the Japanese budgetary

---

[32] Fukui, whose scope is wider than budgeting, argues that party mechanisms can play this role effectively; see his *Party in Power*, pp. 91–94. Such disputes are often willy-nilly left for the MOF to solve, but its comparable difficulties, again for balance reasons, are reflected in the reluctance to organize new cross-jurisdictional activities, and the prevalence of compromises like splitting a program among several agencies or staffing new organizations with officials from other ministries.

process, and its budget bureau is the only full-time participant.[33] The MOF's authority to prepare the budget (*yosan hensei ken*) is jealously guarded against interference from outsiders. With its near monopoly of information on the budget as a whole and its specialized skills, the MOF is in a strong position to implement its own policies if it desires to do so. Balance ideas influence MOF budgeting behavior in all three ways: as an aid to calculation, a strategy, and a value in itself. These are intermingled in practice, but may be separated for analytical purposes.

The most obvious case of balance as an aid to calculation, often cited by officials, is when concrete relationships between two programs dictate that a rise in expenditures for one requires a similar hike in another. The amount for the second program thereby might be set almost automatically. Balancing routine administrative expenses is also relatively straightforward: examples include salaries, unit prices for materials, building maintenance, and numbers of government cars per hundred employees— all established on a government-wide basis so that ministries will not be treated "unfairly." However, balancing administrative expenses often extends beyond those that are obviously routine, as in provision of computers or allotments for travel, where it could be argued that needs of ministries vary widely. Reflecting on this problem in an interview, a budget examiner recalled:

Travel expenses were needed for an international economic conference in Bangkok; here, we balance so that, for example, the Ministry of Construction will not have a full delegation and the Ministry of Agriculture and Forestry only half that number. This is checked with great care . . . it is not a matter of policy questions . . . we really pay attention to this extremely routine work of maintaining balance. This is traditionally what has controlled most thinking about budgeting in Japan.

Though it might be that one ministry really should have sent more participants than the other, such a judgment would require the examiner to investigate the meeting's substance and would irritate ministry officials. It is easier to be equitable.

Such considerations extend beyond administrative to policy expenses. Particularly when expenditures within a single budget category are allocated to different ministries or among different programs, there is a tendency for them to grow at similar rates. A budget officer from a

---

[33] The Budget Bureau, one of the oldest and most highly regarded organizations in the Japanese government, is staffed by over three hundred officials. In its front line are the nine examiners, who specialize in one or more ministries, aided by staffs of seven to seventeen officials more junior in rank. Nearly all examiners are graduates of the Faculty of Law at Tokyo University. They are usually among the most well regarded of their age cohort, and many will go on to top policy-making positions after two or three years' service. Although the Japanese Budget Bureau is comparable to the U.S. Bureau of the Budget (of earlier years) in structure and status, it is not organizationally tied to the chief executive, and has never played the role of enforcing centrally determined policies and priorities upon the government as a whole. See Campbell, *Budget Politics*, and Wildavsky, *Politics*, p. 35.

ministry concerned with public works commented: "If the total budget for public works goes up about 10 percent, the public works budget of each individual ministry should also get a 10 percent hike. Unless there is some special reason, they won't sharply cut or raise only our ministry's public works budget [share]." Partly to maintain balance, public works are handled by a specialized budget examiner. This is not true of the "promotion of science and technology" budget, but as a former high budget official noted, similar considerations prevail:

To some extent, a standard is set [medo o tsukeru] for promotion of science and technology, for example, that it should go up 15 percent next year. The various examiners then keep this in mind while reviewing their ministry's budget. The system is used because of fear of unbalance—for example, among the three Budget Bureau vice-directors, one might be enthusiastic about science, so this budget [for the ministries in his purview] would go up 20 percent, while another with no interest would keep it down to 10 percent.

Again, if a standard growth rate is set for all elements of a category, the need to evaluate and compare individual proposals is largely obviated.

Even when programs are not formally related by budgeting categories, any shared characteristics may be taken as a justification for balancing. The example cited by Kōno Kazuyuki is the "postwar settlement." [34] The repatriates' case in 1967 was extremely difficult for the MOF, not only because of intense political pressures, but also because property records were chaotic and there were no obvious guidelines for deciding the amount of compensation. Accordingly, the MOF held to a position that the grant should be balanced with earlier payments to equivalent claimants, with the precedents of these cases cited as part of MOF proposals on the amount of payments to individuals or households, the total burden on the budget, methods of payment, and a formula to adjust for inflation.[35]

As well as simplifying calculation, such appeals to balance are important strategically. Prime Minister Satō said of the repatriates' case that "since solving the overseas property problem puts the lid on the 'postwar settlement,' I hope it will be kept in balance with other compensation matters." [36] This hope was motivated by a fear that if the repatriates got more than the other groups, these would then demand an equal or better supplement, and the "settlement" would become unsettled.

Conversely, the earlier precedents provided the MOF with its best arguments for opposing the much larger demands from the LDP. The MOF frequently will draw a connection between a program in dispute and some settled matter to claim that the two should be kept in balance.

---

[34] Kōno, "Kōzō to katei," pp. 70–71. See the case study on "Compensating Former Landlords" in Fukui, Party in Power, pp. 173–197.

[35] See Campbell, "Compensation for Repatriates," a paper presented at the Annual Meetings of the Association for Asian Studies, Boston, April 3, 1974.

[36] Asahi, June 15, 1967.

For example, when the Ministry of Health and Welfare asked for a 21 percent hike in public assistance payments for 1963, the MOF replied that this increase should be kept in balance with that in public employee salaries (7.2 percent that year) because both were supposed to meet increases in the cost of living. Such gambits can become rather tenuous. In 1967, this ministry had set its sights lower, asking just a 5.5 percent raise (the same as the previous year), but the MOF offered only 4.5 percent on grounds that the public employees salary raise had dropped off from 7.2 to 6.9 percent over the two years so welfare payment growth should slow down too.[37] The particular logic of each argument is not important; the point is that notions of balance are often used tactically by the MOF in combating demands for individual program increases.

Probably more significant from a strategic perspective is the negative, inhibiting effect of balance on MOF behavior. Its officials are well aware, as a Budget Bureau director put it, that "there is nothing a ministry dislikes more than a 'share-down' in its budget." This means, for one thing, that the MOF must be extremely careful about trying to cut individual budgets, even relatively. The record shows that nearly all the MOF's antispending campaigns have been devoted to across-the-board cuts—equal percentage reductions in certain categories of administrative expenses or subsidies (*hojokin*)—even though MOF officials believe that waste is much more prevalent in some ministries than others and know from experience that such campaigns have virtually no effect.[38] More subtly, even giving an unusually large increase to a certain program of high priority can be dangerous because supporters of other, somehow similar programs will feel that balance has been violated. Since an allocation once offered can never be reduced, there is risk of a general "level-up" that will increase total expenditures significantly. For the MOF, maintaining balance is usually seen as the safest course.

A final interesting example of a positive use of balance as a strategy may be offered. Throughout the 1960s the MOF was plagued by the rapid expansion of two programs with strong political backing: subsidies for rice prices and the government contribution to health insurance. From 1960 to 1969, the deficit in the Food Control Special Account, made up from the General Account (that is, ordinary tax revenues), rose from only 0.7 percent of the total budget to 4.5 percent; in the same period, health insurance costs rose from 3.6 to 7.1 percent of the total budget. At least until the end of the period studied, attempts to restrain these programs were ineffective. However, when the organizational budget breakdown is examined, the Ministry of Agriculture and Forestry share rose only from 9.4 to 10.5 percent in those years, and the Ministry of Health and Welfare

---

[37] *Nihon keizai*, December 6, 1962; *Asahi*, February 13, 1967.

[38] As Wildavsky points out, across-the-board cuts are also much easier to calculate; see his *Politics*, p. 148.

from 10.1 to 13.4 percent.[39] Since both programs are included within the budgets of their respective ministries, this means that the remainder of Ministry of Agriculture and Forestry programs actually declined in budget share from 8.7 to 6.0 percent; for the Ministry of Health and Welfare's remaining programs, the decline was from 6.5 to 6.2 percent (smaller, but perhaps more significant in light of the consensus that Japanese welfare programs should be "catching up" with the West during the 1960s). Operationally, as explained by an agricultural official, "it is a fact that the Foodstuffs Control item has expanded, and this has 'oppressed' [appaku] the budgets for other agricultural programs. [In reviewing our budget] the examiner will sometimes say that the rise in this item makes the rest of the budget 'difficult.' " This is balance again—a view that the budgets for these ministries or these policy areas should occupy some vaguely defined "fair share" of the total. If one component rises swiftly, the others must grow more slowly. In effect, each ministry (or policy area) has a framework (waku) which it should not exceed. Indeed, the Ministry of Agriculture and Forestry counterstrategy here has been to say that rice supports are a separate problem from the rest of agriculture, not controllable by the ministry, and should therefore have a separate framework (betsuwaku). A similar, more general use of this strategy is the frequent MOF demand that any ministry seeking new programs should first eliminate or cut back older programs by a similar amount.[40]

It is logical to ask about the reverse case—a ministry that administers a rapidly diminishing program. Does the MOF compensate for its losses? One such case is the Ministry of Labor; its largest program—unemployment compensation—has fallen off with the growing demand for labor produced by economic development. Statistics indicate that the labor ministry has not kept pace with other ministries: its budget share slipped from 2.4 percent in 1960 (3.0 in 1955) to 1.7 percent in 1969. On the other hand, interviewed officials claimed, and other observers agreed, that new programs proposed by the ministry were approved by the MOF rather more frequently than usual. In part, this relatively soft treatment may be due to the Ministry of Labor's skill at justifying its requests, but quite possibly it is also a function of the MOF's regard for balance as a value in itself, beyond its sheer utility as simplifier or strategy.

The point that the MOF sees balance as a value for its own sake, more than just an aid or strategy, is sustained by examining its view of the LDP's role in budgeting. While conceding that a majority party in a democracy should have a voice in budgeting, the "finance bureaucrats"

---

[39] Figures calculated from Japan, Budget Bureau, Ministry of Finance, Zaisei tōkei [Fiscal statistics], 1970, pp. 65–66; Kuni no yosan, 1970, p. 888; and unpublished tables prepared by the Budget Bureau, August 1969.

[40] The MOF does not decide a specific total amount for each ministry or policy area early in the budget process; "framework" refers to a more generalized idea of an appropriate share of the budget.

tend to be disdainful of politicians, interest groups, and other bureaucrats who seem subservient to them. An examiner was reputed to have said to an official from the Ministry of Transportation: "You are no better than your bosses—the cab drivers." [41] Political intervention in budgeting disturb balance, and the MOF will at times use its own influence as a counterweight to such distortions. It may give less rigorous examination to requests from entire ministries with relatively weak political backing, such as labor or education, or to individual programs within one ministry since the LDP is rarely equally supportive of all ministry activities. In such cases, the MOF makes common cause with spending-ministry officials who are themselves concerned about maintaining internal balance against political pressure. A Ministry of Construction official said:

Interest groups and Dietmen tend to be strong on highway and river projects; in the end, their weight falls here, first in pressure on us and then on the MOF . . . since we know this will happen, at the beginning we really push areas like urban development and housing. The highway and river budgets will go up regardless so we work on the others. If we don't do this and just ask for everything equally, the budgets for housing, sewers, parks, and so forth will be very small. Our strategy is: because it's hard to get, do it first—the Dietmen will take care of the rest.

Finance Minister Fukuda made a remark in 1966 that indicates the MOF's willingness to collaborate in this strategy. He observed that he had to be sure to get sufficient funds for housing into the MOF draft budget because, unlike rivers and highways, it would never get enough political support in the appeals negotiations.[42] The MOF also assists by keeping negotiations with the ministries private, allowing ministry spokesmen to continue making public statements that they are backing up group or party demands to the hilt while actually pushing for less popular programs.

Further evidence of MOF concern for balance is provided by a look at the course of its reforms in the budget process itself. One example is the imposition of a limitation on ministry budgetary requests. The limitation began in 1961 at 150 percent of the previous year's actual budget, was dropped to 130 percent in 1965, and finally to 125 percent in 1968. Such limitations encourage a balanced budget since no ministry can request much larger amounts on grounds of high policy priority, and this in turn diminishes the possibility of a shift in expenditure patterns. The fact that late requests over this limitation have sometimes been allowed merely softens the impact of this reform.

Two other examples both occurred as part of the 1968 "break fiscal rigidity movement," the major occasion when the MOF took the offensive against pressures for more spending. One was called "comprehensive

---

[41] Kusayanagi Taizō, "Okurashō shukeikyoku no samuraitachi" [The samurai of the MOF Budget Bureau], *Bungei shunju*, 46.12 (November 1968): 229.

[42] *Asahi*, January 14, 1966.

budgeting" (sōgō yosan shugi), meaning the elimination of supplementary budgets. Each year, one to three supplements had been passed, amounting to from 2.5 to over 10 percent of the total final budget. It had become customary to devote most of these supplements, beyond the relatively nondiscretionary amounts needed for natural disasters occurring during the year and the mandated local allocation, to two items: salary increases for government employees, decided by the cabinet after recommendations from the National Personnel Authority in midsummer; and the deficit in the Foodstuffs Control Special Account, which depended on decisions, reached by a complicated political process, on the prices for rice paid to producers and asked from consumers. Also, the total amount of the supplements had come to take up most of the natural revenue increase (shizen zōshū), the surplus created by underestimating economic growth and tax revenues in the original budget. This meant that the decisions on salaries and rice prices, which were supposed to be based on "objective" factors, in fact were heavily influenced by the amount of money actually available—if the economy was booming, tax revenues would be strong, and these two items would tend to be large. Not only is this behavior procyclical in fiscal policy terms, but from the MOF's point of view, it allowed these two expenditures to grow more quickly than they should. Under "comprehensive budgeting," provision for the rice subsidy and salaries (as well as disasters) was to be made in the initial budget, covered by a "full" revenue estimate, so these decisions could be brought back into the competition of the regular budget process and thereby kept within overall balance patterns.[43]

Finally, the MOF also proposed to modify the revival negotiations process in 1968. Up to that time, the funds added to various items during this period had come from "hidden resources" (kakushi zaigen), which were secreted away in accounts under MOF control so only MOF officials knew the amount available. In the mid-1960s, this had amounted to some 3 to 4 percent of the total budget. Partly because the mystery of the figures had encouraged the ministries and party to continue asking for more money, the MOF substituted for this system two devices known as "public resources" (kōkai zaigen). One, called "secretariat adjustment expenses" (kanbō chōseihi), was a sum in a range around ¥10 billion (about $28 million) each for the larger ministries, from which the staff of each ministry was allowed to make allocations among the new or established programs it thought most deserving. The other was a larger amount (¥50 billion or more) reserved for "policy-level" decisions—those taken at the level of cabinet minister or MOF-LDP negotiations, and identified in the MOF draft as "adjustment expenses" (chōseihi). These innovations meant that the MOF was formally renouncing the possibility of making these last decisions itself on programmatic or "merit" grounds in favor of simply

---

[43] This attempt failed, as supplements were passed in 1968 and thereafter.

dividing up the remaining resources equitably, allowing the ministries and then the party to decide how to spend them—clearly a victory for balance.

Actually, this reform is not much of a watershed in itself because the degree of its implementation in 1969 and 1970 was somewhat questionable. The reform also seems little more than an institutionalization of a tendency already quite powerful within the MOF; although evidence is hard to gather, it appears that a high proportion of budgetary decisions formally in Budget Bureau hands had already been heavily influenced by ministry opinions. Direct or indirect queries of a ministry's priorities among programs were common in both the September budget request explanations and in later calls from the examiner to the ministry for further information. The most difficult questions were routinely postponed until the revival negotiations where, under either the old or new system, ministry voices are strong. The Ministry of Health and Welfare's budget requests for 1970, which included proposals for forty-eight new items, illustrate the postponement tactic. Of the new items, only one was clearly approved in the MOF draft prepared independently by the Budget Bureau, but at least nineteen more had been approved by the end of the revival negotiations.[44]

This sort of evidence, though fragmentary, indicates that the MOF has in effect been giving up some of its power to decide on individual programs, and the reforms in the budget process noted above both contribute to and symbolize this trend. The point may be made more clearly by contrasting two ideal-type budget processes. In the first, which might be termed "strong MOF," ministries ask for everything they desire; the MOF evaluates their requests and allocates most of the available funds among them as it sees fit. The ministries (and the LDP) then ask again for additional funds for some programs, and the MOF responds by adding on small increments as justified and necessary. The second ideal type could be called "weak MOF." Here, ministries decide priorities among programs before making requests (to stay within the 125 percent limitation); the MOF makes only mechanical decisions on routine items, postponing the difficult decisions. In the revival negotiations, each ministry (and the party) is allocated a lump sum by formula from which it makes its own decisions about programs. Neither ideal type ever existed in pure form, but the process in the mid-1950s more closely resembled the "strong MOF" pattern whereas, by the late 1960s, the "weak MOF" type was not far from reality.

Why did the Ministry of Finance give up so much of its power, for the most part voluntarily? I will attempt a brief and speculative explanation. Budgeting decisions may be divided into two categories: "microbudget-

---

[44] Thirty-five were clearly and twelve probably rejected in the MOF draft. Calculated from official and unofficial documents of the Ministries of Health and Welfare and Finance, and the LDP.

ing," individual consideration of each detailed program; and "macro-budgeting," issues like the size of the total budget, the amount of deficit financing, revenue estimating, and economic regulation through fiscal policy. Traditionally, the MOF had considered itself dominant in both spheres, but three trends in the 1955–1970 period led to a partial redefinition of its mission: (1) in common with other advanced industrial nations, there was increased concern for governmental regulation of the economy, the responsibility for which lay with the MOF; (2) with economic development, governmental programs became more numerous and complicated, and thus informed judgments demanded more expertise in ever more specialized policy areas; and (3) the Liberal Democratic Party was established and grew in confidence and power. The last point is important because the LDP, responding to the interest groups and spending ministries that make up its clientele, has been far more interested in specific microbudgeting questions than in macrobudgeting. The Party did not hesitate to intervene to obtain more funds for favored programs, and these interventions began to impinge on the MOF's autonomy in macrobudgeting decisions and even internal organizational matters. Facing a choice among priorities, the MOF sought to protect its near monopoly over macrobudgeting decisions and its organizational boundaries by allowing control over individual program spending to slip away to the experts in the spending ministries and the LDP politicians.

If this line of analysis is correct, it would follow that most conflict would develop in areas of overlap between microbudgeting and macrobudgeting, where individual programs have an impact on overall budget problems. This has indeed been the case. Most LDP-MOF battles have occurred over items like agricultural price supports, medical insurance, and railroad deficits, when fixed costs have threatened to push up the size of the total budget or inhibit fiscal flexibility (as in the "break fiscal rigidity movement").[45]

How does this shift relate to "balance"? To oversimplify, a major problem in any budgeting system is how to decide on sectoral allocations—the relative amounts to be given to policy areas like education, welfare, defense, and public works—or to each ministry. If the budgeting authority is itself making decisions on each individual program, sectoral allocations will emerge almost automatically from a bottom-up additive process. In Japan, such individual decisions have largely been given over to the fragmented spending ministries and the party. It is still possible for someone to make broad policy judgments—that education, or welfare, or the build-up of social capital deserves greater emphasis this year, and therefore its growth rate should be higher than for other sectors. But to the extent that no participant is willing or able to make such broad policy

---

[45] For a somewhat related analysis, see Daiichi Itō, "The Bureaucracy: Its Attitudes and Behavior," *The Developing Economies*, 6.4 (December 1968): 446–467.

choices, little alternative remains but to confirm the existing pattern of allocations and have each ministry and sector receive about the same budget share as it had previously. This is "balance." And although I must again emphasize that all budgetary systems are terribly complex, that they resemble one another more than they differ, and that all the tendencies illustrated here may be found in every system, I conclude that "balance" is particularly significant in Japan.

CONCLUSIONS

We may now speak of cause and effect. Why should balance be so important in Japanese allocation patterns and elite political culture? And what difference does it make to how the business of the nation is conducted?

An attractive and immediately available explanation of why balance ideas are so prevalent in Japan is that of culture, perhaps even the Japanese "national character." That is, balance appears to correspond to many traits that anthropologists and others consider as typically Japanese. For example, Chie Nakane notes that in Japan "democracy" means that "any decision should be made on the basis of a consensus which includes those located lower in the hierarchy . . . it should leave no one frustrated or dissatisfied." [46] A dislike of open conflict is also frequently noted. A case might thus be made that the Japanese budgetary system inevitably tends toward making decisions through relatively impersonal and mechanistic administrative devices that reward all equitably.

Such an argument has merit and is difficult to contradict. Still, I would prefer to emphasize the equally valid point that all budgetary systems probably have strong tendencies toward decision-making patterns that avoid value judgments. This is both because value judgments among programs are technically and intellectually very difficult and because making such judgments opens the decision-maker to attack from the disadvantaged parties. Therefore, budgeters will attempt to routinize their decisions—and balance is a sensible method of routinization—so long as they are not prevented from doing so.

If, then, balance or something like it is the "normal" mode of budgetary decision-making, what must be explained is not stability in allocation patterns from year to year, but deviations from stability. What factors might influence budgeters to change the decisions they made last year? One common situation is when some programs have to be increased because of inflation or other unavoidable cost increases, but resources are not sufficient to provide equal hikes for all programs. This has often been true in American budgeting, but in Japan rapid economic growth has

---

[46] Chie Nakane, *Japanese Society* (Berkeley and Los Angeles: University of California Press, 1970), pp. 144–145.

produced enough "natural revenue increase" each year to take care of cost increases with some left over.[47] Budgeting is more comfortable.

Table 2*
Change in Budget Share over Ten Years (1961–1970), by Function

Japan	Change in Share (1)	Share (1970) (2)	*United States*	Change in Share (3)	Share (1970) (4)
State Administration	83.2	6.7	Defense	83.7	39.6
Regional Finance	112.7	21.0	International Affairs		
Defense	82.3	7.2	and Finance	52.5	1.8
Special Foreign			Space Research		
Obligations	25.7	0.4	and Technology	248.8	1.8
Land Preservation			Agriculture and Rural		
and Development	86.7	16.6	Development	91.7	3.1
Manufacturing and			Natural Resources	78.8	1.2
Economy	145.3	11.3	Commerce and		
Education and			Transportation	90.8	4.6
Culture	91.6	11.3	Community Develop-		
Social Welfare	110.8	16.1	ment and Housing	765.5	1.5
Pensions	63.7	3.8	Education and		
National Debt	188.9	3.7	Manpower	293.4	3.6
Reserves	132.6	1.4	Health	735.1	6.4
Other	120.9	0.6	Income Security	101.9	21.6
			Veterans' Benefits		
			and Services	75.3	4.3
			Interest	111.6	9.0
			General Government	110.5	1.6

Source: Japan, Budget Bureau, Ministry of Finance, *Zaisei tōkei* (Fiscal statistics), 1970, pp. 212–213; U.S. Office of Management and Budgeting, *The Budget of the U.S. Government*, 1972, pp. 61–65.

* Columns 1 and 3 list the amounts budgeted for each function in 1970 over the amounts in 1961, divided by the 1970 total budget over the 1961 total budget. Columns 2 and 4 show the share of each function in the 1970 budget, as reference. The two sets of figures in this table are even less comparable than in Table 1 because the American figures are outlays (which include net lending) rather than expenditures. All figures are as calculated after the end of the budget periods and include supplements, except for Japan in 1970, which uses the initial budget. As with Table 1, this table should not be employed beyond the purposes specified. A further discussion of both tables will be found in my *Contemporary Japanese Budget Politics*.

Another and probably more important factor is illustrated by Table 2, which lists changes in budget share over a ten-year period (1961–1970) for the standard functional categories of the Japanese and American budgets. It is readily apparent, first of all, that the American shares have changed

---

[47] This analysis contradicts the proposition that high growth brings greater budgetary fluctuation, as suggested by Frederic L. Pryor in his *Public Expenditures in Communist and Capitalist Nations* (London: Allen and Unwin, 1968), p. 299. This book includes an excellent discussion of the problems of cross-national expenditure comparisons.

more than the Japanese shares; in part this is because of the greater year-to-year stability shown in Table 1. But attention should also be directed to the items showing the greatest changes in the two countries. For Japan, these are in large measure items that are nondiscretionary, not part of decision-making on expenditures: "special foreign obligations" are mostly determined by old treaties with countries receiving war reparations; the increase in "national debt" expenditures is a product of the advent of deficit financing in 1965 (a decision on revenue mix, not allocations); and much of the change in "manufacturing and economy" is the increased deficit in the rice-price-supports program, supported by political pressures (leading to a "nondecision") but caused primarily by growing harvests and changing consumption habits, which turned Japan from a rice-deficit to a rice-surplus country.

The "unbalanced" American items have a different character. The enormous increase for "community development and housing" is a figment of accounting peculiarities and should be ignored, but those for the other three—"space research and technology," "education and manpower," and "health"—may be legitimately compared with the Japanese figures. All are the direct result of clear presidential decisions: Kennedy's to reach the moon; Johnson's—in response to the civil rights movement and urban riots—to initiate a "war on poverty." It is clear that the president has had a major impact on American allocation patterns, while no one has had a comparable impact on the Japanese patterns.

Two points may be offered by way of partial explanation of this difference. The first is that Japanese prime ministers have tended not to hitch their political fortunes to domestic issues, at least those requiring money. The chief exception is Ikeda and his income doubling plan, but his policies had more impact on macrobudgeting matters than on allocations (Tanaka is another exception, but his premiership lies outside the period of this study). The second, more structural point is that the prime minister does not occupy anything like the president's key position within the budgetary process. He may conciliate, mediate, and occasionally adjudicate, but he rarely intervenes actively, and his influence over the Ministry of Finance does not compare with the loyalty of the Bureau of the Budget to the president.

A complete discussion of the reasons for such passive prime ministerial behavior in this period would have to include the relative lack of newly formed pressure groups or social movements calling for more spending, the stability of LDP control of the government, a consensus within the elite on national goals, a historically nurtured respect for the bureaucracy, and Japanese styles of leadership behavior in other settings. These are beyond our scope. It is appropriate to point out, however, that the prime minister himself is not unaffected by considerations of balance. He holds his office because he is president of the majority party and, as any study of the LDP will show, maintaining this position requires keeping a majority of

Dietmen satisfied, and balancing off interests of factions and other groupings within the party. The prime minister has most often found that the benefits of strong leadership in domestic policy matters are outweighed by the costs of such a position. Similar calculations apply to the other institutions in a structural position to influence overall allocation patterns, and therefore, none has intervened. Budgeting in Japan has been left to the budgeters. This may well be the primary reason for its expenditure patterns remaining so stable.

What have been the effects of balance and stability? Supporters of programs that are not enthusiastically backed by the LDP, such as public housing, welfare, and some education programs, have clearly benefited by the availability of appeals to fair share. Balance values have served as a counterweight to political pressure. More generally, conflict has been lessened and harmony promoted within the budgetary system. But perhaps the major positive effect of balance has been the avoidance of "boom or bust" financing patterns, which can severely damage the morale and effectiveness of an agency. Under the Japanese pattern, most program decisions are left in the hands of ministry experts. By extrapolating from past budgets, they are able to make accurate estimates of the resources to be available in the future, and thus can plan their activities realistically.

However, at least from the vantage point of a distant observer, the costs of maintaining balance over the long run would appear to be more significant. The annual budget is an expression of the government's policies—responses to the needs of the society. It is inevitable that these needs must change as the society changes. Japanese society has changed during fifteen years of extraordinary economic growth, and while the shape of the budget in the mid-1950s may have been quite appropriate for national needs and goals at that time, by the same token it seems improbable that the same mix of policies would be optimum in the 1970s. Balance tends to prolong the life of programs that are wasteful or no longer required, and to inhibit the shift of resources into higher priority areas and the initiation of large new programs, particularly if they threaten the jurisdictions and budgets of the existing ministries. The responsiveness of the government to its environment is severly limited. One would expect that if balance continues to dominate budgeting for too long, strains and dissatisfactions would build up to a point where they would have to be relieved by rather sudden and large budgetary adjustments. Such a crisis would allow a clearer assessment of the delicate relationships and mutual expectations that make up the Japanese budgetary system.

A Government Ministry: The Case of the Ministry of International Trade and Industry

YOSHIHISA OJIMI

I am pleased to have this opportunity to try to explain the functioning of the Ministry of International Trade and Industry (MITI), but I am perplexed as to where to begin because of MITI's immense size and diverse functions. Among the problems we handle are imports and exports, economic cooperation, the exchange of capital, equipment investments, factory location, and environmental problems. We cover businesses from the largest down to the small- and medium-size enterprises. We cover industries from manufacturing to distribution, including the machinery industry, chemical industry, heavy industry, and textiles. Recently leisure industries, even golf, have been included. The advertising and newspaper industries are also included but, of course, because newspapers are rather frightening, little is done about them. We also deal with consumer complaints and problems concerning energy and power resources. We have sixteen laboratories working on manufacturing technology, and patents are also a big field for us.

As can be seen from this brief sketch, we cover a wide range of activities, several in cooperation with other ministries. Apart from relations with other ministries, there are also frequent problems involving the relationships between MITI and such other institutions as the Diet, the political parties, *zaikai* (financial circles), the *shingikai* (advisory commissions), and the *iinkai* (council).

I will direct my remarks on the question of decision-making in MITI toward the general mood, the basic approach, and common patterns within the ministry. I always have trouble when people inquire about these questions concerning MITI. To many outsiders MITI appears obstinate, tough, and difficult to deal with. Yet, there are always a number of persons who are surprised to find MITI kinder, more understanding, and more dependable than they had expected. Just when one is about to generalize that the pace of the work at MITI is extremely slow, one finds something that is accomplished at lightning speed. Among the projects I participated in, the liberalization of lemon imports, for example, was accomplished in half a day. At best, one can only talk about certain trends and tendencies in discussing MITI.

At the top of MITI's structure is the cabinet minister. Next there are two parliamentary vice-ministers (*seimu jikan*) and an administrative vice-minister (*jimu jikan*). Below that are the bureau chiefs (*kyokuchō*) and then the section chiefs (*kachō*), and all the assistant chiefs in the various units. The work and responsibility of the various bureaus and sections are, as a rule, quite clearly defined.

For the purpose of decision-making in the ministry there are three kinds of important regular meetings (*kaigi*). On the highest level, the *shōgi* (ministry meeting) is composed of the highest officials in the entire ministry and meets once a week. Below this is a meeting called the *shomu kachō* (section-chiefs meeting), which is attended by the highest ranking section chiefs in each of the bureaus. Next, there is the *hōrei shinsa iin* (laws and regulations examiner), an old word that refers to the meeting attended by the subordinates of the section chiefs. These latter two meetings are held twice each week.

Although the minister is the official head of the ministry meeting, he and the two parliamentary vice-ministers rarely attend, and the administrative vice-minister presides over the meeting. Most matters of importance, especially in general areas such as the budget and laws, are decided at this meeting. It does not ordinarily handle concrete issues.

It must seem strange that the cabinet minister does not attend these meetings, but there are frequent meetings between the minister and the vice-ministers. Their relationship is very close. The offices of the minister and the administrative vice-minister are joined by a door. Thus, the two are able to be in constant contact. Since the vice-minister meets the minister every day, he is fully informed of the intentions of the minister and often receives directives from the minister.

As a rule, the matters discussed at the ministerial meeting first pass through the two other meetings but, of course, not everything is discussed at the ministerial level. Some less important matters as well as some highly secret matters are not handled at the ministerial meeting. For example, although not a matter handled by MITI, the revaluation of the yen is a very top-echelon decision. Thus, some of the matters not dealt with at the ministerial meetings are very important. As a rule, however, most matters do pass through the ministerial-level meetings.

Questions of who takes the initiative and who has the real power vary from case to case. Matters of differing degrees of importance are handled differently. Is it a routine matter? Should the matter be broken down into separate parts? Does the matter require a change in the system? Is it a domestic matter? Does it have international implications? Does it have political implications? Is it a matter that requires routine office work, or is it one that must be considered to the fullest extent? Is it a rare, "once only" problem? Is it something that will only happen this year? Is it a problem with long-range significance? There are other kinds of problems, but the preceding list covers the standard ones.

In some matters, lower-level subordinates have a great deal of influence. In others, the bureaucrats who have direct contact with the public—we refer to these as the *madoguchi* (window opening)—have a great deal of authority. Then there are matters that cannot be settled without discussion with the cabinet minister. Normally, however, there are no matters where the power of subordinates is greater than that of superiors. I can make this statement with confidence. Subordinates give their opinions freely and generously, but there are no cases where the actions of the subordinates do not reflect the intentions of their superiors. The system of lower-level drafting of *ringi* documents and other daily routines must be seen in this broader context.

The *ringi* and conferences are also required because of the problems of coordinating work that overlaps the many sections of government. If one ministry does not have its house in order, it causes trouble for the other ministries. And similarly, a bureau within the ministry can create problems for others. As a result, there is a tendency toward increasing the use of such devices as regular meetings and *ringi* to ensure that work is properly implemented.

The work of the bureaucracy goes through a regular cycle. From June to August of each year, we make the policies for the following year. We decide the goals for the following year and the important matters we want to work on. We make a complete schedule for the following year, including budgets, revisions of the tax system, and laws we want passed. We call this the "making of new policies." There are some things, of course, which are not new, but because we have the desire to make something that is new, we give it this name.

The request for the budget is presented to the Ministry of Finance (MOF) in August. The laws and the tax system are done a little later, but these are all part of "making new policies." By the end of the year the draft budget and tax system are settled in conjunction with the MOF. It takes from the end of the year to the beginning of the following year to make final decisions concerning the kinds of laws to be made.

This work is finished when the laws have been presented to and passed by the Diet, the budget has been passed and the tax system revised by the Diet. Thus, when we enter a new year, the policies we have been working on for the previous year begin to take shape. Therefore, we are simultaneously enforcing the policies developed the previous year while making preparations for new policies for the following year.

There are always temporary occurrences that have not been scheduled or allowed for in the budget such as international conferences or discords that must be resolved. It is natural that these sorts of things occur, but unless new systems and policies are handled in the sort of cycle I have outlined, they are difficult to take care of. Of course, the cycle is not completely inflexible, but as a rule, if something is not in the budget by August, it must wait one more year. Thus we have to exert ourselves to the utmost from June to August. All of the bureaus and sections endeavor to find and develop desirable programs. For example, if the minister says, "Can't you come up with a better policy for small and medium enterprises?" we come up with a stack of bills concerning small and medium enterprises. And thus we go through our annual cycle.

As for the general mood in MITI, I think that it can be said that there is a large appetite for new policies. Of course, I do not mean this in comparison with the private sector; I am not qualified to make that comparison. In the government, however, I think it can be said that the appetite for new things at MITI is very large, and because of this there is a lot of friction with other ministries.

To give a recent example, there is the work that has been done on the "information industry." Then there is the plan to reduce the number of automobiles and create a new traffic system. MITI is putting a great deal of effort into these new urban systems. There is also work done on the housing industry, the ocean development industry, the leisure industry. When I reflect on these issues, I am aware that the work to develop a new traffic system is closely related to the work of the transportation ministry, the work on the information industry is closely related to the work of the postal ministry, and the leisure industry is perhaps most closely related to the work of the welfare ministry or some other ministry. These are all matters that reach beyond the confines of MITI's concerns and involve other ministries, but our mood is one of taking them up without any hesitation.

MITI likes to take on problems before others can get their hands on them. I think this is due to the open, flexible atmosphere in the ministry. From some perspectives, it can be said that MITI is conservative. Perhaps it can also be said that work should be done more vigorously. Because it is a big organization, it would be a mistake to generalize too broadly. Yet, although it may not seem so to those on the outside, within the ministry it is quite acceptable for subordinates to argue with superiors over policy. Debate is necessary to our work, and the general atmosphere supports debate. This is because persons in the lower levels of the hierarchy work in narrow, specialized fields, and therefore they are more knowledgeable about details, and they have more time to think about their subject. It is traditional not to put down a subordinate in debate simply because of his low rank. Especially when making the budget or new policies, the atmosphere is one of eagerly looking for new ideas whatever their source.

Do superiors have any influence in this kind of atmosphere? They do if they want something done. It is similar to the situation where the minister says, "Can't you do better than this?" and people reconsider their bills and come up with something better.

There are many other examples of where the opinions of those in the upper levels of the hierarchy have an influence. I would like to relate some of my personal experience on this subject, and please excuse me if it sounds as if I am boasting. When I became administrative vice-minister, I announced the things I wanted to do most. For example, I wanted a new trade and industry policy for the 1970s. I served as administrative vice-minister from 1969 to 1971, and I felt that a new policy could be formulated during my term. The new policy was finally completed one month before I resigned. I resigned right after it was announced.

I also wanted to establish a new system for the information industry. This was met with enthusiasm by those who were put in charge of the project, and they found it stimulating. Another example was my wish to revise the patent laws. This kind of leadership is used not only by the administrative vice-minister but by the bureau chiefs and the section chiefs as well. From the time I became bureau chief, it became standard procedure to announce what I wanted to do during the two or so years in each assignment. I think this helps make the work interesting.

I would now like to turn to the question of personnel practices. There are about fourteen thousand persons in MITI. This figure includes people in the various laboratories, the patent office, and the regional branch offices. Approximately one-fourth of these are actually in Tokyo taking care of administrative matters. Of this number, about one-fifth are civil servants who have passed the highest level of the civil service examination.

I cannot say that all of the bureaucrats work hard, but certainly some of them are very highly motivated. In my view, they work very hard. It is common for them to work until eight or ten or even twelve o'clock in the evening. They have *nabeyaki udon* (a pot of noodles) brought to them in the evening, drink a cup of sake, and work with manly determination. Their pay is not especially high, and it cannot even be assumed that they are respected by all Japanese. Recently economic growth is looked upon as bad. Exporting is bad, manufacturing is bad, being different is bad. Even in the past, MITI's reputation was not particularly good. But these upper-level civil servants continue working until late at night. I used to tell them they were foolish.

Is the work of MITI decreasing? I always thought that the controls of MITI would decrease with trade liberalization. The total number of employees has not changed, but the proportion of MITI officials involved in administration has decreased annually. The total figure has not decreased because decreases in administrative personnel have been matched by increases in the staff of the patent office and laboratories. With liberalization I thought there would be a decrease in the work load, but actually it seems that people are busier than ever. It is a mystery to me, but as the days pass people actually get busier. This may be explained by the fact that the society has become more complex and the demands on the ministry have multiplied.

I also wondered if the quality of the people applying for jobs in MITI might not decrease. I wondered whether MITI would lose its appeal as a place offering top-level career opportunities. But top-level students still strive to enter. So I think it can be said that there are many fools among Japanese students.

DISCUSSION

Nagamasa Ito: Because I spent a little time in Mr. Ojimi's ministry, I would like to mention one of my impressions. I was involved in the preparation of white papers, for which an impressive quantity of good data was collected. But before publishing the white paper, there were always many complaints from the various ministries: "Don't state that so clearly," or "Take this out." The end result would be a document that made little sense. The process of selective omissions was the result of considerable effort on the part of the various ministries, but it also reflected a certain attitude toward responsibility in the bureaucracy. Actually bureaucracies do not take responsibility. If a mistake is made in administrative guidance, for example, those who received the guidance are the ones who suffer. Those who make the mistake, however, do not take the responsibility for it. It was the feeling of those working on the white paper that the bureaucracy does not like a system of clear-cut responsibility.

One other point: Mr. Ojimi mentioned that the policies desired by the cabinet minister usually pass, but from our point of view it was an incompetent system. We kept getting these people who did not know the first thing about economic problems. When Wada Hiro brought his own staff members into office, it looked like their authority was going to be based on their knowledge; but the will to work and the theoretical basis of work is lost when you work under people who speak nonsense.

Yukio Suzuki: I would like to ask about administrative guidance. Mr. Ojimi said that the work of MITI is spreading to new fields, and I think that one of the problems will be to coordinate the activities of MITI and the activities of other ministries to keep them from conflicting. But with these changes, what is happening to MITI's administrative guidance policies? What will be the shape of administrative guidance in the future?

Ojimi: Heretofore, the purpose of MITI's administrative guidance was to aid industrial development, and thus the activities of industry and the bureaucracy were mutually supportive. MITI helped in the coordination of such undertakings as exporting, equipment investment, capital supply. As that sort of work decreases, what will be the pattern of new policies? One new activity which has come to my attention is MITI's role in supplying information to industry. As the Japanese economy and the pattern of economic growth change, MITI will take on the role of supplying precise information to industry.

At the same time, MITI has made it a practice not to interfere in private industry's pursuit of profits. Now, when the activities of industry are seen in some aspects as harmful to society—in environmental pollution, for example—MITI's administrative controls will probably take on a new dimension. Since, as Mr. Suzuki said, these new dimensions are related to the work of the other ministries, in some cases, administrative guidance may require cooperative action by two or three ministries.

Suzuki: This new direction is good, but I think it will present a new set of problems for MITI. Until now MITI was helping industry do what it could not do for itself. When industry could not control its own activities, it called on MITI. It has been difficult to determine whether the control of MITI has been due to its own leadership or whether industry has been controlling itself in the name of MITI. There have been differences among the different types of industry, and I would like to have Mr. Ōjimi explain the internal workings of administrative guidance a little more concretely.

Ojimi: This is a difficult question. As Mr. Suzuki said, the new direction in MITI is toward supplying information and controlling industrial activities that are socially harmful. At the same time, however, it is surprising that the necessity for administrative guidance still remains. For example, I think that it would probably be best to leave the problem of overinvestment in equipment up to the forces of the market, but this has never been tried. Moreover, it now has international implications. For example, the year before last and last year when I went to Europe, I was asked if we could do something to control equipment investment. The Japanese shipbuilding industry, for example, is still investing in equipment. I was asked at what percent of the market share Japan would finally be satisfied. Thus, advising on equipment investment is not a policy that we can easily abandon. Furthermore, as Japanese industry advances into foreign countries, new kinds of conflicts and legal problems arise. Therefore, it appears necessary to keep an ongoing dialogue with industry.

In some ways, MITI may have been used as a tool by industry, and yet there are still problems which cannot be settled without strong leadership from the bureaucracy. There are some problems that are settled simply by MITI's showing its face. An objective, neutral, third party is needed to clear up many problems. Who, if not the bureaucracy, is to play that role?

The *zaikai* groups? The press? The Diet? The parties? When you think about it, this is really the role of the bureaucracy.

Hugh Patrick: I have some questions about administrative guidance. You mentioned that it did not work very well when it was applied to excessive investments. Could we say that it works best when it encourages rather than restricts industry? Does it work best when its goals are those that industry wants? Does this mean that MITI is quite weak as an independent organization but quite strong when it represents business interests?

Ojimi: Administrative guidance is not so simple that we can say it works best when it encourages rather than restricts industry. We can mention examples in which MITI was tough in restricting the interests of industries by administrative guidance. With regard to overinvestment, Japanese industry tends to be overly ambitious, whether the problem is one of excessive investment in equipment or excessive competition. Administrative guidance exists to restrain this excessive aggressiveness. However, MITI policy is basically designed to help and encourage industry. Controls have been used to aid industrial development. Of course, there are cases where there is a vicious circle—because administrative guidance and controls exist, companies feel they can be excessively aggressive since there will be external restraints. There are also cases where industry has been overly encouraged and has been left with scars from overinvestment in equipment when our estimate of prospects were too optimistic. Nonetheless, MITI does endeavor to work for the benefit of industry, not for the benefit of an individual firm of the industry.

M. Y. Yoshino: In looking at the postwar history of MITI, I have been struck by the effectiveness of its leadership. But in the past there has been a strong consensus about the goal of economic growth. It has played a particular role in developing industries like heavy manufacturing and the chemical industry, and in this effort both candy and the whip have been used. The public criticism of industry concerning problems such as pollution, consumer problems, or international problems presents a completely different set of problems for industry in the 1970s and 1980s. There are problems that confront all types of industries, not just a select few. In discussing these things with people in MITI, I have been told that MITI is now making certain structural reforms. What will be the future role of MITI? The problems are different, and yet at the same time they concern the problem of the candy and the whip which are factors that make up power relations. I would like to ask Mr. Ojimi what he thinks the role of MITI will be in the seventies and eighties.

Ojimi: As you said, the way in which MITI has governed industry and the consensus concerning economic growth have complemented each other. It is easy to work when industry agrees with you and you are trying to move things in a direction that will benefit industry. Now, however, the job is to direct industry away from economic growth toward social usefulness. Industry should be kept from polluting, from using too many natural resources, and the like. In taking these new directions, MITI may have to assume leadership because a free economy cannot solve these new problems on its own. On the contrary, as the economy progresses, public control will be required and administrative guidance as well as legislation may still be necessary.

Ivan Hall: I think we can assume that MITI does not operate in isolation from other ministries. Many policies must be decided in cooperation with the other ministries. What is the mechanism of liaison and consultation with the other ministries?

Ojimi: MITI has close relations with the other ministries. These relations are especially close with the other *keizai kanchō* (the ministries related to economic affairs—the Economic Planning Agency, MOF, and the Ministry of Agriculture and Forestry). We also have close relations with the Foreign Ministry. As for the problem of the level at which contacts are maintained with the other ministries, this depends on the issue involved. When a new law or policy requires adjustments in the authority of two ministries, these contacts can be on the level of the bureau chief, administrative vice-minister, or cabinet minister. It all depends on the nature of the problem.

In addition to these kinds of liaison for dealing with special problems, there are also standing procedures for regular relations with other ministries. There is a *renrakukai* (liaison meeting). There is also a semiweekly meeting of administrative vice-ministers from each ministry. Important laws and other matters are all discussed at this meeting, and it serves an important function in the relations among ministries.

Robert Ward: I would like to have some questions about the *ringi* system cleared up. On what occasions are *ringi* documents used? At what level do they normally originate? Once written, is the content of a *ringi* document ever changed? Is it difficult to achieve such change? How important is the *ringi* document as a decision-making device?

Ojimi: To give my impressions, people in the ministries are not much interested in *ringi*; it is a mundane practice. We consider the *ringi* document as part of office equipment along with pencils and paper. The *ringi* document is rarely written at the section-chief level. More commonly it is written by the person in charge of a certain matter below that level. But in some important cases it is sent to the bureau chief, administrative vice-minister, or minister, depending on the content of the document. The simplest routine matters are simply written on a standard printed form as a *ringi* document. And at the other extreme, covering important matters, decisions are made before the *ringi* is ever written and passed around. Of course, *ringi* does serve to make the content of the decision clear, to put things on record, and to keep people in various parts of the organization mutually informed.

As the *ringi* is passed up, it can be revised. To show that a revision has been made, the person making the revision puts his stamp on the *ringi*. There is the story about the man who is reluctant to affix his stamp on the document, and to show his opposition he affixes his stamp upside down. I have never seen anything like this. I think that it is only apocryphal. It shows, however, that, no matter how reluctantly, most people approve a decision once it has reached this stage.

The *ringi* documents that go to the level of the cabinet, however, are treated with great importance in contrast to the *ringi* documents used daily within the ministry offices.

Taishiro Shirai: I am interested in the distribution of manpower in MITI. MITI has very capable people, and I would like to know something about the way in which these people are used. You said that the best university graduates come to MITI and that recruitment is no problem. You also said that they are trained to take on any kind of job. I think this is true. My question may be difficult to answer, but I would like to inquire about *amakudari*, the later entry of former MITI officials into the private sector. How are they introduced to industries? Is this done through MITI, or is it left entirely up to individual negotiation? Is it different for private industry and public groups?

Ojimi: Generally speaking, the lifetime of a top bureaucrat is not very long. I myself resigned from the ministry at the age of fifty-three. Even this was rather old compared with most of my colleagues.

Because the structure is pyramid-shaped, as one climbs to the top, there are naturally fewer posts. With very rare exceptions, we do not put a section chief below a bureau chief who is the same age or younger. This is not such a problem in private companies, but in the bureaucracy it does not work to have an official serving under a younger person. As a result, most bureaucrats, compared with employees in other organizations, resign at a young age. Therefore, they must take new jobs in the nongovernment sphere.

From the point of view of private companies, there is a need for these men. Requests frequently come to the personnel division of the ministry. Thus, placement is usually taken care of by the personnel division.

There are differences between private and public groups. After resigning, a man can immediately go to a public organization, but he must wait two years to enter a private company, or he must obtain permission from the personnel authority, which is under the board of the cabinet. This permission is usually granted; or perhaps it would be more accurate to say that the men search for companies for which permission will be granted. To obtain the permission, it must be a company with which the bureaucrat has not had past relationships in an official capacity. It is easier, therefore, for those lower in the hierarchy and more difficult for those in the upper levels. I have no intention of seeking permission, so I am currently enjoying my two years with no job.

Most people in MITI prefer to go to private companies rather than public organizations. In discussing this with the vice-ministers from some other ministries, I have found that this trend is unique to MITI. They usually say, "Public organizations are more stable than private, most of our people would rather not go to private companies. Your ministry is rare."

Yoshinori Ide: The post that is the hardest to understand in the bureaucracy is that of the vice-minister. Looking at the bureaucracy from the outside it looks like a very elite and tough career. The position of the vice-minister appears to be the most powerful.

Depending on the ministry, the position of vice-minister is very different from that of bureau chief. Up to the position of bureau chief you have your own staff, but when you become vice-minister you lose your staff. You are alone. At the level of bureau chief it is sufficient if you act so that you protect the interest of your bureau. The vice-minister must represent the entire ministry.

You mentioned that when you became vice-minister you announced the policies you wanted during your term. Did you have your own staff in this case? In some ministries, even if the vice-minister proposes certain policies, the absence of a personal staff makes the implementation of these proposals difficult. I would like you to comment on some of your own personal experiences in this regard.

Ojimi: Although the vice-minister can use every part of the ministry, the ministry secretariat is located nearby and he relies on them heavily. The secretariat summarizes policies and daily administrative matters, and there are also sections in charge of matters like personnel and public relations. Moreover, there is a planning office and a research section. The relative strength of the secretariat is different in different ministries. In ministries where the secretariat is strong there is unity in the ministry. When the bureaus are strong, there is less unity. I am not saying which is good or bad because that depends on the work involved.

Anybody who becomes vice-minister has thought about the policies he wants to pursue before he reaches office. When you are in the ministry for a long time and have risen through the ranks—I was a bureaucrat for thirty years—you have ideas and you direct the secretariat accordingly.

If your question is whether or not there is a cleavage between the vice-minister and bureau chiefs which isolates the vice-minister from those below, I will have to say that this is absolutely not true. The administrative vice-minister has the highest authority on all administrative matters. This comes from the position, not from his personality. This is probably not a very good example, but in the case of a power struggle between ministries, it is difficult to find an arbitrator. In a power struggle between bureaus within the ministry, the vice-minister has clear authority to straighten things out. Of course, the vice-minister tries to refrain from rulings which will cause dissatisfaction, but his rulings generally settle matters.

Ezra Vogel: I am interested in the new problems MITI will face, such as environmental protection and consumer protection. I understand that MITI has undergone reorganization to deal with these problems. I have also seen an American article that said that dealing effectively with these problems in any country will require a higher degree of government control than anticipated. What kinds of groups do you envisage working with these problems, and what leverage will the government have in dealing with these problems?

Ojimi: The Kankyō-chō (Environment Agency) of the cabinet is concerned with environmental problems. In MITI we have the *kōgai hoan-kyoku* (Environmental Protection and Safety Bureau). In addition, we have the Chemical Industry Bureau, the Minerals, Oils, and Coal-Mining Bureau, and other specialized bureaus of this sort that can deal with pollution problems in the respective fields. The Environmental Protection and Safety Bureau stands between the various other bureaus in MITI and the Environment Agency of the cabinet, which administers overall policy. One goal of MITI's current reform efforts is to strengthen the sections in charge of environmental and consumer problems. The Diet will also develop new legislation to deal with these problems. I am confident that MITI will be organized to deal effectively with problems of pollution and consumer protection.

PART TWO

Economic Organization

Big Business Organization

KAZUO NODA

This paper aims to present the essentials of organization and top-management decision-making in Japanese big business. To do so for a foreign audience, it is first necessary to deal with certain misconceptions about Japanese management. Some foreign writers, interested in finding the unique "Japanese pattern of management," have tended to reify certain conceptions based on partial observations. The result has been understatement of the extent of change in Japanese enterprises and the extent to which they are similar to foreign enterprises.

In fact, Japanese enterprises, like enterprises in other advanced countries in the free-world economy, must give priority to economic rationality in order to realize profits. To remain competitive, Japanese management has continuously revised unprofitable practices and systems. The elimination of idiosyncratic practices and systems has been particularly marked in the large enterprises that must compete with foreign enterprises in both international and domestic markets. In the long run, Japanese enterprises have tended to respond to international market forces in ways not totally dissimilar to foreign firms.

Of course, some customs and structural features prevalent in Japanese organizations differ in certain ways from those in foreign countries, but "Japanese uniqueness" has been exaggerated because of the confusion between formal and informal practices. As a result of thousands of years of historical development in isolation from other countries, Japan has developed a society that is decidedly homogeneous in comparison with other countries, especially the United States. This homogeneity in race, language, culture, and life style facilitates establishment of informal ties among individuals. Especially in organizations where individuals work together continuously for a long time, informal custom has far more power than the formal system in regulating the daily activities of the system's members. The formally established system that has no substantial function is a phenomenon found also in organizations in the United States, but the extent of difference between the formal and informal systems within the Japanese organization is particularly striking. Since both large enterprises and government bureaucracies in Japan are equipped with extensive formal systems, foreigners sometimes mistakenly assume that the "characteristic Japanese features" of these formal systems essentially explain the actual functioning of Japanese firms.

Defining Big Business

In present-day Japan, most enterprises, from very small-scale organizations to big businesses, are officially classified as corporations (*kaisha hōjin*). There are four types of corporations, but the overwhelming majority are *kabushiki kaisha* (joint-stock companies). Before World War II, many small- and medium-sized businesses in Japan did not adopt the joint-stock-company form. But with Japan's economic growth since World War II, the joint-stock company acquired obvious business advantages, and even small- and medium-sized enterprises gradually adopted this form of organization. Present-day Japanese enterprises referred to as "big businesses" are without exception joint-stock companies.

Despite wide use of the expression "big business," its definition is less clear than that of small- and medium-sized business (*chūshō kigyō*).[1] However, it is not difficult to arrive at a working definition based on widely accepted practice. For example, a company that is listed in the first section of the Tokyo Stock Exchange can be considered a big business. There were 970,000 corporations in Japan as of the end of May 1973, but of these, only 820 (850 at the end of 1973) were listed in the first section of the Tokyo Stock Exchange. Since there are many corporations of comparable scale which are not listed, selection of all companies with capitalization over one billion yen (a criterion for being listed) reveals fewer than 1,500 corporations,[2] or 0.07 percent of all companies.

This group of 1,500 Japanese corporations, however, has great importance. They control 60 percent of all capital, 36 percent of all business revenue, and their business revenue of eighty-eight trillion yen comes to about 6.2 times the government's general budget of 1973. But capitalization over one billion yen is more than a quantitative classification. For

---

[1] The definition in the Fundamental Law on Small and Medium Enterprises specifies the following limitation on scale of operations: (1) For mining, transportation, and other industries, (a) total capital base: less than ¥50,000,000, and (b) total number of employees: less than 300; (2) for commerce and service industries, (a) total capital base: less than ¥10,000,000, and (b) total number of employees: less than 50.

[2] This figure is as of the end of January 1972.

example, corporations with less than one billion yen are overwhelmingly family enterprises (*dōzoku kaisha*), whereas companies with over one billion yen capitalization are mainly nonfamily enterprises.[3] In present-day Japan, a company, regardless of its format, generally outgrows the taint of an individual or family-centered undertaking when it exceeds about one billion yen capitalization. For the purposes of this article, we shall operationally define the big businesses under discussion as those that meet the following two criteria: (1) capitalization over one billion yen, and (2) nonfamily company structure, as reflected in stockholder ratios. Roughly 1,400 companies meet these two criteria—corresponding approximately to the number of companies listed in the first and second sections of the Tokyo Stock Exchange.

BOARD OF DIRECTORS AND
ITS *JŌMUKAI* (EXECUTIVE COMMITTEE)

The Three Legal Organs

Big business, even as defined above, is a broad term which includes hundreds of businesses of many different scales, industrial types, and historical backgrounds. Although it is difficult to generalize about top management organization and the decision-making process for such a diverse group, it is possible, with due caution, to draw some generalizations.

Among the organs defined by the Japanese Commercial Law, the board of directors (*torishimariyakukai*) fulfills the role of top management in business organizations. This is an organ created after World War II (in 1950) when the Commercial Law was greatly revised. Under the old Commercial Law, each director held important legal power in various top management operations and as company representative to the outside. When the Commercial Law was revised, management powers were given to the board of directors, which was composed of all directors as regular members. The board of directors came to make decisions on items covering a broad sphere of top management.

The authority of company representative was delegated to the representative director (*daihyō torishimariyaku*) chosen by the board of directors. Thus, the board of directors became the decision-maker on a broad range of items determined by company regulations, in addition to the following items designated for exclusive decision under the Commercial Law: (1) decision to convene the general meeting of stockholders; (2) nomination of representative directors; (3) nomination of and dismissal of management;

---

[3] A family company is so designated by the law if the three largest shareholders are related and control more than 50 percent of the total company stock. For computation purposes, the number of shares held by minor stockholders who are related must also be counted with those of the major family shareholders.

(4) decision on bond issuance; (5) discretion of turning over nonessential business to outside parties; (6) determination of matters relating to issuance of new stock; (7) approval of the transactions between directors and the company; (8) capital incorporation of the reserve fund; (9) stock split; (10) appointment of representatives in disputes between company and directors.

As defined under the Commercial Law, there are two organs—the general meeting of stockholders and the auditors—which are equal to or above the board of directors. With the revision of the Commercial Law in 1950, the authority of these organs was greatly reduced and in part transferred to the board of directors. In the sense, however, that the right to appoint the directors lies with the general meeting of stockholders, and in the sense that the auditors have the authority to check the business performance of the directors, these respective organs are beyond the jurisdiction of the board of directors. The authority of the three organs (the board of directors, general meeting of stockholders, and auditors) is fixed clearly and entirely by law, with a system of mutual restraints designed to realize profits while preserving the stockholders' rights as owners. However, at least in big businesses, not all organs function in accordance with legal specifications. To overstate the case, neither the general meeting of stockholders nor the auditors fulfill their formally stated functions. Actually, even the power of the board of directors has greatly declined. We shall look first at the actual functions of the board of directors as it in fact replaces the general meeting of stockholders and the auditors.

Separation of Ownership and Control

The general meeting of stockholders is by nature essential to the joint stockholders' company. That the function of the general meeting is undermined as increased scale of enterprise stimulates the "separation of ownership and control" was pointed out with regard to American big businesses fifty years ago. In Japan, the decline of the general meeting of stockholders, already evident prior to World War II, was not connected with the phenomenon of separation of ownership and control until after the war.

The cause lies in the fact that over half of Japan's prewar big businesses were subsidiaries of the so-called *zaibatsu* capital groups and were always controlled, financially and through personnel, by the head companies (*honsha*), which were the stockholding companies. Since the majority of the non-*zaibatsu* big businesses were family companies or quasi-family companies, even if their stock was listed on the stock market, the number of shares actually traded on the market was in fact restricted. Thus the general meeting of stockholders was a mere formality for the main body of stockholders, and the essential decisions, including appointment and dismissal of directors, could not help but be dominated by the will of the large stockholders who were the real owners.

In Japan, unlike America, the "separation between ownership and control" in big business did not result from the natural maturation of industrial society. Rather, it was a by-product of defeat in the Pacific War and the policies for economic and societal democratization imposed by the Occupation forces. The striking elimination of large stockholders and marked increase of individual small stockholders formed the background for the rapid separation of ownership and control and the virtual eclipse of the general meeting of stockholders.[4]

Since auditors were created by the Commercial Law enacted in 1896, they have had little real function in most joint-stock companies. Japan's Commercial Law was strongly influenced by German law, but unlike the German case, broad authority was never given to the auditors. And unlike the situation in England, there was little concern over whether auditorial candidates possessed the experience and knowledge that would enable them to carry out basic auditorial tasks. When, as part of the revision of a series of laws at the end of the Pacific War, the Commercial Law was revised, even the putative legal authority of the auditors was reduced. From the viewpoint of top management, the auditors' functions were negligible. Their importance was further weakened by the provisions of the Certified Public Accountant Act and the Securities Exchange Act, which require all companies listed on the stock exchange (with the exception of financial institutions) to have an external audit performed by a certified public accountant, just as in America.

For these reasons, the auditor—as compared with other joint-stock company executives—has long been considered both by those within and outside the company as a mere title with responsibilities much lighter than those of the director.

Naturally, the decline in authority and function of the auditors and the general meeting of stockholders influenced both directly and indirectly the authority and function of the board of directors. The point is quite clear if we consider the following concrete questions: Who in fact nominates the directors if they are not actually nominated by the general meeting of stockholders? Who in fact checks the directors' business performance and methods if they are not actually checked by the auditors?

As the scale of an enterprise increases, the number of stockholders generally increases, and the relative share of each stockholder is decreased by various factors (such as higher dividends, *mushōkōfu*,[5] and the climb in

---

[4] A government organ called the Holding Company Liquidation Commission confiscated in one sweep the extensive stock that the old *zaibatsu* had held in "child companies" and made it widely available to the general public. According to the stock distribution research of the Tokyo Stock Exchange in the first half of 1950, the proportion of stock held by individuals was an overwhelming 60 percent.

[5] *Mushōkōfu* is the preferential distribution of stock to shareholders at a price considerably

stock value resulting from company growth). With these changes, the majority of the stockholders tend to lose interest in the management of the company as long as their investment desire is satisfied by such means as increase in share value, increased shareholdings, and dividends. Stockholders even fail to exercise their one major right—the nomination of members of the board of directors. Even if one segment of the stockholders endeavors to take an active role, under normal circumstances there is no effective means for rousing the interest of the other stockholders and gaining their timely participation.

Under the provisions of the Commercial Law, the appointment and dismissal of the directors and of the auditors must be determined formally by a decision of the general meeting of stockholders, but we must inquire how this actually works. In fact, it is made possible by a consensus among the members of the board of directors. This is because, except in special cases, the right to convene the general meeting of stockholders lies in the board of directors, and the formulation of the agenda is also a function of the board of directors. The agenda includes such important items as continuance and retirement of present auditors and directors as well as nomination of new auditors and directors. Since it is inconceivable that the general meeting of stockholders will reject the nominations from the board of directors, the de facto right to appoint and dismiss directors and auditors is in the directors' hands.

Jōmukai

The next question is how the board of directors makes such basic decisions. The Commercial Law fixes the decision-making method of the board of directors as a majority vote of directors present, but in fact such voting virtually never occurs. This is self-evident if we analyze the structure of directorships in postwar Japanese enterprises.

In large American enterprises, external directors constitute a substantial proportion of all directors, but in postwar Japan, there are very few enterprises with outside directors. The most notable characteristic of the Japanese directorship structure is that most directors hold regular working positions within the company. Senior executives such as vice-presidents (*fuku shachō*), executive directors (*senmu*), managing directors (*jōmu*) are, without exception, directors. Recently, it has become common even for division level executives, such as chiefs of major factories and branch offices, and the heads of major functional departments like marketing, manufacturing, accounting, and personnel to also be named as directors. These officials are, in fact, appointed and dismissed by the company president, the highest official within the company hierarchy. Generally,

---

lower than the face value or current price. Companies listed in the stock exchange practice *mushōkōfu* when issuing new stock.

the company president is a representative director, appointed by the board of directors.

In most big businesses, the members of the board of directors do not interact as full equals because they have different statuses within the company hierarchy. Moreover, they become directors only after they first achieve their positions within the company hierarchy. Appointment by the company president to an essential position within the company hierarchy is tantamount to appointment to a directorship, and there is no reason to expect that these junior and senior directors will have the same informal power as the representative directors who recommended them in the first place. In Japan, unlike America and Western Europe, the traditional seniority-oriented value system is still strong, and an employee is acutely conscious of his rank. Thus, the board of directors as a voting body is virtually nonexistent, and we can safely say that its decisions are not made by majority rule.

Rather than majority-rule decision-making, the most widespread form of decision-making in Japan is "complete consensus." The most common form of traditional decision-making in Japan, complete consensus decision-making is characteristic of groups in which the members all share basic interests and in which they work together daily for a long period. Since the board of directors of a Japanese big business provides a typical example of such a group, it is natural that complete consensus decision-making should be the rule, except in situations where, for some reason, circumstances produce a grave confrontation among directors. In such cases, the functions of the general meeting of stockholders are often restored.

When we speak of complete consensus it does not necessarily mean that a decision was arrived at after thorough debate and formulation by the entire body of members. There are cases in which, pulled along by the ideas of one or a small number of members with great initiative, the remainder of the members express consent. There are also cases in which, after a variety of differing opinions are expressed, the final decision-maker proposes a single plan that all members agree to follow. In short, it is the *ultimate show* of complete consensus which is essential. Complete consensus decision-making has some shortcomings in comparison with majority rule decision-making, but on the whole it has one decisive advantage for the Japanese.

The advantage is that, when a decision results in failure, responsibility for that failure is not borne by one individual alone; and conversely, when a decision results in success, the glory for that success also does not go to one individual alone. This principle may at first glance seem odd to foreigners, whose value systems and customs differ from those of the Japanese. But for Japanese, it serves more than the simple purpose of emotional satisfaction; it is a practical necessity. From the Japanese point of view, majority rule decision-making often destroys the solidarity of the group. By obscuring its original significance under the Commercial Law and transforming itself into a "cabinet board" for the company president, who is himself a representative director, the board of directors can, as a rule, avoid the type of decision-making that would mar group solidarity. In this sense, it is a most rational system.

Decision-making by consensus is sometimes mistakenly taken to mean that no individual assumes responsibility for a decision or that responsibility is divided among all members. In fact, the final complete consensus is entirely separate from the question of attributing responsibility for success or failure. Even in cases when a decision is made by all members, if the result is a serious failure, the representative director—the company president—either alone or with a small group of senior directors, sometimes takes responsibility for the failure. In other cases, a junior director who has had no actual influence in a final decision may be forced to "commit harakiri" (resign). Of course, it is quite common for responsibility to be shouldered by the persons actually responsible for advancing a given decision. "Responsibility assumption" by Japanese is a complicated subject, but it is sufficient for present purposes to note that decision-making by consensus and responsibility assumption, which leads to praise or blame, are governed by entirely different principles.

A critical condition in complete consensus decision-making is the number of members who comprise a group. When the recovery of the Japanese economy began in the beginning of the 1950s, the number of directors never exceeded ten, even in fairly large-scale enterprises. But after Japan's economic growth began in earnest about 1955, the number of directors in all big businesses suddenly increased, and today a sizable number of companies have twenty to thirty directors. The increase was designed to strengthen top management within each enterprise to ensure that they could cope effectively with the rapid changes in business environment brought about by economic growth. The nucleus of this effort to cope was the establishment of a company organ composed of only senior directors. The name of this organ varies from company to company, but the term *jōmukai* (executive committee of managing directors) is used most frequently.

In addition to the company president (who is usually the chairman), members of the executive committee number five to ten at most and include those holding the positions of company vice-president, executive director, and managing director. Adequate daily communication is easily possible among a group of this size, and on that foundation, it is possible to put into practice the principle of consensus decision-making when it comes to items of serious consequence. When the executive committee system was first introduced, companies were generally in the process of establishing or expanding their general staff department (nomenclature again varies by company, but it is generally called the presidential office [*shachōshitsu*] or planning department [*kikakushitsu*]). Enlisting the aid of this new department, the executive committee is actually able to carry out much greater top-management functions than previously. With the spread of the executive committee system, functions of the full board of directors, which under the Commercial Law was supposed to be the highest decision-making organ, greatly atrophied.

THE RISE OF PROFESSIONAL MANAGERS

The Purge of Prewar Executives

In analyzing the top management of Japanese big business after the war, we must have a thorough understanding of the completely new breed of leaders who were born from the social and economic fabric during the period of Occupation and the revision of the Commercial Law. For approximately seven years after the Pacific War ended in August 1945, Japan was under military occupation. "Demilitarization" and "democratization" were two pressing objectives of the first Occupation reforms carried out by MacArthur's General Headquarters. The latter objective—democratization—was considered a necessary prerequisite for preservation of the former objective—demilitarization. In hopes of democratization, the Occupation forces took firm leadership of the Japanese government and carried out major legal and structural reforms. The democratization measures had a variety of effects on the economic activities of big business, but *zaibatsu* dissolution is the single measure most essentially related to our subject here.

At the close of World War II, the total paid-up capital of ten *zaibatsu* conglomerates amounted to 35.2 percent of the total paid-up capital of all joint-stock companies in Japan. Since twelve hundred companies were listed by the General Headquarters as subsidiaries[6] to the *zaibatsu* for the purposes of *zaibatsu* dissolution, it is safe to conclude that before World War II a large proportion of big businesses in Japan were members of *zaibatsu* groups.

To varying degrees, all main subsidiary companies of the *zaibatsu* were systematically placed in a pyramid-shaped control structure, and at the apex was the holding company, a family company. The finances and leading personnel of the major subsidiaries were completely under the direction of the head company. This pattern of control was eliminated in one swift strike by *zaibatsu* dissolution and other democratization measures. Most dramatic was the large-scale purge of top-level executives from *zaibatsu* holding companies and major subsidiaries, for it instantly transformed the top management of big business.

Immediately after World War II, the government established the

---

[6] A subsidiary was defined as a company in which more than 10 percent of the stock was *zaibatsu*-held.

Holding Company Liquidation Commission under the direction of General Headquarters. It collected large amounts of *zaibatsu* stock from the *zaibatsu*'s leading families, its holding companies, and the subsidiary companies. As a result of this collection and collection of the stock in outside companies held by nationalized companies, which was taken as payment in kind by the Ministry of Finance (shortly after the property tax was initiated in October 1946), the government controlled an estimated one-third to one-half of the paid-up capital in all Japanese companies. By these measures the government swept away the control network which the *zaibatsu* holding company had maintained over its subsidiaries.

The *zaibatsu* dissolution policy was one link in the series of Occupation policies for democratizing the Japanese economic and social systems, but that democratization extended beyond just the *zaibatsu* and their subsidiaries. Non-*zaibatsu* big businesses that had contributed in any way to the war effort were dissolved or restructured by the Japanese government according to the design of the Occupation. Among these were government monopolies, national corporations and banks created for colonial management, and private companies created by mergers under the government's powerful wartime administrative guidance.

Like the policy toward *zaibatsu*, the general democratization policies extended not only to enterprises but also to the individuals responsible for company management. Specifically, the General Headquarters issued directives to the Japanese government, which, through the "Ban from Socially Influential Offices," prohibited large stockholders and upper-echelon executives in 2,500 major wartime companies and banks from holding socially influential offices. The Commercial Law revision prohibited making stock ownership in any form a qualification for appointment within companies. At the same time that the legal powers of the general meeting of stockholders were reduced, those of the directors were increased. Within a few years after World War II, the policy of thorough democratization, including *zaibatsu* dissolution, had forced most top executives in the financial and industrial world to retire. As a result, although big businesses were allowed to continue in some form, most of their directors were replaced and their capital ties with the head companies were severed.

Santō Jūyaku (Third-Rate Directors)

A certain number of the new postwar directors had served as directors even prior to the removal of the senior directors in the purge, but the vast majority had served as such middle-level managers as *bucho* (division chief) or *kacho* (section chief) during the war and became directors to replace those removed from office. During this large-scale replacement, the newly born directors were commonly nicknamed *santō jūyaku* (third-rate directors). There were, of course, some new directors unequal to the tasks demanded by their new positions, and before long they were in turn replaced. But most of the new directors stood up under the heavy responsibility of their positions and, under these difficult circumstances, succeeded in rebuilding their enterprises. Most were in fact not "third-rate directors" lacking in ability and managerial skills, but rather the most promising young middle-level management. The majority of this new leadership class entered the company as "salarymen" and were promoted because of their knowledge, experience, and managerial ability in business administration. In this respect, they are comparable to professional managers in the U.S. industrial world.

Given the shock of defeat and the uncertain future of big business in Japan, it took not only ability but also considerable self-confidence and decisiveness for these new directors to suddenly assume heavy managerial responsibilities. Whatever else may be said about them, most were extraordinarily able.

In one sense, the massive postwar purge of Japan's business leadership was an opportunity to permit fresh young directors to develop their enterprises along bold new lines. Most of these new leaders continued to hold top spots in large enterprises and to lead their companies even after the general relaxation in Occupation policy.

Around 1950, although purge orders had been lifted one after another, very few former top-level executives were returned to their original posts. We can delineate two major reasons for this phenomenon. The first was that since companies had by then developed a sizable corps of capable professional managers, there was little leeway to reinstate former executives. However, even if former executives wished to be reinstated, the new top-level executives did not wish to circumscribe their own authority by returning the former executives to powerful positions within the organization. A second reason was that, in the period of four or five years after the war, large changes in business climate made prewar management experience and know-how obsolete, especially since the prewar managers had little experience or inclination to cope with new unfavorable conditions like the vicious postwar inflation and frequent labor-management struggles. Thus, despite the depurging, former managers themselves had no desire to return to active service.

In this way, the majority of the big businesses that led Japan's postwar economic recovery and growth placed a new generation of professional managers in the top positions. They contributed greatly to the revival of the Japanese economy, which was accomplished in a short period. The unexpected rapidity of Japan's later growth was inseparable from the growth of big business, and the success of both reinforced the influence and authority of this new generation of managers, both within and outside their enterprises.

TYPICAL JAPANESE FEATURES OF
TOP MANAGEMENT IN "REVISED" BIG BUSINESS
SINCE WORLD WAR II

To eager entrepreneurs, the remarkable recovery and growth of the postwar Japanese economy seemed to supply unlimited business opportunities; it did, in fact, produce a considerable number of growth enterprises. But for at least ten years after the war—the recovery period—virtually no small enterprises grew rapidly enough to approach the scale of the big businesses. Even Sony and Honda, outstanding postwar growth enterprises, were listed on the Tokyo Stock Exchange only in 1958 and 1957 respectively. For that reason, until Japan's postwar economic growth began to accelerate around 1955, Japanese big businesses were virtually all continuations of prewar big businesses. Since the capital structure and executive personnel of such businesses had been completely swept away by the Occupation's democratization measures, it might be more accurate to call them "revised" prewar big businesses. The six points discussed below summarize the characteristics of the top-management organization and decision-making system in these big businesses.

1. With the collapse of the power of large stockholders and the return of company control to individual company directors, there was also a great change from the prewar and wartime power structure in Japanese society. The new company directors reflected the more diversified power structure created in the process of Japanese economic recovery and growth. It was a situation similar to the one in a country that is newly independent after a long period of colonial control, where leaders suddenly become aware that they are in a complicated economic and political system.

2. Because the board of directors became more powerful and represented more diverse interests, each director had to assume a role as an interest group regulator, who balanced a number of influences. As the company's controlling group, the board of directors required the teamwork of personnel with diverse specialties, experiences, abilities, and attributes to deal with various interests and cope with crises. This team was easier to create and maintain because most directors were colleagues holding important positions within the company itself. But some directors lacked the capacity for fulfilling the new responsibilities of aggregating interests and working together as part of a team.

3. Since the large majority of the directors in big businesses had advanced all at once from middle-management to top-management positions when their superiors were suddenly forced to retire en masse, they were generally younger and possessed more than average managerial ability compared with the former big business leaders. Prewar directors of big business, as typified by the *bantō* (head clerks) of the *zaibatsu*, had had to

display managerial abilities in representing the interests of the few large stockholders who were in reality the owners of the enterprise. Rewarded with money and advancement, even those head clerks who had originally been mere salarymen gradually came to resemble the owners in outlook. After the war the prototype of the manager in Japanese big business changed from the head clerk to what can be called the professional manager of the postwar era.

4. Despite the provisions of the Commercial Law, decision-making in the board of directors was rarely done on a majority-rule basis. Generally, the board of directors followed the traditional Japanese decision-making procedure of "complete consensus" because, despite the drawbacks associated with this decision-making procedure, it had the advantage of preserving solidarity among team members. Further, it provided a principle for assigning responsibility for the effects of decisions separately from the decision-making system.

5. We might ask whether it was necessary for the board of directors to devote excessive time to laborious consultation in order to achieve complete consensus. This was not and is not the case, because of the parallel and continuing existence of the following practices, which are peculiar features of Japanese organizational decision-making.

a. *Ringi. Ringi* is a procedure for conducting administrative operations that has been in wide practice from before World War II in large Japanese organizations. In particular, in implementing some plan for which the cooperation of a number of divisions is necessary, or whose results will influence many divisions, a *ringi* is produced in almost every case. After being created by the responsible division personnel (a *kiansha,* or plan initiator, generally a section chief), the *ringi* is approved by each division and climbs the ranks hierarchically from the plan initiators through every position of the upper-occupational structure: division chief, managing director, vice-president, and finally the president.

At this point, since the *ringi* has already received the approval of every appropriate party, if the president affixes his seal, the *ringi* is established and its contents are translated into action. (Approval, including that of the president, always takes the form of affixing the seal. For that reason, it is not unusual for the *ringi* to have more than twenty seals affixed to it by the time it reaches the president's desk.) Since the *ringi* arrives at the president's desk by the process of passing through many hands, it is safe to say that the president's final approval is a mere formality in all but the most unusual cases.

Ringi is used daily in large Japanese organizations for everything from disposal of trivial matters to decisions on fairly important issues. Even top-level matters are sometimes handled by the *ringi* system when it was desirable to have formal consensus among all responsible parties, including the middle management in the relevant divisions. Since postwar directors in Japanese big businesses almost all hold important positions as directors within the company hierarchy, their decision-making function is in great part automatically taken care of by the *ringi*.

b. *Nemawashi*. *Ringi* can be called an established system in the sense that it has certain fixed rules and forms despite variations from company to company. The same cannot be said of *nemawashi*, which is simply a modal organizational activity pattern. However, *nemawashi* often has a more important role than *ringi* in the organizational decision-making process.

We cannot say that *nemawashi*—a process of prior informal negotiation and persuasion among concerned parties used in decision-making and problem-solving—is unique to Japan. But when the Japanese, historically a homogeneous people, construct lifetime employment groups, the relative weight of such informal activities is far greater than in foreign countries. For example, when a *ringi* initiator wants to establish a certain *ringi*, he spares no effort in the prior consultation (*nemawashi*) of major concerned parties, especially those whose consent is judged difficult to obtain. Frequently, if the effort in consultation before action is successful, it is tantamount to establishing the *ringi*. In fact, considering the activities related to the decision-making process, the essential decision is often made by the *nemawashi* process and the *ringi* is the formal procedure of writing and detailing the decision.

c. *Ato ringi*. The custom of consultation before action is one factor making complete consensus decisions possible without excessive expenditure of time. For essential matters on which director consensus seems unlikely, it is usual to have meticulous preliminary consultation among concerned parties. For that reason, long discussion during the formal board of directors meeting itself is rarely necessary to reach a complete consensus.

Not every essential item of business is handled by the *ringi* approval system. There are instances in which the *ringi* is sought as a formality in order to authorize a consensus previously reached by all attendants at a board of directors meeting. In such a case, the *ringi* is clearly a post-facto recognition of the actual decision. Such a *ringi* is commonly called an *ato ringi* (after-the-fact *ringi*). In such cases, too, the *ringi* is no more than a formal treatment.

6. Through creation and revision of a large group of laws, including the revision of the Commercial Law, the legal foundations were laid for the group of professional managers to run their companies democratically. There was no reason, however, to expect various Japanese management practices to collapse quickly after the war. However, from the mid-1950s American management formulas and techniques were introduced one after another into almost every sphere of business administration—a phenomenon then known as the "management boom." Under the influence of this boom, most Japanese management practices were

considered premodern and became the object of conscious reform. Naturally, the influence of American business administration on top management and the decision-making system also became noteworthy from 1955 on. The establishment of the executive committee and the strengthening of the general staff division in Japanese companies are typical manifestations of this trend.

CHANGES IN MANAGEMENT SINCE THE MID-1950S

Since the late 1950s, as the Japanese economy maintained more than 10 percent real growth per year, growth was not confined only to big businesses. Many rapidly growing medium-sized enterprises were in turn added to the ranks of the big businesses. There were no more than six hundred companies listed on the Tokyo Stock Exchange in 1955; now about eight hundred and fifty companies are presently listed on the first section and another five hundred and fifty listed on the second section. Therefore, unlike the situation in 1955, the majority of Japanese big businesses today are essentially new organizations born since the Second World War.

Despite the rapid growth and the adaptation required by the Japanese industrial world of the 1960s, neither the revised prewar big businesses nor the rapidly growing medium-size businesses could afford to adopt radically different management systems. That fact must be considered when we generalize about management and decision-making in Japanese big businesses, since it provides a common element among the more than 1,400 companies that otherwise differ in type, scale, and historical background.[7] We can summarize recent developments in the present-day big businesses as follows.

1. Although with the spread of the executive-committee system power has in fact come into the hands of the senior executives of most companies, one exception is the case of subsidiaries of big businesses that have achieved rapid growth since the mid-1950s. They constitute an increasing number of companies on the stock exchange. Even when these subsidiaries are themselves big businesses, the rights of company control do not necessarily lie with the subsidiary company's senior executives, but in large part with the senior executives of the parent companies, which are the major stockholders.

---

[7] The few enterprises that do not fit these general characteristics fall into the following two categories:

1. Among the former *zaibatsu*, (a) companies that were able to produce distinguished leaders among their new directors after the *zaibatsu* dissolution measures, or (b) companies in which powerful prewar leaders returned to positions of leadership after relaxation of the *zaibatsu* dissolution measures.

2. Prewar non-*zaibatsu* enterprises in which owner control did not collapse after the war (especially in the manufacturing sphere, mainly for goods related to daily life, such as food, cosmetics, textiles, and durable consumer goods).

Subsidiaries use the occasion of being listed on the stock exchange as an opportunity to agitate for greater autonomy for themselves. Listing on the exchange is itself premised on the excellence of the company's record, and if growth and excellence continue, the passage of time strengthens the autonomy of the company's top management. This results from the increased trust of the parent-company top management toward the subsidiary-company top management and the increased freedom of subsidiary-company executives to speak out to the parent-company executives.

As long as the parent company continues to exist as a major stockholder, however, there are natural limits to the autonomy of top management in subsidiaries. Even the most outstanding subsidiary company lacks the autonomy to carry on activities that diverge from the parent company's master strategy. However, the more outstanding the performance of the subsidiary company, the more likely it is to accord with the parent company's master strategy. Furthermore, at least one representative director from the subsidiary company participates as one of the enterprise-group leaders in carrying out the master strategy of the entire enterprise group. In this case, the right of subsidiary company control is held by a group of business leaders that also includes leaders of the subsidiary businesses.

2. Although control of a big business is, in principle, in the hands of the executive committee, the forces directly and indirectly influencing that control have continuously grown and diversified. Interaction between these forces and the directors further complicates the picture. The major forces may be described as follows:

a. *Capital groups.* It is well known that the high growth rate of Japan's post-1955 economy was induced by the energetic investment of private enterprise, especially big business. Businesses had to obtain this capital for investment as loans from the large banks, and the banks, in an effort to guide the competition of a growing economy and further their own long-range interests, acted as powerful back-ups by permanently financing selected companies in major industries. The result was the creation of capital groups, which had a powerful bank at the center and included a first-rate company in a major industry. The bank sought to make the promising company an exclusive or main customer, and the company sought capital stability by developing patron-client cooperation. Such capital-group formation became very widespread during the 1960s.

When the capital group consisted of only a powerful bank and its important, semipermanently financed client company, the bank could not exercise the degree of influence over company operations exercised by the parent company in the enterprise group described above. However, powerful trading companies sometimes joined the bank as central institutions in the capital group. If these central institutions and the various companies acquired each other's stock, and the precedent was established for meetings between leaders from the central institutions and the companies in the capital group, then inevitably the capital group acquired both direct and indirect influence over the operations of the various constituent companies.

The old *zaibatsu* capital groups are typical examples of such capital groups. In the Mitsui, Mitsubishi, and Sumitomo groups, the sense of solidarity is firm among the core institutions, including the banks and member companies. There is close cooperation with regard to both expansionary and routine activities. Stimulated by the activities of these groups, a number of other capital groups with large banks at the center were also created during the 1960s. The most prominent of such groupings are the Fuyo Group (associated with the Fuji Bank) and the Daiichi Group (associated with the Daiichi Bank).[8]

In the 1960s, the expression "*zaibatsu* revival" became popular among a certain group of scholars and social critics. However, the connection between capital groups or their core banks and individual companies is completely different from that between prewar *zaibatsu* holding companies and their subsidiaries. Now, as long as the individual companies maintain above-average performance records, they are not in a subservient position to the core banks or capital groups, but more like partners. However, the individual company, because it must maintain and improve its own record, actively uses the core bank or capital group, and in certain cases, must depend heavily on the larger institution. Since certain decisions of the company executives are necessarily influenced by the bank or capital group, there are more than a few companies that have directors who are from the core banks or who are *hijōkin* (holding additional posts in other organizations) directors.

  b. *Gyōkai and Zaikai*. *Gyōkai* is an association or circle that includes all companies from a certain industry. Big businesses with a substantial market share in at least one industry are of necessity finely attuned to the interests of that entire industry. These companies sometimes form an association to lead the industry in a way that maximizes their interests, or at least minimizes harm, and to regulate conflict among companies. Big businesses are always the leading members of such associations, and their senior executives become the executive officials of the industry associations. In addition to collecting together the members of an industry, these groups plan daily contact with politicians and bureaucrats, and occasionally engage in active lobbying for the interests of their association.

Zaikai is not as easily defined as *gyōkai*. Originally, it was a circle or association formed by businessmen from all the enterprises in the business world. Today, it signifies to most Japanese a circle formed by a certain

---

[8] Since the Daiichi Kangyō Bank (the largest single holder of savings in Japan) was established by the merger of the Daiichi Bank and the Nihon Kangyō Bank in 1971, it is presently called the "Daiichi Kangin Group."

group of elite businessmen and financiers who exercise a strong indirect influence over the political activities of ministers and political parties and the administrative activities of the bureaucracies.

Lobbying directed at politicians and bureaucrats is more effective when carried out by *zaikai* than by the *gyōkai*. This is because, at present, the contributions that comprise a considerable part of the income of the LDP are made through groups established and backed by the *zaikai*. Moreover, countless executives of companies and banks are prominently included as "representatives of the *zaikai*" on most of the review boards that have been founded as administrative advisory organs to the various bureaucracies. For this reason, the majority of big-business executives regard *zaikai* activity as an essential function of top management. In industries where governmental policy has an especially large effect on company operations, lobbying as a member of the *zaikai* is on a scale comparable to the operations required for daily management and administration; in some cases, the chairman of the board, president, vice-president, and/or other senior executives may be in charge of *zaikai katsudō* (lobbying through the *zaikai*).

Like the *gyōkai*, the *zaikai* is actually composed of groups, such as Keidanren (Federation of Economic Organizations), Nippon Shōkō Kaigisho (Chamber of Commerce), Nikkeiren (Japanese Federation of Employers' Associations), and Keizai Doyukai (Japanese Committee for Economic Development). Although these four associations have different objectives and different organizational structures, they act as a single unit in carrying out *zaikai* activities and thus, senior executives in the big businesses hold concurrent positions in these organizations. For these executives, a reciprocal relationship grows up in which their positions as senior executives in big businesses are the source of their status and authority as *zaikai* members, and their status and authority as members of the *zaikai* benefit the company.

c. *Political parties.* There is a close relationship between big business and political parties, in particular the Liberal Democratic Party (LDP), which has continued as the party in power throughout the postwar period of rapid economic growth. In exchange for the continued support of the *zaikai,* which expresses the consensus of big business and acts as a large pipeline supplying the capital necessary for LDP activities, the LDP has made the utmost effort to reflect the designs of big business in its policy-making. However, there is very little personnel interchange between the LDP and big businesses or the *zaikai;* almost no politicians have taken positions in big business, and only a very few members of the *zaikai* have entered the LDP (and then, with less than splendid results). Moreover, the *zaikai* has not supported the LDP as a party that shares its own ideology, but as the party that has happened to be in power. The *zaikai*'s attitude toward the LDP is best reflected by the anti-intervention, wait-and-see attitude it has taken each time the LDP has faced a crisis. In reverse, the LDP cannot exercise decisive influence over big business activities via the *zaikai,* nor has it tried to exercise such influence.

d. *Government bureaucracies.* In contrast to the lack of personnel interchange between big business and political parties, the personnel interchange between big businesses and government bureaucracies—although a one-way street from the bureaucracies to businesses—is fairly active. Since the Meiji Restoration, Japan's major bureaucracies have, because of impartial and fervent nationalism, absorbed the outstanding products of the first-rate universities, and this tendency has changed little in the postwar era. As careermen in the various bureaucracies, the members of this promising group achieve important positions at a young age. They are sifted according to ability and character, and some reach the position of *kyoku-chō* (bureau chief)—the highest rank in the bureaucratic organization—at an age of about fifty. Administrative vice-ministers (*jimu jikan*) are chosen from among these bureau chiefs, but since it is established practice that the tenure of both bureau chiefs and administrative vice-ministers will last only one to three years, outstanding personnel in their early fifties are discharged almost every year from the major government agencies.

Since Japanese big business has had to expand its scale, as well as diversify the content of its activities during the process of intense economic growth, it has always sought outstanding personnel for top management. Big businesses in the heavy and chemical industry sectors, whose operations are directly affected by government policy, have especially extensive connections with the bureaucracies and a particular need for personnel who can easily obtain information from government agencies. It is not surprising that each year an increasing number of former high-level bureaucrats wait the required time period after retirement and then enter the business world.

However, if we look at big business as a whole, companies without former bureaucrats are in the overwhelming majority, and even those that have welcomed former bureaucrats onto their boards of directors have, as a rule, not given more than one directorship to a former bureaucrat. In any Japanese company, there is—among not only the company-bred directors but also the rank-and-file employees—strong emotional resistance to bringing in a large number of full-time directors from the outside. Former bureaucrats are well aware of this resistance and, at least initially, they concentrate on their assigned roles without engaging in overt activities.

For this reason, former bureaucrats who have reached such important company positions as president or vice-president exist as unusual exceptions. No matter how great his powers of leadership were in the bureaucracy as an individual, the former bureaucrat exercises little influence over big-business top management.

e. *Labor unions.* From the perspective of company management, legal

adjustment of labor union related practices was, among the democratization measures enforced by the Occupation army, equal in importance to
zaibatsu dissolution. Under the new legal measure, a startling number of
labor unions were born in Japan within a short period of time. Japanese
labor unions developed historically on a company-wide rather than an
industry-wide or trade-wide basis. The rate of labor unionization was
considerably higher in big businesses than in small- and medium-sized
businesses, because big businesses more successfully met the variety of
economic and societal conditions necessary for labor-union formation.

In the initial stage of labor unionization, labor-management relations
were awkward and productive of repeated unnecessary struggles. This was
partially because the period of postwar economic confusion was a time of
ideological instability during which economic livelihood was still a
struggle for workers. Moreover, neither labor nor management yet
possessed the knowledge or skill to utilize collective bargaining and other
techniques. Around 1955, precedents were established regarding Japanese
labor-management practices, and with difficulty at first, individual
enterprises drew upon the newly established practices and developed the
capacity to deal with labor-management relations as a routine task.
Generally, the labor division came to play a larger role within the
company organization, and a senior executive was placed in charge of this
division.

Company unions are a fundamental and distinctive feature of Japanese
labor-management relations. They developed as company unions not so
much because of historical factors but because such established Japanese
practices as lifetime employment and promotion by seniority produced a
strong sense of identification with the company in the union. The Japanese
Labor Law is generally interpreted to mean that those in management at
the rank of section chief and above do not qualify for union membership,
but in all companies the majority of such managers are former union
members. In the seniority promotion path, the average age for appointment as section chief is about forty, and it takes another ten to fifteen years
to reach the position of director. Thus, it is safe to say that the majority of
big-business managers who became directors in the 1960s were former
union members. We must bear in mind that it is not rare for managers to
have served as officials in the company's union.

These facts, however, do not signify full accord between management
and unions within Japanese businesses. In the majority of Japanese
businesses, labor unions display opposition backed by strong union
demands, and labor-management conflicts, including strikes, are as severe
as in other advanced countries. However, Japanese union members never
intend that their activities should create marked disadvantages for their
company in its competition with other companies at home or overseas. Nor
do they desire to undermine company operations. Whenever a group of
radical leaders seeks to guide union activities in that direction, they are

destined to isolation and then exclusion from the company-based union.

Viewing the situation in reverse, the decisions of even top management cannot be implemented if they are opposed by the labor union. Since labor union support is necessary for the executives to exercise successful authority in most top-level decision-making, the executive in charge obtains preliminary approval from the union—or at least, requests union cooperation after the decision. That the majority of people in management are former members of the company union is, of course, a distinct advantage in maintaining smooth communications with the labor union.

f. *University cliques*. Western scholars often emphasize the role of *gakubatsu* (cliques consisting of graduates of a certain school or university) in company relations. There is no doubt that university cliques exist as a statistical artifact: executives in leading companies are disproportionately graduates of certain universities, and certain companies have reputations as strongholds for graduates of a given university. It is dangerous, however, to infer that because such university cliques are statistically significant, they also play a significant role in company relations. Such statistical data describes an elite that was schooled prior to World War II. At that time, there were only a limited number of universities and a limited number of graduates each year. It is natural that these educated few would be selected by the top companies and government ministries.

With the spread of higher education, the eagerness of young people to pursue business careers, and the expansion in hiring during the postwar era, companies have taken graduates from a variety of schools. In utilizing graduates of various schools, Japanese management has learned a valuable lesson: good students are not necessarily good businessmen. During the prewar era, before the separation of ownership from management, the post of head clerk or manager was best performed by a "bureaucratic personality," but postwar company structure requires entrepreneurial talents and innovativeness. It also requires flexibility for dealing with the variety of new tasks. The government ministries, which are less subject to economic pressures, can still afford to emphasize competence in dealing with defined tasks rather than innovation and creativity in their personnel selections, and their young employees are still overwhelmingly from the old national universities. But businesses, under competitive pressure, cannot afford to limit themselves to graduates of certain universities.

3. The seniority principle was gradually institutionalized in the selection and retirement of the directors, except the president, who is a representative director. For a time during the postwar period, after the business leaders had been completely replaced by the democratization measures (including the "purge") of the Occupation army, the seniority principle was somewhat vague. However, with Japan's rapid economic growth and as company expansion stabilized, the seniority system gradually revived. Table 1 shows the results of a 1958 Keizai Doyukai study on top management in 233 Japanese big businesses. Even at that time, we can

already see clear ranking in average age from the chairmen to the ordinary directors.

Table 1
Average Age in Top Management Positions

Position	Age
Kaichō (Chairman)	68.0
Shachō (President)	64.9
Fuku-Shachō (Vice-President)	61.0
Senmu (Executive Director)	59.5
Jōmu (Managing Director)	57.9
Hira-torishimariyaku (Regular Director)	53.8

However, seniority ranking is not—as it is often misinterpreted among foreigners—a practice that ignores or underemphasizes ability, and uses age or tenure with the company as the major criteria for advancement. We should remember that the following three points are basic to any discussion: (1) the authority of Japanese middle management in daily execution of business is very great, and the initiator in the *ringi* system is always the section chief; (2) among the numerous positions in middle management, authority is especially given to the several key positions that are on the orthodox promotion route to a directorship; and (3) promotion and selection of these key positions is more dependent on a total evaluation of character and ability than on seniority. Thus, the seniority system, over the long run, effectively selects the people with ability. Establishment of the seniority system does not imply a rejection of the new concepts of professional management, but the establishment of a distinctively Japanese pattern of professional management.

4. In principle, the decision-making of the board of directors is carried out by complete consensus, but even in this form the decisions of the directors are still often guided by the opinion or will of a particular member. Such cases usually fall into one of the following two categories:

a. *Executive directors in charge of departments.* Since almost all Japanese company directors hold positions within the company, even a junior director is also a chief of a main factory or department where he must practice departmental management. Members of the executive committee usually hold additional positions at a higher-level of top management such as president, vice-president, executive director, or managing director. The responsibility and authority of the senior directors other than the president almost invariably extend to areas such as manufacturing and technology, marketing and purchasing, finance and accounting, personnel and labor, and overseas operations. In each of these areas there is a chief with formal responsibility for managing daily departmental affairs. But in each area, matters that require the judgment of top management generally reach executive committee deliberation through the executive director in charge of that area.

In Japanese big business, the promotion route from talented young employee to director generally includes every major position in the department. In other words, by the time he becomes a director, the employee has the clear stamp of his department. To exaggerate, we could say that every executive director put in charge of a given department has served as the head of that department. He has usually established the close informal ties of *senpai* (senior) and *kōhai* (junior) with department members, with whom he has worked on shared tasks over a long period.

Executive directors in charge of various departments do not formally give orders to the heads of these departments. The decisions of the executive committee are handed down as the president's orders to the responsible parties in each department, but the executive directors of the departments heavily influence executive committee decision-making on items that concern their departments. Usually the other members of the executive committee, including the president, have less information and professional knowledge for forming opinions on department matters. Therefore, the executive director of a department speaks at the executive committee meeting both as a member with professional knowledge and as a representative of the department interests. The executive committee, which viewed externally is the highest organ of company decision-making, is the organ for regulating major department interests when viewed internally. As long as a matter affects a single department, the complete consensus of the executive committee is in effect dominated by the will or opinion of the executive director responsible for that department. When the scope of the decision extends beyond the concerned department, the executive committee naturally assumes the additional function of regulating interests. Once again, the decision-making process is not directly related to the procedure for assigning responsibility for decisions.

b. *President* (shachō) *and chairman* (kaichō). The position of the president in a Japanese company is probably more stable than it is in other advanced industrial countries. Since the members of the board of directors and the executive committee were, in actuality, all appointed by the president as his subordinates in the occupational structure, no internal powers influence the president's course of action except in such extreme circumstances as sudden failure in performance, outbreak of a serious problem within the company, or continued and severe factional quarreling among directors. And as long as the company maintains a tolerable record, there is no external force powerful enough to shake the autonomy of the board of directors. Thus, while decision-making in the executive committee takes the form of complete consensus, there is a natural tendency for it to be dominated largely by the opinion or will of the president.

A former president, however, is one force outside the executive committee that can have a major influence on the current president's decision-making. There is a joke among Japanese businessmen that "only the president decides when the president retires," and in fact appointment of the next president is the prerogative of the outgoing president. Except in cases of forced retirement due to unavoidable circumstances, the reasons for presidential retirement are generally old age, a long period in office, or the coming of retirement age in a firm where this is fixed. But there are very few cases of complete retirement, and the former president normally remains a representative director and assumes the position of chairman. This type of chairman is generally referred to as an "active chairman" because, while he engages in a wide range of activities as a leader of the *zaikai* outside the company, he also exercises hidden power over the important decision-making of the company via his successor.

5. The "management boom"—the movement to modernize existing Japanese management practices on the model of American company management—brought experimentation and reform. The movement made *ringi* the central object of reform for two reasons: *ringi* obscured individual responsibility for the effects of a decision, and its process was too time-consuming.

The focus of the reform was summarized by the phrase "clarification of the job and its authority." In short, every company strove to define objectively the scope and content of major administrative jobs within the company structure and to assign to each job an appropriate sphere of authority. The former would clarify responsibility for results of task execution, and the latter would be used in the overall process of decision-making. The intention was to correct the drawbacks in an organizational format so heavily dependent on the *ringi*. However, it became clear that it was nearly impossible to define objectively the content or scope of administrative jobs. Even when authority was formally assigned insofar as possible, it was unrealistic to expect such changes within the context of the Japanese organizational and personnel practices of lifetime employment, the seniority system, and group decision-making.

During the latter half of the 1960s, there was a general realization of the difficulty of introducing such reforms, and the fever of Japanese big business for modernization of *ringi* and management on the American model suddenly cooled. Along with this came a trend in the industrial sphere toward new recognition of the merits of Japanese administrative practices. Companies that had quickly taken the radical measure of abolishing the *ringi* system had no choice but to revive it.

It is clearly a mistake to think that because the "management boom" broke down without attaining its initial objectives, it made no real contribution to Japanese management. Through the struggle to reform, Japanese companies (1) eliminated or amended several clearly irrational Japanese administrative practices affecting Japan's adaptation to its new economic environment (domestic and international); and (2) wiped out the excessive inferiority complex entertained by most Japanese managers, administrators, and professionals with regard to the American management system and enabled them to evaluate objectively the characteristics, advantages, and weak points of Japanese management practices.

At present the *ringi* system still exists as a formal system in most Japanese big businesses, and it is widely used together with the process of *nemawashi*. Formally, the work of top management is carried out through the executive committee, but in fact the work load of senior executives in big business is lightened considerably just by the *ringi* system. Compared with practices in the 1950s, *ringi* today is a remarkably more refined system and it is employed in a decidedly more realistic manner. Although the modernization of Japanese management practices failed if "Americanization" is used as the yardstick, it produced tangible results in the correction or elimination of weak spots in existing practices.

6. The executive committee was a new system introduced from the outside and modeled on the (senior) executive committee of American big business. That the general staff was either strengthened or newly established at the same time suggests that the executive committee was intended as more than just the company's highest decision-making organ composed of a limited number of senior executives. In fact, the introduction of the executive committee was premised on some degree of change in the existing Japanese decision-making system.

Prior to the period in which the committee was introduced, Japanese senior executives, both as individuals and as a group, lacked an American-style general staff—and they had little need for one. As managers of their own departments, senior executives had the authority to mobilize personnel for use as general staff whenever necessary. In turn, the president could require the senior executives to serve as a kind of general staff to him.

Why then were the executive committee and general staff introduced? In a word, the objective was to strengthen and develop top management jobs. Competent adaptation to the rapid growth of the national economy and the accompanying changes in internal and external environmental conditions, as well as a quick grasp of those changes in order to execute a superior business strategy were the fundamental conditions for company growth. But Japanese big business in the early 1950s lacked certain of these conditions. The majority of directors, including senior executives, was burdened with the daily tasks of departmental management and could not get a long-range or comprehensive view of company management. For this reason, when the executive committee was introduced, companies generally either eliminated or greatly lightened the task of departmental management for executive-committee members.

Gradually it became common for directors who were members of the executive committee—even senior executives in charge of departments—to be requested to evaluate and investigate problems. In order to fulfill such demands, the executive committee members needed a staff that could collect and analyze the information required for general management tasks and at times give professional advice. Since the existing organizational structure of Japanese businesses was usually divided vertically, little staff existed to carry out such tasks, and even if a small staff did exist, there were few opportunities to mobilize it. Therefore, in the context of the introduction of the executive committee system, a real general staff was established for the first time. With this change, the practice of general management by senior executives became institutionalized in Japanese big business.

COMPANY SPIRIT AND ADMINISTRATION

In implementing the decisions from higher levels and adapting to the environmental changes, Japanese executives give great attention to problems of morale and human relations. If Japanese executives have a characteristically Japanese approach to management, it is not so much a specific body of practices but an effort to create a company spirit such that members wish to take part. Seen in this light, the slow increase in salaries in the earlier years of an employee's career and the steep salary increases with years of service is a way of ensuring that company employees not only stay with the company but retain a long-range identification of personal interests with company interests. Various company practices like entering-the-company ceremonies, group living during training programs, company trips, company recreation centers, company-sponsored travel, company facilities for private parties, daily ceremonies, and company sports teams are all efforts to maintain a dynamic involvement with the company. Indeed, many Japanese employees are so involved with company activities that they prefer short vacations and even during vacation become restless to return to the daily life of the company.

In most companies, the management makes a very serious effort to look after the long-term interests of the employee, providing personal attention and assistance in dealing with his individual problems. Compared with the American corporation, which tends to be more "dry" and impersonal, Japanese firms do not make such a sharp distinction between business affairs and personal affairs and assume more responsibility for what Americans consider personal affairs.

Japanese executives identify with their employees and take pride in them. When a young executive is traveling or has business with other companies, his superiors make considerable effort to pave his way by contacting appropriate friends elsewhere.

Japanese company executives consider competing for the employee's spare time—against threats of affluence, ownership of automobiles, and shorter working hours—as a key management issue. For this reason they make every effort to incorporate the spare-time activities of employees within the range of activities provided by the company.

Japanese executives are also constantly concerned about the competition with other companies and make generous use of this sense of competition to inspire employees. Young employees quickly catch this atmosphere of company involvement and sense of competition with rival companies.

Even company ceremonies like anniversaries, commemoratives, welcomings, seeings off, and openings are all consciously designed to reinforce company spirit. The large company expense accounts, which are much larger than in the West, are not only designed to win the favor of people outside the company, but to provide desirable opportunities for those within the company. And company efforts to project lively images are not only for promotional advertising, but also a way of attracting lively, able, devoted employees from among college and high school graduating classes.

The Section as the Company Module

Although there are overwhelmingly similar patterns of administration in Japanese companies and foreign companies, there are some approaches to administration which are perhaps more common in Japan.

In general, it appears that the American executive and his secretary, with possibly some assistants, constitute a kind of module unit within the typical American company. The executive supervises the activities of the somewhat more specialized persons below him, and he is accountable to the rest of the company for everything that is handled within his jurisdiction. In contrast, the basic module of the Japanese company is a section. Personnel are selected for a section in a way that will form a team that can work well together. Team members are matched for temperament and personality as well as capabilities.

The head of the section is always older than the other people working in his section, but he is not necessarily more competent. A section head of moderate ability can be paired with an assistant section head of extraordinary ability. In an American company the second-in-command might feel impatient and frustrated if someone less competent were serving above him, but in Japan the situation works more harmoniously. The Japanese section head, realizing that he possesses moderate abilities, knows that if he does not work well with the abler person under him he will not be able to accomplish the purpose of his section and, hence, will be vulnerable to criticism from superiors. The assistant section head of greater capability will be sufficiently known to superiors that he can be sure he will be rewarded eventually. He also knows that he will eventually rise to higher positions than the person now serving above him, but he also knows that if he hopes to do well in the future, he must get along well with his superior now.

Memos and correspondence in an American office are likely to come from an executive who dictated the letter or memorandum for his secretary to type. In Japan, a more characteristic pattern would be for one, two, or three persons within the section to draw up a document, which is discussed or shown to others for approval and then sent out as a section document. In Japan, there tends to be less of a distinction between secretarial and nonsecretarial personnel, and the duties of various personnel are less sharply defined and differentiated. When one person is out or involved in certain other tasks, it is more likely in the Japanese firm that someone else in the section can draw up the necessary documents in his absence. This pattern places less reliance on any single person and helps ensure that the work of the section will be done even if one or two persons are absent or less than perfectly competent.

Although there has been some discussion in the West on the importance of cliques, no cliques within the Japanese firm are as important for daily activities as is the membership in a given section. The members of a section tend to have close personal as well as work relations, and the superiors in a section, who are almost invariably older, are likely to be supportive and personally helpful to the other members of their sections.

Career Patterns

Because companies intend to keep their employees from school graduation until retirement at age fifty-five or so, they are extremely careful in selection procedures. They want to ensure not only that an employee is capable and reliable, but that he has a special commitment to the firm and that he is likely to remain there. For this reason, in addition to difficult entrance examinations, they provide opportunities for a prospective employee to get acquainted with a number of people inside the firm, and they prefer personal introductions, since this increases the commitment of the individual to the firm.

All those entering a company in a given year start on the same day and spend more time with one another than with others as a way of building solidarity. The time of entry into the firm becomes the basic point of ascription for promotion. Time of entry is much more important than age and even ability in determining the basic relationships between superiors and inferiors. Those who entered in earlier classes are superiors, and those who entered later, inferiors.

Members of an entering class generally all receive the same wages. In the first several years there are almost no title and pay distinctions. Newcomers take part in a wide variety of activities in various parts of the company. Thus, before anyone has moved up the ladder to an important position he will have had broad contacts and experience with all parts of a company. As a result, he will be able to understand the complexities of company activities and have a personal basis for effective cooperation throughout the firm that could not be duplicated by anyone brought in from the outside.

After the incoming group has been in the company for a few years, minor pay differentials may appear, but only after employees have been in the company long enough for their fellows and superiors to have a high degree of consensus about who is more promising. By this time, the incoming class has developed a basic spirit of equality even while recognizing that some among them are more promising. Even after these several years, the initial differentials of pay and position are, in fact, minor, although they may have great symbolic and psychological significance. The abler employees who have been in the company for several years may be assigned to more important sections with more difficult and complicated tasks, but their title and pay may be almost the same as that of their peers who entered with them. A very able young man may become an assistant section head of a very important section at about the same time that a mediocre classmate may become the assistant section head of a less important section. Their pay and titles may be essentially the same, but people within the company are aware of the difference and its significance for prestige and eventual position.

Although emoluments of title and salary are thus based on seniority, the actual task within a section is more closely related to the individual's capacity. The very able young man will be given considerable responsibility despite low pay and title. He will have the informal praise and respect of people around him, which is more than adequate to provide him with the kind of motivation for working hard and doing his best. His role as a promising young man provides terrific motivation. Even though an able young man does not get financial rewards, he expects that he will in the long-run. Although there is no direct short-run relationship between work on the one hand and title and pay on the other, they do mesh in the long-run. Expectations about the future play a very important role in the motivation of individuals at any given time.

The greatest morale problem is among those who are defined as not particularly promising and not promoted to the better sections. Such a young person's superiors generally try to encourage him, communicating that while his performance was not outstanding for the last round of assignments, he still has opportunities. He is then assigned to a new section with entirely different people who were not involved in defining him as a less promising person. In this new section, he thus begins again on his own, and the expectation is that he has a new chance to prove himself, and if he does extraordinarily well, his prospects will brighten. A person is likely to serve in this new position for another period of two or three years, during which the same process may be repeated, and he may then be given a slightly more favorable assignment in the next round.

Although the competition for advancement within a company is strong, the long incubation period prior to the introduction of differentials provides a basis for solidarity, which—with the reinforcement from company spirit and identification with the company—provides personal support even from the least able and prevents competition from completely disrupting the bonds of solidarity.

Since it does not work well for a person to supervise subordinates who are his age and older, the top executives in the company—the president, the vice-president, and the board of directors—assume their positions only after the peers who entered with them have retired. Thus most employees of a company will be retired at about age fifty-five, and only a small group of top executives, selected from the most promising of their age group, will remain on past this age.

The employees who retire at about age fifty-five to sixty are often placed in "child companies," smaller affiliates, or in other companies somehow related to the main company. Although a person may receive less salary on his postretirement job, he is usually pleased to continue working. Sometimes these smaller companies are created in large part to provide employment opportunities for former executives.

The president, vice-president, and other members of the board of directors who remain in the large enterprise were selected from the very ablest of their age group, and they had long looked forward to the prospect of reaching this pinnacle. When they advance to these high positions, they have unquestioned authority based on superior talent, experience, and seniority. The long period of gestation has given them an opportunity to think through what they would do in office. Although they ordinarily do not hold office for more than a few years, the timing of their period of responsibility was quite predictable by seniority rules, and they are prepared to make the most of their brief term.

DECISION-MAKING

Japanese firms prefer to reach a consensus supported by all, but the top executives are capable of making tough decisions when necessary. When they have made reasonable efforts to obtain consensus but there remain two options of about equal weight on which there is no widespread consensus, the executives will generally come down firmly on one side or the other. They prefer to do this, however, only after long debate and discussion and after they have thoroughly explored all the options and all the opinions within the company.

The top executives in a Japanese company prefer to avoid the cool rational presentation of options where advocates neatly present all the arguments for each option. They prefer that an obvious solution emerge from these long discussions with a broad range of company employees so that, when a decision is finally made, the overwhelming majority in the company can see why such a decision is desirable and necessary. In the meantime, the leadership makes every effort to explore all options, sending employees everywhere to acquire the kind of knowledge and skills that will be required to make the decisions. Oftentimes the leaders will go over and over possible solutions before finally arriving at a decision.

This process can be excessively long, especially if the top leadership is wishy-washy. With weak leadership, it may be difficult for the company to reach any decision if clear-cut choices do not emerge from down below. With active leadership, however, the top people in the firm do not simply respond to people under them, but take the initiative in selecting which problems to work on.

In short, some foreigners who have noticed certain specific practices within Japanese firms have tended to ascribe too much to tradition and to "Japanese characteristics." Decision-making in Japan is, in fact, an active, conscious process, and leadership is much more vigorous and adaptable than many accounts of "Japanese traditions" would indicate.

Emerging Japanese Multinational Enterprises

M. Y. YOSHINO

One of the most significant developments in the business scene in the last two decades has been the emergence of the multinational corporations. Until quite recently, this has been primarily an American phenomenon, but now a number of non-American firms, notably European and Japanese, are aspiring to join the ranks. Particularly, the pressures are mounting on major Japanese corporations, both on the domestic and international fronts, to increase their direct foreign investments, which up to this point have been negligible. For one thing, leading Japanese corporations are now confronted with the need to undertake defensive investments to meet the requirements of import substitution policies promoted by a number of developing countries. At the same time, with the rapid increase in the domestic wage level, a growing number of manufacturing firms with labor-intensive production processes are seeking to shift their manufacturing bases to certain developing countries in order to maintain their competitive viability in the world market. The apparel and electronics industries provide a good case in point.

There is another area in which Japanese foreign direct investment is growing. Japan's high dependence on foreign sources for critical raw materials is well known, but until recently the Japanese resource industries had relied primarily on straight purchase agreements with foreign suppliers without equity participation. With the rapid growth of demand for essential raw materials in recent years, it has become increasingly apparent that exclusive reliance on this method is indeed vulnerable; and with their eyes toward attaining a greater degree of stability and possibly lower cost, major Japanese corporations in resource industries are undertaking investments in exploration and development of critical natural resources. While Japan's total foreign direct investment at the current level is no more than $3.5 billion, only a small fraction of that of the United States, it is nevertheless growing at a rapid rate, and according to a recent forecast prepared by the Ministry of International Trade and Industry (MITI), it will reach the level of $26 billion by the end of this decade.[1] Indeed, there is a widespread view in the Japanese business community that transformation into multinational corporations will represent a major thrust for corporate growth in this decade.

American experience has amply demonstrated that transformation of a domestic firm into a multinational one requires major adjustments in the firm's organizational structure, strategies, and management styles. I have recently undertaken a study of how major Japanese corporations are making their initial efforts toward evolution into multinational corporations. The data for the study were gathered through intensive investigations of the thirty-five large Japanese manufacturing firms that have been most active in developing manufacturing abroad. These firms in total operated nearly two hundred foreign manufacturing subsidiaries in twenty-three countries. While the study has probed several critical aspects, this article will examine changes and adaptations that have been introduced in two important aspects of managerial functions—organizational structure and the decision-making process—as the major Japanese corporations have undertaken international expansion through direct investment.

The demands made on management by the establishment and maintenance of manufacturing bases abroad are different from and far greater than the demands of export operations. Comparatively, exporting is little more than the extension of domestic sales activities, requiring a minimum of adjustment in the organizational structure and management processes at the corporate level. This easy adjustment is particularly pronounced in a typical Japanese manufacturing firm because of the common practice of depending almost exclusively on trading companies for export operations. When, however, the firm establishes its manufacturing base abroad, it is, in effect, creating a microcosm of the domestic organization. Once the manufacturing subsidiaries are created, they must be supported, managed, and coordinated by the parent company. Moreover, those charged with the task of managing a foreign subsidiary abroad must, in essence, assume responsibilities for virtually all basic managerial functions, and furthermore, they face an environment substantially different from that facing managers of domestic operations. Indeed, this is the first time that Japanese management is compelled to leave the comfortable sanctuary of

---

[1] *Sangyō kōzō shingikai chūkan tōshin* [An intermediary report by the council on industry structure] (Tokyo: MITI, 1971), p. 42.

a familiar and hospitable environment supported by a highly cohesive and homogeneous culture.

THE IMPACT ON CORPORATE
ORGANIZATIONAL STRUCTURE

In a recent study of 187 U.S.-based multinational corporations, Stopford has demonstrated the existence of three clearly identifiable phases in the evolution of organizational structure as a firm expands its international operations.[2] In the first phase, when the international investment is still small, foreign subsidiaries enjoy a considerable degree of autonomy. The second is the phase of organizational consolidation, ushered in by the creation of a specialized unit in the parent company generally known as the international division to serve specifically the needs of international business. The international division is considered an independent part of the enterprise, not subject to the same strategic planning that guides the domestic divisions. According to Stopford, the continued growth of international business becomes so important to the corporation that it can no longer tolerate control solely in the hands of the international division. Pressures mount toward its dissolution, and eventually the international business is integrated into the mainstream of the corporate activities.

My study reveals that at least in terms of structural development, the Japanese corporations have followed a close parallel up to a certain point. Among the thirty-five firms in the sample, five were in the first phase of organizational development, and the remaining thirty were in the second phase; none was found to have reached the third phase. The fact that Japanese corporations are still in the very early phase in their development of international business through direct investment has afforded an excellent opportunity for firsthand observation and analysis of the forces leading to the creation of the international division, and of how, once created, it evolves and seeks legitimacy.

Forces Leading to the Creation
of the International Division

In the initial stage of development, the motive for direct investment in most cases is a response to the import substitution program of the host countries. It is an ad hoc and often a reluctant response to a specific threat. As in the case of American corporations, the initial move overseas by Japanese corporations was not made as a part of a grand corporate design or strategy, but was based on an effort to counter a real or potential threat. By the time the third or fourth manufacturing subsidiary is established

---

[2] John Stopford and Louis T. Wells, Jr., *Managing the Multinational Enterprise* (New York: Basic Books, 1971), pp. 9–29.

abroad, however, pressure begins to build up within the organization which eventually leads to the creation of a group specializing in the company's international activities. Such pressure comes from several different sources.

In the initial stage, the responsibility for international business is assumed, usually tacitly, by the export department. This is reasonable because at this point foreign investment is no more than a mere extension of export activities, and, moreover, the export department is considered to have the necessary skills. If, for some reason, the export department is deemed inappropriate for this function, a popular alternative is the corporate planning group. The assignment is given to this group not because of strategic implications that foreign direct investment may have for the corporation, but mainly because in a number of companies studied, this is the group that is given an unusual and generally nonrecurring assignment that does not fit into any other existing department.

Under either of these arrangements, foreign investment activities are considered rather marginal and are typically carried out on a purely ad hoc basis as the need arises. But by the time a firm develops three or four manufacturing subsidiaries overseas, however small and insignificant they may be, it tends to generate new investment opportunities. Somehow the company becomes recognized in the business community as an organization interested in international business. Some of the new investment opportunities that come to the company's attention can be ignored completely, others may be dismissed with casual investigation, but there are always a few that must be given serious attention. This requires expertise, specialized knowledge, and, most important of all, management time and attention.

As the work load increases, the department to which international business is tacitly assigned begins to search for ways to rid itself of this evaluation responsibility. The group is likely to be already overloaded, and it is not anxious to divert its energy to an activity perceived as marginal. In addition to the evaluation of new investment opportunities, the established foreign subsidiaries, however small, need some support and attention from the corporate headquarters from time to time. Even at the minimal level this can become a burdensome task.

The second source of pressure lies in the established foreign subsidiaries themselves. At the very early stage, they typically enjoy a considerable degree of autonomy, granted not by conscious design, but as a result of indifference and lack of knowledge on the part of the parent company. It is autonomy implicitly granted by default. The relationship between the subsidiary and the parent company is likely to be ill-structured and, to the extent that the relationship exists, it places a heavy reliance on personal ties. In the course of day-to-day operations, however, the management of the subsidiary invariably faces a variety of problems for which it needs assistance, instruction, and support from the parent company. These needs tend to be tactical in nature, but usually the response must be immediate if it is to be useful. To the great dismay and frustration of the subsidiary management, the parent company is not always responsive to its requests. Sometimes they are totally ignored, but at best the assistance may be delayed or perfunctory. After repeatedly experiencing these disappointments and annoyances, the managements of foreign subsidiaries come to feel a need for an organizational unit at the corporation that will serve as a communication link and a "friend at court" and that will lend sympathetic ears to their needs.

These forces converge in a climate already sympathetic to organizational fragmentation. The permanent employment system and seniority-based promotion practices commonly observed in large Japanese corporations require that individuals be given appropriate status and recognition commensurate with their seniority. Such practices exert strong pressures toward the creation of new sections and departments. During the past few years, however, this tendency toward new sections has been suppressed, though not always successfully, in the name of corporate rationalization; other means devised to accommodate the need for promotion possibilities have been far from satisfactory. Thus, when there is a well-justified cause for creating a new department, such as international activities, the opportunity becomes almost irresistible.

The foregoing represent pressures of a defensive kind. More positive motives are not entirely absent. One such powerful force is an explicit recognition that international business represents a major thrust for corporate growth in the future and that, in order to capitalize on such opportunities, it is essential to create a separate unit to formulate policies and strategies in this area and to coordinate the company's international business activities. Furthermore, more progressive management is well aware that international business needs specialized training, expertise, and knowledge, which, given the Japanese peculiar employment practices, must be nurtured internally. Most commonly, it is observed that the defensive forces exert a strong initial impetus toward the creation of the new unit, the implementation of which is facilitated considerably by the sympathetic organizational climate, with the last factor providing formal justification. Once created, how does the international division evolve with the growth of international business? How does it seek legitimacy?

Evolution of the International Division

Getting Established.—At its inception, an international division is likely to be small, with limited expertise, and its existence is overshadowed by the export department. The freshly assembled staff will have to learn to work as a team and must enhance its limited expertise in the new field. At the same time, the new unit must establish a close working relationship with other organizational units within the corporation.

The initial efforts of the newly created international division to establish itself in the corporate structure are complicated by several factors. For one thing, with the importance which a Japanese organization attaches to informal relationships for task performance, it becomes necessary for the new division to build appropriate relationships with other departments and divisions, and this is usually a slow process requiring painstaking efforts. Another complicating factor is the gap that exists in expertise and experience possessed by the established subsidiaries on the one hand and the new international division on the other. Clearly, the management of foreign subsidiaries view themselves as having knowledge, expertise, and experience in the international field superior to the newly assembled international division staff. The men in charge of foreign subsidiaries are, in a sense, the pioneers and are likely to have little confidence in the ability and judgment of the international division, and, generally, the staff of the newly established division is painfully aware of its own inadequacies. Moreover, established subsidiaries are obviously reluctant to give up the autonomy they have been enjoying prior to the creation of the international division, and resist any actions by the international division that might be interpreted as contributing to the erosion of their power.

For these reasons, the managers of foreign subsidiaries typically expect little from the international division. They view the functions of the new unit as no more than providing a communication link with the parent corporation and performing strictly routine service activities. Certainly, they do not expect policy guidelines in managing their operations. Under these circumstances, the international division has only a limited range of options. It is not in a position to assert itself to dominate the established subsidiaries. It would be sheer folly to do so. The most likely course of action by which the newly created division may win acceptance is maintaining a low posture, avoiding conflicts at all cost, and somehow in the process gaining a minimum of legitimacy to assure its survival. The major thrust of its activities tends to be service oriented. It eagerly processes routine requests coming from the subsidiaries, and attempts to provide whatever assistance in its view the subsidiaries might need. The relationship between the international division and the subsidiaries at this stage tends to be ill-structured and static, since the former has no power to impose an orderly relationship, and the latter, of course, feel no compelling need to establish a formal and exclusive relationship with the division. The initiative for interaction at this stage rests clearly with the foreign subsidiary. It will use the international division only to enhance its own goal, and as it sees fit.

One of the common initial tasks given the international division is to prepare reports on the company's international activities at regular intervals for corporate top management. This requires the collection of certain basic data from the foreign subsidiaries. At the very early stage of development, the international division is so weak that it often has difficulty obtaining even the most routine data from the subsidiaries in the form required and by the deadline established.

The managers of foreign subsidiaries are likely to continue to communicate with various departments in the parent company through informal networks they had developed prior to the creation of the international division. Naturally, the latter is anxious to become the channel for all communications with the corporate headquarters, but it lacks power to instigate, let alone enforce, such a policy. Moreover, from the viewpoint of the subsidiaries, the circumstances are such that direct communication with relevant groups is more desirable. At this stage, the foreign subsidiaries themselves are likely to be still in an early phase of development as a mere extension and integral part of the firm's export activities. They perform only a minimum of manufacturing activities and naturally they receive almost all necessary component parts and raw materials from the parent company in Japan. Frequent communications are required to facilitate the flow of these materials, and they are likely to be channeled directly between the foreign subsidiary and a relevant group in the parent company, usually the export department. Likewise, in key dealings with the parent company such as negotiations on transfer prices for items supplied by the parent company, it is natural for the subsidiary to take up the matter directly with the export department. Thus, the existing informal communication links are likely to persist with the reluctant acquiescence of the international division.

Let us now examine how the international division attempts to establish its relationship with other corporate staff and line groups. The international division by its very nature must depend heavily on other groups in performing its functions since it possesses few technical capabilities of its own. For example, in evaluating a new investment opportunity, it must rely on the expertise available in several different groups, such as finance, marketing, planning, engineering, construction, and personnel. This high degree of dependence complicates its relationship with other groups, particularly at the initial stage, when the expertise and experience of the international division is limited and close cooperation from other groups is needed. But at this stage, the international business is so small and marginal that the international division cannot provide tangible incentives to those whose assistance is so critically needed. Thus, it must rely largely on their good will and personal relationships, or on their sense of organizational loyalty.

A common strategy followed by the international division in its effort to establish itself within corporate groups is quite similar to the pattern already observed—that is, to emphasize its service functions. It stresses its role as an agent to facilitate smoother flow of information between various corporate groups and the subsidiaries without usurping what may be considered their vested interests or prerogatives. It also attempts to assume much of the time-consuming and less rewarding activities that were previously performed, albeit reluctantly, by corporate groups. For example, until quite recently, the proposal for a new investment had to be screened by the Japanese government, a time-consuming and frustrating process which no department or individual would relish. This is one of the first tasks that the international division takes over. An emphasis on service orientation avoids conflicts and reduces resistance from well-entrenched and powerful corporate groups, particularly the export department, which may look on the creation of an international division with a certain ambivalence.

Thus, at the initial stage, the international division is strongly service oriented, maintaining a low profile. Certainly at this stage, it plays a very limited role in the areas of policy and strategy formulation.

Quest for Power.—Entry into the second stage is predicated on the continued growth of international business. As it grows, the international division becomes increasingly dissatisfied with its secondary status. Once achieving a cohesive and well-functioning team, the division begins to search for opportunities to extend its control over the foreign subsidiaries. At this stage, there are usually two or three subsidiaries that were organized after the international division came into being, and it is likely that the international division is able to exert greater influence over them. But even with the older subsidiaries, the international division can seize on certain opportunities, such as a change in the management, to increase its control. New managers, if their experience in international business is limited, are likely to look to the international division for information, guidance, and support.

More subtle means of gaining influence are available. One is to lobby for desirable assignments for managers returning from abroad. The Japanese managers overseas, like their American counterparts, often experience certain career dislocations on their return. While continued employment is assured by the very nature of Japanese employment practices, reentry into the mainstream of the corporation may pose weighty problems, particularly for senior managers. Some are fortunate enough to have former associates or superiors in influential positions who have looked after their career interests during their absence, but not all can expect such benefits. The international division, though it may be limited in its power, can perform this career-watching function. In the best Japanese tradition, the demonstration of concern and effort is often as important as the results achieved.

The power of an international division is further enhanced as its capabilities to provide meaningful services and support for the subsidiaries increase. By this time, the core of the international staff has gained substantial expertise and experience in the field. They have been exposed to a wide variety of problems encountered by different subsidiaries. They have also had opportunities to gain firsthand experience by frequent field visits. They can anticipate problems that a subsidiary is likely to face rather than merely reacting to the requests from the field. Also, by this time the division has enough internal competence to handle many of the recurring problems without referring them to other corporate groups. Even in those cases where outside assistance is needed, the international division can interpret the requests from the subsidiaries in terms that are meaningful to other groups to elicit a more relevant response. Moreover, it has developed sufficient organizational knowledge and personal contacts to be able to tap the right sources of information in the parent organization.

By this time also there emerges the increasing need for greater involvement of the international division in the management of foreign subsidiaries. As the subsidiary grows, it is likely from time to time to face such strategic problems as major expansion of production facilities, diversification into new products, friction with joint-venture partners, or pressures of various sorts applied by the local governments. These problems go beyond routine management, and certainly their solutions call for a competence not generally available in the export department. Also at this point, the once strong relationship between the subsidiary and the export department is becoming weakened or even strained. For a variety of reasons—including growing uneasiness felt by the local government or local partners concerning the subsidiary's continued dependence on the parent company for parts, components, or raw materials—pressures are exerted to reduce imports from the parent company. In addition, local management, including personnel sent from the Japanese parent company, becomes less satisfied with being a mere appendage to the export department and begins to seek its own identity. These developments will lead to a subtle shift in the subsidiary's organizational identification away from the export department and toward the international division. In this process, an informal coalition emerges between the international division and the subsidiaries against the export department.

These forces tend to facilitate consolidation of the international division's power, which has grown out of the secondary role of performing merely routine service functions. The international division now has standardized procedures whereby operating data are regularly reported to it by subsidiaries, and it can openly discourage direct communications between the subsidiary and other parts of the parent company. Persons sent overseas must first be transferred to the international division, from which they are then assigned abroad.

In this stage, however, the international division has not yet been totally successful in gaining a dominant position vis-à-vis the foreign subsidiaries. It has not been able to cast itself in the role of forming policy and setting strategy for international business. New investments are still made without specific policy guidelines and evaluation criteria, and the relationship between the subsidiary and the international division, though closer than that existing in the first stage, still is not well defined. Informal coalition between the international division and foreign subsidiaries is of limited scope, applying chiefly in relation to the export department. The division's attempt to gain greater self-assertion is likely to introduce elements of conflict in its relationships with the subsidiaries, leading to jockeying for power. The subsidiaries, perceiving threats to their autonomy, become defensive. Also, another type of conflict is likely to appear. In acting as an intermediary, not infrequently the international division is caught in a position of having to arbitrate conflicting interest between the corporate groups and a subsidiary. When the division finds itself in the crossfire, its initial response is naturally to work out a compromise, but failing in this effort, it must take a stand. In this difficult position, the natural inclination for the international division, which is still searching for a greater degree of acceptance in the eyes of powerful corporate groups and operating divisions, is to apply pressure on the subsidiary to conform to the parent company's point of view. Under these circumstances, the foreign subsidiary, already uneasy over the growing power of the international division, is reinforced in its suspicion of the emerging role and organizational allegiance of the division. Thus, the relationship between the division and the foreign subsidiary at this stage can be characterized as fluid, unstable, and ambivalent.

Attaining Maturity.—Only at a third stage of its development, with the attainment of maturity, does the international division finally achieve its long-sought acceptance. Its relationship with subsidiaries as well as with other departments in the corporate headquarters has gained a considerable degree of stability. For the first time, it can exert a major voice in determining international policies and strategies of the company and play a central role in coordinating the activities of foreign subsidiaries. It has become much less vulnerable to pressures from the influential subsidiaries or from powerful corporate units and freer to take its own position toward either group without being overly concerned about the possible impact of its action on its relationship with other units.

To achieve this stage, the company's international business must have developed to a point where the following conditions at least are present. First, the firm's international business activities must have achieved a significant importance. The definition of "significant importance" is elusive. The relative importance of foreign subsidiaries in total company sales and profits is certainly a key consideration, but by no means the elusive one. The phrase implies that, however it is measured in the perception of corporate management, the international business does have a measurable impact on the performance of the corporation as a whole, and the corporate resources committed to international business have become considerable. With the growth of the international business, not only does the number of potential investment opportunities increase, but they tend to become more significant in size, necessitating formal systems of evaluation and screening.

Second, at least some of the subsidiaries have reached a state of maturity and have gone a long way toward achieving self-sufficiency. Their dependence on imported materials and components diminishes, and as a result their relationship with the export department approaches termination; conversely, their dependence on the international division increases substantially. By this time a subtle change in the parent company's point of view also takes place. No longer does it view foreign units as mere extensions of export activities, but as full-fledged enterprises that must be profitable on their own.

The third important development is the growing opportunity as well as the need for coordination and integration of activities among foreign subsidiaries. As the subsidiaries expand and mature, the potential benefits of such practices as product specialization and the crosshauling of certain products among several countries become increasingly apparent. The appeal of these benefits encourages the corporation to move away from a fragmented single-country approach and attempt some semblance of integration, at least among the more mature subsidiaries. Sometimes, such integration is forced on the subsidiaries by pressures from the host countries to export a part of their output. As the subsidiary becomes well established and begins to fill much of the local need, it is likely to come under increasing pressure from the local government to export its products to other countries. Since the overwhelming number of Japanese manufacturing subsidiaries are located in developing countries, such pressures indeed have serious implications for the operations. Here, the international division can perform a variety of useful functions from identifying promising markets, soliciting the assistance of the export department, and setting policies and programs for crosshauling of products, to actually coordinating and managing an integrated production system among several subsidiaries. Building and maintaining an elaborate logistic network does indeed require careful central planning and coordination.

Another element, though sometimes elusive, tends to increase a subsidiary's dependence on the parent company. The great majority of Japanese manufacturing investments are joint ventures in which at least one partner is a Japanese trading company. During the initial stage of development, partnership between the manufacturing firm and the trading company is mutually satisfactory, but as the subsidiary gains sufficient experience and expertise, and increases its self-sufficiency, the trading company's value to the joint venture diminishes substantially. Moreover, given the very ad hoc manner in which the partnership is formed in most companies at the time of market entry, a manufacturing firm is likely to have several trading companies as its partners in different joint ventures. Such arrangements tend to complicate any effort toward integration. Understandably, this changing relationship leads to strains and tensions between the two partners. Many of these conflicts can be resolved, or at least compromises can be reached at the local level, but more serious ones must be negotiated through the parent company, and in these discussions the international division serves as a focal point.

By this time the international division's capacity to provide meaningful assistance to the subsidiaries is further enhanced by the wider experience of its personnel. For one thing, a number of the staff members in the international division have had at least one foreign assignment, giving them greater insight into problems of local subsidiaries. This increases the division's credibility with the subsidiaries as well as with other corporate groups. Moreover, the managements of foreign subsidiaries are partly staffed by personnel from the international division. Such interchanges of personnel contribute to improved communications.

Only when this third stage is reached does the international division achieve a position whereby it can exert strong influence in shaping policies and decisions in the evaluation of new investment opportunities and the management of established subsidiaries. The division can now openly claim to be the focal point of communication between the subsidiary and the parent company. It can establish and enforce a system of planning that reflects the views of both the division and the subsidiaries. Its suggestions to the foreign subsidiaries for possible improvement are now relevant and respected. And it can now claim to be the main transfer agent of corporate resources and experiences.

Of the thirty companies with an international division, only three such divisions were observed to have reached the third stage of maturity. The international divisions in the remaining twenty-seven companies were believed to be at various points of development in the second stage, which is telling evidence that international operations are still a comparatively recent phenomenon even in leading Japanese manufacturing firms.

The classifications we have proposed here are obviously crude and tentative, and the line of demarcation between stages is much less clear-cut than implied. Nevertheless, it gives a picture of how a new organizational unit evolves in the search for legitimacy. The international division is ostensibly created to manage and coordinate the firm's international activities and to serve as the focal point in the company for its international business, but the study has clearly demonstrated that only in the last stage of development can the division really fulfill this function.

The American experience has shown that even this stability is transitory. As international business gains in its relative importance, it becomes vulnerable to pressures from other interest groups in the corporation, which will finally be resolved in favor of some form of integration into the total corporate activities. As we shall see in the ensuing section, given the peculiarities of the decision-making process in large Japanese corporations, the international division in Japanese corporations is not likely to be as autonomous as its American counterpart even at the very mature stage. It would be interesting to speculate on the impact that the de facto integration achieved through the peculiar pattern of decision-making will have on the viability of the international division. For example, an intriguing question to be examined by further research is whether or not such built-in integration implicit in the *ringi* system of decision-making would have a delaying effect on the dissolution of the international division.

ADAPTATIONS IN THE
DECISION-MAKING PROCESS

Having examined structural adaptation of corporate organization to the growth of international business activities, let us now examine the extent to which development of international business activities has altered the traditional decision-making method in large Japanese corporations. During the past two decades, Western, particularly American, management concepts have been selectively adapted into Japanese corporations. But it is generally recognized that the very core of Japanese managerial practices, such as the decision-making process, has remained virtually unchanged. This is an area that is strongly culturally bound.

The Japanese decision-making process commonly followed in a large bureaucratic organization is known as the *ringi* system. The system is often described as the approval-seeking process where a proposal (*ringi-sho*) prepared by a lower functionary works itself up through the organizational hierarchy in a highly circuitous, snail-paced manner; at each step it is examined by the proper officials, whose approval is indicated by affixing a seal, and somehow a decision emerges from the process. Such a description, while partially true, does not capture the essence of the system. It represents only a procedural aspect whereby the decision already reached is formally approved. The substance of the *ringi* system is far more dynamic, and this is the aspect that is relevant to the present consideration.

Indeed, the *ringi* system defies a neat and clear definition. It is characterized as a bottom-up, group-oriented, and consensus-seeking process. True, the *ringi* system possesses all of these elements, but its essence is found in the dynamic interaction of all of them. It operates in the climate of the traditional Japanese concept of organization, characterized by ambiguity and elusiveness, where the group rather than individuals constitutes the basic unit of organization, where the task is assigned to groups, and where the functions and the role of each individual member of the organization is virtually undifferentiated. The *ringi* system is also intricately related to the strong emphasis the Japanese have traditionally placed on implicit understanding. One such consequence is an aversion to explicit definition of organizational goals and policies, and their strong preference for dealing with each major decision on an individual basis as the need arises, evaluating it on its own merits. It is bottom-up in the sense that the need for decision is first recognized by those at the operating level, typically the middle management. It is group oriented and consensus seeking in the sense that the various interest groups that may be affected by a decision as well as those that must implement it, all participate in the decision-making. A final decision emerges in this process of group interactions rather than being made explicitly by an individual who occupies the formal leadership role. This consensus-building process is carried out through informal means. Discussions, consultations, persuasions, bargaining, or arm-twisting are all carried on through rather subtle, informal, interpersonal interactions.

These dynamic but informal interactions, which characterize every stage of decision-making, are the very essence of the *ringi* system. From the very early stage during which a decision itself is being shaped, different ideas, and various alternatives, are explored, albeit very informally. Different interests are accommodated, and compromises are sought. At the same time, the process of education, persuasion, and coordination among various groups takes place. Thus, by the time the final decision is made, virtually all the major elements of decision-making except implementation have been completed. Another elusive element in the *ringi* system is the role of the formal leader. In this system the formal leader is not a decision-maker in the classical sense. In the Japanese organization, while the status of a leader is meticulously defined, his role in the decision-making process is little differentiated from that of other members of the organization. The leader participates with his subordinates in the decision-making process. Thus, the degree to which the leader's view is incorporated into a decision depends largely on how well he is accepted and respected by his subordinates and on the kind of relationships he enjoys with them.

For the *ringi* system to operate effectively, certain conditions must prevail. First, heavy reliance is placed on informal personal relations. Much of the discussion, negotiation, bargaining, and persuasion are performed through mobilization of personal networks. To make this possible, organizational and physical setting must be such as to encourage regular and frequent face-to-face interaction. Moreover, not only are such opportunities necessary for the process of making a specific decision, but more importantly they are essential to building in the first place and maintaining the personal relations on which the system is based. The need for frequent and close contacts is further reinforced by the very nature of interpersonal relationship in the Japanese cultural setting. Chie Nakane, an authority on Japanese social structure, characterizes the nature of the interpersonal relationship in the Japanese setting as local and tangible. She goes on to note that in order to build and maintain interpersonal relationships in such a system, frequent face-to-face interaction is essential.[3]

---

[3] Chie Nakane, *Japanese Society* (Berkeley and Los Angeles: University of California Press, 1971), p. 136.

Another basic condition to make the *ringi* system effective is a strong pressure of shared understanding and values among participants. Moreover, they are expected to be totally familiar with the climate of an organization and to have unswerving loyalty to it. Since anything important is not likely to be explicitly defined, the participants in the system are expected to have a good feel for what is acceptable and possible within a given organizational context—how a decision is to be presented, who must be consulted, and how each must be approached. Moreover, communications often take the most subtle forms. In a system where individuals are bound to an organization for their entire working career, disagreements and conflicts on a particular issue must be managed in such a way as not to disturb any subsequent relationship. Communications under these circumstances must be subtle, discreet, and indirect. Participants are required to understand the implication of the most oblique cues. They must be able to read a real meaning into what for outsiders may seem to be a most casual comment. To be able to do so requires a strong sense of shared understanding and common interest.

In large Japanese corporate organizations, shared understanding and organizational commitment are developed in a most elaborate manner. It begins with the recruiting system and is reinforced through subsequent personnel practices. Young men are carefully selected from among the graduates of outstanding universities who have survived a series of rigorous screening processes, and who are already highly homogeneous in their ability, training, background, and values. On joining the company, from the very first day they go through the most intensive socialization process, during which they are indoctrinated with the value orientation of the particular firm. After a number of years, as they go through the well-structured advancement system, they develop a high degree of shared understanding and commitment. In the *ringi* system, there is no explicit control mechanism whereby the outcome of a particular decision is closely monitored and measured. The eventual outcome of a particular decision becomes known to virtually everyone concerned with that decision, and such knowledge becomes, no doubt, an important input in subsequent decisions proposed by the particular group. Through the presence of a shared understanding and organizational commitment, the participants can be reasonably certain that the decision, once made, will be implemented in the best interest of the organization.

My study reveals that virtually no change has been introduced in the decision-making practice in the international operations of Japan's leading corporations. The basic concepts and practices of the *ringi* system prevail, in spite of the fact that distance and physical isolation make the workings of the *ringi* system difficult and less effective. The relative absence of the essential prerequisites have not been explicitly taken into account, and no conscious attempts have been made to devise a different decision-making process for international operations. The authority and functions of the management of foreign subsidiaries are no more clearly defined than are those of a domestic division. Given this ambiguity, the management of a subsidiary must have almost intuitive understanding of what types of decisions can be made at its discretion, and what must be referred to the parent company. A good criterion, of course, is that if a particular decision requires any significant commitment of the parent-company resources, it must be decided by the parent company, but in practice the question is infinitely more subtle. The subsidiary management must exercise considerable judgment, which, in turn, requires close knowledge of the climate of the parent company.

As is typical in domestic operations, the consideration of a decision in the international sphere almost always originates at the subsidiary level and follows a similar process. The subsidiary managers who are physically isolated and lack ready access to those who could affect the decision at the parent company are seriously handicapped in their participation in the process. Particularly difficult is the initial stage of exploration, perhaps the most critical phase in the entire process, during which views and reactions concerning a tentative idea are informally elicited from relevant groups. Given the very local and tangible nature of human relations in Japan, personal ties, painstakingly cultivated prior to a separation, are bound to suffer during a long absence, and their effectiveness is considerably reduced.

An important task of the subsidiary management is to arrest serious deterioration in personal relationships with relevant members of the parent company. This requires considerable attention and effort. For example, the renewal of personal ties becomes a central concern on trips to the parent company. Moreover, the subsidiary management devotes a considerable amount of time to private correspondence with former associates at the parent company to keep abreast of the climate of the parent company. The effectiveness of these efforts varies considerably among individuals, but they are at best only a poor substitute for frequent and regular face-to-face interaction. Thus, the subsidiary management is much less familiar with the prevailing climate of the parent company, its power relations, and any pending proposals that may have direct relevance to a particular decision soon to be proposed by the subsidiary. Also, it is understandably difficult to participate from a distance in the discussion, negotiations and bargaining necessary for the building of a consensus. Because of these factors, a longer lead time is necessary for the foreign subsidiaries to achieve this purpose. The exploratory stage is particularly difficult and time-consuming, since the subsidiary management has only limited opportunities for face-to-face discussions to assess the feasibility of a proposal, to size up the proper way of structuring and presenting a proposal to increase its chances of acceptance, and above all to obtain implicit commitment of support from relevant groups.

An intriguing question in this connection is the extent to which the international division can serve as a surrogate for a foreign subsidiary in performing these functions. Here, the patterns vary. If the international division is perceived as weak (stage I), the subsidiary has little choice but to undertake much of the exploration itself directly with the relevant groups in the parent company. Under these circumstances, the division plays only a very limited role. In addition, at this stage, because of the general unfamiliarity with the foreign environment among the headquarters personnel, considerable educational effort is required, and the foreign subsidiary is in a much better position to perform this task.

If the international division is in the second stage of development, the situation can be more complicated since the relationship between the division and the subsidiary is fluid and even strained at times. The subsidiary may insist on assuming many of the functions itself, because it lacks confidence in the division's ability to serve as its surrogate. Also, the subsidiary managers, anxious to minimize their dependence on the international division, may wish to maintain their own ties with various departments in the company. At this stage also, the subsidiary is far from certain as to how much support it can obtain from the international division if conflict in points of view should arise between the subsidiary and a powerful corporate group, and therefore it is anxious to protect itself through direct participation. The international division, however, may resent the subsidiary's direct communication with the parent company and may have gained sufficient power to apply pressures to discourage such a practice. Against these considerations, some form of compromise emerges. Typically the subsidiary and the international division reach an agreement to "cooperate" jointly in the initial exploration. But there are likely to exist unnecessary duplications of efforts, both parties often working at cross purposes, giving rise to considerable tension and confusion.

In the third stage, the international division has attained sufficient power that its support becomes a critical factor in the decision process. Thus, one of the first essential steps for the subsidiary is to assess the views of the international division concerning a given proposal, and only after having received its support, and with its implicit understanding, can it approach other departments. The subsidiary management must also compete for higher priorities and for greater support within the international division among various proposals submitted by other foreign subsidiaries.

Another intriguing aspect of decision-making in international operations is that when an important decision is involved, all the available personnel resources of the subsidiary are mobilized to lobby for that decision. As the senior management of the subsidiary begins its discussion with relevant individuals and groups in the parent company, various staff groups of the subsidiary are also likely to begin their own informal exploratory discussions regarding the particular aspect for which each is responsible. Typically, these men still enjoy personal contacts with their former departments in the parent company, and they are in a position to engage in informal educational efforts and lobbying for the project. No doubt, informal feedback from the respective units will be reflected in the proposal to assure their approval when it is formally presented. Informal lobbying, negotiations, and discussions will also help fill the informational gap as well as create a sympathetic climate in each group for the decision under consideration prior to its formal presentation. These activities supplement in important ways the efforts made by senior management. Given the cohesive and powerful ties that bind those who have had common experiences and similar organizational affiliations, the personnel of various units in the parent company, whether in a plant, product division, or staff department, are likely to demonstrate a special sense of allegiance to those in the foreign subsidiary they consider their counterparts. Thus, the plea for support coming from these men tends to be much more effective in mobilizing support than a request routed from the international division or even from the head of the subsidiary. Since in the *ringi* system, every relevant department participates in the decision-making process and can support the decision with varying degrees of enthusiasm, it is vital to build a sympathetic climate within every unit concerned with a given decision.

As in the domestic situation, the process is gradually formalized only after considerable informal exploration, discussion, and negotiation, during which the tone of the decision is shaped. At this stage, teams may be sent to evaluate the proposal, formal meetings will be called, and technical advice is officially sought. While the inputs from these processes are vital to the refinement of a decision, they seldom alter the nature of the decision itself. Finally, a formal proposal is prepared and circulated for approval and confirmation.

Thus, Japanese management has extended the *ringi* system of decision-making to international operations with virtually no alterations. It was simply a matter of extending abroad a management practice found effective domestically. In fact, the *ringi* system is so ingrained a part of the Japanese managerial system that it is highly questionable whether even the slightest doubt has occurred to the Japanese managers concerning the desirability of extending it to their international operations. Surely, it has not occurred to them to examine the basic premises that made the *ringi* system effective in Japan. Moreover, it is impractical and inconceivable to devise another decision-making system just for the foreign subsidiaries when the major part of the organization is still managed by the *ringi* system.

The extension of the *ringi* system to management of foreign subsidiaries has, however, had several immediate as well as long-range implications. Looking first at immediate ones, it has created some practical difficulties for the managements of foreign subsidiaries, because it is they who must somehow bridge the gap that is created by their physical separation and isolation from the parent company. This diverts their attention from the pressing needs of management of the local enterprise and is often a great source of frustration for them. Furthermore, the decision process can be extremely time-consuming when circumstances require rapid responses. This may result in serious competitive disadvantages for the subsidiary.

Perhaps the single most serious long-term implication of extending the *ringi* system to international operations is that it makes the participation of non-Japanese nationals in the decision-making process extremely difficult, if not impossible. For one thing, most of them lack skills in communication sufficient to enable them to engage in these rather subtle interactions. Even more basic is the absence of a shared understanding and credibility. Significantly, the Japanese nationals who are recruited in foreign countries are almost as seriously handicapped in this regard, and they are almost invariably relegated to secondary roles in the Japanese corporations abroad. Japanese management is a closed, local, exclusive, and highly culture-bound system, and the *ringi* system epitomizes it. Only those who have gone through the most intensive socialization process at the corporation headquarters for a sufficient period of time can meaningfully participate in the *ringi* system.

A closely related and fundamental implication is that the *ringi* system requires the management of the subsidiary to be heavily staffed by Japanese nationals from the parent company. Indeed, my research reveals that the Japanese subsidiary tends to have a far greater number of personnel from the parent company than similar subsidiaries of American or European corporations. Not infrequently, virtually all line and staff positions down to the middle-management level are filled by Japanese nationals from the parent company. The *ringi* system is not the only reason, but no doubt it is an important one. For one thing, the senior managers sent from the parent company are products of the *ringi* system and unfamiliar with any other system of management. The concept of formal delegation of authority is foreign to the Japanese managers, for they are the product of an organizational climate in which authority and responsibility are ill-defined and often implicitly assumed by subordinates in the traditional manner. Where authority cannot be delegated with any degree of explicitness, the participation of local nationals in the management process is extremely difficult.

A large complement of Japanese are also required for effective participation in the corporate-wide *ringi* system. The presence of representatives of key functional areas is highly desirable, if not essential, for effective communication and lobbying. The performance of such tasks by local nationals would be all but impossible.

The foregoing factors make Japanese foreign subsidiaries extremely vulnerable. For one thing, they are already under serious attack in a number of countries for their heavy dependence on Japanese nationals.

Continued reliance on this practice prevents Japanese corporations from having ready access to high-talent manpower resources in the host countries, and it will obviously place a heavy strain on the managerial resources of the parent corporation. This strain places an inherent restriction on the growth of Japanese corporations in the international field. Serious efforts are now being made in a number of Japanese corporations to replace Japanese managers with local nationals, but unless rather fundamental changes are made at the very core of the Japanese managerial practices—not only in the foreign subsidiaries, but also in the parent company—local nationals will always be relegated to a secondary status.

A bold forecast now predicts the rapid growth of Japanese foreign direct investment in the next decades, but the feasibility of attaining this growth depends, among other things, on one critical development: that the Japanese depart from their highly culture-bound managerial practices and evolve a system more relevant to other cultures. Is Japanese management capable of achieving such a basic adaptation?

The Japanese ability to adapt foreign concepts, institutions, or technology to the Japanese setting on a selective basis with a minimum of social disruption has been well demonstrated throughout the nation's history. This ability has been credited as a major factor responsible for the remarkable results achieved during the past century in Japan's rapid modernization and industrialization. Those who are familiar with Japanese practices in this regard are aware of the fact that the process goes far beyond stereotyped imitation. It is much more dynamic. What is now demanded of Japanese management is just the reverse of their time-tested practices. Can the Japanese achieve a similar success in adapting their system to accommodate heterogeneous cultural elements and make it relevant to diverse environmental settings?

The Japanese management system has evolved in a homogeneous, cohesive, and insulated environment and it is therefore strongly culture-bound. As a means for organizing and motivating people, it relies more heavily on culturally induced values and less on explicitly defined formal organizational mechanisms. This presents a striking contrast to the American pattern where, among other things, the need to cope with rather heterogeneous and diverse values gave rise to a management system which relies heavily on formal and explicitly defined organizational structures and control systems. Compared with the Japanese, the American system is less culture-bound, has greater flexibility, and has a considerable degree of tolerance for heterogeneous elements. It is not unreasonable to suspect that this has been a factor in facilitating the international expansion of American corporations. In contrast, the Japanese management system, which has been so effective within Japan, has only very limited tolerance for heterogeneous elements. Since the very strength of the Japanese system derives from the highly homogeneous and strongly shared values, the introduction of heterogeneous elements to any significant degree is likely to be disruptive and disintegrative.

Japanese management faces a serious dilemma. In order to undertake major expansion internationally, the Japanese must bring about basic changes in their management system. The extent to which they can achieve such a feat is by no means certain. But, more important, in the process they may well lose those very elements which have made their system so effective internally. The optimist would cite the remarkable ability of the Japanese to achieve what appears impossible through their ingenuity and diligence; he would also point to the great success of the Japanese in selective assimilation of foreign institutions and technology. Clearly, however, what is demanded now of Japanese management is fundamentally different from the adoption of certain elements of foreign cultures into the tight and homogeneous cultural setting. The past offers no assurance in this regard, and the outcome is by no means certain.

Decision-Making
In the Japanese Labor Unions

TAISHIRO SHIRAI

JAPANESE UNION ORGANIZATION

Two fundamental factors determine patterns of decision-making in Japanese labor unions. First, Japanese unions have a short history compared with those of other advanced industrial nations. Second, Japanese labor unions are generally organized on an enterprise-wide basis rather than according to trade or industry as in the United States.

Labor unions were not free to organize in prewar Japan. Even in 1936, at the apex of prewar union organization, union membership totaled only four hundred and twenty thousand, constituting only 7 percent of all employed workers. This low rate of unionization resulted not only from pressure exerted by government and employers, but also from instability caused by ideological controversy within the unions. On the whole, these prewar organizations lacked the capability to engage effectively in collective bargaining.

Under the protective policy of the early stages of the American Occupation, the Japanese union movement progressed rapidly. As democratic thought—imposed by the Occupation authorities—was a concept alien to Japanese workers and employers, industrial democracy as an overall system of thought and behavior is still not firmly established. However, both workers and employers in postwar Japan adjusted rapidly and, for the most part, successfully to the concepts and institutions associated with union legitimacy and collective bargaining.

Japan's labor unions have continued to expand since World War II, particularly under the conditions of rapid economic growth since 1960. In June 1971, union membership stood at 11,684,000, a figure second in the Free World to that of the United States. The present rate of organization in Japan is 35 percent, exceeding the rate in the U.S. and equaling that in West Germany. Peculiar to the Japanese situation, however, is the dispersion of this great industrial power among thirty thousand separate union organizations. More than 90 percent of Japan's organized workers are in so-called enterprise unions. Unions conforming to the Western concept of craft and industrial organizations are rare exceptions.

Enterprise unions have several distinctive characteristics. In the first place, eligible members are limited to workers and staff with regular employee status in a specific enterprise. Second, an enterprise union, in principle, excludes those who represent the interests of management, and it exists as the sole representative of all regular enterprise employees; workers are not organized separately for different crafts or occupations. With few exceptions, both blue-collar and white-collar employees are grouped in the same organization, and this practice certainly has some merits: unionization of white-collar workers in Japan has been easier than in other industrialized countries where the tradition of blue-collar unionism is strong; and the enterprise union can utilize the knowledge of white-collar workers to formulate union policies and to strengthen its position in the negotiation with management.

The same feature, however, may give rise to internal conflict between the two groups, which, as is often the case, may develop into a split in the union with white-collar workers taking the lead in forming breakaway unions. In Japanese unionism the idea and practice of sectional representation and separate bargaining units are almost nonexistent. The practice of decision-making through majority vote is coupled with the concept of egalitarianism, which is pervasive among union members; in the unions, much as in other Japanese organizations, "democracy" is synonymous with "egalitarianism." Some white-collar workers, particularly knowledge workers in the higher professional, technical, and administrative categories, tend to be dissatisfied with the union and its policies. They tend to become more committed to the management side than to the union side.

Third, enterprise-union officers are elected from the employee list of a particular enterprise. Accordingly, professional union leaders are comparatively rare in Japan. Fourth, an enterprise union is an autonomous organization whose sovereignty is recognized within the whole union power structure. Enterprise unions generally affiliate to form federations on an industry-wide or regional basis, and these bodies in turn affiliate to form national centers. Although national centers and industrial federations are becoming increasingly significant, they seldom have the power to control or sanction the policies, activities, or management of individual enterprise unions.

Although Japanese enterprise unions are generally organized on a relatively small scale, this does not mean that there are no large unions in Japan. Of all Japanese labor unions, 60 percent are in enterprises of more than one thousand employees, and some enterprise unions have more than fifty thousand members. Industry-wide federations with more than twenty or thirty thousand members are not unusual. Bureaucratization is inevitable in organizations of such size.

Despite the relatively short history of Japanese labor unions, their activities are more diverse than those of American "business unions" in the sense that Japanese unions are more heavily committed to political activities such as national and local elections, legislative action, the socialist party, and peace movements than their American counterparts.[1] The influence of the Japanese Communist Party (JCP) is also quite strong in the unions, often resulting in severe internecine ideological warfare.

PROCEDURES AND MECHANISMS OF DECISION-MAKING

In order to understand the processes involved in union decision-making, it is first necessary to identify the types of institutions involved in union government and their peculiar characteristics. Generally, institutions of union government and administration can be divided into legislative and executive bodies. There is little difference between Japanese and American unions with regard to the types of institutions that exist and the formal

---

[1] Professor Solomon B. Levine suggested at the conference where this paper was originally presented that Japanese labor unions are broader than American labor unions in their political discussions but narrower in that they focus primarily on wage-increase and employment-security issues rather than on all the complicated economic- and shop-arrangement issues that American labor unions face. He further suggested that this might be one reason why Japanese unions do not require professional organizers.

Professor Levine may be correct as far as bargaining issues, particularly nonwage issues, are concerned. I realize the difficulty of making comparisons concerning union functions. It is true that Japanese unions have been primarily concerned with employment security and wage increases. However, the scope of collective bargaining on employment security and other nonwage issues has become larger and more detailed as unions have grown, the practice of collective bargaining has become more widely accepted, and continued economic growth has improved the situation of workers on the labor market. Up until the early 1960s, employment security was pursued by unions mainly in resistance or opposition to management's attempts at mass discharge. Now employment security includes fairly detailed control of job content, the size of the work force, work load, production speed, transfer and retraining, welfare, safety, and even promotion and demotion. Needless to say, whether a union takes up one of these issues, and how effectively it handles the issue, depends on the union's ability and power to cope with the management. This may be essentially the same as the situation in America. However, it is worth noting that in Japan: (1) the history of collective bargaining has been relatively short; (2) negotiation of such problems will not necessarily result in a detailed written contract or agreement, as in the United States, but is more likely to take the form of a de facto workshop practice; (3) the personnel division of the management or the supervisors often act as though they are representing the workers' interests; and (4) informal workshop groups (as distinct from unions' shop organizations) may have some authority or influence on these issues, so unions may not deem it necessary to take up these issues as collective-bargaining items.

and functional relationships between them. Several differences are apparent, however, in their operational styles and in the distribution of power among the various organizational levels. On the whole, in Japan these differences reflect the ascendancy of legislative organs over executive councils and the predominance of collective decision-making. This means that the scope of decisions left to the discretion of the Japanese union leaders is relatively narrow. Popular control takes precedence over administrative efficiency.

The Union Convention

As in the United States, the highest authority in the Japanese union power structure rests with the union convention. The convention has sole power to revise the union platform and constitution, ratify activity reports, set action programs and administration policy, elect officers, perform budgeting and accounting tasks, decide on strikes, ratify collective agreements, and take disciplinary action against officers or members. There is little difference between Japanese and American unions with regard to the formal and constitutional requirements governing the role of the convention in union government. Nevertheless, the management and procedures of the convention are unique in Japanese unions.

In the first place, Japanese unions have more frequent conventions. Union organizations on all levels convene at least once a year. In fact, Japan's labor union law specifies that in order to qualify as a registered union, an organization's constitution or bylaws must provide for annual conventions. This law was promulgated in order to ensure democratic administration, but legal prescriptions aside, annual conventions are a minimum prerequisite for the smooth operation of a Japanese labor union. Most unions find it necessary to have several extraordinary conventions each year in addition to the plenary meeting. This is because conventions offer union executives an opportunity to forge a membership consensus through debate among their own membership or among affiliated unions, and to test the balance between status quo supporters and opposition forces.

Hence the habit of frequent conventions is not based on such ideological or ethical considerations as respect for democracy or the principle of decision through mass participation and debate. Rather, it is due to organizational weakness caused by the internal contradictions pervading Japanese enterprise unionism. On the enterprise level, various employee interest groups form coalitions and conflicts with other groups: white-

---

At any rate, whether or not Japanese enterprise unions engage in collective bargaining on such nonwage issues has nothing to do with the lack of professional functionaries. These nonwage issues are specific to individual enterprises, so that they are more easily and effectively handled by nonprofessional leaders within the enterprise union, who generally have more detailed knowledge of the daily operation of a certain institution than professionals from the outside. Moreover, workers are not likely to rely on professionals from outside to solve such problems.

collar versus blue-collar, young versus old, well-educated versus poorly-educated, those who are intensely loyal to the firm versus the disloyal, those with higher seniority versus those with lower seniority, and so on. In addition, there are divisions based on ideology and political factionalism.

At the industrial-federation and national-center levels, splits frequently occur over such factors as differences between unions in large and small enterprises; conflicts of interest among unions that belong to competing enterprises marketing the same type of commodities or services; incompatibility between unions in the private and public sectors; and confrontations based on loyalty to contending political parties and ideologies. These conflicts often lead to organizational splits and lend a distinctly political coloring to the decision-making process in Japanese unions. Frequent conventions are essential to ameliorating these conflicts through conciliation and compromise, and forming a new consensus.

The second peculiarity of Japanese union conventions concerns quorum requirements. In general, the constitutional quorum requirements are comparatively strict in order to prevent manipulation of the convention by the leadership or by a vocal minority of the membership. In the United States, even the United Auto Workers, noted for being particularly democratic, requires only "twenty-five percent of all the delegates seated at an International Convention" to constitute a quorum.[2] The interval between conventions in American international unions is longer than in Japan, but most local membership meetings take place once a month. As far as I know, the most rigid quorum requirement for a local meeting in the U.S. seems to be about 25 percent of the membership, and in some locals, meetings are held with only about seven members present including the executive officers. Some American locals do not even have a quorum requirement.

In Japan, however, on the national, industrial, and plant levels, a quorum is generally two-thirds of the eligible delegates or, in the case of small local unions, two-thirds of all the dues-paying membership. Despite growing apathy among young Japanese union members (which has not yet reached American levels) almost all Japanese unions closely adhere to quorum regulations. One reason is that enterprise unions can hold meetings on company premises, where it is easy for members to attend. A more important reason is conflict among various groups or factions in the union or federation; if quorum requirements were lax, certain groups could be over- or underrepresented, upsetting the balance of forces. Third, the leaders need the convention as a mechanism for achieving the greatest possible majority of supporters.

Another distinctive characteristic of Japanese labor conventions is the system for selecting convention chairmen. In the United States, almost without exception and regardless of the level of union organization, the

---

[2] U.A.W. Constitution, art. 8, sec. 3.

union president automatically becomes the chairman of the convention. In most cases, he is also empowered to appoint members of such important committees as resolution, credentials, constitution, auditing, order of business, and grievance. As convention chairman, he even has the right to call on speakers from the floor. Such a one-man concentration of power would be unthinkable in a Japanese convention. Japanese unions make a great effort to keep the legislative, executive, and judiciary functions separate in order to avoid concentrating power in a single individual or office.

The purpose of the Japanese convention is to examine, evaluate, and criticize the actions of the executive committee. The president along with the entire executive committee, which he represents, is put in the role of defendant. Thus, the president would not be allowed to take the chair in order to manage the convention in a way advantageous to the incumbent executive committee. Convention chairmen are chosen on an ad hoc basis by vote of representatives or of the entire membership. On the industrial-federation and national-center levels, a "body of chairmen" is often chosen rather than a single individual—a further act to reinforce or correct the existing balance between contending factions and interest groups in the organization. The elected chairman, or body of chairmen, has supreme authority over convention management; the executive officers therefore are temporarily subjected to his control. Of course, when the president has the support of a majority of the union membership, the delegates will most likely choose a chairman acceptable to him. He is then able to manage the convention from behind the scenes, and in fact this is common. Nevertheless, there are comparatively fewer opportunities in Japan for manipulation by strong leadership.

Intermediate Legislative Bodies

Another peculiarity of the government and administration of Japanese unions is the widespread use of interim legislative bodies in national centers, industrial federations, and even the large-scale enterprise unions. These intermediate bodies have supreme authority over governmental and administrative matters in the interval between conventions. They are usually convened either to alleviate the financial burden of frequent plenary and extraordinary conventions, or to cope with emergency problems which cannot wait for convention decision. They have various names, depending on the union: *chuō iinkai* (central committee), *hyōgikai* (council), and *daihyōsha kaigi* (representative conference). The frequency of their meetings varies, but most union constitutions stipulate two to six meetings a year. Power to convene intermediate bodies rests with the union president, and he usually assumes the chairmanship. Most union constitutions specify the range of issues to be decided by the union conventions and intermediate bodies respectively and prescribe the relationship between the two bodies. The intermediate body acts both on matters explicitly delegated to it and on matters that require immediate decisions, but must be ratified by the union convention afterwards. Generally speaking, decisions made by the intermediate body are minor compared to those reserved for convention decision.

The jurisdiction of the intermediate bodies vis-à-vis the convention is sometimes only vaguely delineated, and their spheres often overlap. Both organs ascertain the will of the membership, reconcile opposing opinions and interests, and set official union policy; this union policy, in turn, guides and regulates the activities of the executive committee. The intermediate body serves as a sounding board for the rank-and-file's reaction, evaluations, and criticisms of the executive committee. Accordingly, it is not unusual that executive officers ask for a vote of confidence from the intermediate bodies.

The Executive Committee

The executive committee is responsible for putting into effect the policy resolutions passed by the legislative organs, but its specific jurisdiction is often not clearly defined. Theoretically, the executive committee has authority over all affairs of the union that are not specifically delegated by the constitution to the legislative bodies. Furthermore, to the extent that the handling of a given matter is not provided for specifically in the constitution, the executive committee is free to determine whether it will consult a legislative body. On the whole, however, union executive committees are careful, even timid, about exercising their prerogatives. In addition, there are several specific restrictions on their rights and duties.

In contrast to the American practice, Japanese executive committees are standing committees which operate under the principle of collective decision-making. In collective decision-making, the individual rights and jurisdiction of top leaders, such as the committee chairman (union president) and secretary-general, are often ill-defined. Hence the executive committee also meticulously avoids concentration of power and authority in one or a few men or offices.

In the AFL-CIO and most American international unions, the executive board, or executive council, is not a standing body, and meets only two, four, or at the most six times a year. In other words, its role resembles that of the Japanese intermediate legislative councils. Although these American bodies are called executive boards, they actually act as advisory councils to the top leaders—the president and secretary-treasurer. Since they are not standing committees, they do not require full-time members. Their members attend meetings and offer their services on a part-time basis. This is the case in most unions in Great Britain as well.

In Japan, however, executive committees are standing committees, and according to union constitutions, must convene at least once a week. Many of their members are full time and, just as in a government cabinet, each member is responsible for a certain area of union affairs; executive committee members head various departments, including finance, education, planning, research, wages, and organization. In addition to regular meetings, the committee can be convened at any time, and in principle, any important issues that come up to the executive committee are decided by an agreement of at least a majority of the members.

The specific and exclusive power and duties of Japanese executive officers are not clearly defined, although the authority of the union president and secretary-general is more narrowly limited than in American unions. In the collective decision-making process, the officers are on an equal footing with ordinary committee members. The constitutions of many unions set forth the jurisdiction and duties of the president in an abstract and vague manner: "to coordinate union activities and represent the union." Even where presidential duties are spelled out in more detail, they are usually limited to activities such as convening the convention and central committee and signing the agreements, contracts, and official documents issued by the union. The vice-president aids the president and represents the union in the president's absence. The secretary-general is responsible for carrying out the daily business of the union, coordinating the activities of the specialized departments, keeping records of meetings, storing union documents, and so on.

Judging from union constitutions, the jurisdiction of top union leaders often extends only to a bare minimum of essential union business. The main decision-making and executive functions are carried out collectively by the officers through the executive committee, avoiding concentration of power in individuals. At the same time, the principle of shared responsibility operates in all the executive organs.

PSYCHOLOGICAL FACTORS IN DECISION-MAKING

We have seen two areas in which the rank and file have strict direct and indirect control over decision-making by union leaders: in the structural forms and administrative practices of the legislative and executive organs; and in the distribution of power among the levels of union organization and among union officials. As Sidney and Beatrice Webb have pointed out, the conflicting needs for popular control and administrative efficiency have shaped the history of the labor movement.[3] In the Japanese case, it appears that administrative efficiency is sacrificed to popular control. One reason for this is the structural weakness of unions organized on the basis of enterprise. In addition, however, there are certain psychological factors which prevail in the Japanese union movement.

---

[3] Sidney and Beatrice Webb, *Representative Institutions* (1913), part 1, chap. 2 ("Industrial Democracy"), p. 58. This edition was printed by the authors for the students of the Workers' Educational Association.

The Psychology of Group Orientation

The first psychological factor of significance is the marked "group orientation" pervading all organizations in Japanese society, including unions. There is a tendency to resist any special privileges or responsibilities that would distinguish between one member, or one group faction, and another. Most leaders fear being isolated from rank-and-file membership and whenever possible seek a membership consensus. In other words, they try to prevent open confrontations over conflicting opinions or interests between leaders and members, or among the members themselves. The members expect their leaders to follow the principle of collective, consensus-oriented decision-making, and leaders who fail to meet their expectations in this regard tend to lose their positions. Before a leader hands down a decision, he listens to the opinions of other leaders and members, tries to reconcile differences, and gets as many others as possible to participate in the decision-making process. This is what the labor movement calls the "mass line" or "mass debate." When a decision is made collectively, the responsibility is widely shared.

Hence the union democracy ideally conceptualized by Japanese union members and their leaders is similar to the "primitive democracy" discussed by the Webbs: "In this earliest type of Trade Union democracy we find, in fact, the most childlike faith not only that 'all men are created equal,' but also that 'what concerns all should be decided by all.' " [4] Most Japanese union leaders as well as members are far from childish; the unions, in fact, diverge from this type of "primitive democracy" as their organizations get larger and their functions diversify. A certain degree of bureaucratization is inevitable. The faith, however, that "what concerns all should be decided by all" is retained in the deeply rooted belief that important decisions should be made collectively by committee members or a delegates' meeting duly elected by all of the membership.

Distrust of Union Leaders

Another important psychological predisposition derives from the ideological conflict of the prewar union movement. Prewar leftists, particularly Communists and their sympathizers, often attempted to undermine confidence in rightist labor unions. In line with a strategy of "boring from within," they sometimes launched individual attacks on rightist union leaders to discredit them in the eyes of the rank and file. A favorite expression of leftist vocabulary at that time was *darakan* (corrupt leader). The term was used to slander labor leaders by implying that they had sold out the workers in order to reach a modus vivendi with the government, police, and employers; that they were making illicit profits; or that they

---

[4] Ibid., part 1, chap. 1 ("Primitive Democracy"), p. 8.

ran their unions in an authoritarian manner. These "corrupt leader" attacks became common in early postwar Japan as well. Most of the slander had no basis in fact, but it had strong appeal, given the predisposition of the average Japanese worker. The workers often mistrusted the leaders and were quite receptive to suggestions that the leaders, if given broad powers, would put their own interests before those of the workers they were supposed to represent. This frame of mind has led to the belief that the rank-and-file members and their representatives must seek to observe and control even the day-to-day decisions and activities of their leaders. The leaders themselves often attempt to avoid "corrupt leader" charges by restricting the scope of their leadership and authority as much as possible. The leaders, too, have benefited from the system of collective leadership, because collective sharing of power renders the role of the leader less responsible and thus less hazardous.

Respect for Institutional Prerogatives

A type of authoritarianism does prevail in Japanese unions. If we may exaggerate somewhat, the respect commanded by a given decision does not stem from the sagacity, insight, appropriateness, speed, or rationality of the decision itself. Nor is it a consequence of the great past accomplishments of or respected position of the individual leader who supposedly made the decision. Rather, the legitimacy of the decision hinges on whether it was processed by the appropriate governmental organs of the union—convention, intermediate legislative body, or executive committee —via the duly established and orthodox procedures. If the decision is made "by action of the convention," or "by action of the central committee," and passed with the proper formalities and procedures, it will be granted full legitimacy and respect.

How thoroughly the convention or committee debates the content of the decision and how large a majority of the membership participates in the discussion are only secondary considerations. What matters is the consensus effect—whether the action of the union's highest legislative organ confirms the support of all, or at least a majority, of the membership and affiliated unions. In other words, even though collective deliberation by union organs is often nothing but ceremonial play-acting, this formality constitutes an important criterion for legitimacy. In fact, ceremony often covers up for the leadership's lack of persuasiveness and the membership's shortcomings in comprehension.

ACTUAL OPERATION OF THE
DECISION-MAKING MACHINERY

Administrative Inefficiency

Needless to say, the system for decision-making in Japanese labor unions includes much administrative inefficiency. The Japanese union decision-making process is often criticized as excessively time-consuming. During collective bargaining, for example, the management side is often irritated by the inability of union negotiators to reach a decision among themselves. The more urgent and important a problem is, the more likely the negotiators are to postpone discussions in order to consult with the committee. Such irritation is often shared even by the public-interest members of dispute-settlement machineries.

Excessive decision-making time means inefficiency in the use of manpower and finances. The total amount of money spent by Japanese labor unions, in real terms, seems greater than that used by unions in many countries of Western Europe; in comparison with wage levels, it exceeds even that required by American industrial unions such as the United Automobile Workers and the United Steel Workers. A large portion of Japanese union expenditures goes for the salaries of full-time officials; Japanese unions usually have one full-time official for each three to four hundred members—a rate unheard of except in Japan and the United States. Furthermore, craft unions, which are the major cause for such high figures in the United States, do not exist in Japan.

A considerable part of the manpower, time, and energy of Japanese unions is spent planning, preparing, and recording the countless meetings required to deliberate and produce policy decisions. One of the largest items on the union expenditure list is conference costs—the charges for renting meeting halls, delegates' travel and accommodations, communications, and so on. Inefficiency in the use of manpower, finances, and other resources is among the most difficult problems faced by Japanese unions. It is not, however, frivolous waste. Rather, it is an essential cost for maintaining the solidarity of union members.

The decisions made through these inefficient procedures are not as rigid as usually thought; they do not restrict the freedom of judgment and action of the union leaders as severely as might be supposed. Often, in fact, the decisions are impractical. Accordingly, there are times when the decisions are respected, but not observed. This is especially true of decisions regarding collective bargaining.

How an Actual Decision Is Made

The best example of the actual decision-making process occurs annually during the spring "wage offensive," when decisions concerning wage

demands are made. The process is a complicated one. The wage proposals
discussed at workshop and plant level membership meetings are collected
by the headquarters of the enterprise union. The executive officers make
proposals based on information on the labor market, commodity prices,
living costs, enterprise profits, and wage levels in other industries and
enterprises. These proposals are communicated down the organization
hierarchy to the membership below. Industrial federations, affiliated
unions, and national centers cooperate in collecting information.

After this process of information exchange is completed, a union
convention is held. The executive committee makes a proposal, and after
discussion by the assembled delegates, the union wage-hike policy is
formulated and issued. It may say, for example: "We demand the
employer grant an average monthly wage increase of over ¥15,000 per
worker. Should we fail to receive this amount, we will go on a strike of
unlimited duration."

After reaching a decision, the convention delegates and executive
committee swear solidarity and announce their determination to succeed.
On the plant level, workers wear armbands or headbands with slogans like
"Yōkyū kantetsu" (Achieve our demands), and perhaps hold demonstrations.
Nevertheless, everyone knows that the wage-hike decided on at the
convention can never be achieved, and also that the union will not resort
to an unlimited strike.

The wage demand decided on at the convention is conveyed to the
management side, and collective bargaining begins. In the interval before
management replies to the demand or makes a counterproposal, the union
may execute a strike of four to twenty-four hours' duration. This strike is to
hasten management's reply or to tell management, "We really mean it!"

In order for negotiations to proceed, however, the union must revise its
wage demand to a more realistic figure. At this stage, the central
committee, or even an informal representative conference, convenes and
decides on a "Realistic Wage-Increase Proposal" along with a schedule of
strikes and other tactics. This time, the original demand for a ¥15,000
increase falls to ¥12,000. The original vow to carry out a "strike of
unlimited duration" is dropped in favor of a plan for a series of
twenty-four hour strikes. These intermittent, short strikes are used to force
up the amount of counterproposals from the management side.

As a result, the positions of management and the union begin to
approach each other, and the bargaining reaches the crucial juncture
when the union will make its final decision. The management side will
have already made a final proposal of, say, a ¥10,000 increase (both
management and union make repeated use of "final proposals," but this
one is really the last). The union side, at this point, must decide to accept
the wage-hike offered by management and terminate the struggle, or to
reject the proposal and initiate a much longer and more difficult strike
with a limited chance of achieving gains. This decision is made either by

the executive committee itself or by an expanded central struggle committee. This is the time when the leadership capabilities of the top leaders are displayed. A leader's intuition, analytical skill, and judgment become crucial; he must assess such factors as the mood surrounding the negotiations, the relative bargaining power of union and employer, the ability of the union to persevere in a long strike, the movements of anti-mainstream groups within the union, the benefits that may be expected to accrue from a longer strike as against the possible losses, and so on. Then he must be able to persuade his fellow committee members of the wisdom of his position.

The members of the executive committee or the central struggle committee finally reach agreement, and the struggle is usually terminated. The executive committee then must convene a meeting of the central committee, or a convention, to explain the course of the negotiations and seek membership approval for the decision reached. The necessity for compromise has considerably reduced the original wage-hike figure decided on by the convention, and instead of a strike of unlimited duration, only a few short strikes have been called. In order to improve the management counterproposals, the executive committee may have made concessions on working conditions that had not been approved in advance by the convention. These moves have flaunted the sacred "collective decision by convention or central committee."

The executive committee members who have committed these infractions must be examined by the central committee and their "misdeeds" sanctioned. When we remarked earlier that the executive committee is placed in the position of defendant during conventions, we were referring to this type of situation. Here, too, is a crucial test of the executives' leadership qualities. The leaders explain the reasons for their decisions to the assembled delegates and seek to persuade them of the inevitability of the results. Regret over the "executive's failure to abide by the convention's "decision" prompts "self-criticism" and a vow to do better in the future, but sometimes the dissatisfaction of antimainstream, opposition elements in the union cannot be easily dispelled. If the executive committee feels that, as things stand, the convention will not ratify their actions, the committee calls for a vote of confidence in the leadership. This time, they go on the offensive. The membership is forced to decide whether to express overall confidence in the incumbent leadership, and hence ratify their specific decisions, or to vote them out and accept the leadership of an anti-mainstream group. In either case, the convention or central committee itself makes the decision.

Behind-the-Scenes Decision-Making

The intellectual capabilities, eloquence, and persuasiveness of the leaders influence decision-making at the convention and central-committee levels, but these qualities are not entirely sufficient. Since decisions of the legislative councils are by consensus or majority vote, the top leaders must engage in various political maneuvers to obtain majority support. The executive officers are weak in statutory rights and duties, and decisions are made collectively; hence, it is essential that the officers retain the support of their trusted factions and caucuses. If the leader's faction does not command a stable majority, he must negotiate with other factions, even those in overt opposition, in order to move the convention in the desired direction. Hence, behind-the-scenes negotiation or, as it is termed in Japanese, *nemawashi* (binding the roots of a plant before pulling it out), is carried out prior to the formal debate and vote. In many cases, the formal decision on the floor is little more than a ceremony to confirm the decision already reached behind closed doors. In such cases, decision-making is done in places and through procedures totally unknown to the rank-and-file union member. Great ability and wisdom in such political maneuvers is one of the most important qualities of a union leader. If a leader has majority support, violations of decisions collectively made by the convention, or even unilateral changes in policy in the course of collective bargaining, will usually be accepted by the rank and file.

Decision-Making at the National Level

National industrial federations have become increasingly involved in collective bargaining, although their role is generally still confined to coordination of the policies and activities of their affiliated unions on an industrial level. The national centers such as Sōhyō (General Council of Trade Unions of Japan) and Dōmei (Japanese Confederation of Labor) also play an important role in *shuntō* (the annual "spring wage offensive" for wage increases). Particularly Sōhyō, which jointly with Chūritsurōren (Federation of Independent Unions) organizes the Joint Struggle Committee for *shuntō*, is responsible for setting common targets, exchanging information, and organizing a scheduled united drive of affiliated unions which includes mass meetings, demonstrations, slowdowns, and strikes. However, Sōhyō and other national centers do not take part in collective bargaining. It has been very rare, at least so far, for Sōhyō's top leaders to meet and negotiate with the prime minister or cabinet ministers to settle a general strike of the transportation and communication industries.

While some of the characteristics of union decision-making described thus far are also applicable to the national centers, the national centers have some unique characteristics of their own, since their function is more political than economic. This is particularly true of Sōhyō, which, unlike Dōmei and Chūritsurōren, is composed largely of unions in the public sector—those of national and local civil servants including teachers, and employees of public corporations such as railway, postal service, telecommunications, and national forestry. Union members from the public sector constitute two-thirds of all Sōhyō membership, and their activities are intrinsically politically oriented, since their employers are government or semi-governmental agencies, which limit or forbid the unions' right to bargain or to strike.

One of Sōhyō's most difficult and controversial decisions is on which political party to support. The decision is simple for Dōmei because it is committed to support only the Democratic Socialist Party (DSP), but Sōhyō's convention must decide whether to support only the Japanese Socialist Party (JSP) or two parties—Socialist and Communist. Socialist party supporters have a caucus called the Socialist Party Members Council, which has been able to command the majority position so that they have been called the "mainstream faction." Communist party supporters also have their caucus, and they join with non-Communist leftists to form the "antimainstream faction." In addition, there is another group of unions from private industry which supports the DSP, but this group is of minor importance compared with the other two factions.

In every Sōhyō annual convention, open strife takes place on the floor between the two factions over the issue of supporting a political party. In such a highly ideological issue there is no compromise. Unlike the issue of wage increase, the executive officer cannot make the kind of proposal that is accepted by the convention but later actually modified or negated. The choice between the alternatives can only be decided by taking a vote of the delegates to the convention.

The vote is taken in two ways. One is the vote cast by individual delegates, who are allocated to each affiliated organization in accordance with the number of its registered (Sōhyō dues-paying) members. In this kind of vote, big organizations with hundreds of thousands of members have the decisive power. The second type of vote is for each affiliated organization to cast one vote as a single unit. This type of vote is designed to counterbalance the power of big unions.

Naturally, the two factions compete with each other in various ways to attract unions and their delegates to their respective sides as effectively as possible. Therefore, this process of decision-making reflects exactly the actual balance of power between political factions within Sōhyō. It is difficult to predict what will happen when the vote is ultimately taken on the convention floor. This may be even more true in the near future, since the political situation within Sōhyō is supposed to become more complex and unstable.

RANK-AND-FILE REVOLT

Despite many administrative inefficiencies, it appears that the Japanese union movement has been highly successful. Union membership has risen steadily to the present high numbers. Wages have risen at a speed unprecedented in Western industrial nations. Job security has increased along with overall improvement in hours and working conditions. The many large-scale discharges and long strikes of the 1950s, which often caused union splits, have become rare exceptions in the 1960s and 1970s. Despite the increasing apathy among young workers toward the union and union activities supposedly revealed by recent attitude polls, support for unions among workers as a whole is quite strong.

Table 1
Growth of Union Membership by Selected Years

Year	Number of Unions	Union Membership	Total Number of Employed Workers[a]	Estimated Rate of Unionization
1955	18,013	6,285,878	16,620,000	37.8%
1960	21,957	7,661,568	23,820,000	32.2
1965	27,525	10,146,872	29,140,000	34.8
1970	30,058	11,604,770	32,770,000	35.4
1971	33,830	11,797,570	33,820,000	34.9

Source: Ministry of Labor, "Labor Union Basic Survey."

[a] The total number of employed workers in the figure as of June according to the Labor Force Survey, Bureau of Statistics, Office of the Prime Minister.

Hence, union organization has been a huge success in terms of wages and employment conditions. In large measure, the achievements have been due to such favorable environmental conditions as rapid economic growth, a shortage of labor, high labor productivity, and the strong competitive power of Japanese goods on the world market. Unions have done little more than act to protect their interests under such favorable economic conditions. However, in the process it seems that union leaders have been guaranteed a stable position. Hence, even though procedures have been inadequate in the eyes of a certain segment of the membership, a high level of satisfaction has been the rule.

Nevertheless, the leadership crisis is the greatest problem facing the Japanese labor movement. Within the last two years or so, several eminent and capable leaders of powerful industrial federations and national centers have been forced to resign. In some cases, rank-and-file members have criticized the leaders for their decision-making and administrative practices, and either ousted them with a vote of nonconfidence or pressed them to resign.

Prominent leaders who lost their positions in 1971 included Takaragi Fumihiko, president of the Japan Postal Worker's Union, and Nabasama Yutaka, president of the Japan Seamen's Union. Both of these men were supported by large majorities of their union members and commanded great respect both within and outside their unions. Both, however, were forced to quit by a revolt of the rank and file. President Takaragi fell victim to rank-and-file discontent when he made concessions without consulting union members at the close of a "struggle" against the government. In President Nabasama's case, the membership refused to accept the rate of wage increase obtained through compromise by the leadership, since it was considerably below the amount previously specified as desirable by the union convention (though it was not below the average increases obtained by other unions).

Rank-and-file revolts, because they often include an emotional or ideological element, sometimes become quite intense. Young workers are usually in the forefront. We cannot say that rank-and-file workers—particularly the younger generation—have never criticized or been dissatisfied with the decision-making and administrative practices of the leadership in the past. But in the past, the authority of the leaders has been protected by majority support in legislative councils, and the membership has recognized, at least in form, the mechanisms of union democracy designed to alleviate such unrest. To the extent that rebellion against decision-making under formalistic democracy has continued to take the form of apathy and indifference, no serious organizational problems have arisen. But the resulting lack of public criticism of the leaders contributes to facile self-confidence, widening even further the large gap between the leadership and the rank and file.

We can isolate several reasons why the previous apathy on the part of the mass membership has given way to revolts against leadership in some of Japan's large labor unions. First, the demands of young workers have become stronger and more diverse. Young workers have been in a very advantageous position in the labor market. Even though their wage increases have been more rapid and continuous than those received by their elders, they feel dissatisfied with a wage system based on seniority. In addition, they feel that high wage levels have been due more to the effects of supply and demand in the labor market than to the efforts of the union and collective bargaining. For this reason, they ask unions to take a more militant position for bigger wage increases. Furthermore, young workers and union leadership have different standards for evaluating the fruits of management-union wage compromise. The leaders' emphasis on experience as a guide is no longer convincing to the younger union members.

A change in the value structure of young workers is a second cause of revolt against union leadership. Increasing labor mobility and a higher level of education among young people have accelerated value change in postwar Japan. This has had a great impact on all organizations in Japanese society including the unions and has contributed to a growing generation gap between union leaders and rank-and-file members. The value changes are diverse, but with regard to union government there are two: the denial of the legitimacy of established authority, and the demand of young workers for a more active role in making decisions that affect their working and living conditions. The younger workers do not tend to value the existence, continuity, and stability of the union organization as ends in themselves. Rather, they are interested in the benefits the organization can bring to them as individuals. Nor do they necessarily value for its own sake the established authority deriving from past accomplishments and diverse experience. They are not willing to be manipulated by such authority. Formerly, union leaders were able to bolster their negotiating position in collective bargaining by mobilizing the aspirations and energy of young workers. After that, the leaders could obtain approval of their decision from legislative organs. Now, however, the young union members are no longer satisfied with their former passive role in the decision-making process. They demand the right to be heard directly and to participate actively in decision-making. They strike out at the alienation of workers under the leadership of bureaucratized labor unions and call for a "restoration of humanity."

It is true that the attitudes of the young workers and the actions and demands that grow out of these attitudes are often emotional and impetuous and do not always serve the long-range interests of the union structure. However, the unions are confronted with the distressing fact that these attitudes are now being shared by an increasing number of older workers. In other words, the mistrust of established decision-making and administrative procedures is gradually broadening. Japanese labor unions, which have enjoyed unprecedented growth in the postwar years, have been jolted by these problems, and are facing a critical juncture.

The Company Work Group

THOMAS P. ROHLEN

Although their labels have been diverse, few writers comparing Japan with other industrial societies have failed to give a central place to the strong tendency toward group involvement one finds in Japanese institutional life. This group emphasis is generally understood to predate the modern period, and thus it is a major element in the discussion of such issues as cultural continuity in modern Japan and the reinforcement of modern organizational patterns by traditional values. The consensus about the importance of group involvement is not, however, enriched by a very extensive understanding of just what Japanese groups are like, how they vary, and what factors are causing them to be refashioned. Obviously the term *group* is a vague category encompassing numerous quite distinct entities. This paper aims to bring into sharper focus one crucial subcategory—the company work group. The discussion is based primarily on material from a one-year fieldwork study (1968–1969) of a bank of three thousand employees and a three-month study (1972) of a plastics manufacturer employing six hundred people in two factories and a head office.[1]

[1] Support from a NIMH predoctoral fellowship for the earlier study and from an additional NIMH grant for the more recent fieldwork is gratefully acknowledged. A more detailed account of the bank's work groups and the general organizational context of white-collar work is contained in Thomas P. Rohlen, *For Harmony and Strength: Japanese White-collar Organization in Anthropological Perspective* (Berkeley and Los Angeles: University of California Press, 1974). This paper relies more heavily on material from white-collar groups. For further detail on the character of blue-collar work relations, see Robert J. Cole, *Japanese Blue Collar: The Changing Tradition* (Berkeley and Los Angeles: University of California Press, 1971); and Arthur M. Whitehall and Takezawa Shinichi, *The Other Worker: A Comparative Study of Industrial Relations in the United States and Japan* (Honolulu: East-West Center Press, 1968).

THE GENERAL CHARACTER OF WORK GROUPS

A key variable in most employees' response to their company is the quality of their face-to-face relations in office or factory groups (usually called *ka*). Informants frequently cite teamwork and related qualities prominent in company ideologies in their descriptions of good relations,[2] and those dissatisfied point to interpersonal problems in work groups as the source of their unhappiness. Management takes a similar view of the importance of work-group relations. Regarding white-collar work in particular, personnel departments show a preoccupation with improving office morale as the solution for problems as different as emotional instability and declining productivity. As further evidence of managerial concern, personnel departments, which are charged with improving work-group morale, typically have far greater status and authority in the Japanese company system than in American firms. In sum, management regards good relations at the small-group level as crucial to maintaining high levels of energy and attention. This perspective did not originate with modern theories of personnel management (although the thinking of the Mayo School has been influential), but rather it echoes ideals and psychological predispositions characteristic of premodern Japan.[3] The large organizational framework places various constraints on this pattern, and yet any attempt to characterize Japanese companies without recognizing that their dynamic is generated, fundamentally and quite intentionally, in small-group contexts would obscure a most significant quality.

General Structure.—No one works totally outside a group context. The president and his council of executives have considerable independence, yet ideally they decide matters through frequent joint meetings. All employees, even those with the most isolated tasks, have a place in some work group. Almost all white-collar employees and many blue-collar workers are assigned first to a group and then to a specific job. Rank, skill, and actual task are correlated, but their final sorting out accommodates the requirements of the group first. Nakane notes that Japanese companies hire potential, not skills,[4] and to a lesser degree this observation holds for the way employees enter company work groups. On-the-job training often brings individual potential into line with group requirements. Regular employees are sorted by a rank system, which gives a pyramidlike

---

[2] Japanese managers are inclined to enunciate rather elaborate statements of company goals, ethics, and other ideals. See Rohlen, *For Harmony and Strength*, for a detailed account of the bank's ideology.

[3] See, for example, Kawashima Takeyoshi, *Nihon shakai no kazokuteki kōsei* [The familistic construction of Japanese society] (Tokyo: Nihon Hyōronsha, 1950); Kawashima Takeyoshi, *Ideorogii to shite no kazoku seido* [The family system as ideology] (Tokyo: Iwanami shoten, 1957); and John C. Pelzel, "Japanese Kinship: A Comparison," in Maurice Freedman, ed., *Family and Kinship in Chinese Society* (Palo Alto: Stanford University Press, 1970).

[4] Chie Nakane, *Japanese Society* (Berkeley and Los Angeles: University of California Press, 1970).

structure to the work groups. In manufacturing firms, clerical and engineering workers tend to be organized into one rank system, while blue-collar workers are organized into a separate rank system. Even more than for white-collar workers, promotion up the blue-collar ranks is a direct function of years of service.[5]

The result is a hierarchy in most work groups that closely corresponds to age. Exceptions occur if (1) older women are present, since women are rarely promoted above the lowest few ranks,[6] (2) older people with short company service are present, or (3) men who have been promoted either very slowly or very fast are present. In the blue-collar situations, the first two factors were the primary causes of age-rank discrepancies, whereas the third possibility was most influential in white-collar situations. In both companies there is also a small percentage of persons (such as temporary workers and custodians) who are not regular employees, and thus of lower status. They are typically older and unobtrusive to a fault. The group's informal social activities seldom include them.

Size of groups varies considerably. The smallest branch in the bank and the smallest factory section both have less than six people, while the largest units number over forty. Whenever size passes something like twenty-five, subdivisions become the loci of face-to-face interaction and interpersonal relations. This can be a source of confusion, and furthermore some larger units lose the valued atmosphere of small-group involvement. The bank's managers recognized the special problems of its large branches in this regard.

The ideal office, from the point of view of smooth relations, has ten to twenty people and an ascending distribution of ages within its hierarchy. Groups of ideal size and symmetry are not likely, given the varying work requirements and the numerous ways age-rank disjunctures may arise. In the bank, the youngest section chief (*kachō*) is thirty-eight, but many are in their late forties and early fifties. In the manufacturing company, section leaders are as young as thirty-three, and before age fifty they tend to be promoted to the position of department chief (*buchō*) without any change in their actual leadership responsibilities. Factory supervisors (*kantoku*), the highest blue-collar rank, are all over fifty. Whenever the leader of a work group is old, younger men are usually crucial in subordinate positions to

---

[5] At least this is true of the promotion system of the plastics manufacturer studied.

[6] The bank employs a large number of women (one-third of the total personnel), and offices almost invariably have a ratio of two men for each woman. The women are all unmarried and almost always young. They must leave employment upon marriage. Factory work groups, by comparison, have unmarried and married, old and young women, and there is a much greater variation in the proportion of women in each group, since work requirements vary greatly from unit to unit. Recently, the bank promoted three women above the lowest rank. This "first ever" move was made to boost morale among working women, but it did not result in women supervising men. The manufacturer, thirsting for inexpensive but steady workers in its rural plant, has taken to hiring local farm women on a half-day basis. They are mostly middle-aged and without previous factory experience.

keep close relations with the very young, lead the group's recreational activities, and generally serve as a bridge between the generations. This bridge is missing in some cases, and there the generation gap, so prominent in Japanese public culture, emerges full blown. Older men, furthermore, reportedly resent working under a younger man, but few such problems actually occur in either company. It seems that because the younger leaders are sensitive to the problem, they give less cause for resentment.

Group Competition.—Competition among the branches of the bank and the sales teams in the manufacturing company is regular and highly conscious, but it is carefully avoided among individuals within groups. Each branch of the bank is assigned a quota for new deposits, and it is well understood that the standard of success is relative to the record of other offices. Branches that do well are given public notice at awards ceremonies. Other classes of recognition (for effort, cooperation with other branches, enthusiasm, and office efficiency) are also distributed to the most successful branches, and awards given to deputy-group leaders (*dairi*) almost invariably reflect office-group performance. Only the lowest ranking employees appear to receive awards without particular consideration for the record of their offices. Although branch chiefs seldom receive individual rewards, any honors to their office are honors to them and strong indications that they are looked on with favor by those who decide promotions.

Neither company gives a commission or other direct-pay incentives. There are cases in the bank of individuals with good collection records actually giving credit for their deposits to others whose records are down for the month. Similarly, sales in the manufacturing company are handled totally on a team basis. The result is a situation in which (1) group leadership is emphasized, (2) leaders find themselves in competition with one another, and (3) leaders must rely on their followers for support and further promotion.

Morale is, thus, not simply a matter of the group, but also a question of loyalty to the group leader. Although the production side of the manufacturing firm does not lend itself to intergroup competition, the sense that motivation is in proportion to the group's enthusiasm for its leader still exists.

Morale.—Several general patterns of organization characterize the normal activities of office groups. These are manifested in the adjustments of the group to two basic requirements—work output and group maintenance.

The two patterns are a formal hierarchy and an informal circle. The arrangement of desks within any office reveals much of interest in this regard. Typically, the chief's desk is at the back-center of the office. His deputies' desks are on either side and a bit forward. From there, the desks of the rest of the staff are gathered in small infacing clusters that form a haphazard ring. Whether they become an actual circle is less relevant than the fact that the desks are arranged to face one another. The exact pattern is determined by the space available and the preference of the chief, but never will one see a section arranged so that people are looking at the backs of others in the same group. Even with this group orientation, the positions of importance are easily determined at a glance. The chief, at a slightly larger desk, is clearly the focus of the arrangement and his location permits him to take in all that transpires within his section in a glance.

The office at work generally follows the lines of hierarchy that link employees to deputies and deputies to chiefs, but there are qualities that distinguish it from an impersonal kind of office hierarchy. First, the general group relationship is expressed by the inward directioning of desks. Second, the character of vertical ties within the office is direct and close, for no barriers are set up between the leader and his followers.[7] There is a striking absence of any sense of individual isolation or of mechanical relationship in this pattern. The office is arranged to maximize the group sense, and interferences such as noise are not considered serious enough to justify separation or seclusion. Furthermore, authority does not require the creation of impersonal distance.

In factory situations, one finds the foreman moving about discussing problems, helping with a piece of work, talking to outsiders and instructing the inexperienced. With the exceptions of lunch and evening quitting times, break-taking and consultation are not formally regulated but determined rather by the flow of work. The intermediate ranks in most factory work groups share some supervisory responsibilities, but they also have regular tasks that limit their movement. General get-togethers for the communication of messages occur at a brief daily meeting before work starts, and more extended discussions of common problems take place after work, without overtime pay. The same is true for office meetings.

An informal circle is the common arrangement for relaxation and fellowship. Group morale and commitment and the intensification of individual friendships are sponsored through activities arranged to reduce the sense of rank, age, and even sex differences. The circle form stresses the fact of common membership. If the essence of the working order is hierarchy, the essence of the group principle is the circle. It is not difficult to perceive the interplay of the two in most office activities, for seldom is the pattern strictly linear or circular. Each activity and context calls forth slightly different arrangements, and the group finds it quite normal to shift from one to another. One characteristic of vital work groups, in fact, is their frequent but orderly shifts from one arrangement to another,

---

[7] Most offices have special side rooms for meetings with visitors, but only men of directorial rank in the bank and the president of the manufacturing company have private offices. The very high cost of office space in Japan could be cited as a reason for the minimal development of the individual office pattern, but this is far too simple an explanation given the emphasis on familiarity in work-group relations and the availability of side-room space.

permitting realization of the spectrum of possible official and personal relationships within the group.

It is, of course, imperative that hierarchy regulate the daily affairs of the office. The shifts to informal, group-centered activities require effort and time (and are most vulnerable to the debilitating effects of complex organization and patterns of modern living). The general expectation that group relations will be satisfying can produce a breakdown or loss of motive force in the working order unless discussion meetings, parties, and other maintenance gatherings are forthcoming. It is part of the leader's job to be sensitive to this general need and to meet it energetically.

The work of group maintenance, above all, requires time. Just working together in a hierarchy is not sufficient. For the group to coalesce and realize the potential for cooperation and team motivation, informal social activities after work and on weekends are needed. This is why administration and office leaders plan, conduct, and partially pay for a heavy schedule of group social affairs. These activities are ostensibly voluntary but virtually all members participate—some out of group loyalty, some out of interest, and a few with a sense of being coerced.

The emotional momentum and sense of group solidarity are largely cultivated during such social activities.[8] The annual calendar of office events typically includes two overnight trips (*ian ryokō*) at company expense, monthly Saturday afternoon recreation at company expense, and an average of six office parties held to celebrate one thing or another. In the manufacturing firm economic stringency has caused the company recently to stop paying for work-group trips, but most groups have continued to go at least once a year at private expense. Also for financial reasons that company has no monthly Saturday recreation program, believing that company-sponsored sports teams and summer camp-outs are the more effective means of satisfying its young people. Several basic differences between the two types of companies are indicated here. First, company prosperity and size are correlated with greater expenditure on such recreation and, second, the branch banking system offers no alternative to office groups as units for the organization of leisure, whereas a factory or main office readily accommodates sports teams, youth groups, and other alternatives. We should also note that hikes, after-work drinking expeditions, mahjong and bowling, involving some but not all people in an office (age and sex being the primary sources of separation), are frequent activities in both companies.

The drinking party is a particular and important part of many work-group social relations, although the blue-collar workers report its decline. The reasons for its influence can be appreciated from an analysis

---

[8] Such activities are common to most Japanese work groups. A teachers' group party is illustrated in John Singleton, *Nichū: A Japanese School* (New York: Holt, Rinehart and Winston, 1967).

of its dynamics and the expression of emotional participation involved. The first stage is marked with the serving of food, toasts by leaders, and much reciprocal pouring of drinks within the group. To keep up with the generosity of neighbors, one is constantly obliged to drain a glass or cup only to have it refilled by another waiting patiently with bottle in hand. The purpose is primarily to get everyone loosened up and happily inebriated, but the exchange of offerings and acceptances provides opportunities for the subtle expression of feelings of affection, admiration, and even repentance among persons who in normal circumstances are circumspect with one another. The gesture of filling another's glass is a convenient bridge across strained relationships. No one is forgotten. No one need pour his own drink. Support and attention for all revolves within the group, and a swaying, relaxed fellowship is created. This first stage prepares the atmosphere for the rounds of solo singing performances that often follow.

It is no easy thing to stand before a group and sing. Trembling hands, shaking voices, and nervous faces reveal the stress many suffer at the moment they are selected. The group responds sympathetically, however, with clapping, encouragement, and sometimes by actually joining in the song. When the ordeal is over, it is normal for the performer to experience a rush of relief and a feeling of gratitude to the others for their help. From that point he is deep into the group emotionally, for he has revealed his humanity and been accepted by the others; what occurs is much like a confession-forgiveness sequence. Each also acts as part of the group in helping other soloists through the ordeal and receiving them into the fellowship. With the solos over, restraint decreases noticeably, and the drinking has brought the men, at least, to a plateau of drunkenness. The process of uniting the group has ended, and there is no further obligation for full participation. Those in the mood are left to continue the party.

I estimate that in a week the bank office groups spend fifty-six hours working together and four to six hours socializing. Drinking parties do not occur more than every month or two, but they do represent pinnacles of emotional involvement that are not soon forgotten. The point that the work group does considerably more than simply share an office and a set of tasks is evident. This fact colors all that transpires within the hierarchical framework.

Decision-Making.—At the office level, discussions are another activity that serve maintenance functions. The manner of arriving at conclusions, however, varies greatly. The chief is empowered with the authority to make all decisions, and if he wishes he may maintain a strict order in which he alone decides. On the other hand, since the entire group is involved in the work of the office, the chief is free to submit decisions to discussion and, again if he wishes, to the rule (a rather flexible one) of group consensus. He may also encourage open discussion but decide the issue himself. There is no fixed procedure; among the crucial determinants are the nature of the issue, the type of group, and the personal style of a given leader. Group processes require considerable time, and to push for an early consensus or to fail to involve everyone can often lead to resentment and opposition. It is difficult to hurry discussion, and one simple rule influencing office decision-making is: the more urgent a decision, the more likely it will be made according to hierarchy. People favor group discussions, however, and have an expectation of participating in considerations of group affairs. This includes the joint consideration at the office level of new company-wide policies and directives. Opening an issue to general office discussion may take time, and may even reveal an embarrassing gap in opinions, yet the sense of unity and the identification with the solution that usually results make the practice worthwhile from a leader's point of view.

The subtle question of the delegation of decision-making power arises in this context. A chief, anxious to utilize the positive effects of group discussions without relinquishing his own control over major decisions, may hold numerous meetings but submit mainly issues of minor significance, retaining his authority over crucial matters. He may also choose to discuss his own decisions with the group. The alternative of introducing a question for the group's consideration only after being certain that his opinion will previal is also available. The conclusions may be foregone, but the fact that discussions have been held is very important since a chief is expected to share his opinions, ask for advice, and permit dissenting voices to emerge. His trust and respect for the others and his acknowledgment of the group's importance are symbolized by the discussion process.

These general considerations only begin to accommodate the range of variation. Some offices are characterized by a steady stream of meetings, others may have no more than one a month. What are the differences involved? In the factory, production units do not gather frequently for discussions. They are not free to leave their tasks, and unless the issue is serious, they do not feel inclined to stay around after work just to take up minor matters. For the most part the unit leader consults with his men individually, and sometimes there are huddles of three or four men over some problem. Routine and minor adjustment characterize the situation, and there is little for group consideration except when new production goals or the Zero Defect program are discussed. At the opposite extreme are design engineer teams, sales teams, and groups empowered to formulate new programs. Meetings are frequent, open, and animated with leaders taking rather nonassertive roles, but always formulating the conclusions. Offices characterized by a high degree of routine, such as accounting, meet less frequently.

The degree to which central authority delegates decision-making power to groups is another crucial matter. Characteristic of the management of both companies is the practice of assigning specific goals and expecting the work groups to develop the means to achieve them. Obviously, groups with established routines will need many meetings only when the goals assigned create a crisis because the routines must be overhauled or new ones established. In the factory it is notable that blue-collar groups are strongly inclined to regard the established procedures of production as their domain. The resident engineers do not have control over regular production, and supervisors (men at the top of the blue-collar ladder) are given the time and latitude to solve problems in conjunction with their subordinates that would quickly draw intervention from higher (outside) authority in American plants. This is most true of units using techniques and equipment of long standing, since experience has led to mastery. In the case of new forms of production, however, engineers are much in evidence. While such considerations help explain the degree of variation in small-group autonomy, the general rule that goals come from above, implementation from groups below, remains characteristic.

I should add that stagnation and demoralization can result from a lack of direction and encouragement from managers (usually the department chiefs) intermediate in the hierarchy between the work group and the general goal-setting top level. What the group-level leader needs is a guarantee that his group's actions will be accepted, supported, and brought into coordination with the total organization. Forceful middle managers are those who form close personal relations with group leaders below them and encourage them to dynamic action.

Handling Deviance.—Turning back to the internal processes typical of small groups, we should consider briefly the way the group responds to deviance. Actions at variance with the expected and required behavior within the group seldom if ever take the form of open confrontation with authority or a refusal to perform required work. Numerous factors, including the ethic of cooperation and the general restraint of expression in Japan, inhibit direct confrontations in the office. Deviance and opposition take more private and qualified yet discernible forms, and the response of the rest of the group to even mild nonconformity is worth considering.

Deviation is most often expressed by withdrawal from participation in the group and with its leader. The individual who is unhappy or in strong disagreement, but who cannot express these feelings, is likely to set himself at odds with group norms in areas of behavior where matters of personal preference and the standards of the group intersect. Some typical examples would be avoiding office social activities, excessive make-up, drinking too much, joining a leftist youth group, and remaining silent during group discussions. These kinds of actions disturb the sense of unity, but cannot be labeled insubordination and summarily dealt with. They are conventional symbols of dissatisfaction and isolation from the group. It is true that some people quit in protest against a group or its leader, but to do so without a prospective job can be a form of career suicide, especially for white-collar men. Such eventualities are avoided by restraint and a sensitivity to the nuance of individual participation.

Conformity and full participation are, in one sense, offerings individuals make to the common existence. They should not be forced from them. The individual right to disagree and criticize through acts of nonparticipation is recognized, and the group must attend sympathetically to such indications of a problem. Often acts of "resistance" (*teikō*) to the group or its leader are understood as analogous to the rebellious behavior of children toward their families, particularly when hurt feelings rather than principles are at the heart of the matter. The individual's natural state of existence is within some group, it is assumed, and resistance is easily interpreted as a sign of unhappiness and an indirect expression of personal need, which should be answered with sympathy and special attention that create a sense of belonging. The group's members, especially its leaders, experience considerable irritation to be sure, but these reactions should and usually are repressed. Understanding and tact are required, reminiscent of the general expectation that parents will be flexible and tolerant in the face of their children's recalcitrance. That order and participation begin with individual feelings and cannot be forced through rules and punishments is the crucial assumption.

What about difficult individuals, we might ask? How does the group deal with the contentious, the overly ambitious, the lazy, and other similar types? This question is of interest primarily because personalities are seldom typed this way in small group contexts. Actions that would fit such categories are not absent, but the practice of writing people off into immutable character boxes is avoided, and in its place one finds a faith in the possibilities of group socialization to smooth rough edges. Much of the most effective smoothing occurs as part of senior-junior relationships, and the group's informal social activities offer further opportunities to generate a cooperative spirit in the less well adjusted. Even so, there are people who come to be recognized as permanently difficult, and the solution is to place them in isolated jobs (company librarian, warehouse attendant, truck driver, and so on) that effectively separate them from work groups even though they remain attached to one or another group for formal purposes. Rarely is a troublesome person treated with anything but sympathy and constraint, and this in turn undoubtedly generates constraint and cooperation from most potentially difficult people. The calm surface of mutuality, however, can be accompanied by much hidden disenchantment and resentment.

When most of the group object to their chief, it is likely that complaints will find channels to higher authority, particularly the personnel department. In the bank such a leader is likely to be transferred, but in the much smaller manufacturing firm such shifts are more difficult, and attempts to change the leader's ways is the likely outcome. In either case, quitting or the threat of it from established employees is a certain spur for the reconsideration of a group's situation by management.

Short of such extremes, it is usually necessary to live with a degree of problems, and the chances of redemption often hinge on the departure of those who do not fit in, or the arrival of a new chief or deputy able to draw the office back together. Even so, efforts to engineer cooperation and full participation, through focusing increased attention and affection on those withholding themselves from group life, are highly predictable. The effectiveness of these methods is not as predictable, however, partly because of the very fact that they are expected. Finally, it is my impression that the white-collar world is less likely to show the tension of work relations than the blue-collar, perhaps because open hostility is even more inappropriate.

SUPERIOR-SUBORDINATE RELATIONS

Employees in both companies share a vocabulary of labels for work place relationships, and while their typology is not fully discreet, these labels do mark the basic starting place for the distinctions that constitute the interpersonal world. As such they deserve enumeration and clarification, but we should be forewarned that like most typologies, they only begin to sort out the situation.

As in most organizations the most crucial face-to-face relationship is the one between a superior and subordinate who work together. In Japanese company organization these are regularly employees of different rank who are assigned to the same work unit.

Because of seniority in promotion, it is highly likely that a superior will be older. No man in either company had a woman superior, and only a small percentage of women had another woman as her superior. Two terms, *uwayaku* and *jōshi,* refer to superior or boss, and the term *buka* refers to subordinates. The characters for "above" and "below" are used to write these words, indications of the clarity of the hierarchical order involved. When addressing one another, subordinates and superiors have a different set of terms. One may address his boss using either his family name (plus the suffix *san*) or his rank (for example, *kachō*). The superior has the option of using the subordinate's family name suffixed by *san* or the more intimate *kun*. (Only once have I ever heard a woman subordinate addressed with *kun,* however.) While details of address may seem rather mundane, they provide an outline of some of the basic dimensions of the relationship. It shows that hierarchy is a constant in both address and reference and that the option of openly expressing intimacy is given only to the superior. The mutual use of family name (plus *san*) offers an egalitarian form of address that bank policy urges, but in practice both official titles for addressing superiors and *kun* for male subordinates is often preferred. People say there is more flavor and a sense of connectedness to these expressions. While women may be addressed familiarly by their first names, the widespread use of the intimate *kun* for male subordinates reflects the centrality of male-male relationships in business organization. Male-female relationships are essentially appendages to a central core of hierarchical male ties.

Much of this will not seem particularly unfamiliar to Americans with experience in complex organizations. Clearly hierarchy, degrees of intimacy, and sex distinctions are part of our own systems of address and reference. Our language, however, provides greater flexibility for the establishment of degrees of intimacy and equality (such as the use of first names or initials), and we may obscure hierarchy altogether by using first names to address superiors. .Sense of hierarchy is more constant in Japanese.

One's boss may or may not be personally close. It is his official position alone that makes him a *uwayaku* or *jōshi,* and this becomes clear when we contrast the superior-subordinate dyad with another relationship, the *senpai-kōhai* (senior-junior) relationship that is also hierarchical but centered on interpersonal involvement. While *senpai* often means any person senior in age, it is common in a company or other specific organizational context to use the word to refer to (and occasionally address) one or a few older people who are especially close and supportive. Ideally, one's superior in the official hierarchy is close and supportive ("like a father or older brother"), but for a variety of reasons, the ideal is generally hard to realize. It is, therefore, necessary to distinguish the official roles of superior and subordinate from the interpersonal *senpai-kōhai* relationship even though both are hierarchical and both can, and ideally should, overlap. The distinction is crucial to any analysis of the nature of authority in face-to-face relations in Japanese organization.

Before discussing authority, however, it will be useful to examine the senior-junior relationship, for it provides an ideal model for its official counterpart.[9] To begin, the Japanese have a comparatively positive attitude toward hierarchical relations involving explicit age differences. They do not assume that hierarchy precludes the opportunity for intimacy. The term for senior, *senpai,* is a compound of two characters: the first meaning before or ahead, and the second meaning companion. A *senpai* is understood to be a person who proceeds or leads with the

---

[9] There is much more to be said about *senpai-kōhai* relations in Japanese companies. For further information and discussion, see Cole, *Japanese Blue Collar,* Nakane, *Japanese Society,* and Rohlen, *For Harmony and Strength.* It is worth noting that (1) most relations of this sort are significant while the younger man is still unmarried, (2) that it serves important socialization functions, and (3) that it is near universal for young men in their late teens and early twenties but of greatly diminished importance afterwards, except as the basic relationship within the cliques that exist at the managerial level. The great majority of *senpai-kōhai* ties among young men derive from working together, living in dorms together, or playing on a sports team together. The relationship among older men is based more on mutual career interests and/or mutual recognition of ability.

implication that those who follow are his companions in the same pursuit, career, or institution. *Kōhai,* literally "companion that is behind," expresses the other half of the relationship. The complete image created by the characters is one of "friends," one ahead and the other behind, passing along the same path of endeavor.

While all those who are older in a company are, in a general sense, seniors, the term is used most often to refer to one or a few specific older individuals of the same sex who are particularly close and protective. A senior, however, may have more than a few juniors—one of a number of interesting correspondences between this relationship and that of parent and child. Among the reasons for the division along sex lines is the implied comradeship between senior and junior, a form of comradeship that does not easily cross the boundaries of sex.

The basic characteristics of the relationship are:

1. The senior is older than his junior, has worked longer for the company, and is in a position of relative power and security. This position enables the senior to assist the junior.

2. The senior is beneficially disposed toward the junior, and befriends him.

3. The junior accepts the friendship and assistance of the senior.

4. These acts and related feelings are the basis of the relationship. There is no explicit agreement.

5. Ideally, the junior feels gratitude to the senior for his beneficence, and this feeling is accompanied by a desire on the part of the senior to become a good *senpai* for those younger.

The similarities between this and parent-child and older-younger sibling relationships are more than coincidental. It appears that family relationships provide the underlying model for the senior-junior pattern. Interviewees occasionally stated that "seniors are like older brothers"—a revealing analogy, particularly if we examine the ideology of the Japanese family. First, interdependency and continuity are central to the family ideal. Second, the emphasis on continuity translates into gratitude toward past generations and obligations to assist future ones. Third, affection and hierarchy are understood as mutually reinforcing rather than contradictory. Last, the dependency of the younger, weaker party is not only accepted, it is the focal point of the relationship. These are basic elements in one major Japanese code of interpersonal relations, which make seemingly dissimilar situations and involvements, such as a family and an office group, in essence quite comparable. Because of this code, company senior-junior relationships receive powerful reinforcement from the patterns of interpersonal relations throughout the society since all repeat the same basic message.

The kind of assistance expected of a senior varies greatly. Not only will he advise, console, and protect his junior, but like a good older brother, he is also likely to be a strict judge of performance and a stern task master. A good senior is one who fosters the growth and adjustment of his junior with a strong mix of encouragement and criticism, all in the context of a close friendship. Socialization of young men into the company is primarily accomplished within this and the larger work group contexts.

The pattern describes an image of one kind of ideal working relationship, one that is secure, beneficial, reciprocal, and selfless to a degree. The ideal of close involvement between older and younger, experienced and less experienced, more established and less established is often applied to the relationship of superior and subordinate in the official system of organizational roles. Company leaders, for example, are occasionally referred to as *senpai* in company publications. The paternal and familistic philosophies (*onjō shugi* and *kazokuteki keiei*) espoused by most companies also suggest that leadership should be as sympathetic, protective, and unselfish as good *senpai*. While clearly the ideal may go unrealized, it does establish a set of expectations about proper leader and follower conduct.

Returning to the question of authority in the superior-subordinate relationship, we should note that legalism (such things as explicit rights and duties) is not characteristic of official hierarchical relations in Japan. Instead, short of leaving the organization entirely, a subordinate has no recourse for contending directly with his superior. Open argument with him, refusal to obey orders, other forms of "insubordination," and open appeal to higher authority are all possibilities so rare in the Japanese context that they never occurred during my observations. There are no rules that would condone or permit such actions. People with exceptionally strong grievances usually hide them behind a screen of silence until they can leave the organization or the authority of their superior entirely. Thus, the superior has absolute authority, but without legal basis. Like parental authority, it derives from general custom and the compliance of subordinates. In the companies I studied, no union power or set of company rules stand between a superior and his ability to exercise authority. Nor are there any reports of dramatic scenes of inflamed passion or righteous resistance to an unfair boss. The only times such overt expressions occur is when union and management adopt recalcitrant and hostile stands toward each other; at this juncture the company is likely to cease existence in organizational terms. Such a rare occurrence underlies the fact that in face-to-face relations Japanese are, by Western standards, unused to and unable to cope with open expressions of resistance to authority.

In another equally real sense, however, the superior finds his authority strongly limited by the general expectation that he will look after the best interests of those who work below him—that he will be their guardian or patron in the senior-junior model.

It would be erroneous, however, to view Japanese superiors either as pseudo-parents or as extraordinary and unlimited tyrants. These two extremes, although possible, are hardly ever realized in actuality. Confusion does arise about the nature of authority in instances of trouble, since the expectations of obedience and paternal regard can become separate and opposing interpretations in times of discord.

The possibilities inherent in the Japanese superior-subordinate situation are of even greater complexity. On the one hand, there is a strong tradition, particularly emphasized in the military heritage, for a very strict form of order and discipline, and it is not unusual to come across scenes in Japanese offices highly reminiscent of the most thoroughgoing military procedure. At other times, however, one may find leaders and their followers gaily drunk together after work, staggering arm-in-arm down some back alley. This is part of a tradition of co-worker camaraderie. Superiors seldom hesitate to ask subordinates to do unpaid overtime work (at least in the white-collar world), yet it is equally common to find them involved in helping a subordinate with a private problem at considerable personal sacrifice. Such seemingly contradictory patterns are actually characteristic of common themes such as group involvement, an emphasis on feeling, and little capacity to separate the people from their roles.[10] Definitions of what is proper vary with the people involved and the context, not with some contracted or administrative formula. The energetic, warm leader creates for himself great power, whereas the opposite commands no more than a mechanical authority based on his position alone. In Japanese companies, loyalty to an immediate leader is obviously a crucial aspect in the flux of motivational levels. The more important group motivation is to accomplish the work at hand, the more important leadership becomes.

It is ironic, then, that companies (on years of service considerations) regularly place many men in group leadership positions who lack the capacity to motivate their followers in the highly personal manner required. In such cases, the ideal model, with its heavy demand for personal involvement, actually serves to generate disappointment and resentment among subordinates. Companies have a particular dilemma in this regard since they consciously seek the benefits of group-ordered work, yet are bound by other factors to retain a promotion system based on considerations other than leadership capacity.[11] High group morale is hard to produce and impossible to guarantee in large organizations, and

---

[10] Pelzel asserts this view when he writes, "I argue that no attention is in fact paid to what may be called the social personality of the individual member. It is the emotional aspects of the personality that are instead given outlet in the procedures of the Japanese small group, and a wealth of standard behavior patterns can only be interpreted in this light." See Pelzel, "Japanese Kinship," p. 247. Nakane's emphasis on the emotional quality of group relations is also a closely allied perspective. See Nakane, *Japanese Society*. In Japanese the central concept and value of *wa* (translated as "harmony" but better grasped as teamwork, high morale, and general group vitality) emphasizes this same quality, particularly as it is coincidentally the group's internal ambition and the means to accomplish its external goals.

[11] I have in mind the factors of seniority and promotion based on technical skill in particular.

this fact has encouraged Japanese companies to establish supplementary efforts of a different kind. Increased emphasis on ability in promotions, on character-building programs, and on penalties for poor performance are all aimed at the individual rather than the group.[12] These attempts, although minor, are indications of management impatience with the inadequacies of the group-motivation approach.

MODERN OBSTACLES TO THE WORK-GROUP IDEAL

The effects of large-scale organization and modern life styles on the effort to establish satisfactory work-group relations can be pointed out, but to measure their impact requires historical and comparative frameworks beyond the scope of this paper. Among the most significant organizational constraints to note are the absence of any work-group-level control over recruitment and promotion.[13] Transfers may be initiated by problems in office or factory groups, but no group leader has much power over who will be assigned to his unit. The personnel department in the manufacturing firm does on occasion attempt to place factory workers with an eye to special connections (such as kinship, regional affiliation, and personal obligation), but this practice is very rare for white-collar work groups and, in fact, requests by section leaders for individuals are generally discouraged. Since promotion is presently governed by seniority considerations, some are given leadership positions for which they are unsuited. The fact that the rank of section leader is a meaningful career goal, a reward for service, and a mark of status complicates the problem of establishing greater coherence between the work group and the promotion system.

Personnel turnover is another source of work-group problems. Transfers are greatest in the bank with its many branches, less frequent for office workers in the manufacturing firm, and almost negligible (except on a voluntary basis) for blue-collar workers.[14] Although the men in the bank

---

[12] On promotions and penalties, see M. Y. Yoshino, *Japan's Managerial System* (Cambridge, Mass.: MIT Press, 1968), pp. 225–253; and Rohlen, *For Harmony and Strength*. For a discussion of a company character-building program, see Thomas P. Rohlen, "Spiritual Education in a Japanese Bank," *American Anthropologist* 35.5 (1973): 1542–1562.

[13] The account of the role of foreman labor bosses in early factories offered in Mikio Sumiya, *Social Impact of Industrialization in Japan* (Tokyo: Japanese Commission for UNESCO, 1963), describes them as having the power to recruit for and promote within their own work group. The control of these functions by management came after World War I. It would appear that one legacy of this early work-group autonomy is the continuing view that someone at the "foreman" level is more the workers' than the management's man. The plant engineer's general reluctance to interfere with production groups might also derive partly from these early circumstances.

[14] The plastics firm has recently opened a new factory in a rural prefecture, and the lack of private housing suitable for city families coupled with the long commuting time from suitable housing has made the move to a rural area rather unpopular, despite the much improved facilities, lovely scenery, and lack of pollution. Bachelor men at the new plant, housed in dormitories, complain of the absence of city amusements. All of this is instructive in the light of the Tanaka government's plan to move industry to the hinterlands as a solution to the devastating urban pollution and congestion.

retain a long association with their company, their participation in any particular office group is interrupted by periodic transfer. We can estimate an annual turnover in any office of 15 percent, and the bank's personnel department offers the additional information that the average length of time spent in an office is 3.75 years. Transfers involving women seldom occur and only when it is possible for them to commute from home to a different office. In the manufacturing firm, transfer rates in general are much lower, with only salesmen being shifted at approximately the same rate as men in the bank.

Thus continuity, so characteristic of a man's relationship with his company, is not characteristic of office work groups, an interesting point regarding the nature of Japanese organization.

Office groups are also seriously affected by the high turnover rate of women who leave to marry. One in four (in both companies) leave each year for this reason. For male blue-collar groups, quitting and mid-career entrance (a few each year among three hundred factory workers) are the major sources of change. In one factory the quitting rate for young people in their first five years of work was almost 50 percent and in the other 30 percent. We must conclude that the small work group in modern companies does not resemble the traditional family, the village, or the small commercial enterprise in this respect. The ideals and procedures may be the same, but the depth of acquaintanceship and involvement are certainly affected by the greater turnover. The intense interest in creating good group relations shown by the bank is partly explained by its high rate of transfer, just as the manufacturing company's emphasis on youth-oriented leisure activities is best explained as a response to the high turnover rate among its new, young workers.

The size of office and factory groups is not determined by considerations of group dynamics, but by the work load and other external factors. In consequence, many groups are too big to be organized on a small-group model. Attempts at subgroup arrangements are seldom satisfactory since the lines of cooperation in work cannot be easily aligned with boundaries established by informal involvement.

Private living patterns also have considerable impact on work-group relations. Dormitories, for example, draw residence and work together, whereas dispersed private housing tends to reduce the time co-workers interact, particularly if commuting time is great.[15] The worker's degree of involvement with social ties outside the company (such as family, neighborhood, and voluntary associations), as well as the strength of his

---

[15] For descriptions of company dormitories, see Rohlen, *For Harmony and Strength*, and Cole, *Japanese Blue Collar*. For descriptions of the living patterns of married white-collar workers, see Ezra F. Vogel, *Japan's New Middle Class* (Berkeley and Los Angeles: University of California Press, 1965); Rohlen, *For Harmony and Strength*; and Christie W. Kiefer, "Personality and Social Change in a Japanese *Danchi*" (Ph.D. dissertation, University of California, Berkeley, 1970).

desire for private as opposed to company-oriented leisure, weigh in the final balance of after-work time allocation, and this in turn has much to do with the capacity of work groups to hold lengthy discussions, enjoy parties and otherwise maintain close personal involvement.

Both companies, while not intending to increase family-type company housing, still emphasize dormitories for unmarried employees and have recently built new ones. Dormitory life is a major source of friendship for many young people (only for men in the bank, but for both men and women in the factories). Wherever dormitory social life is dormant, there is the complaint that modern salaries have provided luxury which in turn has caused young people to separate socially. Individual rooms, private stereos and TVs, the independence of a private automobile, and other similar factors all appear to have reduced the inclination or opportunity for communal forms of leisure. Dating, clearly on the increase, also has this effect. Where dormitory life is active, on the other hand, young people prefer it to socializing with older co-workers. Activities popular with the young such as sports, camping, hiking, bowling, and weekend travel are all forms of relaxation in which older people have difficulty participating. There is, in short, a trend toward more age-segmented after-work leisure, and while this is often encouraged by management because it satisfies the young, it also points to the widening gap between the ages in work-group situations. The bank has gone further than simply recognizing the trend. It has recently created formal associations for its unmarried men and women.

We need to remind ourselves that although Japanese company people are remarkably company oriented by contemporary Western standards, modern living is eroding this involvement at what managers see (using the criteria of the Japanese work-group tradition and the present ideal) as an alarming rate. In the two companies studied, for example, it was no longer shocking to hear of a group leader so much absorbed in his own private affairs that his after-hours socializing with co-workers had become minimal. For workers, marriage and family, while by no means Western in character, have increased in significance, particularly with the growth of family-oriented leisure. Furthermore, people with very long commuting times, new homes or an unusual interest in outside affairs or hobbies— matters that are regarded as modern trends—find it hard to give time to work-group relations. Watching television, the most mundane of these, has for some become a nighttime preoccupation.

The separation of young and old is another common topic everywhere, and both ends of the spectrum comment on how hard it is to understand and talk frankly with the other. There is no better way of measuring the solidarity of a work group than to ask about the relationship among the generations. Only where the group is well knit and the leader personally involved does the age gap seem inconsequential. Such cases are certainly in the minority, particularly among factory workers, but they do illustrate the fact (and hope) that when successful the work group has considerable potential to integrate young and old regardless of their very different experiences, attitudes, and life styles.

Perhaps the most debilitating of all on work-group relations is the general decrease in identification with and enthusiasm for company and work, something that apparently derives from both the scale of organization and the nature of contemporary public culture. While there are employees of all ages thoroughly involved in their work, there are many who mention as reasons for uninvolvement such things as the distance between themselves and top management, the lack of a sense of common purpose, the attractiveness of private forms of leisure, and their sense of a conflict of interest in company-employee relations.[16] Alienation may not be nearly as strong in Japan as in America, but it is present and does affect the morale of work groups. There is no easy way to gauge its general increase, but the increased company-to-company movement of young blue-collar workers is a strong signal. On the other hand, many of the young people most expressive of a modern sense of alienation are likely to adopt a different, more accepting stand with age. Finally, it is well to remember that any general organizational arrangement can tolerate a good deal of dissatisfaction, particularly if it is rarely expressed openly as in the Japanese case.[17]

WORK-GROUP DYNAMICS

My case material indicates, then, that solidarity in work groups is something to be achieved and that, compared to the ideal, groups are likely to be viewed as imperfect. Basic understandings and values create a

---

[16] There are literally hundreds of opinion surveys that document the general shift in attitudes (particularly among the young) away from conscious preference for company and work-oriented lives. Kiefer reports that while overtly denying any special company loyalty, the behavior of white-collar workers in the apartment building (*danchi*) he studied actually expressed deep involvement with their companies and work groups. See Kiefer, "Personality and Social Change," p. 194. Undoubtedly, at the individual level the number of potentially contradictory layers of opinion, feeling, and unconscious assumption are great enough to require a very cautious use of any single expression (for example, to a questionnaire, a TAT, a Rorschach or an interviewer's question) as representative of the respondents' actual or predictable behavior.

[17] Japan's recent economic contraction (late 1973 on) will greatly affect the trends discussed in the preceding paragraphs. Those companies that suffer the greatest setbacks will undoubtedly witness considerable strife and alienation as reorganization of personnel policies, lay-offs and the like occur, however the long-term effects of an economic retrenchment are likely to reinforce the importance of (1) an individual's tie to a particular company, and (2) the perception that company and employee interests are fundamentally allied. This will come through the general contraction of available jobs, the greater relative success of some companies, and the decrease in voluntary labor mobility, particularly among younger workers. All of these shifts will serve to arrest and perhaps even reverse some of the trends toward greater individual autonomy just discussed, depending, of course, on the duration of the economic problems. Furthermore, a decrease in youthful alienation and mobility will be accompanied by less company emphasis on youth-oriented activities and an increase in worker concern with good personal relations with their seniors and superiors. In other words, jobs and good companies will replace workers (especially young ones) as the scarce commodity.

dimension of concern that not only points to goals, but also highlights existing inadequacies. Acknowledging the various qualities of small groups to be matters of degree compared with a set of ideals, creates the basis for examining the dynamics of the situation in terms of shifting conditions within the group. When the sense of solidarity is down, for example, hierarchy is less agreeable and more apparent. The reverse is also true. Solidarity itself is essentially a subjective quality or mood that arises primarily from the emotional aspects of the group, particularly the relationship between the group leader and his subordinates. When things go well, when the leader is followed out of affection as well as because of his formal position, the internal structure of the group appears quite useful and proper. The three general factors of positive emotion toward the leader, solidarity, and structure are interrelated in essentially the following manner: (a) positive emotion and working solidarity are mutually beneficial, (b) structure as a means of ordering work may also contribute positively, but (c) when structure comes to stand for separation and difference, then it is viewed negatively. To prevent the ever-present hierarchy from becoming onerous the group has recourse to activities of the circle kind. The leader's style and energy are also crucial, particularly as he must be able to create a mood of respect and fellowship.

The most poignant source of stress in this situation is the requirements of work itself. Pelzel is perfectly justified in underlining the importance of the task orientation of Japanese groups.[18] Without a common task, office and factory groups would have nothing to justify their existence, and their enjoyment of one another informally would seem frivolous. Yet, it is the demands for greater production, the problems of sharing the work, and the responsibility and fatigue of strenuous effort that most tax the emotional ties and the sense of mutuality within office and factory groups. This pressure falls particularly on the chief, for he faces the demands and criticisms of top management.

It is interesting to note the response of employees in the bank to the characterization of their organizational life in terms emphasizing their close personal relations and sense of unity. These, they say, are qualities a foreigner (using a cross-cultural perspective) might choose to emphasize, but such a description ignores the daily problems and inadequacies of Japanese organization. When the problems are discussed, however, comments from the same people imply that models of close relations and solidarity do exist. Outstanding groups are the ones with good working relations, and they provide standards for comparison. Cross-cultural perspectives, we may conclude, are significant precisely because they highlight a particular conceptual framework and a set of ideal models, and therefore provide a perspective of reality that will deal adequately with the thought-action dynamics in real problem-filled situations.

---

[18] Pelzel, "Japanese Kinship."

The question of authority is a central issue in any cross-cultural comparison of bureaucratic organizations. Recently Crozier, citing cultural differences as significant, has suggested how impersonal authority problems in French bureaucracy are closely related to various themes and patterns of French culture.[19] Face-to-face dependency and warm primary group relations in work are difficult for the French, and the result is a high degree of impersonality. Crozier's general approach, one that views the response to authority as varying with such things as dependency, is of special interest in the light of the fact that Japanese work groups seem so different from the French.

The acceptance of dependency (with limits) is a definite part of successful work relationships in Japan, and there is much evidence that dependency is very often regarded as a positive aspect of social relations.[20] But dependency does not automatically lead to the "acceptance of most arbitrary discretion," another of Crozier's preconditions for bureaucratic success.[21] We have seen that work-group discussions and situations of informal intimacy are regular aspects of the program designed to maintain participation in the group and acceptance of its leader's prerogatives. Without such efforts to maintain a sense of unity, the group ideal of mutual interest would soon disappear. For the office leader, the ability to be arbitrary one moment depends greatly on his readiness to be responsive to the group the moment before and the moment after. This shifting of emphasis, which serves to preserve the acceptance of leadership and trust mentioned by Crozier, is supported by official company policies and is therefore institutionalized and expected to a large degree.

Although Japanese procedures indicate much the same authority/compliance complex discussed by Bernard (1938) and those after him, the actual practices of American and Japanese work groups are quite different.[22] For the Japanese, the procedures of discussion and participation are institutionalized, office groups are far more sensitive to the process of inclusion, and their leaders are far more inherently equipped to manage

[19] Michel Crozier, The Bureaucratic Phenomenon (Chicago: University of Chicago Press, 1964).

[20] For discussions of dependency from a variety of perspectives, see Doi Takeo, Amae no kōzō [The structure of dependency] (Tokyo: Kōbundō, 1970); William Caudill, "Around-the-Clock Patient Care in Japanese Psychiatric Hospitals: The Role of the Tsukisoi," American Sociological Review 26.2 (1961): 204–214; William Caudill and David W. Plath, "Who Sleeps by Whom? Parent-Child Involvement in Urban Japanese Families," Psychiatry 29.4 (1966): 344–366; William Caudill and Helen Weinstein, "Maternal Care and Infant Behavior in Japan and America," Psychiatry 32.1 (1969): 12–43; Kimura Bin, Hito to hito no aida [Between person and person] (Tokyo: Kōbundō, 1972); and Ezra F. Vogel and Suzanne H. Vogel, "Family Security, Personal Immaturity, and Emotional Health in a Japanese Family," Marriage and Family Living 23 (1961): 161–166.

[21] Crozier uses dependency in a less psychological and more organizational sense, making it necessary to discuss the acceptance of authority as the intersection of psychological predispositions and the basic arrangement of small-group interaction. See Crozier, The Bureaucratic Phenomenon.

[22] Chester I. Bernard, The Functions of the Executive (Cambridge, Mass.: Harvard University Press, 1938).

this form of direction.[23] In fact, the terms for authority (*ken'i* and *kenryoku*) are not used in everyday descriptions of group dynamics. Acceptance (*nattoku*), participation (*sanka*), resistance, and opposition (*hantai*) are the key dimensions, and neither impersonal rules nor formal role definitions are of much significance in adjusting behavior from the negative to the positive sides of these dimensions. Instead, the leader's virtue, his concern for others, and the general esprit within the group are the most effective means to gain individual acceptance and participation. Involvement and trust, once established, do indeed permit considerable "arbitrary discretion." Pelzel attributes essentially the same qualities to Japanese household groups. He writes:

The tolerance for authoritarianism is perhaps higher in the Japanese than in many Western or Chinese situations, but in Japan no head can expect well-motivated action on any decision that has not been deliberately accepted by members who have the right by interest or competence to be heard.[24]

In Weber's terms, Japanese work groups might appear to be highly traditional, but in Crozier's they are remarkable examples of the reinforcement of bureaucratic requirements by the psychological predispositions and small-group patterns of the parent culture.

CONSEQUENCES OF WORK GROUPS
FOR THE LARGER ORGANIZATION

The general nature of work groups is acknowledged by the treatment they receive from above. We have already noted the common practices of encouraging competition between groups and of judging section chiefs according to their group's performance with the result that rivalry is often strong among men of that rank. A team form of motivation is heavily relied on, even in cases where the lack of comparability makes intergroup competition impossible. This complex has the following general correspondences with the larger organizational setup:

1. The role of group leader has special significance: its status is high; it is crucial to most operations, particularly nonroutine ones; and careers are either made or destroyed primarily at this level.

2. Individual forms of reward, especially immediate ones, do not receive

---

[23] Our everyday understanding of authority assumes that (1) close personal involvement undermines the latitude to make hard decisions about personnel, and (2) familiarity drains respect and status from leadership positions. In Japanese companies the first is a problem, but the second is not. Since close personal involvement is virtually built into the work-group hierarchy, special means are necessary to maintain discipline. All crucial personnel decisions are made in the personnel department far removed from the work-group situation. Furthermore, group leaders often ask intermediaries (usually the *senpai* of troublesome or recalcitrant group members) to privately caution others. In other words, the power of the most intimate ties, usually those between *senpai-kōhai*, are brought to bear on cases we would label disciplinary.

[24] Pelzel, "Japanese Kinship," p. 246.

strong emphasis by American standards in the salary and promotion systems.

3. It is difficult to organize activities between work groups without direction from a higher authority.

Work groups, because they are recognized as independent social entities, are allowed considerable autonomy in the Japanese company system.[25] Experts are not utilized to solve operational problems for specific groups; this would be regarded as outside interference and would undermine morale and leadership. The bank does have an inspection team, which visits each branch once every few years, and engineers are called in to solve technical problems in the factory, but basically the work group has full latitude to handle its own daily affairs. If it does not do this well, a new leader is likely. Even central administration policies may not have a binding force on the conduct of groups. In the bank, for example, most offices still were ignoring the 5:30 P.M. quitting-time policy one year after it was made the official rule for Wednesdays. On such matters, work-group compliance is encouraged, but not forced. If the issue has great overall concern or less consequence to the internal conduct of the group, however, central authority can be thorough and swift. Management watches the performance of work groups with a keen eye, but it is reluctant to interfere unless quite necessary. Finally, the sense of domain and the expectation of discussion and consensus in small groups means that much of any effort to change work methods must be directed at gaining the voluntary participation of each group. The manufacturing firm, for example, instituted a "Zero Defect" program only after each factory section had reviewed and endorsed it. Similarly, the bank management frequently calls for branch-level discussion of company problems. New programs are often initiated at a ceremony attended by representatives of each office group.

Neither company has a written set of rules defining the decision-making procedures for any level. Obviously, the hierarchy of ranks and the establishment of central authority serve these purposes to a large degree; but even at the highest levels, group discussion and consensus are acknowledged, although their significance varies with the situation and the arrangement of power at the top.

Above the president in the formal organization of companies is the board of directors, a group that contains the company's top executives. They meet often and are ostensibly the small group that runs the company.[26] Other meetings to discuss, to decide, or to recommend

---

[25] There are fascinating parallels between this autonomy and the autonomy from direct governmental control of villages in the Tokugawa period. See Kurt Steiner, *Local Government in Japan* (Palo Alto: Stanford University Press, 1965, pp. 9–18.

[26] The board of directors may or may not be the locus of power. In "one-man companies" the group is usually a rubber stamp for the policies of the president or chairman, and in many companies including those divided by factions, decision-making can be located in

characterize the intermediate levels of organization above the work group. Branch chiefs, section chiefs, and managing directors' groups meet frequently, usually on a weekly basis. These middle-level meetings rarely decide issues, but they are important for the purposes of creating general acceptance of policies made above, for recommending new policies, and for improving lateral coordination and cooperation. While I do not possess sufficient material to satisfactorily discuss the variable procedures actually involved in decision-making above the office-group level, it is evident that even at the top, many of the group procedures and many of the same alternatives in decision-making patterns that characterize low-level work groups characterize the interplay of leadership and group discussion within the realm of management.

A final way the large organization and the work group are related is through the influence of the ideals of small-group conduct on the manner of administering the entire company. The image of a company comprised of people dedicated to the same goals, personally involved, and united by interest and common spirit underlies company ideology. Executives, rather than consciously concocting such an image, tend to regard it as an assumed goal of any company and any group of employees, and numerous events, policies, and statements of regret about contrary tendencies all point to the underlying model of the company as a small group.

The fascination here is the obvious fact that any organization over a certain small size will find it exceptionally difficult to preserve a sense of personal, emotional connectedness that extends beyond the work group and other face-to-face relationships. It is precisely on this point that Nakane Chie's general characterization of company organization is weak, I think, for while she is correct about the way Japanese small groups should work, she does not clarify sufficiently the basic differences between the small group and the large organization. Nakane's approach does have the virtue of describing the nature of informal cliques and personal ties often in the background of high-level influence, but companies are far more rationalized and impersonal than her account implies. It is as if her primary focus never leaves the small group and thus factions, cliques, academic circles, and other small entities within larger organizational spheres dominate her analysis.

The total company situation is more complicated. While the nature of work groups is best approached from the question of their fundamental conceptualization, it is less likely that an ideology emphasizing small-group values will have the same significance for large organizations. Company leaders may be devoted to such values, but they are not in a position to unite the personnel of a company in the same immediate way

several places due to the impossibility of open discussion and consensus in a central group. In such a situation, the board of directors is a place for formal approval of plans already laid by separate elements within management.

group leaders are, and the best they can accomplish is to make a success of the directors' and other high-level small groups. The effect of an ideology of small-group togetherness on management-policy decisions is impossible to gauge, but certainly one major result is the frequent expression of regret that the small-group ideals must be overlooked in the face of larger organizational realities. Companies have been able to elaborate a wide manner of activities of symbolic participation (such as ceremonies, gatherings of representatives, company-wide outings, and civic and charitable programs), but none of this will be sufficient to secure the sense of connectedness of individuals to the whole, a crucial matter to Japanese companies.[27] This, it seems, can be accomplished in one or several of the following ways: through the value of a company's public image (size and status), through the opportunities for rapid advancement (growth), and through the satisfactions of company work (above all social relations). Work groups occupy a central position in the last consideration for they are the primary environment in which the individual and the organization are interrelated, with all that means for such matters as authority, motivation, and individual satisfaction.

---

[27] See Rohlen, *For Harmony and Strength.*

Apprenticeship and Paternalism[1]

GEORGE A. DE VOS

Organizational structures cannot continue to operate effectively without some mutually reinforcing isomorphic resonances originating in the personality structure of the participants. Such a general contention is central in a psychocultural approach to a study of any society. To illustrate, I shall attempt to compare and delineate some cultural differences between the implicit attitudes of superiors and subordinates in Japanese industrial organization and those of their counterparts in the United States. The firsthand empirical evidence and the experience indirectly brought to bear on the subject is that obtained by Hiroshi Wagatsuma and myself in the course of our research among the merchants and artisans of Arakawa Ward in Tokyo.[2] However, the reports and writings of others as well as the plots of films and literary works give credence to the wider social application of the generalizations partially derived from our empirical research.[3] We believe that what we observed as underlying social attitudes embedded in the roles of apprentice and patron in Arakawa is also operative more generally in the economic and cultural historical processes at work in the course of Japanese industrialization. We

---

[1] This paper is adapted and modified from parts of vol. 1, chap. 22 ("Conclusions and Implications") in George De Vos and Hiroshi Wagatsuma, *The Heritage of Endurance*, 2 vols. (Berkeley and Los Angeles: University of California Press, forthcoming).

[2] Ibid., I.

[3] See, for example, J. G. Abegglen, *The Japanese Factory: Aspects of Its Social Organization* (Glencoe, Ill.: Free Press, 1958); Chie Nakane, *Japanese Society* (Berkeley and Los Angeles: University of California Press, 1970); Ezra Vogel, *Japan's New Middle Class* (Berkeley and Los Angeles: University of California Press, 1963); Ronald Dore, *City Japan: A Study of a Tokyo Ward* (Berkeley and Los Angeles: University of California Press, 1958); and Robert E. Cole, *Japanese Blue Collar: The Changing Tradition* (Berkeley and Los Angeles: University of California Press, 1971).

do not prophesy how long these attitudes will be maintained in the face of countervening sociological forces. Suffice it to indicate that their present existence as influences has helped set the tone of contemporary Japanese organizational behavior.

PSYCHOCULTURAL REASONS FOR THE RELATIVE ABSENCE OF DISRUPTIVE INDUSTRIAL STRIFE IN JAPAN COMPARED WITH THE UNITED STATES AND WESTERN EUROPE

In the course of the past century, at an ever-increasing rate, the Japanese population has shifted demographically from rural villages to urbanized industrialized communities. Compared with the United States, however, Japanese cities give much less evidence of social unrest or personal disruption. Why has the population migration been so relatively nontraumatic?

There are, for example, statistics on numerous mental health breakdowns attendant upon migration in the United States.[4] Admittedly these cannot be considered symptomatic in all situations of urbanization. There are special minority status features in the United States that cause stress in urban migrants. Urbanization is apt to be relatively more traumatic when the migration takes place between rather than within cultures.[5] One cannot conclude that the urbanization experience itself explains social disruptions when they occur. One must look to other pertinent societal factors such as the relative degree of direct *impersonal* exploitation of the urbanizing workers, or the degree to which urbanizing workers are constrained to accept a continuing minority social class or ethnic status within an urban community. Such conditions can lead not only to social unrest but personal emotional breakdown. In the United States, the reported high rates of mental ill health among both European immigrants and black migrants from the rural South must be considered a symptom of cultural dislocations and social discrimination rather than a symptom of the urbanizing process per se.

Social conditions aside, there are also cultural factors. Contrary to the experience of some migrating groups, Japanese who move both within Japan as well as externally to North or South America generally maintain

---

[4] B. Malzburg and E. S. Lee, *Migration and Mental Disease; a study of First Admissions to Hospitals for Mental Disease* (New York: Social Science Research Council, 1956); also Benjamin Malzberg, "Are Immigrants Psychologically Disturbed?" in S. Plog and Robert Edgerton, eds., *Changing Perspectives in Mental Illness* (New York: Holt, Rinehart and Winston, 1969).

[5] George A. De Vos, ed., "Response to Change," unpublished. Anthropologists studying urbanization in a number of different cultural settings, such as Edward Bruner in Sumatra and Alex Inkeles in his well-controlled comparative survey of six highly different cultures in the process of urbanization, would indicate that urban immigration within a given culture need not lead to interpersonal or social disruption.

integrative family and community life and manifest no forms of increased crime or delinquency that could be attributed to either urbanization or migration per se. There are obviously strong socially integrative cultural traditions at work, which can overcome even the severe social discrimination that occurred in the United States. One must consider, therefore, that in some situations, at least, cultural patterns may overcome social conditions.

Labor conflict is another possible disruption attendant upon industrialization, and more a symptom of social rather than personal ill health. Compared with the history of labor grievances and labor unrest in the United States, one finds the history of the Japanese labor movement relatively nontraumatic. One can question whether this is due simply to a relative lack of social exploitation in Japan, or again, to the countervening force of cultural patterns. I believe the latter is the case.

Several of the economic disruptions experienced in Japan from the beginning of industrialization until World War II have been cushioned by a culturally available pattern that encouraged the family's reabsorption of displaced or unemployed workers back into the rural areas. Japan has also been able newly to reemphasize some practices and attitudes derived from the premodern cultural past to establish job security for most workers.

In the course of Japanese industrialization, former merchants, artisans, and farmers have been recruited into the cadres of industrial workers, who have been either hired in the large, modern, industrial plants or apprenticed in the small, urban-house factories that remain as part of Japan's dual economic structure.[6] Yet from what we witnessed in the microcosm of the Arakawa area of Tokyo, urban migration has been neither personally alienating nor socially disruptive. We found no evidence of any form of general disaffection or of anomic disorganization in the more newly formed urban communities. We did find evidence of how the newly constituted communities functioned to integrate the individual and his family into more or less encompassing, if not entirely satisfying, larger units of social organization. In Arakawa one can document the pattern by which the so-called *shitamachi* (downtown)-traditional-townsman culture of northwest Tokyo had moved steadily into the newly settled areas of northern Tokyo; as it moved, it maintained considerable organizational force, which encompassed the new recruits from the countryside enough to counter the possibly disruptive processes generated by the large-scale industrial movements of people.

Even granting the integrative force of the community-organizational features of Japanese local neighborhoods, one must still turn to the cultural features that influence experience within the work situation itself to explain the relative lack of alienation experienced by Japanese workers. There are mutually complimentary attitudes between subordinates and

---

[6] De Vos and Wagatsuma, *Heritage of Endurance*, I, chaps. 1, 3, and 4.

superiors in Japanese hierarchical social organizations; these extend through social class barriers and are a strong force against the development of the type of class alienation that Marx predicted so well for Europe in his analysis of the development of industrial society. Marx's predictions do not seem to work for Japan. Why is this so?

THE EXPRESSIVE FUNCTIONS
OF JAPANESE PATERNALISM

In Arakawa Ward at least (perhaps to an embarrassing extent for Japanese Marxist theorists), one does not find the kind of social alienation or class consciousness among Japanese industrial workers that one quickly recognizes in contact with Italian or French workers;[7] nor does one find the less ideologically tinged but equally strong hatred of management that is characteristic for American industrial workers. The reasons for this difference between the Japanese industrial situation and that of Western Europe and the United States can be found in the cultural, historical continuities of Japanese social organization. Especially pertinent is the way individuals within Japanese families are socialized to fit into the pervasive, usually hierarchically structured social networks within which they spend their later lives. Reasons are also found in the consequent expressive satisfactions of Japanese paternalism—both in the way one plays the superordinate role as a boss, or the subordinate role as either an apprentice or a long-term, faithful, factory employee. One has to examine more carefully, therefore, the cultural forms of secondary socialization into occupational roles, which follow upon the primary socialization occurring within the family.

In the traditional Japanese social system, a youth was usually introduced into a network of occupational expectations around the time of puberty as an apprentice who would be taught a particular skill. The apprentice role was defined in quasi-familial terms and became part of a network of mutual expectations—both instrumental and expressive in nature. Since some of the apprentice's expectations could be actualized only in the distant future as part of his work role, he was also being trained to develop a future-time orientation. He had to maintain sufficient faith in his future gain to forego immediate material or emotional payment. He was resigned to what an outsider might consider harsh, exploitative treatment for the sake of the future promise of continuing paternalistic support. This sense of reciprocity through time was reinforced generally by the social attitudes of his own family and others.

In Japan today this type of apprenticeship role is being redefined as the social atmosphere affords less reinforcement for the sanctions that maintain the individual in his subordinate role. Youth are increasingly

---

[7] Cole, *Japanese Blue Collar.*

more apt to quit than to put up with constrictions of sustained discipline. We found in Arakawa Ward, however, that the external social sanctions of the society were still applied in the person of the police and with general social approval. One of the police functions in Arakawa was to arrest apprentices who had absented themselves from work. The apprentice role, therefore, was socially defined in terms similar to that of a student in school. The police, in both instances, were expected to enforce required attendance.

By degrees the individual is expected to gain a sense of pleasure from his increasing competence, as he gradually internalizes the standards of excellence related to his craft. Ideally, he would also be increasingly rewarded with signs of appreciation for his growing skill. Hence, there is a gradual socialization of inner satisfactions to be gained by approximating the standards of skill set by the master or teacher within any given tradition.

In this secondary period of occupational socialization, socially expected attitudes of gratitude and repayment were turned from the parents onto occupational mentors in the quasi-familial master-apprentice situation. The boss or master was not free to ignore the dependent expectations of his former apprentice. His own sense of actualizing his master's status derived from a capacity to meet some of these expectations and to do well for those who had been depending on him.

In sum, the Japanese were socialized to gain certain reciprocal expressive satisfactions on all levels of dependency or interdependency. Such gratifications act as a counterforce against the potentials for alienation in an industrial society. One finds evidence that this attitude of mentorship on the part of older men toward younger workers continues even in industrial units. The Japanese working in modern industry still seek out relationships with some nurturing paternal figure with seniority. The bonding together of nonage-graded "brothers" in labor organizations does not seem to satisfy many Japanese the way it does workers elsewhere.

One reliable index of social alienation is delinquency among youth. After a fifteen-year postwar surge in youthful delinquency among lower-class youth in Japan, the overall rates are going down rather than up.[8] Instead of finding restive alienation among the lower-class youth in Japan today, one finds that it is the youth from relatively higher-status backgrounds in the universities who express more social criticism and feelings of social alienation. There is an obviously increased malise about the impersonal, albeit vastly expanded, system of advanced formal education. College students are exhibiting more signs of personal social

---

[8] George A. De Vos, *Socialization for Achievement* (Berkeley and Los Angeles: University of California Press, 1972), especially chaps. 13 and 14.

stress than the youth who go to work in either large- or small-scale industries. The students from middle-class families seem to lack integrating personal interaction with occupational mentors. The teacher's role has become not only distant but much more impersonal than in the past. In contrast, industrial workers, or college youth after they enter business concerns, quickly become part of an organization and take on a sense of personal belonging.

In contrast to the American society with its more stringent forms of age segmentation and peer-group orientation, and its high rate of unemployment among all youth but especially minority youth, the more hierarchically organized Japanese society still, to some degree, bridges the generation gap induced by rapid social change. It is the Japanese upper-middle-class youth, during their time spent as noncommitted students, that manifests crises related to occupational choice. The period of worker apprenticeship, whatever its hardships and strain for the individual, is not a period of protest or alienation for most. In brief, to the degree that it is still maintained in Japan, the apprenticeship system remains a force for maintaining social cohesion in modern Japanese society. The same cannot be said for the university.

Let us consider certain organizational and psychological features of Japanese culture in turn. They are inseparable aspects of observed social behavior. Nakane Chie in her recent volume, *Japanese Society*, distinguishes between two types of belonging: "attribute" and "frame." [9] Attribute groups include both those entered by ascription through birth and those entered by acquiring an occupational specialization. In the first instance, the groups may take the form of clans or kinship lineages; in the second instance, the individual enters a group designated by class position or some given occupational definition such as plumber, carpenter, or professor. In contrast to all such attribute groups is the second major type of group of identity produced by "frame." For Nakane, a frame is a situational-historical definition of belonging such as what happens to you when you join the Ford Motor Company or become a member of the *New York Times* staff, regardless of the actual position. In this sense, partially at least, the U.S. labor movement might serve as an illustration: the CIO organized industrial unions on the basis of frame, whereas the AFL organized workers on the basis of attribute.

The strongest sense of occupational commitment or loyalty found in Japan is in a frame group. One joins such a group for life. Within a frame organization of one kind or another, Japanese subjectively experience working together on common objectives as satisfying to their own inner sense of purpose. These groups, by definition, are internally cooperative; no overt displays of competition are permitted. Any existing competitive-

[9] Chie Nakane, *Japanese Society*.

ness, such as seeking some special recognition or advancement, must be disguised in terms of overall group objectives. Fixed ranking is used to minimize competition, and the principle of seniority is often exercised as the major criterion of precedence. Nakane's principal contention about Japanese social organization, past as well as present, is that frame interpersonal organizations have been more important within Japanese culture than attribute organizations such as kinship structures. This is despite the fact that kinship terminology is used to indicate the familylike atmosphere that is supposed to unite groups. In fact, individual Japanese do characteristically identify themselves as a permanent member of some group like the "*Asahi* family" rather than as a janitor or newsman who happens to be working for the *Asahi* press. A sense of belonging with other members of the *Asahi* is more important than maintaining some formal occupational-class cohesion with other janitors or reporters working elsewhere. Nakane further cogently analyzes how cooperation is emphasized in team efforts shared by all members in a hierarchically defined frame cluster such as a manufacturing company, or even the university, which tends to function in direct competitition with other similarly constituted social units.

From a psychocultural standpoint, I contend that the propensity to join a frame organization, whatever its compelling organizational features, is integral with Japanese socialization experiences that continually emphasize the interdependency of individuals within the primary family. The family is also organized around a sense of precedence in time by seniority among branches and within sibling relationships. The sense of order in precedence or seniority learned within familial relationships is transmuted into one's occupational role.

The traditional sense of tragedy in Japan involves conflicts of loyalty between that accorded one's occupational status and that felt toward the primary family. The acceptable moral resolution of this quandary has usually been structured in favor of the occupational role. In this respect, too, Nakane's analysis makes good sense.

Nakane's description of the vertical structures in Japanese social organizations helps spell out why there is so little evidence of class alienation in Japan compared with Western and even Soviet industrial societies. It is my contention, however, that this cohesiveness must be further explained in the special features of Japanese paternalism as it is experienced in an emotionally satisfying way by Japanese. The expressive satisfaction to be gained sets behavioral limits on the superordinate role. It mitigates against the more widespread appearance in Japan of alienating and exploitative abuses of workers as impersonal objects; workers in the West can deal with such abuses only through the formation of conflicting organizations, which exercise a protective power reinforced by legal contracts.

NURTURANCE, AN EXPRESSIVE NEED:
ACTUALITY AND ILLUSION IN JAPAN

Central to a psychocultural analysis is a thorough consideration of the nature of the subjective experience of exploitation from an expressive as well as an instrumental standpoint. One has to examine, for example, how particular emotionally satisfying or expressive features of a subordinate role can conflict, in the inner experience of the Japanese employer, with the instrumental advantages to be gained by uninhibited economic exploitation of subordinates. Conversely, one has to examine how the exercise of culturally patterned dependent expectations on the part of subordinates can, in certain instances, distort perception of the actual situation so that they hide from themselves the degree to which they may have been victims of exploitation on the part of their superiors.

One can make the extreme contention, for example, that instrumental or economic exploitation does not exist as a social problem until it is consciously perceived and defined as such by the individual subjected to it. This lack of readiness for the Japanese worker generally to perceive himself as exploited is a point of considerable frustration to the leftist political parties in Japan. One may generalize that the majority of Japanese workers choose to continue to think in positive personal terms about their superiors rather than to perceive themselves as used impersonally by them simply as a means toward economic gain.

One is constrained, therefore, to consider the fact that in Japan a Western type of alienating class consciousness is countered by a type of economic and social paternalism that is still experienced as relatively satisfying by both those in the subordinate as well as those in superordinate positions. Such an expressively satisfying paternalism can offset the alienating processes involved in more directly impersonal instrumental situations of class exploitation. From a psychological-motivational point of view paralleling Nakane's structural analysis, the paternalism in Japan works because there is a reciprocal, personal, psychological identification between subordinate and superordinate individuals. Status differentials in Japan do not completely impersonalize or distantiate, causing a lack of emotional concern between those on different levels of Japanese status hierarchy. Therefore, there is possible an emotional interchange of a type that is very rarely experienced between present-day superiors and subordinates in Western economic settings.

One has to examine whether the Western manager or owner has learned to think so completely impersonally about his work force as a consequence of his social history or as a consequence of his trained capacity to think in impersonal abstract terms. Impersonal abstract thinking is notably lacking in the Japanese tradition. Western economic theory is, by and large, impersonal. The operative forces are economic forces. Decision is "rational." Personal, emotional concerns and what are

defined in Western economics as irrational considerations are handled
with difficulty in economic formulae. The presence or absence of paternal
attitudes, therefore, has only a secondary role, if any, in economic theory.
The laws of supply and demand are impersonal, mechanical forces;
human decison-making starts with the assumption that man given the
opportunity will maximize his material benefits rather than impose
irrationally based constraints on himself.

An examination of Japanese legal structure demonstrates how the
subordinate has been in effect at the mercy of the superior. What is
imperfectly understood even by the Japanese themselves in examining
social science theory is the degree to which there remain implicit, legally
unenforced constraints that limit the decision-making of the superior.
These constraints are not established in law, but enforced simply by
Japanese psychology.

Paternalism in Japan is real. Those in the *oyabun* (parent role) positions
do indeed relate very often to their subordinates as if they were charges.
They are not simply dealing with impersonally conceived contract labor
from whom one seeks to obtain maximum productive output. The
subordinate is not depersonalized or treated as a machine. Even in
Western capitalism there is now some knowledge of the fact that one has to
oil the morale of one's workers at least as well as one's machines to
maintain proper functioning without too much disruption or need for
constant, costly replacement.

The master who takes on an apprentice might be seen from outside the
system as one who economically exploits the labor of the young by paying
them pitiful salaries under the pretext that they need years of training in
order to learn a skill well enough to function independently. The same
behavior perceived internally and subjectively may be phrased quite
differently by the participants; this internal cultural perception at times
demands the capacity for considerable denial or distortion away from the
raw objective fact of exploitation. In their mutual internal perceptions, the
Japanese see the apprenticeship situation as a reciprocal payment of
present labor for future-oriented training in a skill. Although apprentices
are paid poorly, if at all, the apprentice is learning a necessary trade
through which he will later realize himself and earn his own living.
Indeed, very frequently an apprentice inherits his master's job, even his
family. This is not to gainsay that in many occupational situations in
Japan there is a lifelong perpetuation of *kobun* (child status), where the
individuals remain subadult and maintain an emotional and financial
dependency on an *oyakata* (parent figure) who periodically rewards his
followers by symbols of appreciation or nurturance. Such ties remain
highly emotional, internally reinforced by potential guilt should the
subordinate not repay his benefactor. And what is often missed by the
Westerner and even by the modern Japanese is the fact that guilt arises on

the part of the benefactor should he fail to give proper care to his subordinates.

Some Western observers might concede that an apprenticeship situation can be tolerable when one can identify with the future privileges to be reached by seniority. This is probably more quickly understandable to some than situations of satisfying lifelong dependency. Those espousing modern Western concepts that all individuals in a society should strive for a sense of independent adulthood are disturbed by the readiness in some cultures to espouse the permanently dependent role as a positive feature of a society. Western theorists do not like to consider the fact that Japanese paternalism also gratifies an expressive need for dependency on the part of many. Such gratification is considered irrational in both impersonal and economic terms.

Interdependency

The propensity to continue dependent gratification is related emotionally to the way many Japanese are socialized in their early primary family experiences. William Caudill and others who have studied Japanese socialization in considerable detail find that a primary feature of Japanese socialization is the manner in which strong dependency needs are developed and sustained by culturally typical patterns of maternal nurturance directed toward the young.[10] This early childhood pattern is reinforced in later secondary occupational socialization by the manner in which passive compliance is periodically rewarded. The individual learns to seek continuing gratification in this manner. He not only learns to expect it, but learns to some degree to distort his perception so that he will achieve fancied gratification from those in superior positions to him.

This latter observation of how Japanese characteristically distort toward the experience of fancied care and gratification from others is well brought out in descriptions of Naikan therapy very often practiced with delinquent youth.[11] The individual sits and contemplates or meditates on how he has been ungrateful in the face of the supposed benefices given by his or her parents, mother-in-law, or other parental authority who are culturally expected to gratify the individual's need for nurturance.

This is a highly complex process to be further explored psychologically and culturally. Japanese characteristically seek to quell internal resent-

---

[10] William Caudill and Helen Weinstein, "Maternal Care and Infant Behavior in Japanese and American Middle-Class Families," in René König and Reubin Hill, eds., *Yearbook of International Sociological Association* (Switzerland: Broz, 1966).

[11] For an English summary, see I. Kitsuse, "A Method of Reform in Japanese Prisons," *Orient/West* 7.11:17–22. In Japanese, see I. Yoshimoto, *Naikan yonjūnen* [Naikan-forty years] (Tokyo: Shunjūsha, 1965); R. Ishida, *Naikan bunseki ryōhō* [The *naikan* method analysis], *Seishin Igaku* 10(1968):478–484. See also Takie Lebra's perceptive analysis of *naikan* in relation to guilt in Japanese culture, "The Social Mechanism of Guilt and Shame: The Japanese Case," *Anthropological Quarterly* 44.4 (October 1971).

ments by distorting toward a not infrequently illusory perception of gratification within the family; in like situations in the West, the individual might more candidly observe a non-nurturant family environment and turn outside the family to religious beliefs. He is taught not to expect nurturance from those who cannot give it, but to overcome resentment by turning to a universal source. In fact, the seeking after dependent nurturance only within the family is culturally discouraged. Individuals are supposed to learn to be less emotionally dependent, less "hung up" about what to expect from others. We cannot overemphasize this cultural historical difference in ways of achieving emotional security as it relates to religious belief systems. One central function of Christian beliefs is to give the individual the assurance that there is someone who cares for him and will take care of him; someone who recognizes his deepest needs, understands, and accepts. This person is not a real figure in the actual social environment but either the Virgin Mary or Jesus Christ. God the Father for many is too aloof an authority figure to concern himself individually, but his compassionate son or the mother of his son are considered approachable figures, from whom to receive a sense of care and concern. In turn, one "gives" himself over to Jesus. One finds a release from the petty resentments of life and can then experience a flow of love. The Japanese generally have no such religious recourse to a Jesus figure, although some have found emotional satisfaction in reliance on figures such as Kannon, an oriental goddess of mercy.

In most instances, however, Japanese are constrained to find the illusion, if not the reality, of "giving" within the primary family or in some occupational transmutation of the primary-family relationship, so that individuals in parentlike roles tend to be imbued with capacities and desires to give what they may not actually possess. Japanese are wont, therefore, to feel gratification from individuals who have in actuality done very little to deserve such attachment. It is often curious to Westerners when they find Japanese expressing gratitude for behavior that they themselves had given little thought to. They do not well understand the Japanese need to feel that someone has cared, has given special attention—has indeed inspired him, released his energies productively, and freed him from the necessity of feeling resentful toward an impersonal ungiving world.

When these nurturant expectations are not fulfilled, the Japanese have a cultural reluctance to place blame or resentment on external society or on particular individuals; under duress, their only object of blame readily available tends to be the person's own body.[12] This psychological pattern makes resentful social protest or persecutory personal paranoia culturally less frequent. Japanese paranoid individuals in my experience, for example, more characteristically exhibit delusions of grandeur than of

---

[12] See De Vos, *Socialization for Achievement*, chap. 4.

persecution. There are in any Japanese population a number of benignly paranoid individuals whose delusionary system includes some beneficial act, which he is bestowing upon the entire world, such as the creation of new inventions or the writing of some book that will unite conflicting societies. In effect, these are grandiose delusions of bestowing benefits upon a needing world that blot out the hard fact of being ignored or forgotten as an individual. Japanese would rather distort reality in a direction of experiencing gratification from understanding superiors than distort in the direction of experiencing themselves subject to a melevolent, impersonal, exploitative social system in which they are being used, broken, and cast away as rubbish. Such a view of life for many a Japanese would elicit an unmanageable sense of irreparable outrage.

Seeking to continue dependent gratification in the adult occupational role is related emotionally to the way that many Japanese are socialized in early primary-family experiences. A primary feature of Japanese socialization is the manner in which strong dependency needs are developed and sustained by the culturally typical patterns of maternal nurturance directed toward the young. This nurturance pattern is reinforced in later, secondary, occupational socialization in a sufficient number of instances to make it a culturally prevalent belief system. Passive compliance is rewarded in emotional currency.

Not every individual has to have these learning experiences in his childhood and reinforcement of them in his later adulthood for the cultural belief system to persist. In a culture that puts heavy emphasis on a nurturant mother, some individuals may not experience such a nurturant mother; but since it is a shared belief transmitted in interpersonal communication that one is to expect a nurturant mother, one will tend to distort one's own experiences toward the maintenance of the belief that he too experiences the type of giving for which he should feel grateful. In the West, the figure of Jesus or Mary as a giver of care and concern is used symbolically in the religious system; in Japan, the mother, or parents, or later the boss is perceived as a potential source of nurturance. If the wish is not reinforced by the immediate experience, it is reinforced by the communication of a social belief in which the particular individual participates.

Endurance

This emphasis on dependency and interdependency is related psychodynamically to a second feature of Japanese socialization—the capacity to sustain oneself through present adversity toward the realization of a future goal. The virtue of endurance is recognized in Japanese culture and expressed through a number of terms with various shades of meaning in given circumstances. Endurance is a continual test of a capacity to win out in the end. "Succeed" is an English word that still carries both senses of its meaning in Japanese. That is, to succeed is both to accomplish and to inherit—usually on the part of someone who has played an inferior role for a long time in anticipation. For a Japanese there is nothing personally demeaning in being a pupil for a long time or in submitting oneself in a seemingly passive way to the active dominance of someone playing the master's role. There is the balancing anticipation that by submitting one will eventually learn the necessary secrets of power and mastery. So too, as a nation Japan could learn from the West because there was no sense of pride being permanently wounded by taking in knowledge when one knew it was for the purpose of future mastery, independence, and perhaps, dominance.

Vicarious Identification

A third feature typical of Japanese socialization is how the development of empathic capacities for vicarious identification is crucial for the exercise of paternalism. I have elsewhere noted the psychological identification of a mother with the success of her male child, or with the success of the lineage into which she has been adopted by marriage.[13] There is the same capacity for vicarious identification on the part of an inferior with the behavior of the individual in a superior role. It is less frequently noted but true, however, that the individual in the superior role identifies in some ways covertly, if not overtly, with the person in the inferior role. This last type of identification is usually on the part of older men toward younger men, since men are less permitted to cross the barrier of sexual roles and identify with women in their subordinate status. Men can be rather unsympathetic or unconcerned with the feelings of women or even their own children while quickly sensitive to the feelings of male subordinates outside their own family. Nevertheless, although it is generally disguised, there is a potential for guilt on the part of males toward their long-suffering mothers, if not their wives. As a consequence, potential for guilt on the part of superiors toward inferiors becomes a deeply internalized part of a Japanese sense of status responsibility.

It is necessary to take into consideration such patterns of vicarious identification that are emphasized in Japanese socialization; one cannot explain simply from a social structural point of view why the Japanese society is so well knit together in vertical structures by expressive affectional ties instead of by the externally visible instrumental contractual bonds required in the West.

In Japanese society, the capacities to endure in order to succeed and to identify vicariously with one's superior reach their apotheosis in the role of married women. Women identify readily with males carrying out their

---

[13] Ibid.

expected roles. This identification is an essential part of the woman's capacity for a deep sense of accomplishment as a mother; and her capacity for endurance permits her to go through what seems to be almost incredible acts of metamorphoses in the later stages of her life cycle. The meek bride is, in effect, the pupal stage of the later horrendous mother-in-law, just as the eager male apprentice is the larval stage of a potentially dominant master in the future. Many males, of course, carry on a continuing larval existence as more or less well-cared-for drones. The fact that the final stages of metamorphoses do not occur for all in the same way does not negate a Japanese cultural climate of relatively high worker morale.

Psychologically at least, if not in actuality, it is as if Japanese are in various stages of "becoming" during their life cycle. This gives them a sense of forward thrust into an optimistically conceived future. If the subsequent stages of metamorphoses do not occur during one's own life, there is the hope that they will see realization in one's children. While looking forward, one remains at the same time in a dependent position within hierarchical relationships. Premature assertion of independence would be disruptive. The individual would be destroyed and, therefore, would never reach the final stages of development, which require waiting and patience. Better to wait for an opportunity than to destroy one's chances by a premature assertion of independence that will not be sanctioned by the existing social reality.

The Western image of paternalism connotes an instrumental-exploitative use of a dependent labor force with whom there is no sense of personal involvement or belonging. The Japanese, in contrast, tend toward strong belief in political and social myths about their nation, company, group, or family collectivity. The boss or *oyakata* is supposed to have parentlike feelings. Indeed, the social expectations of his role often cause him to manifest overt behavior suggesting such feelings whether they are present or not. The good parent is assumed by the group or the community to provide for his dependent children—no matter what internal emotional reality is experienced. There are positive fantasies of protective consideration directed toward such superiors as bosses or company presidents that reinforce an internalized sense of responsibility on their part. They are not psychologically free to dehumanize their employees into numbers or abstractions of statistical tables giving projections of maximal efficiency. Many Japanese industrial leaders as well as the small-scale entrepreneurs we have researched are caught with an inner necessity to play out the benevolent aspects of an idealized wise company president spontaneously concerned with the welfare of his workers.

Some of these individuals who have succeeded from humble origins in the expanding national economy of Japan can hearken back in their imagination to their own previous status as young apprentices. They take pride in their rise through adversity, and maintain within themselves a personalistic capacity to identify with an eager younger man who seems dependent on an older leader. On a deep psychodynamic level, one finds in Japanese an age-status network of affection binding persons of sharply different status into relations with one another. This sense of expressive rapport transcends status differences that more characteristically alienate individualistic Westerners from one another. The Western identification is more easily directed horizontally, whereas the Japanese sense of identification extends itself up and down in vertical relationships—characteristically defined as age-graded patterns—in which the individual has earlier experienced the lower stages and anticipates his experience of higher stages with succeeding age.

Since the subordinates have no instrumental power in the Japanese status hierarchy, they can only hope to induce kindness in their superiors by invoking potential feelings of nurturance and appreciation from them. This capacity, which is called *amaeru* in Japanese, has been very simply and cogently discussed by Takeo Doi.[14] If fate puts one in the hands of a harsh authority, one has no recourse but to endure and to hope for change in the future. Japanese must depend on the positive expressive aspects of their dominant-subordinate relationships to be rewarding, since they have only recently begun to create in their social institutions the instrumental guarantees that ensure or secure what Westerners consider rights or justice for the weak.

It is often difficult for modern Western observers to consider a combination of nurturance and control that works both ways: not only is nurturance used to control, but control sometimes is a means to the bestowal of nurturance. The fact that he had early gratification of his own dependent needs constrains many a Japanese boss to find social means to bestow on others what a Westerner would view as almost maternallike nurturance. Such constraint comprises a profoundly significant part of Japanese social consciousness and sense of social responsibility. Wagatsuma and I have described the not unique incidence of a company president of a tiny five-man factory who turned back his extra income to his workers, realizing for himself his idealization of being a warm, paternal figure.[15] Robert Bellah has provocatively contended in a cogent argument that the traditional image of the emperor contained maternal attributes.[16] While agreeing with the essential arguments forwarded by Bellah, I would put it that what one calls maternal in Western parental role concepts can be readily fantasied as part of paternal authority behavior by Japanese. It is indeed true that the experience of such nurturance is derived from the mother-child experience; nevertheless, one frequently finds Japanese

---

[14] Takeo Doi, *The Anatomy of Dependence* (Tokyo: Kōdansha, 1973).

[15] De Vos and Wagatsuma, *Heritage of Endurance*, I.

[16] Robert Bellah, "The Emperor as a Maternal Symbol," colloquium paper, Center for Japanese and Korean Studies, University of California, Berkeley, 1967.

males behaving toward one another with maternal-like nurturance attitudes.

A system of reciprocity in expectations between superiors and subordinates only works when there is sufficient belief on the part of the subordinates that they will be rewarded if they perform properly in their subordinate position. The system therefore implies a reciprocal sensitivity to the expressive needs of subordinates on the part of superiors, not a simple exploitation of the weak on the part of the strong. In processes of socialization found frequently in Japan there is indeed a particular kind of internalization socialized into those who will later assume positions of authority. This process starts with a strong dedication on the part of the mother to her role as responsible socializer. This dedication requires considerable desexualization and the general foregoing of immediate gratification.

PUBLIC DEDICATION: THE CLEAVAGE BETWEEN SOCIAL THEORY AND PRACTICE

It was also the expected, or at least idealized, role of the samurai bureaucrat in the premodern culture to be as truly dedicated to his job as a mother to her children. We are wont to hear more, much more, about the samurai as a swordsman, who would cut down inferiors, than about the samurai as a dedicated administrator, who was relatively uncorrupt and who would attempt to govern with an unusual degree of equity and fairness. Craig and Shively, in a number of chapters in their volume, present instances of notable samurai who performed as dedicated governors and administrators.[17] Administrative authority may have been feared in Tokugawa Japan, but there was also an overall general respect for it. This is not to gainsay the periodic peasant rebellions against improper treatment. These were indeed symptomatic of misrule and corruption in local instances, but generally the system worked because there was enough relative honesty to keep it going. Therefore, individuals who held authority positions were generally invested with a certain moral ascendancy by their subordinates. The obvious split in the West between the idealized spiritual authority of the church and the rebellious self-righteous hatred of corrupt state power does not appear in Japan. In the West the individuals in the religious hierarchy were supposed to be more dedicated, while those in the secular hierarchy were expected to be less trustworthy. If there were any counterpart in Japan to Western religious authority, it is curiously enough found in the role of the dedicated civil bureaucrat.

Present-day police and governmental administration in Japan, compar-

---

[17] Albert Craig and Donald Shively, eds., *Personality in Japanese History* (Berkeley and Los Angeles; University of California Press, 1970).

atively speaking at least, inherit considerable public respect. Whatever the negative feelings engendered, authority is never perceived as so dishonest that it is distrusted, and for the most part it is granted a degree of respect rare in the United States. This attitude of respect is more feasible for Japanese emotionally. It is mobilized as an implicit expectation that gratification will be awarded for compliant behavior. The Western sense that moral obedience gains God's reward of nurturance is seldom extended to civil authorities; in Japan it is indeed toward the civil not the religious authority that one traditionally directs respectful obedience.

Such a pattern of emotional interaction in a hierarchical social structure is highly repellent to Western theoreticians and, of course, to modern Japanese Marxist theorists as well. They choose to ignore its operational force in present-day Japanese society or to see it as socially pathological. They choose the Western model of society as the ideal basis for social analysis. Japanese social historians, also influenced by Marx, emphasize rational instrumentality and ignore, if not abhor, the continuing force of expressive needs that permeate occupational as well as familial hierarchical structures in Japanese social organization. They do not like to see the relation between high industrial morale and what they term feudalistic social patterns. In the West, industrialization separated social classes rather than bringing them together. The lack of identity between classes in Western nations has become an alienating factor. Not only is there a lack of emotional ties, but there are direct and continual experiences of impersonal exploitation. The results are strong feelings of mutual class antagonism and a further separation between the different occupational strata of Western societies. Western nations, despite their capacity to arouse ethnic or national patriotism in wartime, are not knit together like Japan with a mythology of quasi parentage, or extended quasi-familial networks of obligations that act as nonlegally specified internal constraints against raw exploitation.

It is difficult, however, for Japanese to extend their administrative organization overseas to include non-Japanese. The implicit role patterns that allow mutual understanding of noncontractual operations within a totally Japanese social organization do not function well when members of alien cultures are involved. During their period of military expansion, the Japanese found that they could not readily identify downward with subject members of alien populations, and moreover the expected types of deference were not forthcoming from subordinates. In this situation, the Japanese potential for a racist-type of arrogance was quickly manifest, alienating even the previously subordinate populations who had initially viewed the Japanese as liberators.

Even today the implicit understanding that makes decision-making and interpersonal communication possible in Japanese occupational hierarchies cannot work with a minimum of formal legal contractual structuring when non-Japanese are involved. The Japanese are constrained to adapt themselves in their external dealings to programs lacking the expressive aspects of psychological functioning that continue to operate peculiarly within Japanese organizational life.

Economic Realities and
Enterprise Strategy

PETER F. DRUCKER

A great many books and papers have been published in the last few years pointing out, especially to the Western businessman, the differences between the way business is conducted in Japan and in the West. There have been discussions of Japanese personnel policies, of the decision-making process in Japanese business, and of the relationship between business and government. But the area in which Japanese management seems to differ most in behavior from what Western executives are wont to take for granted is the area of business strategy.

In the first place, Japanese business does not, it seems, put great stress on "maximizing profit." Second, Japanese business enterprise, for all its vigorous selling efforts, does not usually market and sell its own products. Indeed, it relies on an outside "trading company," which handles a great diversity of products for a great many different producers in the domestic Japanese market as well as in the export markets.

Finally, Japanese business enterprise aims at maximizing volume. Increased sales, rather than increased profits, seem to be the first objective. The Western company, American and European, that enters into a joint venture with a Japanese company, invariably reports receipt of a most comprehensive sales plan from its Japanese partner. But rarely does the Japanese partner seem to pay much attention to the profit planning which the Westerner has come to regard as the necessary foundation of rational business strategy.

Businessmen notice these phenomena, but are understandably not much interested in explaining them. Scholars also have made few attempts at explaining Japanese business strategy. The Japanese tend to take it for granted; and Westerners tend to fall back on such bromides as "Japanese tradition," or "Japanese values," or some variant of the "inscrutable Orient."

Yet an understanding of such basic differences in business strategy should contribute greatly to our understanding of Japan and of the Japanese economy; the nature of cultural differences; and the economists' "theory of the firm" that is our model of microeconomy and of economic behavior. The Japanese have built and are running exceedingly successful businesses; yet their basic business strategy not only violates everything a Western executive "knows"; it is incompatible with the economist's (including the Japanese economist's) theories of economic behavior and of microeconomics.

It is the thesis of this paper that the business strategy of Japanese enterprise, while indeed different from that of American or European business, is not "mysterious" nor "nonrational" nor "culturally conditioned." It optimizes, in perfectly rational fashion, the specific structural realities in which Japanese businesses operate, especially those of banking and capital markets and those of wage system and wage structure. And these structural realities, in turn, are not the result of Japanese tradition or of Japanese values. They are of recent origin—mid-Meiji at the earliest. When introduced, they were genuine innovations and not adaptations of new tasks to old institutions or old traditions. They resulted from accidents of personality or from highly specific socioeconomic and political conditions at a given moment in time. This paper will attempt to place the Japanese structural realities and the resulting Japanese business strategies in context by comparing them with both American and European realities and resulting business strategies.

CAPITAL MARKET, BANKING STRUCTURE, AND THE ROLE OF PROFIT

There is evidence that the Japanese business enterprise puts profits much lower on its scale of values than any Western enterprise. By any of the conventional measurements, the profitability of the Japanese business enterprise appears low. Measured, for instance, as percentage of sales—the most widely used measurement of profitability and profitability objective —Japanese business enterprises, especially large businesses, perform at a much lower rate of profitability than enterprises in similar lines of business in the United States or in Europe.

And yet it is also clear that the Japanese economy operates at a higher rate of profit than any Western economy. Japan has, ever since the Meiji period, managed to run its economy at a phenomenally high rate of savings and investments measured as a percentage of total gross national product. This would not be possible unless profits—a major, if not the major, component of capital formation—were consistently very high.

The explanation for this apparent paradox lies in the structure of the Japanese banking system and capital market. As the result primarily of a historical accident—the ascendancy of Iwasaki Yataro, the founder of Mitsubishi, during the formative years of Japan's modern economy— "profit" is not what the business enterprise shows as such. The profit that matters to the economy is what the banks return, especially the *zaibatsu* banks that finance the *zaibatsu* industries.

In the early Meiji years when Japan started to build her modern economy, banking was already seen as central to economic development. Fukuzawa Yukichi stressed the need to develop a banking system in his very early writings. And the most brilliant of the young economic leaders in early-Meiji government, Shibusawa Eiichi (1840–1931), resigned from one of the most powerful positions in the Ministry of Finance at the age of thirty-four to become a banker and thus to serve his nation more productively and forcefully than he could even as a powerful civil servant and government leader.[1]

At that time, the model of banking that dominated the developed world was the English banking system. Fukuzawa Yukichi focused on it in his writing. The early banks, started around 1870 or so, were meant to be joint-stock banks on the English model. But this model of what Americans call the "commercial" bank was not suitable for Japan.

The English banking system had been developed before the Industrial Revolution. It was a child of the Commercial Revolution of the late-seventeenth and early-eighteenth century and focused on trade, not industry. When industry developed almost a century later, it developed essentially outside the banking structure and without the benefit of the banking structure. Banking remained focused on the commercial, the trading transaction. The English capital market, and following it, the American capital market grew up almost entirely outside the banking system and contributed venture capital directly to local industry.

This original pattern has persisted to this day in Great Britain. No major British industry has been built by the banks, whether the joint-stock or merchant banks. The most comprehensive history of a major British industry does not even mention banks and bankers as factors in the founding, growth, or even the merger of the multitude of companies out of which Imperial Chemical Industries was created in 1926.[2] While the entrepreneurial banker had a major role in the United States between 1870—when J. P. Morgan returned from Europe and started his own

[1] On Shibusawa, see the essay by Johannes Hirschmeier S.V.D., "Shibusawa Eiichi: Industrial Pioneer" in *The State and Economic Enterprise in Japan*, ed. William W. Lockwood (Princeton: Princeton University Press, 1965), which also contains an extensive bibliography especially of Shibusawa's writings and of the literature on him in Japanese.

[2] W. J. Reader, *Imperial Chemical Industries: An History*, I, :Oxford, 1970.

banking house in New York—and World War I, the capital market in the United States started outside the banking system and during the Depression was moved away from the banking system into separate institutions.

This was not a pattern Japan could adopt in 1870. To this day most Japanese books on banking are couched in language such as that used by nineteenth-century English banking theorist Walter Bagehot in his historic book, *Lombard Street*. But the English banking system was incompatible with Japanese reality. Industry had to be developed before there could be trade, and the English banking system, either in its original or in its modified American version, could not do this.

At the time of early Meiji, a second banking model was being designed. The continental European model, which has become known as the "universal bank," was a "deposit" bank unlike the English merchant bank.[3] Its purpose was entrepreneurship: to find and finance industry, and to provide venture capital. The aim was to nurse an infant enterprise to the point where its securities would become marketable. At that point the bank would sell off part of its holdings in the enterprise at a substantial capital gain and recoup its investment. The bank would, however, retain sufficient stake in the enterprise to assure for itself the firm's commercial banking business. And it would continue to have a controlling voice, since the private investors, with whom the bank had placed the shares of the enterprise, would continue to hold their shares in the custody of the bank and vote their shares through the bank.

This universal bank was the model Japan needed, and the founder of Japanese banking, Shibusawa Eiichi, clearly had this model in mind. Indeed, as a young man shortly before the Meiji Restoration, Shibusawa had spent a year mostly in France—where the idea of the universal bank had originated—and it is highly probable that it is this experience that impressed him with the importance of both banking and business.

The universal bank was indeed founded to deal with a situation exceedingly similar to the one that existed in early Meiji Japan. The universal bank had truly developed in Germany—a country of small workshops and no industry but where there was, however, a heavy emphasis on education as the main engine for development and where the government had made economic development a major priority, if only to obtain and maintain military strength. Georg Siemens, who developed the model and served as the first head of the Deutsche Bank—the dominant financial institution on the European continent within a few short years—had, like Shibusawa Eiichi, started out as a young government servant, risen extremely fast to high position and then, contrary to all

---

[3] For the "universal bank" and the various models of banking, see the chapter "Georg Siemens and the Deutsche Bank," in my book, *Management: Tasks; Responsibilities; Practices* (New York: Harper & Row, 1974).

social tradition, left at a very early age to go into banking as a better way to serve his nation.

The bank that Shibusawa Eiichi founded as Japan's universal bank, the Dai-Ichi Bank, did eventually, within the last few years, become Japan's largest bank. Yet Japanese banking did not follow Shibusawa Eiichi's logical line, and the reason is one man: Iwasaki Yataro. Unlike Shibusawa, Iwasaki believed in profit maximization. He also believed strongly that it was unsound to sell shares of enterprises to the general public; an enterprise had to be controlled completely by one man. He grudgingly accepted the need for incorporation, but he made sure that control would remain vested totally in the family head and that the shares owned by other members of the family would be held in what, in effect, was a family voting trust, with the head of the house exercising voting power. As for nonfamily "outsiders" holding shares, this appeared to him to make management impossible.[4]

Iwasaki did not represent a "Japanese" point of view. His beliefs were shared by most of the major business builders of the late-nineteenth/early-twentieth century. Even in the United States, it was strongly held, for instance, by Henry Ford. In Germany, Siemens's idea of the universal bank, which mobilized individual savings for direct investment in the equity capital of business, faced tremendous resistance from industrialists as well as from a government that did not want to have public savings directed into share ownership. Indeed, Siemens had to go into politics and get himself elected to the German Parliament to fight the governmental resistance to the idea of public ownership of businesses and of a stock exchange. And he did not win out until the very end of his life, when a historical confrontation with his own cousins, the heirs of the great Werner von Siemens who had founded the electrical company that still bears his name, forced Werner's sons to accept direct public ownership of Siemens shares and interference from representatives of the public—that is, from the bankers—with company management.

Iwasaki Yataro also saw banking as central, as indeed, any intelligent observer of 1870 Japan must have done. But his idea of a bank was as an institution to attract capital for investment in the industries and businesses of the Mitsubishi *zaibatsu* in such a form that the public would in no way acquire title of ownership or control. The public would come in as depositors, and not as "investors." In other words, he looked upon a bank not as a means to create a capital market, as Georg Siemens and Shibusawa did. He looked upon a bank as a substitute for a capital market. And it was Iwasaki who prevailed.

As a result, Japanese industry is financed primarily by what legally are

---

[4] For a discussion of the basic approaches of Shibusawa and Iwasaki to the economic development of Japan, and of the clash between them, see my book, *The Age of Discontinuity* (New York: Harper & Row, 1969), pp. 123–126.

bank loans. Economically, most of this money is equity capital. But it is not invested in the equity form, but in the form of short-term indebtedness. As a result, Japanese business is legally financed to only about 20 percent of its total investment by equity, that is, by common shares; 80 percent of the investment is in the form of loans. In the United States, the proportion is almost the exact opposite: 30 percent indebtedness and 70 percent equity. On the Continent, the proportion of equity is slightly lower in a large company than it is in the United States, but it rarely falls below 50 percent or so of total capital employed. Where most of the nonequity portion of Japanese capital is in the form of short-term bank loans, the continental European business tends to rely heavily on long-term bonds held by outside investors. In other words, the proportion of money in the form of bank loans is probably no higher in Europe than in the United States and may well be smaller.

The form of financing makes very little difference regarding the total return on the invested capital with which a business has to operate. The "cost of capital" is remarkably similar, especially in the period since World War II with its international and highly mobile capital market. It can be said that for the period 1950–1970 all business enterprises of any size whether American, continental European, British, or Japanese have had to earn 12 percent or so pretax income on total capital invested to earn the cost of capital.

Because of the different structure of banking and capital markets, the strategy needed to earn the cost of capital is totally different in the three areas. A Japanese business must earn enough money to pay the interest on what is legally a bank loan but economically is equity investment in business and industry. The profit in the Japanese economy—the return on venture capital—is essentially the difference between what it costs a Japanese bank to attract and hold deposits, and the interest it charges for the loans to industry. Therefore, Japanese banks have traditionally kept interest rates on deposits exceedingly low—in effect nothing. The interest they charge their industrial customers, on the other hand, is rather high and runs at least one-third, if not one-half, above interest rates charged for truly commercial loans. This is, of course, completely legitimate considering that most are not truly commercial loans and therefore include a much larger risk premium. As long as the interest on these loans is secure, the bank is satisfied. Business earnings over and above what is needed to cover the interest charge with a fair safety margin are of no benefit to the bank. The bank's income is fixed, and therefore it exerts little pressure on its customers to increase earnings over and above the interest required.

There is also little reason for the Japanese business executive to try to increase earnings on that fairly small portion of his total capital that is in the form of common shares and legal equity. By old tradition—which is only now beginning to change—companies can only issue additional shares at par value. They cannot, as in the centuries-old Anglo-American business tradition, issue shares at their market value, even if the market value is many times the original-issue value. A Japanese business does not acquire the capacity to obtain capital at more advantageous cost if its share price goes up. In effect, successful Japanese enterprises issue new shares as a form of stock dividend, a distribution of earnings, and not as a way to obtain new capital at advantageous cost.

The Japanese business manager, therefore, has little incentive to increase earnings above what is needed to cover the bank's interest charges and earn a modest return on the shares outstanding in the hands of the public—which itself is a post-World War II innovation for the *zaibatsu* companies. Although his minimum profitability is high for interest charges, this needs qualification. Since legally his profit is paid out as interest on debts, the tax collector does not consider it profit, but a deductible business expense. Insofar as the tax on corporation profits is indeed a tax on profits—rather than a tax on the consumer as most economists would contend—the Japanese business has a decided advantage over its Western competitors. Increasing profits also do not make it possible for him to decrease his dependence on the bank and increase the amount of equity capital he can raise outside in the growing capital market. The tradition that forces him to offer new shares at par shuts this escape hatch.[5]

From the point of view of the Japanese business executive, however, faced as he is by the high cost of the capital on which he depends, minimizing the cost of capital is the most rational business objective. Maximizing profit makes no sense to him: there is no benefit to his company and incidentally, with stock options being practically unknown in Japanese management, no benefit to him personally. But minimizing the cost of capital—that is, trying to operate the business with the very minimum of borrowed money—is indeed a major rational business objective. His business strategy, therefore, focuses on profit only to the extent to which it represents a minimum requirement. That minimum is quite high by Western standards. It is nonsense to say that the Japanese executive is not profit conscious. But he is not "profit-minded" in the sense that profit is an objective. It is a necessity; "minimizing the cost of capital" is the objective.

That this is the result of structure and not of values is clearly shown by the way the different banking and capital market structures determine business strategy in other areas. In the United States, where the commercial banking system traditionally has been kept out of the capital market, and where the capital market has furnished funds primarily in the

---

[5] This, it should be said, is changing fairly fast. In another few years, it may have become commonplace in Japan to sell shares of successful companies at the stock exchange price, that is, at a price that reflects earnings rather than "par"—with, in all likelihood, tremendous impact on Japanese business behavior and business strategy.

form of equity capital, profit maximization is a rational objective. It is the way a business is enabled to obtain the capital it needs at the lowest possible cost—the strategy calculated to produce "minimization of the cost of capital." The American business that depends on a capital market will have to pay less for new money the higher its shares are priced in the market. The price-earnings ratio, therefore, determines to a large extent—though not entirely—the cost of capital for the larger, publicly held American business. Maximizing profit on equity is, therefore, the way in which the American manager minimizes the cost of capital. Maximizing earnings per share are rational objectives for him. At the very least, it is a rational means to the same objective of "minimizing the cost of capital" which leads the Japanese manager to a very different strategy.

On the continent of Europe, the rational strategy is neither to maximize earnings per share nor to minimize the cost of capital, but to maintain the dividend on the common share. With the bank as the determining shareholder—even though its direct holdings may be only a fairly small proportion of the share capital—maintenance of this dividend best suits the needs of the decisive shareholders. The bank depends on dividends from its business investment to pay its liabilities—the interest it owes to its depositors. It has a fixed obligation, which is met out of the distribution of business profits. Maintenance of the dividends is, therefore, far more important to the German or French or Italian universal bank than rapid growth of earnings. Fluctuations in the dividends are intolerable and dangerous. For the continental European business, this means a policy aimed at maintaining dividends at a reasonable but not necessarily very high level and building reserves during years of high profit to make dividend maintenance possible in poor years. Again, maximization of profits is a secondary goal. Stability of dividends comes first.

In fact, all three systems can be said to have the same objectives: minimizing the cost of capital and minimizing the risk of not being able to obtain capital. These two objectives are the only rational foundation for a valid "theory of the firm." They are also the only valid objectives for rational business behavior. But the structural, institutional conditions that result from accidents of history rather than from cultural traditions dictate different strategies for the attainment of these objectives in different economies.

The profitability level of the economy is dictated by objective forces, especially by the objective need of an economy for capital. For this reason, profitability of the Japanese economy—an economy developing from a low base, with poor natural resources, and with a conscious policy of not depending on capital from abroad—had to be very high. And it has been high except during periods of severe economic depression like the early 1920s or the 1930s. But because the true venture capital of the Japanese economy is not investments of the public in equity or even investments of banks in equity but bank loans, the individual Japanese business enterprise does not base its strategy on profit maximization. To do so would be economically irrational. Instead, it bases its strategy on minimizing the cost of capital.

THE TRADING COMPANY

The trading company and its role in Japan are also, in large measure, a result of the structure of banking and capital markets rather than of tradition or of Japanese values. And again, it is instructive to compare the situation in Japan with that of the United States and Western Europe.

The Anglo-American banking system was essentially created to provide medium-term credit. It is the medium-term credit, the credit with a maturity of ninety days to five years, which is the typical and indeed constitutive credit in a commercial economy. It is also the credit for which need expands the fastest with economic growth.

In England, the credit demands of an emerging commercial economy were satisfied through two different institutional channels which developed side by side: (1) the deposit bank, primarily for short-term loans needed for domestic purposes such as seasonal loans on crops or loans to artisans; and (2) the merchant bank, founded to provide medium-term loans, especially for foreign trade. In fact, the merchant bank is what was meant when people talked about banking in the mid-nineteenth century. Its highly developed institutional structure, organized around the discounting of foreign trade bills of exchange, is essentially what Walter Bagehot presented as the model for the banking system in *Lombard Street* more than a century ago. To this day, the commercial law of continental European countries, codified as a rule in the mid-nineteenth century, centers on what the Germans call *Wechselrecht*, the law relating to the instruments of medium-term credit.

In the United States, the merchant bank did not develop. The American bank that came into being instead—perhaps first with Alexander Hamilton's founding of the Bank of New York in the closing years of the eighteenth century—was designed to attract short-term deposits and to lend them out medium term. The American banking system is predominantly a medium-term banking system, designed to finance domestic trade rather than foreign trade like the English merchant banks.

On the continent of Europe, the universal bank embraces medium-term finance at least in theory. In actuality, the Continent never built an adequate medium-term banking system. In part this resulted from the availability of the City—that is, of the medium-term market in London, organized around the merchant bankers. This supplied the medium-term money needed to finance foreign trade well into this century—that is, until World War I. In part the universal bank, founded as a bank for enterpreneurship and for the development of industry, focused on its industrial group in the supply of medium-term money. Businesses outside of a bank's orbit found it, as a rule, difficult to obtain medium-term money. The main reason, however, was probably legal. By concentrating on the formal instruments of medium-term credit, and especially on the bill of exchange—an instrument that never found true acceptance in the United States—the banks focused, in their medium-term lending, on transactions rather than on borrowers. The American banks, by contrast, soon began to finance businesses rather than transactions and thereby developed increasing expertise in medium-term finance. To this day, the American commercial bank has the leadership in medium-term finance, which explains, for instance, why in the last twenty years the major American banks have been able to establish themselves as financial leaders in European business and even in that citadel of old merchant banking, the "City" of London.

In Japan, medium-term finance remained almost undeveloped. The *zaibatsu* banks had set a pattern of banking as the provider of venture capital, and this absorbed all their available resources. Medium-term financing for foreign trade became available very early in the form of the instruments developed by the Europeans. But Kobe financed its cotton imports in London and Liverpool rather that in Tokyo or Osaka. Medium-term finance in Japan has been scarce and hard to get, even for large and successful businesses.

Yet it is medium-term credit that grows the fastest as an economy or a business expands. We do not have reliable figures, but it is safe to say that for every dollar of equity financing required for business expansion, three to five dollars are required for medium-term finance. At least, this has been the experience of the last twenty years in respect to financing the tremendous expansion in world trade.

For structural reasons, therefore, Japanese business faces a continuing shortage of medium-term finance, and at the same time a particularly high need for it. While equity finance primarily finances production, medium-term finance is required for distribution, and the Japanese distribution system is one that ties down large sums of money for long periods. At the same time, such habits as the semi-annual bonus militate against developing instruments to mobilize medium-term finance, such as installment paper.

Shibusawa Eiichi saw this clearly. In his various writings—especially his 1876 booklet on banking, which can be read as a polemic against Iwasaki and his banking policies—Shibusawa stresses the need to preserve liquidity to provide medium-term credit, particularly for distribution. Again, Iwasaki won—in part because the Japanese government (as is common among governments) gave distribution low priority compared with production and therefore sided with Iwasaki. As a result, medium-term money is the true need of Japanese business, and not only of the smaller and medium-sized businesses.

The trading company does not seem to have roots in pre-Meiji Japan. It is not the successor to the Osaka merchants. It was created to handle the buying of foreign machinery and materials, such as cotton, for the nascent Japanese industry. It was created primarily because an expert was needed for the contacts with the "inscrutable Occident" rather than because it served an economic function. Apparently it was not until late in the nineteenth century that the trading company began to move into handling trade within Japan for Japanese-produced goods. Then the trading company developed very fast. And the faster the Japanese home market grew, the more prominent the trading company became.

Outside observers are quite right in pointing out that as the market becomes larger, the need for the merchandising services of the trading company diminishes. They are also right that it makes no sense from a business point of view for a major petroleum company, such as Mitsubishi Oil, to distribute its gasoline to its network of service stations through Mitsubishi Shoji, a trading company that handles thousands of other products as well as gasoline. They are quite right in pointing out that a goodly number of foreign companies—Coca Cola is the best-known example—have been successful in marketing their merchandise directly without a trading company.

These critics, however, miss the point. The trading company is indeed unnecessary, maybe even quite uneconomical from the point of view of distribution. It means, in effect,[6] that the responsibility for production and marketing are divorced. But the economic rationale for the trading company is not merchandising. A trading company is the one way in which the Japanese economy manages its medium-term credit problem, for the trading company optimizes the need for medium-term credit. The trading company creates its own money pool, or what bankers call a "float"—a reservoir of money that can be used whenever the need arises and that can be turned over a great deal faster than money invested in any one distribution channel or cycle. It creates a medium-term money market, and does so very effectively.

Again, a reference to the situation in other areas is instructive. In the United States, where medium-term credit is the specialty of the monetary and banking system, medium-term credit has actually become central. Because a century and a half ago American bankers conceived of medium-term credit as something given to a business rather than as the financing of a transaction, the producer is the focus of American distribution. If a bank lends to a business instead of financing a transaction, the financial strength of the business becomes the critical factor. This, in effect, means visible assets. Therefore, the more fixed

---

[6] Paradoxically, this probably makes the Japanese industrialist more marketing conscious than his Western counterpart. He has no control over the people who market his product and has to satisfy them in a way that the American or European industrialist, who is the "boss" of his marketing people, can hardly conceive of.

investments a business has in the American system, the more borrowing capacity it will have for medium-term money. This clearly favors manufacturers, rather than wholesalers, who as a rule have very little by way of fixed assets. In other words, the producer—and to a lesser extent the retailer—have become the centers in the American system. The wholesaler has no power because he does not have the financial capacity to attract medium-term money. In turn, the manufacturer is expected to finance the wholesaler, and to a large extent his distribution altogether. As a result, distribution costs for the American economy are comparatively low—maybe the lowest of any major economy. But distribution costs to the manufacturer are very high, since he is expected to provide the financing.

In continental Europe there is a hybrid situation. For those companies that belong to a major bank's group—most of the larger companies—the bank will provide medium-term money. Other companies cannot obtain it easily. Indeed, for medium-sized family companies, medium-term money is dangerous. It makes them dependent on a bank and is likely to lead to the demand that they join the bank's group, which means that they hand over control to the bank rather than retain it in the family. The wholesaler on the Continent, therefore, is in a much stronger position vis-à-vis the medium-sized business. A large business that is not part of a bank concern, such as Krupp before it had to capitulate to the banks in the 1960s, has to organize its own wholesaler to obtain trade finance for its distribution. Thus, in Europe the wholesaler is either nonexistent, as is the case for most of the products of large publicly owned companies, or he is in a strong and rather dominant position. In respect to medium-term finance, Europe exhibits both the characteristics of the American system in respect to large publicly owned companies, and the characteristics of the Japanese system in respect to family-held small- and medium-sized companies.

But the central role of the trading company in Japan is a reflection of banking structures and money market realities. It represents the most rational optimization of the existing structures, under which medium-term finance is critically short and inadequately taken care of by the existing banking system. In many ways, the trading company is not a "trading company," but a "finance company." Just as the *zaibatsu* bank is the capital market of Japan, so the trading company is its money market.

PRODUCTIVITY AND THE MAXIMIZATION OF VOLUME

Even if the Japanese business does not aim at profit maximization, it seems to be obsessed by volume. Larger sales, rather than larger profits, are clearly the first objective.

In the West, sales are of course important. And growth, as such, has been seen as good in itself again and again. But the periods in which "growth" was the most important objective of business have always been few and far between in the West: the 1830s, the 1870s, the 1920s, or the

1960s. Of course, economists and businessmen in the West know of the "economies of scale," but their approach to volume essentially tries to balance the advantages of larger sales against costs and risks. This does not appear to be the typical Japanese attitude. Volume comes first, and questions about its cost come long after, if at all.

Such behavior is completely rational within the structure of the Japanese wage system, which affords automatic increases with seniority and job security until retirement age.[7] But neither Japanese nor Westerners seem conscious of the implications of the Japanese wage system for productivity and for the impact of volume on business results.

If wages go up automatically with length of service and independently of job or skill, and if employees have to be kept on the payroll until retirement, then raising volume is the only way to increase productivity rapidly. Not to raise volume is a prescription for rapidly falling productivity and loss of competitive position. Since, by and large, employees in Japan can be hired only for the entrance position (the only significant exceptions have been senior civil servants who move into top management positions in business upon their retirement from government service at age fifty-five), the only way to accommodate expansion of volume is by hiring new people into the entrance grades.

As many students of Japanese organizations have stressed, this practice creates substantial problems. It makes it particularly difficult for a new business to grow fast, which in turn explains in some measure the advantage of a "joint venture" for a new business. In a joint venture, the established partner can furnish experienced managers, foremen, and skilled workers to a new enterprise, which otherwise would have to staff itself entirely with inexperienced people just entering a career.

The advantages to the Japanese wage system have rarely been considered. Since the beginner is traditionally paid a fraction of what the mature and experienced man receives for the same work, and since most workers, especially rank and file, produce pretty much the same regardless of length of service, rapid expansion means that the persons brought in to do the additional work cost only a fraction of what the employees already at work cost, and what the employees doing the same work for the competition cost. Their productivity per man-hour may be somewhat lower than that of experienced employees, though the difference is not particularly great in most routine jobs. But the productivity per unit of wages is as much as three times that of the man who has been on the payroll for twenty-five or thirty years. The business that can expand faster than its competitors, therefore, has a tremendous—almost an unbeatable —advantage in labor costs and productivity. Conversely, with automatic

---

[7] That this does not mean inflexibility of employment or wages needs to be stressed; see my article, "What We Can Learn from Japanese Management," *Harvard Business Review*, March/April 1971.

increases in wages with length of service, the business that cannot increase its volume very rapidly finds itself losing productivity.

The objective of maximizing volume is, therefore, completely rational given Japanese economic realities. In fact, it is the only rational strategy in the situation. The Japanese executive can assume, with considerable probability, that his profitability and his economic results will not be endangered by rapid volume increase even if prices decrease. In other words, he does not need to worry as long as the price he receives covers his present expenses. He knows that the true cost of the additional production is likely to be much lower. In the economists' terms, he knows that incremental revenue pricing, in which the additional volume does not have to cover anything but out-of-pocket expenses, is almost certain to be adequate to prevent a loss and, in fact, obtain a profit.

This is in marked contrast to the position of his Western colleague, who pays primarily for the job rather than for length of service. There, the fact that the new employee is likely to be less productive than the experienced man while still, especially in unionized businesses, receiving the same—or almost the same—wage as the man with seniority on the job, means that additional volume has to produce significantly greater returns to be profitable. This does not rule out "incremental revenue pricing," but does limit it to capital-intensive industries, in which capital assets are not adequately utilized. In the Japanese situation no such limitations apply. Under the Japanese system labor is, in effect, a capital expenditure and one in which, contrary to all other capital expenses, the fixed charge increases as the "investment" gets older.

This is so obvious to any Japanese business executive that he rarely mentions it. At the same time, it is so completely different from anything any Westerner has seen that he barely notices that his Japanese colleague operates with different ground rules. It is more amazing, however, that the economists also do not seem to have recognized that volume has a different impact on the economic results of a business in Japan than in the West. They have not noticed that to the Japanese executive increasing volume is the way to increase productivity, and with this the return on the total economic resources employed.

Again, we deal with a Japanese structural reality that is not grounded in Japanese history or Japanese tradition. I cannot, from the sources accessible to me, find out when payment by seniority coupled with lifetime employment became general, but it was unknown for rank-and-file employees before the 1920s. It may have been fairly common for managerial employees before that date, and apparently it had become fairly common for government employees even before that time. Yet there is no precedent for it in pre-Meiji times. The Samurai of a Han had lifetime employment, but they were paid by position not seniority. The employees of the pre-Meiji workshop had a lifelong relationship, though it would be exaggeration to call it lifetime employment. Like today's employees in Japan's preindustrial sector, the obligation was fairly one-sided; the employee could not move, but he could be discharged and often was. And there was no payment by seniority, just as there is none in today's preindustrial sector. In other words, though quite clearly in tune with Japanese ideas of human and social relations, payment by seniority is a post-Meiji innovation. It clearly was not introduced for reasons of economic rationality, let alone to make possible expansion of volume with a built-in increase in productivity. But this has been its effect. As a result, maximization of volume is a rational business strategy in Japan way beyond its role in the West.

Indeed, the much-vaunted rapid increase of Japanese productivity since 1950 represents in substantial part—perhaps as much as half—nonrecurrent shifts in the labor force rather than genuine productivity increases. Japan, during the last twenty years, has been able to move into its modern sector—its large-scale manufacturing and service firms—enormous numbers of young people receiving very low salaries in relation to the average salary. This was the result in part of the tremendous shift of young people from the farm to the city and in part of the short but fairly sharp baby-boom Japan underwent in the early fifties. As a result, Japan went through a period in which the ratio of young employees, whether blue-collar, clerks, or managerial (middle-school, high-school, or university graduates), was unusually high. And while their wages went up very fast, the wage pyramid was highly biased toward the youngest—that is, the cheapest—category and toward the categories with the highest productivity per unit of wages. Since these employees also were very well educated compared with their predecessors, they might well be assumed to have had higher productivity altogether, or at least not to be less productive despite their lack of experience.

This period is at an end. The Japanese birthrate dropped precipitously in the mid-fifties, which means that from now on the number of young men entering the labor force each year will be significantly lower than it was in the sixties. At the same time, the movement of young, well-educated people from the farm to the city is essentially over (except, perhaps, for young women finishing middle school). In other words, the tremendous availability of young people—those of high productivity per unit of wage—is likely to be replaced by a relative scarcity of young workers in all categories (except perhaps university graduates for managerial positions, whose supply is likely to continue to grow throughout this decade at the price of a sharp cut in the supply of young middle-school and high-school graduates for blue-collar and clerical work).

It is not possible to guess what proportion of the Japanese increase in productivity can be attributed to the Japanese wage structure rather than to actual productivity increases. It may run as high as 50 percent. In other words, what looks like consistent Japanese ability in the last twenty years to increase the productivity of labor year after year may, in large measure, reflect demographics rather than managerial ability or worker motivation. And the democraphics are almost certain to turn in the other direction and to make increase in productivity based on the influx of young and comparatively low-paid workers increasingly less important. There is indeed reason to wonder whether Japanese productivity figures are not in for a sharp drop—regardless of what Japanese management or government do. The drop would be as much of a statistical illusion as the increase has been; it would reflect a shift in age structure rather than a shift in productivity. But the net effect would surely be a basic change in the reality of Japanese business, which would make maximization of volume far less attractive to Japanese business and far less rational as a business strategy.

CONCLUDING OBSERVATIONS

The foregoing discussion does not pretend to be an analysis of Japanese business or of Japanese society. It attempts to present some aspects of Japanese business behavior and business strategy that are rarely discussed, and thereby to contribute to the understanding of the Japanese economy and of the behavior of the Japanese business enterprise. But the main aim of this paper was not essentially to contribute to the understanding of Japan. Nor would the author presume to speak as an "expert" on Japan. The aim was primarily to raise two questions regarding the study of institutions and of Japanese institutions in particular.

The student of institutions is prone to start with a "model," whether he is conscious of this or not. He then tends either to impose the model and to describe behavior in terms of the model, disregarding the inconvenient fact that actual behavior does not follow the model. This has been true, for instance, for the economists' "theory of the firm" with the ludicrous result that while everybody admits that no business behaves the way the theory says it should, everybody also claims that the theory nonetheless explains what business is doing and why. The tendency has been equally true with respect to the study of political institutions, such as the attempt to impose American models of pressure groups on Japanese or European political reality. Or the analyst, realizing that his subject does not behave according to the predictions of his model, falls back on the explanation that people are "not rational."

The example of Japanese business strategy suggests, however, that the most fruitful starting point for institutional analysis and for understanding the behavior of people in institutions might be the assumption that they are behaving rationally and that they rationally optimize their realities. The assumption might be that different behavior is best explained in terms of different realities and that it is the job of the institutional analyst to find out what the realities are. This in turn might explain why people behave in what, to the analyst, seems to be such an "irrational" manner.

The Japanese businessman behaves perfectly rationally. His strategies optimize his realities. So does the American businessman, in terms of the realities of his capital and labor market, or the German businessman in terms of his. The realities are different. They are not, admittedly, easily seen from the outside, but they are usually fairly easy to find, once one starts looking for them.

The second observation is equally methodological and relates to the study of comparative institutions and the comparative study of society. We have two dominant approaches in these two fields. One might be called the ideological approach, of which the Marxist approach—that has been applied with such dubious results to Japanese history and Japanese society—is only one example. The other one might be called the approach of cultural anthropology with its emphasis on the values, the history, and the conditions of a people and of its society. Both are obviously fruitful, but are also only heuristic principles.

The examples of Japanese business strategy given in this paper suggest that these two approaches need to be complemented by a structural or institutional approach—an approach that neither assumes a universal theory nor cultural and historical determinism; that accepts, and indeed, rejoices in the diversity of human experience, of human ingenuity, and of human personality; and accepts that different historical situations, different personalities, and different historical accidents lead to the fashioning of different tools for the same job and different solutions to the same problem.

To the academic scholar, this is not very inviting. One can only see such reality in practical experience. It cannot be deduced from first principles, since it usually does not derive from first principles, but from expediency. One cannot, as a rule, identify it through values, traditions, or beliefs, since it usually has little to do with them, but represents innovation. And yet an understanding of behavior and of the dynamics of a society, a culture, a political system, and an economic system may not be attainable without an understanding of the structural realities that institutional behavior tends to optimize, and usually in a rational manner.

ECONOMIC REALITIES AND ENTERPRISE STRATEGY: A COMMENT

Hugh Patrick

Professor Drucker's paper is deceptively ambitious. What at first seems a rather general discussion has imbedded in it a sophisticated theory of the behavior of the firm—a theory into which Japanese large firms fit, in terms both of basic business strategy and of the structural or institutional realities affecting that strategy. I first summarize his argument as I understand it, and then appraise it.

First, the theory is about large firms with professional managers and control vested in the management rather than the diffused and fragmented stockholders. Management is subject to constraints, both those specifically institutional and those more broadly termed the economic environment. Managers behave rationally, optimizing their goals subject to the institutional realities.

Second, these firms have two goals. One is to minimize the cost of capital. The other is to be assured that they have or can obtain capital when they need it—to minimize the risk of not having access to capital.

Third, the firm's business strategy is thus to optimize these goals and to respond rationally to the existing structural realities of the economic environment. That environment has been determined historically, in part by such "historical accidents" as the nature of and differences in leaders' personalities, in part by highly specific socioeconomic conditions.

Fourth, Japanese firms, in determining their business strategies, have to respond to three important institutional realities, which lead to apparently different behavior from Western firms, but which are based on trying to achieve the same ultimate goals. These three realities are: the high debt-equity ratio; the use of independent trading companies to handle sales; and the nature of the employment and wage system. Each deserves further elucidation.

The high debt-equity ratio imposes high interest costs on a firm. Most debt is in the form of bank loans, which are a substitute for equity. Firms feel under greater pressure to cover their interest burden than to maximize the profit residual after interest payments. Therefore, they try to maintain and enhance the volume of production and sales. A corollary is that managers have incentives to sacrifice rather than to maximize profits; it is most important to pay interest charges, and next to pay some stable rate of dividends. Managers have few, if any, stock options. Rather, firms try to minimize costs of capital in other (unspecified) ways.

The extensive use of large, general trading companies is mainly due to the lack of medium-term (ninety days to five years) finance for distribution. Professor Drucker makes the important point that trading companies in practice are large financial intermediaries that borrow from banks and finance customers.

The system of permanent employment and seniority wage increases tends to raise the unit costs of production. The only way to offset this cost pressure is to expand volume. Dynamically, this lowers the average age of the work force since new hirings concentrate on young people. Statistically, with wage costs relatively fixed, it pays to maintain a full-capacity level of operation. Thus, maximizing volume and its growth holds down unit labor costs. (Note that this explanation does not require technological change or economies of scale, though both help.)

I find this an exciting and challenging line of argument. However, I have some reservations about the logic of the argument, and particularly about its empirical support.

Let me begin with the two goals that dominate the behavior of firms. Minimizing the risk of not obtaining access to capital is important; in its extreme form it means that a firm wants to stay alive, not to go bankrupt. Yet it relates to growth rather perversely. The best, and indeed complete, access to capital is a firm's own cash flow from depreciation, reserve allowances, and retained earnings. By limiting its growth rate to that financed from internal sources, the firm minimizes its risk of access to capital. But it also means substantial growth and profit opportunities foregone by the firm in a high-growth economy.

The minimization of the cost of capital is also an important goal. The article is somewhat unclear, but Professor Drucker has indicated that he includes both internally generated funds and external sources of funds in capital costs; the firm equates the cost of each, so that it is neutral between internal and external funding. The two goals conflict: minimizing availability risk means emphasizing internal funds, whereas minimizing cost may mean heavy reliance on outside funds. It is important thus to know how firms weight (trade off) the two goals. Professor Drucker does not provide us an answer.

More important, these two goals do not adequately describe the behavior of most large Japanese firms, which have grown rapidly and borrowed heavily to do so. This does not mean that Japanese managers are not rational or not optimizing—I agree with Professor Drucker that they are—but that the specification of basic goals is incomplete. We need to add additional, more dynamic goals for an adequate theory of firm behavior.

I agree with Professor Drucker about the importance of specific institutional or structural realities in behavior. However, it is unclear whether Professor Drucker regards these as constraints that firms must take into account in optimizing certain goals—just as, for example, they must take into account constraints of the law—or whether these institutional features have a greater role, somehow determining intermediate goals directly. Moreover, Professor Drucker's argument seems to reject the theory of Chandler and other business historians that strategy determines structure; rather, for Drucker structure determines strategy. However, Chandler is concerned with corporate structure, whereas Drucker is concerned with the structure of the external environment within which the firm operates. I see a dynamic interaction over time between strategy and structure. The strategy of one period results in a new structure, which then becomes a constraint on strategy in the next period. For example, the rapid growth objectives of Japanese firms in the 1950s and 1960s resulted in the new structural condition of high debt-equity ratios.

This brings me to more empirical issues. I focus on financial issues since others are better qualified to discuss the other two structural realities of trading companies and of the employment and wage system. I want to make several brief points. The financial role of trading companies is an important point that needs further research. Why have banks been willing to lend more, and at lower cost, to trading companies than to large producing companies? Or do they, relative to the demand for funds? Professor Drucker points out that general estimates of industrial productivity growth may be exaggerated, since they reflect in part a substantial differential between the relatively high productivity and low wages of young workers. I find this somewhat confusing. His underlying demographic point is relevant: the average age of the industrial labor force will rise in the future because there will be relatively few new young entrants.[8]

I agree with Professor Drucker on the nature and importance of the banking system and capital market for Japanese large firm behavior. The large, fixed interest charges of heavy borrowing are an important constraint on firms; it encourages them, as do any fixed costs, to maintain production and cut prices in periods when demand declines. I disagree with his assertion that such bank loans, or indeed any portion of them, are economically "equity capital." The bank's loan claims on income and assets come before any equity claims. With the equity base small the risk may seem high. But in fact this has not been true. Loan losses in postwar Japan have been and are negligible; actual risk has been low.

I regard Professor Drucker's historical interpretation of the role of finance for Japan, and for the United States and Europe, to be exaggerated. First, Goldsmith's data show that new equity-share issue through capital markets has not been a major source of finance, in the aggregate, for any industrial economy.[9] This does not deny that at certain periods for certain firms, new stock issue, openly in the capital markets or to investment banks, has been an important source of funds. For example, large American firms do not raise the bulk of their capital in equity issue; most is from internal sources, with bond issue next. Share issue is about the same proportion of total fund sources for Japanese and American firms; the main difference is that the former rely heavily on bank loans.

I find Professor Drucker's discussion of Japan's historical financial development somewhat confusing. Shares were actively traded in the 1880–1890s, but in Japan, more than in other countries, bank loans were important. However, prior to World War II business borrowing was not great relative to their net worth position; the debt-equity ratio was about one-third. Firms financed a significant proportion of expansion from internally generated funds. Only after World War II have the debt-equity

---

[8] Incidentally, I estimate that an increase of one year in the average age of a large firm's work force would raise its wage bill by about 3 percent; this effect has been swamped in recent years by the large annual average wage increases, averaging about 15 percent.

[9] Raymond W. Goldsmith, *Financial Structure and Development* (New Haven: Yale University Press, 1969).

ratios become so high; it was due primarily to the rapid expansion of company investment, much too large to be financed internally. Thus the strategy of rapid growth, in response to profit opportunities as well as competition for market share, caused the present structural reality of high debt-equity ratios and high fixed interest costs.

I do not regard this situation either as inconsistent with profit maximization or as making profit maximization unimportant. In contrast, one could argue within the context of Professor Drucker's theoretical framework that firms should maximize profits in order both to minimize the degree of dependence on borrowed capital and to be able to borrow more. There is also a strong growth incentive to maximize profits in the long run. Of course some fims, such as Shiseido, have been able in a protected market situation to generate sufficient profits to grow rapidly without much borrowing.

Professor Drucker apparently accepts the view that Japanese large firms do not maximize profits. Certainly there have been fewer incentives to do so for management in Japan than elsewhere: no executive stock options or bonuses directly tied to profitability; and substantial inability (until very recently) to raise funds relatively inexpensively by new stock issue at market price based on profitability. My own view is that Japanese firms, despite what they say, behave in a way in which long-run profit maximization is approximated. I think Japanese management has a longer time horizon than American management; at least executive incentives are structured somewhat that way. However, the principle of the maximization of profits is not strongly supported by Japan's value system, in contrast to American business ideology. Thus Japanese management justifies the firm's role in terms of benefits to its customers (consumers), to its employees, and even to the nation. We clearly need much more empirical research on Japanese management, particularly in distinguishing between stated and actual motivation and behavior.

PART THREE

Cultural and Educational Organization

Intellectuals in the Decision Making Process

HERBERT PASSIN

INTRODUCTION

English intellectuals, a prominent Japanese writer tells us, have close relations with the upper strata of government, Parliament, and the business world, but they are cut off from the masses.[1] French intellectuals are cut off from the upper strata, but have very close relations with the masses. Japanese intellectuals, however, have the worst of both worlds: like the English they are cut off from the masses, and like the French they are cut off from the upper strata.

Leaving aside the correctness of the observation about the British[2] and the French,[3] is it in fact the case that Japanese intellectuals are isolated and without power? This paper will not try to give a definitive answer to this question but to explore some of the issues involved in approaching an answer. In the broadest sense, our problem is the relationship of intellectuals in Japan to the "establishment" (the power structure, the system). A brief accounting of the history of this relationship may, therefore, be useful.

---

[1] Katō Shūichi, *Nihon no nai to gai* [Japan: Inside and Outside] (Tokyo: Bungei Shunjusha, 1972), p. 153.

[2] "In Britain," writes English sociologist T. B. Bottomore, "intellectuals have not possessed such great social prestige as in France, nor have they been so prominent in political life." *Elites and Society* (Hardmondsworth: Penguin, 1964), p. 75.

[3] Mattei Dogan found that more than one-half of the elected members of the French Chamber of Deputies were intellectuals. "Political Ascent in a Class Society: French Deputies 1870–1958," in Dwaine Marvick, ed., *Political Decision-Makers* (Glencoe, Ill.: Free Press, 1961).

In Japan of the early and mid-Meiji period, the intellectuals constituted a small, cohesive group. This small group was very much part of the then-existing establishment.[4] The diverse elements of which it was composed were initially held together by the *bunmei kaika,* the "civilization and enlightenment" ideology that formed the basis of the Meirokusha (or Meiji 6, that is, 1873 society). As a small group the intellectuals all knew one another, and their views weighed in heavily with the political elites. Whether in public office like Mori Arinori, or resolutely outside of it like Fukuzawa Yukichi, most of them were active participants in the public life of their times through writing, lecturing, reporting, teaching, advising, and operating modern institutions. Toward the end of the Meiji period, this unity of the intellectual classes began to break down. The increasing number of graduates produced by the new universities began to replace the Restoration generation.

With this new development, the intellectuals divided into three broad streams: a pro-establishment clerisy, respectable and supportive of the established institutions; an anti-establishment intelligentsia, dissatisfied with the new institutions and with their own place in society; and a nonpolitical stratum of professionals, technicians, and specialists concerned primarily with their own work and only secondarily with politics. As the sheer number of intellectuals grew, their relations with the other elites underwent important changes.

The stream of anti-establishment intellectuals, first adumbrated in the early-Meiji Jiyū Minken (Freedom and People's Rights) movement, broadened steadily, despite frequent setbacks. Their critical position with regard to the central institutions of the society led them into growing moral and political opposition—a position that crystallized around a variety of movements based on Christianity, socialism, pragmatism, liberalism and, after World War I, Marxism.

The opposition to the forms that the modern Japanese society was taking was based on a combination of motives. One was the traditional samurai contempt for trade, moneygrubbing, and the pursuit of private advantage. Since the samurai were highly overrepresented among the early Meiji intellectuals, their ethos permeated the intellectuals' outlook. To this aristocratic disdain for the vulgarity of a materialist, capitalist (later "mass") society were joined traditionalist and nationalist reactions against westernism (and after World War II against the United States), populism, working-class discontent, agrarian distress, and egalitarian impulses and concepts that rapidly diffused their way through Japanese thought and institutions.

The discontent following World War I, combined with another

---

[4] See Herbert Passin, "Modernization and the Japanese Intellectual: Some Comparative Observations," in Marius Jansen, ed., *Changing Japanese Attitudes towards Modernization* (Princeton: Princeton University Press, 1965).

quantum jump in the number of university students and the appeal of the Russian Revolution, strengthened the progressive, liberal, and radical forces and led to the well-known confrontations with authority of the late 1920s and particularly the 1930s. Despite severe repression and the frequent surface conformity, anti-establishment radicalism remained a strong latent force in literature, journalism, and the universities.

The end of World War II found the progressives—newly released from the restraints of the militarist period—stronger than ever. The atmosphere created by the American Occupation's democratization program was favorable to them. So was the emergence of other newly liberated elements such as the trade union movement, the radical political parties, liberalism, progressive thought, and women's emancipation. During the first few years of the Occupation, not only the established intellectuals but even liberals, progressives, and leftists were active in public life, particularly in the development of the reform programs.

But with the sharp polarization caused by the cold-war issues, the progressive forces moved sharply away from the establishment. By the end of the Occupation period it would be fair to say that the progressives had become the majority, if not of the intellectuals as a whole, then at least of the principal articulate intellectual elites. The tradition, which had already begun to show itself during the twenties and thirties, was now firmly entrenched. In general, the intellectuals, along with the labor unionists and the students, could be counted on in the "progressive camp." The progressive intellectuals have come to play a dominant role in most of the principal intellectual institutions, including the universities, the mass media, and publishing.

From the end of the Occupation to the mid-1960s, at the same time that the intellectual stratum as a whole was growing by leaps and bounds, the progressive, anti-establishment strain within it was growing even faster. But as Japan approached "maturity," the relatively advanced condition of the post-industrial society, new developments began to make themselves felt. On the one hand, a new polarization developed with the separation of student activism from the intellectual mainstream. The older intellectual generation, whether pro- or anti-establishment, appeared increasingly irrelevant to the new preoccupations. The younger intellectuals, drawn from the recent New-Left-dominated student movements, were more than ever alienated from the centers of power.

On the other hand, however, there was some diminution of the sharp polarization among the older intellectuals. As Japan's economy maintained its steady, high-speed growth, the stratum of scientists, researchers, technicians, specialists, and professionals was expanding and also becoming more involved in the operations and decision-making processes of economy and government. As measured by all the indicators—consultation, research, research funds, public attention, and publication—the demand for the services of intellectuals, which has always been higher than is generally realized, appears to be going up. As Japan becomes increasingly a knowledge-based society, intellectuals become even more indispensable than before, and their position in relation to the other elites improves. The relative balance among the various intellectual sectors also changes. The literary, humanistic intellectuals have lost some of their prestige as those with scientific-technical expertise have come into increasing demand.

WHO ARE THE INTELLECTUALS?

As in other advanced industrial societies, the number of people engaged in intellectual work in Japan has increased enormously. In consequence, the intellectuals have become, like all large groups in modern society, differentiated, even stratified, and they form, for certain purposes, a political constituency of their own. The borderline dividing them from other groups becomes hard to draw, and their relations with other elites become complex.

For our purposes here, intellectuals will be taken as people who "devote themselves to cultivating and formulating knowledge." [5] Normally they will be engaged in the professions—university teaching, scientific research, writing, journalism—that require them to spend most or a good portion of their time in creative intellectual work. We shall, however, also have in mind those whose primary work is elsewhere but who engage in intellectual work some of the time.

People primarily engaged in the occupations within which we would expect most intellectual work to fall constitute about 5 percent of the labor force in Japan. If we use the census category of "professional and technical" occupations as an indicator of the intellectual occupations, we find that in the twenty years between 1950 and 1970 they have increased four times as rapidly as the labor force as a whole (see Table 1).

If we look more closely at specific occupations of an intellectual character, the trend is even clearer (see Table 2). The number of university teachers increased about nine times faster than the labor force as a whole, scientific researchers about seven times faster, writers more than five times faster, and the legal profession more than three times faster. Using a somewhat different census classification, we find that in the five-year period between 1966 and 1970 alone, there has been a 34 percent increase in the number of scientific researchers. This is roughly four times the growth of the labor force in the same period (about 9 percent).

Very often, when people use the word "intellectual," they have the small intellectual elite in mind. Just as the business, political, or military elites constitute a very small part of their constituencies, so do the intellectual elites of theirs. But if we include not only the chiefs but the

---

[5] Robert Merton, *Social Theory and Social Structure* (Glencoe, Ill.: Free Press, 1949), p. 162.

Table 1
Growth of Intellectual Professions

	Index of Professional and Technical Occupations[a]	Index of Labor Force as a Whole
1950	100	100
1955	119	110
1960	130	123
1965	163	134
1970	217	147

Source: My calculations, based on census data. The 1965 data are based on the 20 percent sample analysis, and the 1970 data taken from the one percent sample reported in *Nihon no tokei—1971* (Statistics of Japan—1971), ed. and comp. Prime Minister's Office, Statistics Bureau (Tokyo: Ministry of Finance Printing Office, 1972).

[a] This is calculated from the regular census breakdown entitled "Occupation (Minor Groups) of the Employed Persons 15 Years Old and Over by Employment Status and Sex." In this breakdown, professional and technical employees (*senmonteki, gijutsuteki shokugyō jūjisha*) are usually listed first in the eleven categories. The category usually contains thirty-seven census lines including technicians, teachers, medical personnel, artists, writers, the legal profession, accountants, and social workers.

Table 2
Growth Index of Selected Intellectual Professions, 1950–1970

	Writers[a]	Scientific Researchers	University Faculty	Legal Profession[b]	Labor Force as a Whole
1950[c]	100	—[d]	100	—[d]	100
1955	170	100	156	100	110
1960	215	135	160	182	123
1965	254	261	209	234	134
1970	322	426	457	257	147

Source: My own calculations, based on census data.

[a] This census category includes "writers, editors, publishers."

[b] For 1955 and 1960, I have grouped two census lines, "judges, prosecutors, lawyers" and "other legal"; for 1965 and 1970, there is only one line, entitled "legal."

[c] The classification used in the 1950 census is somewhat different from the later ones.

[d] Not identifiable in the 1950 census.

rank and file, as it were, the apprentice along with the master craftsmen, or to use Shil's terms,[6] the reproductive and executive intellectual, as well

---

[6] Edward Shils, "Intellectuals, Tradition, and the Tradition of Intellectuals: Some

as the productive, we may very well be talking about millions of people. Not only do they attract other people to their ideas, but their own votes alone are sufficiently numerous to be important. Politicians, however contemptuous they may be, cannot disregard them. There are over a million teachers alone. Even if we reserve the term "intellectuals" for teachers in higher education, there are still 160,000 of them.[7] The university, with its 1.5 million students in addition to its 120,000 faculty, plus all the others involved in its administration and maintenance, has become a constituency of noticeable heft (See Table 3). This is especially clear when we realize that about 45 percent of this population is concentrated in and around Tokyo. Most of the 310,000 in the census category of "scientific researcher" (1971) are also located in the Tokyo area, and their weight can be added to this political force.

Table 3
Higher Education, 1971

	Universities	Colleges[a]	Higher Technical Schools[b]
Institutions	389	486	63
Full-Time Faculty	78,848	14,910	3,369
Part-Time Faculty[c]	43,973	17,558	2,018
All Faculty	122,821	32,468	5,387
Faculty Ranks[d]			
Presidents	364	460	62
Professors	24,353	5,063	728
Assistant Professors[e]	17,732	2,928	1,036
Instructors[f]	10,741	4,108	948
Assistants[g]	25,658	2,451	595
Students	1,468,538	275,256	46,707

Source: Compiled from *Nihon no tōkei—1973* (Statistics of Japan—1973).
  [a] *tanki daigaku*, two- or three-year postsecondary institutions.
  [b] *kōtō senmongakkō*.
  [c] Most part-time faculty hold the rank equivalent of lecturer.
  [d] These figures refer to the full-time faculty only.
  [e] The *jokyōju* rank includes both the American associate professor and assistant professor.
  [f] *kōshi*, often also translated as "lecturer."
  [g] *joshu*.

In thinking about the place of Japanese intellectuals, this concentration of national activities in Tokyo should be kept in mind. Tokyo, like London and Paris, is a true national capital—not only the political, but the industrial, financial, intellectual, academic, artistic, and taste center of the

---

Preliminary Considerations," *Daedalus*, Spring 1972; and *The Intellectuals and the Powers and Other Essays* (Chicago: University of Chicago Press, 1972), particularly chap. 7.
    [7] As of 1971, including both full- and part-time university, college, and higher technical school facilities.

country. In the United States (as in other decentralized systems such as Australia, Brazil, and Germany), there is no single capital: Washington is the political capital but the financial, artistic, publishing, and media center is in New York, the industrial center is in the Midwest, the movie center is in the Far West, and the university population is dispersed throughout the country. In Japan, with the exception of the small Osaka *zaibatsu*, virtually all elites are centered in Tokyo. This means that in a way that is not true in decentralized systems, the elites are constantly in contact with one another. Japanese intellectuals form a community: they know one another, associate with one another, read the same newspapers, books, and journals, and share a far wider range of common understandings than, for example, do Americans. They also rub elbows with top businessmen, politicians, journalists, actors, writers, and bureaucrats much more frequently than their American counterparts do. Tokyo metropolis constitutes about 12 percent of the total population of Japan, but it includes not only half of the university population, but the main newspaper, magazine, and publishing enterprises, most of the television and radio networks, and close to 100 percent of virtually all categories of intellectual, artistic, and cultural activity. This high degree of concentration strongly conditions the position of the intellectuals in the network of elites in Japan.

DECISION-MAKING

The ideas of economists and political philosophers, both when they are right and when they are wrong, are more powerful than is commonly understood. Indeed, the world is ruled by little else. Practical men, who believe themselves to be quite exempt from any intellectual influences, are usually the slave of some defunct economist. . . . I am sure that the power of vested interests is vastly exaggerated, compared with the gradual encroachment of ideas. . . . Madmen in authority, who hear voices in the air, are distilling their frenzy from some *academic* scribbler of a few years back.

J. M. Keynes

Having identified in a broad sense who the intellectuals are, we have now to examine briefly what we mean by "influence" and "decision-making." For some people the word *influence* calls up the image of a decision-maker leaping to his feet at the intellectual's words and falling all over himself to put into effect the ideas proposed. "Even in a society which is officially an aristocracy," as Irving Kristol writes, "the ruling class never has that kind of instant power and instant authority." [8]

Another frequently held model of influence is the intellectual advising the power holder (president, prime minister)—in the extreme case even dictating his policy, but in one way or another having a say in his decisions. Japanese intellectuals often refer enviously to Kissinger as an

---

[8] Irving Kristol, *On the Democratic Idea in America* (New York: Harper & Row, 1972).

example, even though Kissinger himself has argued the limitations of the relationship.[9] In its malevolent form, the intellectual becomes a Rasputin or a Dr. Strangelove, the evil genius who exerts a malign influence over the ruler and corrupts the decisions of state. In the more benevolent version the intellectual is seen as the expert or philosopher contributing specialized knowledge or wisdom to the respectfully attentive secular powers. The extreme case is Plato's philosopher-king; although history provides many less than edifying examples of the intellectual-turned-ruler, the image continues to attract.

If this is our model of the influence of intellectuals, certainly there is little of it in recent Japan. Japan does not have a Kissinger; nor has it had, at least in the postwar period, a Rostow or Bundy. But the reason for this difference may tell us less about the relative influence of intellectuals in the two countries than about the relative weight of career bureaucrats. The Japanese Foreign Office has more weight within its governmental structure than the U.S. State Department, and its members have much more prestige than their counterparts in the U.S. Since the allocation of foreign-policy talent is somewhat different from that of the U.S., the relative weight of in-house experts and outside consultants is correspondingly different.

If we look on decision-making as a process, with the actual decision the product of a series of inputs by competitive forces, we then look not for some single decisive influence but rather for a structure of decision. When are the intellectuals themselves one of the political constituencies involved in a decision and when are they not? What is the relative weight of each of the actors in the decision? What are the points, or stages—innovation, judgment, planning, formulation—at which intellectuals make their inputs in the process?

Different kinds of decisions call for different actors, or participants, and each will make a different kind of input. The mix for decisions on military matters will be very different from that for transportation. In a major decision on, let us say, the introduction of a new weapons system, the decision-making mix will include not only the professional military but many other actors as well: the Defense Agency, the cabinet, the Liberal Democratic Party (LDP), the Diet, high-ranking officers in the self-defense forces, the Finance Ministry, the munitions-related industry, and the business community. In addition, there would be important inputs from strategic specialists (both inside and outside the Defense Agency), some of them coming from the universities, research institutes, newspapers, and think tanks. The Defense Agency input itself is very likely to have been made up of the inputs of various factions within it: ground versus naval or air interests, line versus staff officers, military versus civilian elements. The

[9] Henry A. Kissinger, "The Policymaker and the Intellectual," *The Reporter* 20:5 (5 March 1959).

final outcome would also be affected by the opposition parties, the press, factions within the LDP, mass movements, student movements, and public opinion in the broad sense.

Whether any of this intellectual input is "decisive" would be hard to say, but in the modern bureaucratic decision-making process, it would be hard to say whether *any* single input is decisive. Nevertheless, intellectuals are likely to have been involved from the very first policy-planning stages. They will be among the specialist consultants from the universities, research institutes, or think tanks. Opposition, or anti-establishment, intellectuals would also have made their weight felt, if not through the decision-making apparatus itself, then through the opposition parties, the press, the civic organizations, and the mass movements.

In this total process, how can we isolate out the influence of intellectuals?

THE INTELLECTUALS AND POLITICS

Although this paper is concerned mainly with the participation of the intellectual in the process of decision-making in the narrow sense, his participation in the broader political process is, if anything, even more important.

In certain areas intellectuals themselves are one of the main constituencies. Scientific development and education are obvious examples, and in these areas the influence of intellectuals is most effectively brought to bear through organized bodies. Some organizations purport to speak in the name of intellectuals as a whole—the Japan Science Council is the elected representative body of the natural and social sciences. Others represent particular constituencies (the teachers unions), or professions (the Japan Medical Association), or scholarly fields (the Japanese Political Science Society). Some are more political in character, like the Democratic Scientists Association. Although there are many professional organizations, so far, with the sole exception of the Japan Medical Association, they have been politically weak as pressure groups. Since the intellectuals seldom achieve consensus, even on the issues closest to their own interests, it is not surprising that they can only rarely put forth a unified view to compete with others on the field of political battle.

In the more general political process, it is no less true of Japan than of the United States that "intellectuals, more than most other groups, have the power to create, dignify, inflate, criticize, moderate or puncture" the "galloping abstractions" of public life.[10] Their influence is transmitted through their teaching, their books and articles, which form the basic parameters of public discussion, and the mass media. Through these

---

[10] Charles Frankel, "The Scribblers and International Relations," *Foreign Affairs*, October 1965.

means they have an influence, and often a decisive one, on public opinion and therefore on one of the key factors in the background of decision-making.

In many countries the intellectuals are isolated from the mass media. In Japan this is not the case. Although professing dismay about the vulgarity of the media, intellectuals play a very active part in them. The level of journalism, particularly of the national dailies, which occupy the bulk of the market, is very high, and there is also a vigorous intellectual journalism in weeklies, monthlies, and the pages and columns of the great dailies.

Japanese journalism has two traditions that are important in connection with the political role of intellectuals. First, it is strongly oppositional. Since its inception in the Meiji period, it has been, except in the period of militarist control in the 1930s, almost always on the opposition side. Although the national press professes a strict neutrality with regard to parties, its general thrust has been against the party in power. This, along with the fact that the majority of journalists tend to be progressive, has created a hospitable environment for independent and anti-establishment intellectuals.

Second, it is a very individualized journalism with a European-style *feuilletoniste* tradition. The newspapers carry many signed articles and frequently invite outside contributors. Leading Japanese intellectuals, in consequence, have newspaper outlets that are normally not available to Americans, other than celebrities. It is common, in a way that is not the case in the United States, for intellectuals, scholars, and writers to be called upon for comment on the news, analytic articles, roundtable discussions, and general social commentary. This kind of journalism not only gives intellectuals an outlet for their views, but also a high degree of public visibility (the leading press is national and runs to millions in circulation) and a significant addition to income.

The weekly and monthly journals consist virtually entirely of signed contributions rather than of unsigned staff articles. At least fifty of them provide outlets for intellectuals to express their views and opportunities for them to earn extra income. Although the intellectual journals (*sōgō-zasshi*) do not match the huge popular weeklies in circulation, they are by no means "little mags"; they reach national audiences, and they play an important role in maintaining a high degree of unity and communication among intellectuals.

To this high demand from the print media has been added the virtually insatiable demand of radio and television. Here too intellectuals are active on the artistic as well as the intellectual side. They appear frequently as commentators, news analysts, panelists, and lecturers. The relations between practicing intellectuals and the intellectualized staffs of the broadcasting media is much closer than in many other countries. Here again the broad access that intellectuals have to television and radio gives them an important outlet, enhances their influence by turning them into celebrities, and makes them more viable by adding to their income. The demand from all of these sources is sufficient to support a large corps of free-lance critics (*hyōronka*).

During the postwar period intellectuals have provided important leadership for or identified themselves closely with all the major mass movements, particularly those involving protest against authority. Writers Hirotsu Kazuo and Uno Kōji played a decisive role in the development of the Matsukawa movement which finally led, after twenty-one years, not only to full exoneration and payment of damages to the defendants, but also to major impact on the judicial system, investigation and trial procedures, and the American Occupation's criminal-code reforms.[11] Although "union support and mass letter-writing campaigns helped create the impression of popular backing for the movement," writes Chalmers Johnson about the Matsukawa case, "it was the involvement of famous Tokyo intellectuals that made the headlines and filled the columns of commentators." [12]

For further examples of the influence of intellectuals one has only to think of the close relationship of the Peace Problems Symposium (Heiwa Mondai Danwakai) in the 1960 movement against the U.S.-Japan Security Treaty.[13] Or one can think of Ōta Minoru in the post-1960 antitreaty movement, or Nakajima Kenzō in the movement for the normalization of relations with China.

Intellectuals are often influential even without the backing of a specific mass movement. The shift of national priorities from the "growth first" to the "balanced growth" policy, which gives greater emphasis to welfare and environmental protection, has been decisively affected by their views. There are, to be sure, many other factors that go into that shift, but the influence of the intellectuals in pushing it against the reluctance of business and government is clear.

Another way of assessing the weight of intellectuals in decision-making is to look at the social demand for their services. While intellectuals, especially the academic intellectuals, like to complain about how ignored they are, there are many who would argue that they are, if anything, too much involved with the powers. Are they, in fact, as powerless as some would like to make out or, on the contrary, too much "the handmaidens of whatever political, military, paramilitary, and economic elite happens to be financing their operations," to borrow a phrase from Roszak's charges about American intellectuals? [14]

---

[11] Chalmers Johnson, *Conspiracy at Matsukawa* (Berkeley and Los Angeles: University of California Press, 1972), particularly chap. 5, "The Two Zolas."

[12] Ibid., p. 237.

[13] See George R. Packard III, *Protest in Tokyo* (Princeton: Princeton University Press, 1966), pp. 26–31.

[14] Theodore Roszak, ed., *The Dissenting Academy* (New York: Pantheon, 1968).

Let us take the example of the academic intellectuals. If we look at the total round of their activities, we find that although most of their time is spent in teaching-related activities—that is, teaching, preparing courses, grading papers, conducting examinations, seeing students, and sitting on university committees—a significant amount is also spent in outside work. This outside work, called *arubaito* (from the German *arbeit*), is very important.

There are two sides to the professor's outside work. On the one hand, he needs extra income because his salary is low. The outside work helps him make ends meet. On the other hand, outside work is also a measure of social demand. Both of these aspects undoubtedly enter the balance sheet.

International comparisons of wages are notoriously difficult methodological exercises. We cannot, therefore, be dogmatic about whether Japanese academics' salaries are low or high on any absolute scale, and whether their share, compared with that of other components of the labor force, is appropriate or not. What can be said is that although they are lower in money amount (as measured by international exchange rates) than American or Western European academic salaries, within Japan they are on the same level as the civil service. This means they are not as good as equivalent positions (and equal years of service) in large-scale private industry, but that they are better than smaller companies and elementary and secondary schools. Although there are differences between public and private universities and great variations among the private universities, academic salaries in Japan range between (at 1973 exchange rates) $7,000 per annum for a full professor just starting and $14,000 for a senior professor with upwards of thirty-years seniority. They can also be expected to go up about 10 percent a year.

But for the great majority of professors, particularly in the better universities of the Tokyo area, salary is only one portion of total income; and in the case of the popular, well-known professors who are in constant demand, a very small portion indeed. Figures are hard to come by, but a good estimate is that for the well-known professors of leading Tokyo universities, the stars or celebrities of the academic profession, university salary often represents no more than one-third of total income. Table 4 gives the results from a 1965 survey on the sources of income for national university faculty members. Table 5 reports the results from a 1967 sample survey of public as well as private universities.

If we compare the Japanese and the American university professor, we can say that the American university salary is higher than the Japanese. Outside work is important for academic income in both countries, but there are three important differences. First, the Japanese professor receives a smaller proportion of his total income from his salary. If we assume that American professors derive 90 percent or more of their total income from salary (there are, of course, many exceptions), on the whole Japanese

Table 4
Sources of Income, National University Faculty, by Age

Age:	20–29	30–39	40–49	50–
Total Income	100%	100%	100%	100%
University Salary	56.3	80.5	82.3	86.3
Outside Work	10.9	10.6	14.8	11.6
Other Family Income	32.8	9.0	2.8	2.2

Source: Kokuritsu daigaku kyōkai [National University Association], "Kokuritsu daigaku kyōkan no kyūryō kaizen ni kansuru ikensho" [Memorandum on the improvement of salaries of national university faculty members], *Jurisuto*, no. 356 (October 15, 1966): 97. Adapted from table as reported in William K. Cummings, *Nihon no daigaku kyōju* [Japanese university professors] (Tokyo: Shiseidō, 1972), p. 104.

Table 5
Academic Moonlighting

Proportion of Total Income from Outside Work	Proportion (%) of Respondents
Some	77[a]
10% or more	43
20% or more	24
50% or more	8

Source: Adapted from Cummings, pp. 105–106.

[a] Compare this figure with the 62 percent for U.S. social science professors having outside income reported by S. M. Lipset, "American Intellectuals: Their Politics and Status," *Daedalus*, Summer 1959.

professors would receive more on the order of 70–80 percent in this form. Second, the Japanese academic's salary buys him a somewhat less satisfactory standard of living than the American's. Third, the mix of elements that makes up his outside income is somewhat different. Outside income for the American professor usually comes from research, teaching, lecturing, and consulting. In Japan, a much larger proportion would come from writing (both for the mass media and in the form of books) and from panel discussions in the public media, and significantly less from research.

A checklist of outside work opportunities for Japanese professors would look somewhat as follows:

1. Writing articles—in the mass media, general journals, specialized journals.

2. Writing books—textbooks, general books, scholarly books.
3. Lectures, panel discussions, public speeches.
4. Teaching elsewhere—in other universities, governmental training programs,[15] private business training institutions.[16]
5. Research grants.
6. Contract research—with government, private business, research organizations, public associations.
7. Consulting (for the same as 6 above).
8. Government advisory commissions.
9. Editing.
10. Private practice (lawyers, doctors).
11. Private business (architects, engineers, etc.).

Obviously, opportunities for outside work vary by field of specialization. Doctors, dentists, and lawyers can have private practices. Chemists, engineers, and architects often have corporate as well as governmental consulting outlets. They will also have access to considerable research funds. Among social scientists, economists are in the greatest demand, rather like engineers. However, there is increasing demand for sociologists and political scientists as well. More practically oriented fields, such as business administration, labor-management relations, and urban planning increasingly call upon social scientists. For the humanist scholar, there may be fewer outlets in government and corporate consulting (although these are not entirely absent), but a larger world of cultural and intellectual activity is open to him: the mass media, cultural journals, editing, public speaking, and civic associations.

INTELLECTUALS AND GOVERNMENT

Despite the prevalent view that intellectuals have little or no influence on government, a close examination of the actual decision-making process shows a number of areas of impact, or at least potential impact.

In a broad sense, there are three general postures from which the intellectual can exert influence on government: (1) as an insider, a civil servant holding a nodal position in the internal decision-making process (including high-ranking administrators, scholars in government institutions, policy planners, and even middle-ranking bureaucrats); (2) as a consultant called in to provide advice, information, critical review, or new ideas; and (3) as an independent, very likely an opponent, exerting his

---

[15] The government runs at least forty schools or training institutes. Most of them are at the university or postuniversity level and are called *daigakkō* or *kenshūsho*. Examples are the Defense Academy, National Police Academy, National Defense College, Foreign Service Training Institute, and Social Insurance Training College. In most of these there are *arubaito* opportunities for academics.

[16] Aside from technical and vocational schools, there are something on the order of one hundred higher schools in private industry at the college level, of which the Tokyo Denryoku Gakuen (Tokyo Electric Power Academy) is a good example.

influence through the mechanisms available in a democratic polity—the mass media, civic movements, and political parties.

Whatever one's position in regard to the establishment, all three modalities are available, if in differing degrees, to intellectuals. While pro-establishment and neutral intellectuals are not likely to take to the streets, nor anti-establishment figures to take positions of official responsibility, such developments are by no means unknown. In general, however, there are likely to be more pro-establishment and neutral intellectuals among the insiders and consultants, and anti-establishment intellectuals are likely to figure more heavily in the third group.

Insiders.

Insiders are often spoken of as *goyōgakusha,* the term for the scholars during the Tokugawa period who provided their services for pay to the Shogunal or domainal governments. The term is, of course, a pejorative one, implying that to work for the "powers" is to prostitute oneself. Pro-establishment intellectuals, or indeed any intellectual who happens to be in agreement with the government position, may find himself tarred with this brush. The term *goyōteki-shingikai,* for example, is commonly applied to official advisory commissions that appear to go along with what the government wants.

However we judge the moral and political issues involved, it is clear that there are large numbers of people we would classify as intellectuals who work directly for government. They may be found first of all among the corps of highly qualified upper civil servants. Japan's higher civil service, along with the French, certainly ranks as one of the most competent, dedicated, and powerful in the world. The stringent competitive requirements assure that many of them will be intellectuals, some actually scholarly in their inclinations. They will also be highly responsive to the academic community, often maintaining close personal associations. Many of them are known as intellectuals to wider publics through their writings, and others have an accepted standing in their own professions, such as economics, social policy planning, engineering, or area study. In addition to purely administrative line functions, policy-planning positions fill a good part of their careers.

Intellectuals are also widely employed in government for their specialized knowledge. The exact numbers are hard to estimate, but some indications can be found. There are, for example, about ninety national government research institutes employing about twenty-five thousand research scientists.[17] (The total number of employees is much higher.) The

---

[17] Some of these have regional branches as, for example, the Ministry of Agriculture's Regional Fishery Research Laboratories. In addition to the national government, local government entities maintain 551 research institutions (data as of 1 April 1971).

incidence of intellectuals, scholars, and specialists varies by government department. Some, such as the Economic Planning Agency, will have proportionately more than, say, the Ministry of Posts. But even the Ministry of Posts has its intellectuals, at least in its higher administrative ranks, its Electrical Wave Research Institute, the Communications College, and its specialized technical departments. Most of the intellectuals here are, of course, engineers, natural scientists, and technicians— scientific-technical rather than humanistic intellectuals. The largest number of intellectuals will be found in the Prime Minister's Office, the Economic Planning Agency, the Ministry of Finance, and the Ministry of International Trade and Industry (MITI). In general, the more "technocratic" the field, the greater their weight. Important inputs come mainly in engineering and economics, or in areas that involve both such as regional planning, developmental economics, urban problems, and systems analysis.

What impact do they have on government policy? The answer would have to be that in virtually all policy matters within their area of concern, their input of information and their formulation of the issues is very important, but that their direct influence varies in accordance with the particular constellation of forces involved. On purely technical issues, with relatively small political content, their influence can be important. The views of structural engineers, for example, carry great weight in the actual outcome of decisions on bridge-building, although the question of location is often a very political issue. In general, the Japanese government is very respectful of technical expertise. Even on economic issues, which lie near the border of the scientific-technical and the humanistic, the work of the Economic Research Institute (Keizai kenkyūsho) of the Economic Planning Agency is very influential, even if it is not the only voice involved in decisions.

Some government research institutes carry little weight in their own area of decision. This may be for many reasons: that their sphere is too peripheral to the major priority areas, that powerful pressure groups are involved, that they are incompetent, or that they are badly positioned in the bureaucratic structure. Some semigovernmental research institutes, which depend primarily on government support, for example, are regarded as little more than a place to pasture retired bureaucrats.

It is often argued that the government scholars are not true intellectuals, that they do not decide problems on their own but simply apply their skills within the framework of problems set for them by the government. Such a view is far too simplistic. Much of the work of government research institutes is scarcely different from that done in institutes located in the universities. The sociologists, mathematicians, social psychologists, and demographers of the Welfare Ministry's Population Problems Research Institute, or the scholars in the Institute of Mathematical Statistics located in the Ministry of Education do much the same kind of scholarly work as those in nongovernment institutions. Since they have budgets, equipment, staff, continuity, and an audience, they are often better off and can do more self-initiated research than outside organizations. To be sure, some of the institutes do a good part of their own research in response to direct government requests or to their perception of national problems. But applied or policy research need be no less scientific than basic research. Much of the work of nongovernmental institutes, in the universities or elsewhere, is also applied research—often contracted for—whereas the work of, say, the governmental Institute of Mathematical Statistics is much more far-ranging and independent than that of many academic survey institutions.

Nor would it be correct to think that government institutions have no freedom at all to initiate research even in basic fields. Some of them, such as the National Institute of Genetics or the National Cancer Institute, are involved primarily in basic research, and it would be more correct to see them as national scientific facilities supported by the government, just as much a part of their field as a university institute. They are also quite capable of producing analyses that are critical of government policy or recommendations that are at variance with current policy. The real problem is more often that decision-makers pay no attention to the work of the government institutes, and not that the institutes have no freedom.

Although the impact of the government scholars and research institutions varies, the influence of the bureaucrat-intellectuals cannot be doubted. They are found among the senior permanent civil servants, whose tenure outlasts the government in power and is more secure. The ministers and the parliamentary vice-ministers (*seimu jikan*) come and go, but the *jimu jikan* (administrative vice-minister) goes on forever.

The Intellectual as Adviser.

The work of modern governments has become very complicated and, with the increasing welfare obligations that they have accepted, an enormous range of expertise is required. Not all of this can, or should, be provided from within the government itself. Government finds itself constantly in need of fresh inputs from the outside, which may be for many different reasons—ranging from the need for information, evaluation, or reactions, to a desire for validation or for legitimation to particular constituencies. It is not at all uncommon for top bureaucrats and even ministers to call upon academic authorities for their views. *"Osetsu o haichō shimasu"* (Let me hear your distinguished views) can often be heard in bureaucratic chambers.

The principal way that nongovernment intellectuals make an input into the decision-making process is through serving as consultants of one kind or another. The system of advisory councils, of which the *shingikai* (advisory commission) is a typical example, started in 1947, under the influence of the American Occupation's desire to build more citizen-participative institutions in what it perceived as a nonresponsive bureaucracy.[18] Many different types have developed, some permanent and established by law, others ad hoc, some investigative (*chōsakai*), and some deliberative in character. Although the principle has been more often honored in the breach than in the observance, the advisory commission is expected to include in its membership representatives of all the important constituencies involved in the particular issue, plus relevant experts, as well as representatives of the public interest. All major constituencies, such as business, agriculture, labor, and women, are represented on the councils, although in varying degrees, but intellectuals (mainly academics) rank second only to businessmen in numbers. Therefore, literally thousands of intellectuals sit on hundreds of government commissions that have variable but on the whole important influence on public policy decisions. Almost all government commissions will have some scholars, whether for their expertise or purely for public name value and window dressing.

Every government ministry, with the exception of foreign affairs, makes use of the advisory commissions. Altogether, there are about 240 (as of August 1972), with an average membership of 30, ranging between 5 and 180.[19] They vary in importance, impact, size, internal composition, and degree of representativeness, depending on their subject matter, the department concerned, and the timeliness of their central mission.

They also vary in the extent to which they provide a source of significant outside income to the committee members. Most committees pay purely nominal consulting fees, so that participation is considered a financial loss by many intellectuals. A famous writer was recently reported to have resigned from the Central Education Council when he learned how small the consulting fee was; he could make much more efficient use of his time, he said, by appearing on well-paying television or on panel discussions about educational problems. In a few cases, however, the consulting fee may become significant enough to raise questions about people being "bought." The Public Service System Council, which deals with very sensitive issues and very sensitive constituencies, has representatives from labor and management, and pays its members monthly fees.

As expected, the councils vary widely in their impact. One of the major functions of the advisory commissions is to adjust the conflicting demands of the major constituencies involved in a particular issue. The Rice Price Council, for example, has representatives of the farmers, consumers, workers, businessmen, and the general public. When it agrees on a plan,

---

[18] For an excellent summary in English, see Yung Ho Park, "The Government Advisory System in Japan," *Journal of Comparative Administration* 3.4 (February 1972).

[19] These represent the advisory commissions established by law. If we take into account the various study groups and commissions established by ministerial ordinance or even more informally, there will be several hundred more. See ibid., p. 437.

the Council's recommendations carry great weight and are hard for the government to reject. The advisory commission's input may be decisive under other circumstances as well: as final arbiter when the major elements cannot reach agreement, or as a pressure group pushing its own recommendations. In other cases its position may be an important, even if not always decisive, input into the departmental deliberations. Often the advisory commission's position, through publication or reporting in the mass media, plays an important role in establishing the frame of reference for debate and in forming the public opinion that influences the government or Diet decision. This is seen clearly in the role of the Central Education Council, or the People's Livelihood Council of the Economic Planning Agency.

Characteristically, the advisory commission will be one of the decisive elements at certain stages of the process.[20] The Boston Consulting Group analysis of the development of Japan's computer industry gives us a valuable picture of how the advisory commission articulates with other elements in an ongoing process.[21] The government's computer development program started in 1953, but the first real fruits came only in the late 1960s. The process therefore required a sustained effort of about fifteen years. In 1954, after a false start by the Ministry of Education, which, through Tokyo University scientists, had actually developed a vacuum-tube computer, the Science and Technology Agency (then within MITI) began the development of a computer logic using transistors as one of its many internal research activities. In 1955, MITI organized a research committee on the computer whose composition "was typically Japanese, representing all constituencies with substantial interest: MITI officials, prospective manufacturers, Japan Telegraph and Telephone managers, and university research scientists were members." [22] In accordance with the Electronics Industry Development Provisional Act, passed by the Diet in 1957, MITI established an advisory commission—the Electronics Industry Deliberation Council (in 1971 renamed the Electronic and Machinery Industries Deliberation Council). It consists of "approximately 40 members including vice-ministers of the Ministry of International Trade and Industry and the Ministry of Finance, presidents of major electronics hardware manufacturers, the managing director of the industry's trade association, the president of the industry's computer renting company, and distinguished scholars." [23] Although "effectively, the Coun-

---

[20] In its first years, the Central Education Council's reports, for example, were "almost totally devoid of real influence on the formulation of policy," but its 465-page 1971 report was "touted as the prelude to Japan's third educational revolution." T. J. Pempel, "The Bureaucratization of Policymaking in Postwar Japan," unpublished, 1972, pp. 12–13.

[21] In Eugene J. Kaplan, *Japan: The Government-Business Relationship—A Guide for the American Businessman* (Washington: U.S. Government Printing Office, U.S. Department of Commerce, Bureau of International Commerce, February 1972).

[22] Ibid., p. 80.

[23] Ibid., p. 81.

cil is dominated by its secretariat," [24] its 1966 report was "the most important document in the industry's history." [25] Thus, the advisory commission was only one of the factors making its impact over the fifteen-year period—along with the industry, the bureaucracy, the business community, and the Diet—but at certain stages its actions were of decisive importance.

In addition to the more or less permanent advisory commissions, the government frequently appoints expert or public commissions of various kinds to make inquiries or recommendations concerning specific problems. These are as variable as the permanent advisory commissions in their impact.

Many people find the structure and powers of these commissions unsatisfactory. One of the most important criticisms is that the government defines the issues for them and the first drafts embodying the commission's deliberations are usually written by the bureaucrats. The commission members simply read over the prepared report, express agreement or disagreement, and propose changes. The bureaucrats then pull these together and issue the final report, which therefore tends to be fairly close to the government's preferred position, or at least not too critical of it.

Another criticism is that the government assures a favorable outcome, or reduces the prospects of an unfavorable outcome, by carefully selecting the members. The first panel of the commission appointed to investigate the famous mercury-poisoning case (involving the question of the Shōwa Denkō Company's responsibility) was criticized for returning a report favorable to the government position. The commissions are often criticized as mere window dressing, lending respectability to a predetermined government position, and in the worst case as pure whitewashing. Anti-establishment intellectuals, as well as labor people and the supporters of the opposition parties, are therefore very wary about some of the advisory commissions. Taking part, they fear, means being co-opted or accepting the underlying premises of the establishment. Many intellectuals also refuse out of fear of being branded a tool of the government by the constituencies they are concerned with. Faculty members of some national universities, for example, were hesitant about sitting on several Ministry of Education commissions because of the opposition of radical student organizations.

Nevertheless, in spite of their many weaknesses and defects, "their deliberations and reports," as Park says, "often constitute an important preliminary in the totality of Japanese policy-making; and there are numerous instances of commissions having authorized persuasive reports which culminated in administrative policies or legislation." [26]

---

[24] Ibid.
[25] Ibid., p. 91.
[26] Park, "Government Advisory System," p. 457.

Government-Supported Research

Another way that intellectuals, particularly academic intellectuals, make some input into consideration of public-policy issues is through research commissioned or supported by the government. Although the volume of Japanese governmental support for outside research is not as great as the American, the outlay for research and development in all fields is rising rapidly. As illustrated in Table 6, for example, in 1970 Japan spent ¥217.4 billion (¥152 billion from the government; the rest from private sources) for the support of university research in science, engineering, agriculture, and medicine.[27] The corresponding American figure is $2.6 billion. On a per capita GNP basis, however, this figure is much better than it appears: it is certainly better than in many European countries, including the United Kingdom; it is 22.5 percent higher than the preceding year in Japan; and it is on a more steeply rising curve than the American figure.

Table 6
Research Expenditure, 1970
(Unit: 1 billion yen)

Users	Total	%	Public	%	Private	%	Foreign	%
				Sources of Funds				
Total (yen)	1,195.3	100	301.4	25.2	893.5	74.7	0.4	0.0
	100%		100		100		100	
Companies (yen)	823.3	100	10.9	1.3	812.2	98.7	0.2	0.0
	68.9		3.6		90.9		45.1	
Research Institutes								
Total (yen)	154.6	100	138.5	89.6	15.9	10.3	0.2	0.1
	12.9		46.0		1.8		35.5	
Public (yen)	140.0	100	137.1	97.9	2.8	2.1	0.1	0.0
	(11.7)		(45.5)		(0.3)		(3.3)	
Private (yen)	14.6	100	1.4	9.6	13.1	89.8	0.1	0.6
	(1.2)		(0.5)		(1.5)		(32.2)	
Universities								
Total (yen)	217.4	100	152.0	69.9	65.4	30.1	0	0.0
	18.2		50.4		7.3		19.4	
Public (yen)	147.8	100	146.2	99.0	1.5	1.0	0	0.0
	(12.4)		(48.5)		(0.2)		(11.2)	
Private (yen)	69.7	100	5.7	8.2	53.9	91.7	0	0.1
	(5.8)		(1.9)		(7.2)		(8.2)	

Source: Summarized from *Kagaku gijutsu hakusho* (Science and technology white paper) (Tokyo: Science and Technology Agency, 1972), p. 83.

Although Japan was rather a slow starter in research and development, the investment from both public and private sources has been rising

---

[27] About $604 million at the 360–1 exchange rate, which prevailed in 1970.

sharply. In 1970, total research expenditures reached ¥1,195.3 billion[28]—
one-quarter from government and three-quarters from private sources (see
Table 6). The governmental budget for the promotion of science and
technology in 1971, which came to ¥305.5 billion, was 15 percent higher
than in 1969 and 4.9 times higher than in 1961. National budgets for all
varieties of research show a sharp upward trend. University research
expenditures rose over 80 percent between 1967 and 1971. Support for
relatively high priority research areas shows steep rises in the past few
years: atomic power research, up 57 percent from 1969 to 1970; space
research, up 158 percent from 1967 to 1970; and oceanography, up almost
50 percent in one year. Government subsidies and contract research funds
for scientific and technological research went up 27 percent in the two
years between 1969 and 1971.

Although the funds available for social scientific research are much less
generous than for pure sciences and technology (18 percent of all
researchers, but only 8 percent of total research expenditures in 1971),
they have also been going up proportionately in both commissioned
research as well as grants and subsidies. Virtually all government
departments give such support, although they vary considerably according
to their particular area of operation. The greatest support for social
scientific research comes from the Ministry of Education, the Economic
Planning Agency, and the Prime Minister's Office.

Government research funds are available to scholars in several forms. A
number of government agencies offer pure research grants. The ministries
also have research funds available in one form or another through the
research institutes attached to them or through their administrative
branches. General support grants may be made to scholars on application
for any worthwhile project; or the ministry may invite application only in
specified fields. Apart from outright grants, ministries may also give
selective support for fields in which they have a particular interest and
invite scholars to conduct research that has some relation to their own
areas of program responsibility.

Think Tanks

Since the 1960s there has been a remarkable new development on Japan's
intellectual scene—the think tank. Although some institutes have been in
existence since the 1950s, their real development has come since the
Nomura Research Institute was launched in 1965. Since then—partly
under the influence of such American models as Rand, the Stanford

---

[28] At the predevaluation exchange rates, $3.2 billion. In 1971, the figure went up to
¥1,355.5 billion, a 14 percent increase in yen amount. Calculated at the then exchange rate
of 308-1, it is equivalent to $4.4 billion, a 40 percent increase in dollar amount.

Research Institute, and Battelle—about forty-five think tanks have been established or planned.[29] Some institutes work for a single client; the Mitsubishi Sōgō Kenkyūjo works for the Mitsubishi group of companies. The Nomura Research Institute, on the other hand, although it does much work on behalf of its parent Nomura Securities Company, also conducts research on broader questions, including molecular biology. The institutes characteristically bring together an interdisciplinary mix of specialists centering on the interface of economics and technology: economists, engineers, designers, planners, survey specialists, and statisticians. Each institute creates its own distinctive mix.

In addition to the government-oriented institutes, the business community has supported the establishment of a policy sciences institute, and each major business group either has established or is in the process of establishing one: the Mitsubishi Sōgō Kenkyūjo (Mitsubishi General Research Institute), the Mitsui Knowledge Industry (MKI), the Toyota Keizai Kenkyūjo (Toyota Economics Research Institute), the Midori-kai (The Green Association, of the Sanwa group), and the Sumitomo Jōhō Sangyō Kaisha (Sumitomo Information Industry Company). Typical general think tanks are the Nippon Sōgō Kenkyūsho (Japan General Research Institute), the Shakai Kōgaku Kenkyūsho (Social Engineering Research Institute), and the Mirai Kōgaku Kenkyūsho (Future Engineering Research Institute).

The announcement the day after Tanaka Kakuei's election as prime minister—that a think tank would be organized to put into action his pre-election plan for the "Reconstruction of the Japanese Archipelago"—indicates how entrenched the think tank concept has become. The chairman of the LDP's Policy Affairs Council announced in July 1972 that "he was looking for qualified persons . . . 10 to 15 eminent academicians and a few capable party members . . . to start off its work on how to resolve problems of congested cities, environmental pollution, housing shortage and insufficient welfare." [30] In July 1973, the government announced that it was in the process of establishing a giant think tank funded at the ¥100 billion level.[31]

Although these institutes are new, it looks as though they may become an increasingly important channel for sophisticated research input into the government and corporate decision-making process. They also provide an arena in which many scholars and specialists can deal with public-policy issues and make a contribution of high potential impact. Their very existence further enlarges the sphere of consulting and free-lance intellec-

---

[29] Tallied from tables in Tsūsanshō daijin kanbō jōhōka taisakushitsu, ed., *Nihon no shinku-tanku—sono kadai to bijon* [Japan's think tank: Its problems and vision] (Tokyo: Dayamondo-sha, 1971), pp. 330–336.

[30] *Japan Times*, 9 July 1972.

[31] To be under the Economic Planning Agency.

tual work in Japan. The consulting fees, research funds, and various forms of compensation available through the think tanks and other research institutes are not insignificant for the changing economics of Japanese academic life.

Local Government

Political power in Japan tends to be concentrated in the central government; local autonomy, despite the efforts of the American Occupation, is still weak. Since so much power is concentrated in the capital, the opportunities for consulting work or for influencing the centers of decision-making are to be found almost exclusively in Tokyo, around the central government, corporate headquarters, and the mass media, rather than in the provinces.

Nevertheless, local government entities provide some channels for intellectuals to take part in public activities. Tokyo's Governor Minobe, himself a former professor of economics, has many academicians who serve as consultants and researchers in his various programs. Tokyo metropolis's Tokyo Tosei Chōsakai involves many academic experts in its work of monitoring environmental pollution and social indicators and proposing solutions for Tokyo's manifold urban ills. The Chōsakai is the most active agency engaged in the recently popular "civil minimum" research. The importance of academic opinion, in Tokyo, if not in all of Japan's great cities, may be seen in the fact that even the conservative candidate who ran against Minobe in the April 1971 elections, Hatano Akira, had his platform—the "Hatano Vision for Tokyo"—drawn up by academics who supported his candidacy.

Even in the remote provinces, some participation of intellectuals in policy deliberatiohs will be found. In general, however, intellectuals, including social scientists and humanists, find themselves closer to policy making in areas where "progressives" are in office. As of summer 1973, there were 6 prefectures with progressive governors,[32] and 6 out of 8 cities with populations over one million had progressive mayors.[33] In all, there are progressive mayors in 134—or 22.3 percent—of Japan's 579 cities.

In the remote provinces, local intellectuals and academics often find an honored place. They write columns and learned commentaries in the local journals, and they are listened to on the lecture circuits. They are called upon for advice, for entertainment, or for gracing an occasion. Their

---

[32] Tokyo, Kyoto, Osaka, Saitama, Okayama, and Okinawa. Four others—Akita, Yamanashi, Gifu, and Akita—have nonparty governors elected with the support of both the government party and the opposition Japanese Socialist Party (JSP).

[33] Tokyo, Osaka, Nagoya, Kyoto, Yokohama, and Kobe. The only two with conservative mayors are Sapporo and Kita-Kyushu.

opportunities may be fewer than in the metropolis, but so are their competitors.

INTELLECTUALS AND THE POLITICIANS

Intellectuals rarely enter professional politics and still more rarely conquer responsible office. But they staff political bureaus, write party pamphlets and speeches, act as secretaries and advisers, make the individual politician's newspaper reputation which, though it is not everything, few men can afford to neglect. In doing these things they to some extent impress their mentality on almost everything that is being done.

Schumpeter

The political opinions and the behavior of intellectuals are seldom to be taken seriously.

W. H. Auden

Table 7
Intellectuals in the House of Representatives, by Party
(as of February 1973)

	Number of Intellectuals (A)	Total Number of Seats (B)	% A/B
LDP	44	284	15.6
JSP	22	118	18.9
JCP	21	39	53.8
Kōmeitō	6	29	20.6
DSP	4	20	20.0
Independent	1	1	100.0
Total	98	491	19.8

Source: My calculations, based on biographical data about Diet members reported in Miyakawa Takayoshi, ed., *Konpyūta ga henshū-shita seiji handobukku* [Computer-edited political handbook] (Tokyo: Seiji Kōhō Senta, April 1973), pp. 3–90.

Despite their passionate preoccupation with politics as ideology, philosophy, value integration, and morality play, most intellectuals' interest in routine electoral politics is somewhat less than enthusiastic. Few have run for public office, particularly administrative offices such as governorships or mayoralties. A Minobe, a former professor of economics and a celebrity, elected governor of Tokyo by huge electoral majorities, is the exception. Perhaps, he is the forerunner of a new type of intellectual politician.

In the representative bodies, however, particularly at the national level, candidates who can be broadly characterized as intellectuals have fared better than might be expected. Approximately 20 percent of the members of the House of Representatives have intellectual origins (see Tables 7 and

Table 8
Intellectuals in the House of Representatives, by Profession
(as of February 1973)

	LDP	JSP	JCP	Komeito	DSP	Independent	Total
Journalist[a]	18	3	1	2	1	1	26
Writer	1	0	1	0	0	0	2
Professor[b]	6	4	0	0	0	0	10
Lawyer	9	1	11	0	1	0	22
Television	3	0	0	0	0	0	3
Education[c]	5	12	6	1	2	0	26
Doctor	2	2	2	1	0	0	7
Dentist	0	0	0	1	0	0	1
Composer	0	0	0	1	0	0	1
Total	44	22	21	6	4	1	98

Source: My classification, based on Miyakawa.

[a] Includes journalists and editors in all aspects of publishing.

[b] Includes all ranks in university-level education.

[c] Includes schoolteachers, principals, members of boards of education, etc., at primary- and secondary-school levels, and officials of Japan Teachers' Union (Nikkyōso) and other associations connected with education.

8) as against 10.4 percent from business[34] and 18.9 percent of bureaucratic origin.[35] The Japanese Communist Party (JCP) has the largest proportion of Diet members of intellectual origins (53.8 percent), more than half of whom are lawyers. The JSP is particularly strong among teachers, and the LDP has the largest number of legislators from the mass media.

In the upper house (Councillors) about 28 percent of the members are intellectuals by origin (see Tables 9 and 10). The proportion is higher on the opposition side than on the government side. Educationists constitute the largest single group, most of them with the JSP, because of JSP dominance in the Japan Teachers Union. These figures stand in contrast to about 8.9 percent of councillor members from business and 24.3 percent (overwhelmingly LDP members) of bureaucratic origin.[36]

Since the mid-1960s, a number of *tarento* (talents)—movie stars, television personalities, and popular writers—of whom novelist Ishihara Shintarō is a well-known example, have made a modest appearance on the political scene (see Table 11).[37] Since their strength, based on media

---

[34] Businessmen, owners, and executives (my own calculations). The largest group in most of the parties appears to have come up through political channnels—through the party machinery, local assemblies, and (in the JSP) the trade unions.

[35] Those who had most of their prepolitician career in government service.

[36] My own rough calculations from Miyakawa Takayoshi, ed., *Konpyūta ga henshū-shita seiji handobukku* [Computer-edited political handbook] (Tokyo: Seiji Kōhō Senta, April 1973), pp. 92–138 Political workers represent about 17.4 percent, the majority of which (25 out of 43) are JSP members.

[37] Ishihara, an Akutagawa Award winner, was elected to the upper house in 1968 with the largest number of votes in the national constituency—over three million. Before his six-year

Table 9
Intellectuals in the House of Councillors, by Party
(as of March 1973)

	Number of Intellectuals (A)	Number of Seats (B)	% A/B
LDP	22	136	16.2
JSP	23	61	37.7
JCP	4	10	40.0
Komeito	10	23	43.4
DSP	3	11	27.2
Independent[a]	3	6	50.0
Total	65	247[b]	27.9

Source: My calculations, based on Miyakawa, pp. 92–138.

[a] Includes the Dai-ni Club (a minor conservative grouping) and others.

[b] Five seats are vacant; the full statutory membership is 252.

Table 10
Intellectuals in the House of Councillors, by Profession
(as of March 1973)

	LDP	JSP	JCP	Komeito	DSP	Dai-2 Club and Others	Total
Journalist	4	5	1	5[a]	0	0	15
Writer	1	0	0	0	0	0	1
Professor	3	0	2	1	0	0	6
Lawyer	3	1	0	0	1	0	5
Television	0	1	0	0	1	2	4
Education	3	12	0	2	1	1	19
Doctor	1	1	0	0	0	0	2
Dentist	1	1	0	2	0	0	4
Composer	0	0	1	0	0	0	1
Nurse	1	0	0	0	0	0	1
Theatre	2	1	0	0	0	0	3
Religion	2	0	0	0	0	0	2
Singer	1	0	0	0	0	0	1
Pharmacist	0	1	0	0	0	0	1
Totals	22	23	4	10	3	3	65

Source: My classification, based on Miyakawa.

[a] Four of the five are on the party newspaper.

term was completed, he resigned to run for the lower house from Tokyo's Second District on December 10, 1972. The District elects five members, and Ishihara won in first place by a large margin.

popularity, is diffused throughout the country rather than concentrated in one single district, all twelve ran in the national constituency elections of the House of Councillors, which is a kind of national popularity contest, rather than in the more narrowly political House of Representatives competition. In the 1971 elections, *tarento* candidates won the top three places in the national constituency, the only ones to win with more than a million votes. They are all in their first term (which lasts for six years), and they have not yet established a particularly distinguished record. Whether they will last remains an open question. Nevertheless, their popularity is an asset that political parties, both government and opposition, do not lightly disregard.

Table 11
Tarento Diet Members, House of Councillors
(as of March 1973)

By Party		By Field	
Party	*Number*	*Occupation*	*Number*
LDP	5	Television[a]	4
JCP	0	Storyteller[b]	3
JSP	2	Athlete[c]	2
Komeito	1	Writer	1[d]
DSP	1	Singer	1
Dai-2 Club	3	Actress	1
Total	12[e]	Total	12

Sources: My calculations, based on Miyakawa.
  [a] Announcers, writers, masters of ceremonies.
  [b] Vaudeville and traditional narrators.
  [c] Baseball and volleyball.
  [d] A Buddhist priest known for his popular writings.
  [e] There were originally thirteen, but one resigned in mid-term to run for the lower House.

Even though the extraparliamentary politics of demonstrations, mass movements, civic organizations, petition campaigns, and agitation is more their métier, many intellectuals still find themselves drawn to party politics in the narrow sense. Except in the case of the left-wing parties, they do not expect this activity to be at the Jimmy Higgins level; the nonstaff intellectuals serve as advisers, theorists, analysts, and planners for various parties and factions.

Ultimately all political decisions must come through the Diet's voting procedure or through a single mind, whether that of the prime minister or of whichever decision-maker is involved. Each decision-maker differs in how he reaches his decisions, whom he listens to, what he reads, the forces that influence him. The fact that until now most of Japan's leading political figures have come from a small number of elite educational institutions has given them in some respects a common culture. Although they differ in their particular views, they often share, even with extreme opponents, elements of a common outlook, a kind of common responsiveness.

The Shōwa Kenkyūkai

One prototype of the relations of the intellectual to the powers was the Shōwa Kenkyūkai (Shōwa Era Study Group). Konoye Fumimaro's brain trust, brought together in 1933 by Gotō Ryūnosuke.[38] Gotō gathered together some of Japan's leading antifascist philosophers, thinkers, historians, sociologists, political scientists, economists, and natural scientists to bring the best available intelligence in the country to bear on the problems confronting Konoye, the liberal hope against the militarists.[39]

Established specifically as an organization of intellectuals, bureaucrats and politicians were excluded from the Shōwa Kenkyūkai from the outset. Many of the members had been regarded Marxists and leftists. By the time the group was dissolved in 1940 it had involved, at its height, some three hundred intellectuals every year in its work. During its seven years of existence, the Shōwa Kenkyūkai carried on a vigorous panoply of activities—studying national problems in detail, preparing position papers for Konoye, and endeavoring to expand the participation of intellectuals in the determination of public policy. In 1936, it spun off a Shina mondai kenkyūkai (China Problems Study Group), and in 1938 it formed a Bunka kenkyūkai (Cultural Study Group) to deal with the cultural aspects of Japanese-Chinese relations. In July 1938, it also established the Shōwa Dōjinkai (Shōwa Comrades' Association), which brought together middle-level bureaucrats, business leaders, and politicians to spread the ideas it was developing. In November of that year it established a school, the Shōwajuku or Shōwa Academy, to train successors in its methods. In November 1940, under the pressure of the wartime mobilization regime that saw the eclipse of Konoye, it dissolved itself.

It will also be recalled that from the China Incident on through the Pacific War, establishment institutions such as the Southern Manchurian Railway and the Cabinet Planning Board involved intellectuals, even leftists and progressives, in their work. To some extent this reflected a respect for academic expertise, but it was also a device to provide refuge for liberal intellectuals. By and large, with the exception of Communists and a few others, Japanese intellectuals offered little resistance to the war.

[38] See Baba Shūichi, "1930-nendai ni okeru Nihon chishikijin no dōkō [Trends among Japanese intellectuals in the 1930s]," Tōkyō daigaku kyōyōgakubu, Shakaikagaku kiyō, vol. 19, 30 June 1970.

[39] The group included Miki Kiyoshi, Funayama Shinichi, Sasa Hirō, Shimizu Ikutarō, Kasai Junichi, Nakajima Kenzō, Nakayama Ichirō, Yabe Teiji, Ryū Shintarō, Kata Tetsuji, and Rōyama Masao.

Although some went into isolation or silenced their voices and pens, most offered at least passive and some active support for the war effort.[40]

After the War

Although the Japanese military did not like the intellectuals very much, the American Occupation did. Intellectuals were brought into various aspects of the Occupation's work at an early point, providing American officers—who knew little about the society they were commissioned to reform—with expert information. Intellectuals also helped in the formulation of major Occupation programs. During the early postwar years, the Occupation looked on the liberal academic intellectuals as friendly allies. For some of the liberal reforms, the intellectuals, not the "masses," were the main constituency, especially if there was no particular mass base as, for example, in the reform of the criminal code. Intellectuals played a major role at many stages in the formulation of the new constitution, the reforms of the civil code, the educational reforms, the land reform, the civil liberty laws, and many others.

Since the end of the war there has been nothing to compare with Gotō's intensive mobilization of liberal intellectuals to work with Konoye. Ikeda Hayato probably came closest, bringing a small, informal group of journalists, academics, and businessmen in to look at broad questions of policy for him. Since Ikeda had a strong background in economics, he drew a great deal on professional economists for advice. They undoubtedly exerted a significant influence on the development of the economic programs for which he is well known, particularly the income-doubling plan.

Satō Eisaku, on the other hand, appears to have had no regular mechanism, formal or informal, for seeking outside advice. Nevertheless, he did make a practice of personally meeting many specialists, including foreigners, and seeking firsthand information from them. In economic and foreign policy questions, he listened to a few experts, sometimes at the breakfast meetings for which Japanese politicians are famous. It has been suggested that he was more responsive to favorable advice and information than to criticism. But he was most likely to seek expert advice through the formally constituted groups established by the prime minister's secretariat or by the LDP. One outstanding example was the Okinawa Kondankai (Okinawa Discussion Group), under the chairmanship of Obama Nobumoto, former president of Waseda University. This group, which carried on research, inquiries, public discussions, conferences, and both formal

---

[40] There is by now a considerable literature on this subject, particularly with regard to writers. Among recent pieces, see Kikuchi Masanori, "Chishikijin to sensō sekinin kaihi no ronri" [Intellectuals and the logic of evasion of responsibility during the war] *Ushio*, August 1973.

and informal soundings of influential American views, undoubtedly influenced the government's stance on the nonnuclear issue during the negotiations with the U.S. on the Okinawa problem in 1969.

It is perhaps too early to assess Tanaka Kakuei's style of relations with intellectuals. Since he is the first postwar prime minister who did not graduate from one of the elite universities—in fact, he is not a university graduate, and he has a business rather than a bureaucratic background— he did not come to office with a natural inclination toward associations of this kind. It is not clear whether he had a regular group of consultants, but he drew the information that he needed mainly from the network of middle-level bureaucrats that he created during his incumbencies as minister of MITI and of Finance. His well-known "Plan for the Reconstruction of the Japanese Archipelago" was widely considered to have been written up by younger bureaucrats in MITI.[41]

Most of the leading conservative politicians, at least those with prime-ministerial ambitions, have their own advisers and at times even something on the order of a brain trust. Leading candidates usually have some kind of formally established support organization that holds regular meetings and study groups; in some cases there is also a regular journal or other publications. In these groups, intellectuals often play an important role.

Although the various politicians may have their own brain-trust entourage, the parties tend to operate mainly with their own in-house personnel. The LDP, for example, has a number of study groups (*chōsakai*) that work on policy. Essentially an arena for the party to hammer out a position, the study groups usually consist of politicians and party staffers, and conduct their own studies without outside help or consultation. The party committees on the U.S.–Japan Mutual Security Treaty and on Normalization of Relations with China have played an important role over recent years. But intellectuals are not very involved in these committees.

The Democratic Socialist Party (DSP) has the support of the Democratic Socialist Study Group, an association of intellectuals modeling themselves on the relationship of the Fabian Society in England to the Labor party.[42] Although they provide support and undoubtedly influence the general intellectual atmosphere within which the party functions, they probably do not have much direct influence on the party's legislative program.

The Shakaishugi Kyōkai (Socialist Association) plays a somewhat

---

[41] Translated into English as *Building a new Japan—A Plan for Remodeling the Japanese Archipelago* (Tokyo: Simul Press, 1973). A popular joke at the time was that, when the Prime Minister heard that his book had become a best-seller, he said, "I guess if it's so popular, I'll have to buy a copy and read it too."

[42] They publish a monthly journal, *Kaikakusha*.

similar role for the JSP.[43] But since the JSP leaders consider themselves to be intellectuals and theoreticians, intellectual organizations function essentially as just another pressure group on the left rather than as an advisory body.

The Kōmeitō engages in a wide range of study activities, but these primarily involve party members. Nevertheless, the Kōmeitō is somewhat respectful of the views of intellectuals and its parent, Sōka Gakkai, supports a major intellectual journal, *Ushio*. *Ushio* is a high quality journal that draws contributions from a wide range of the political spectrum. The party also invites intellectuals and specialists to take part in its frequent study groups. However, the formal deliberative bodies of the party are made up of party members who range widely in their information and idea inputs.

CONCLUSION

Let us now look once again at our original question: is it in fact the case that Japanese intellectuals are isolated and without power?

First, as we have seen, they are a major political constituency in terms of numbers, wealth, institutions, and power. Second, they are one of, if not *the* most important of the opinion leaders in Japan. Public opinion, the perceived interests of different elements of the population, the activities of organized movements and parties, and ideological attitudes are all very important in the competition of political forces, and in all these areas the intellectuals play an important role.

Third, their writings often influence the very formulation of the policy decisions at issue, even if their particular position does not happen to win out. When a distinguished professor of Tokyo University's Faculty of Law writes a book or an article, or makes a statement on some public issue, the decision-makers may not leap to obey him, but they are not entirely unresponsive; his work often strikes an echo. Most of the key civil servants, and even many of the leading politicians and businessmen may have been his students or his classmates. In any event, he will be a respected *sensei* (teacher) whose works they will have studied and who has had a role in shaping their thought. They will therefore reverberate to his views, his language of thought, his posing of the issues, even if they do not agree with his specific political position.

A 1971–1972 survey of leadership opinion, for example, showed that 36 percent of the responses to the question, "Who should be mainly involved in the establishment of national goals?" referred to intellectuals in one form or another (mass communications, think tanks, intellectuals and men of culture, religious organizations, and academia) as against 27 percent that referred to the established political institutions (Diet, cabinet, LDP,

---

[43] Their journal is called *Shakaishugi*.

and local government), and 13 percent that referred to anti-establishment organizations (opposition parties, the student movement, and labor unions).[44]

Nor is this respect for intellectuals confined to the elites. The Japanese masses might not rise to Victor Hugo's call as the French masses presumably do:

> Peuples! Écoutez le Poète!
> Écoutez le reveur sacré!

But Japanese intellectuals have always had great moral authority. The *gakusha* (scholars), the *sensei* (teachers), the *bunkajin* (men of culture), the *chishikijin* (men of knowledge) are listened to. Their presence graces the occasion and validates the cause.

Intellectuals have been active politically, and they have often been extremely effective through the organizations and movements in which they have participated. No one can doubt their influence on national politics and even on particular decisions, even if they have not always won all of their demands. The 1960 anti-Security Treaty demonstrations did not, in the end, bring about the abrogation of the treaty, but the Kishi government was brought down and Japanese politics was never quite the same afterwards.

Fourth, intellectuals are extensively involved in all phases of the public decision-making process from the original conception through the planning, information input, development, and final decision stages. This participation is increasing, although the process is uneven. Literary-humanistic intellectuals are probably losing ground while the technical-scientific intellectuals are gaining.

Every policy area evokes a different mix of constituencies and creates its own structure of decision. In some, the intellectuals are important; in others, they are not. But whatever the particular situation or outcome they must be ranked among the decision-makers along with the bureaucrats, politicians, businessmen, journalists, and leaders of civic organizations. In short, they are not as influential as they think they should be, but they are more influential than they think they are.

---

[44] Tanaka Yasumasa, Koyama Kenichi, and Yasuda Jūmei, "Nihon no kokka mokuhyō ni kansuru chōsa—kisō shūkei hōkoku" [Research on Japan's national goals—report of preliminary compilation], mimeo (Tokyo: Kokka Mokuhyō Kenkyū Project Team, June 1973), table I:1, p. 19. This is a survey of leadership opinion on national goals in which the respondents were drawn from the following areas: politics, government, business, academia, mass media, literature, labor unions, and women's activities. (All the calculations in this paragraph are my own.)

Competition and Conformity:
An Inquiry into the Structure
of the Japanese Newspapers

NATHANIEL B. THAYER

Independent newspapers speak with an independent voice. But Japanese newspapers speak in unison. Why? Some critics answer that a cabal runs the newspapers. Since these newspapers are critical of the ruling conservative party and tolerant of the opposition parties, these critics further suggest the cabal is leftist. An American ambassador espoused this thesis at a Senate hearing a few years ago. Within the Japanese newspapers, he said, were more than two hundred communists.

The ambassador did not say where he got that figure. The Japanese police said they did not give it to him. The newsmen said they did not know how many communists had jobs on the newspapers but the ambassador's figure was far too high. Others said the ambassador had understated the figure by half. All agreed the CIA had bungled. No one got back to the original question: what reasons impel the newspapers to conform? That answer is now my purpose in these few pages.[1]

---

[1] This article is partly the result of personal experience, partly the result of conversations with newsmen, and partly the result of documentary research. I was press attaché in the American embassy from 1962 to 1966. Three newsmen who have particularly helped me in the preparation of this article are Horikawa Atsuhiro, now an editorial writer but formerly a political reporter on the *Yomiuri*; Yoshimura Katsumi, now a director for Fuji Television but formerly a deputy-managing editor of the *Sankei*; and Matsuyama Yukio, who has served variously as a political reporter, overseas correspondent, and as deputy editor in the foreign news section of the *Asahi*. I have made reference to *Shinbun no shuzai* [Newspaper reporting], 2

I start with a description of the Japanese newspapers. There are the noncommercial newspapers which are published by political parties, religious groups, unions, industrial organizations, and clubs. I know of no accurate count of them. Newspapers whose purpose is to make a profit have organized a federation—the Japan Newspaper Association. It has published a list identifying commercial newspapers.[2] This list includes special audience newspapers: sports, foreign language, shipping, industrial, and entertainment. Most newspapers, however, are general interest papers and they divide into three groups: local, regional, and national. Finally, there are two wire services.

Since all newspapers contain articles on local, domestic, and international events, content is an inadequate criterion by which to separate the lesser from the mightier papers. Only a few papers, however, maintain reporters in most of the government agencies in Tokyo and correspondents overseas. No locals, only a few regionals, both wires, and all the nationals fall into this category.

THE PRINCIPAL NEWSPAPERS

In western Japan this is the *Nishi Nippon*. Its home office is in Fukuoka, and its market is chiefly on the island of Kyushu. In central Japan is the *Chūnichi Shinbun*, with its home office in Nagoya. Its market is the ten prefectures between Tokyo and Osaka. Several years ago, the Chu-nichi purchased the *Tokyo Shinbun*, which it runs almost as a separate entity. *Tokyo Shinbun* has its home office in Tokyo. Its market is the three prefectures surrounding the capital. In northern Japan is the *Hokkaido Shinbun*. Its home office is in Sapporo. Its market is the island of Hokkaido. Collectively, these newspapers are known as "the bloc" newspapers. Since their markets do not overlap, the bloc papers have arrangements to share facilities and news. It is not uncommon to see articles by one newspaper's foreign correspondent appearing in another newspaper, though domestic stories are more rarely shared.

The major wire services are *Jiji* and *Kyodo*. Their responsibility is to supply news to the regional and local newspapers, though today other organizations as well purchase their services. Initially, these two wires agreed to divide reporting responsibilities: *Jiji* was to handle the economic and commercial news; *Kyodo* was to handle the social and political news. This agreement is no longer honored. Both services compete to cover every story.

The nationals make up the final category. These newspapers now have

vols. (Tokyo: Nihon Shinbun Kyokai, 1968). I am grateful for the interest and support given me by both the Social Science Research Council and the East Asian Institute of Columbia University for research into the mass media of Japan. Neither the individuals nor the organizations bear any responsibility for the views I have expressed herein.

[2] *Asahi Nenkan*, 1972, p. 239–241.

their home offices in Tokyo but distribute papers throughout the country. The largest national is the *Asahi*. It has 263 domestic bureaus and 22 overseas bureaus and almost ten thousand employees, of whom better than three thousand are editorial personnel. It publishes eleven morning editions and three evening editions. The morning editions run twenty-four pages and their circulation is six million; the evening editions run twelve pages and their circulation is three million. A network of sixty-two thousand newsboys delivers 99 percent of the newspapers to the home.[3] Comparable in facilities but slightly lower in circulation are the *Mainichi* and the *Yomiuri*. These newspapers are known as the Big Three.

Another national is the *Nihon Keizai*. It started out as a financial newspaper much like the *London Financial Times* or the *Wall Street Journal*. In recent years, its interests have broadened and its circulation has grown. The fifth national is the *Sankei*. It started as a regional newspaper serving the prefectures around Osaka but has since moved its headquarters to Tokyo and now distributes almost nationwide. Its circulation has been slipping in the recent past.

In recent years, these nationals have expanded into new fields. All now publish weekly, monthly, quarterly, and annual magazines. Most have English language publications and have television and radio stations. They also do outside printing and publish books. Some are in real estate, sound recording, and travel service. Although these ventures seem to be quite profitable, the newspapers remain the core of the empires.

Table 1
List of Principal Newspapers in Japan
(circulation figures are in thousands)

Newspaper	Year Established	Circulation[a] Morning	Evening	Number of Employees
Asahi	1879	5,994	3,979	9,406
Mainichi	1872	4,667	2,823	8,071
Yomiuri	1874	5,512	3,330	7,627
Nippon Keizai	1876	1,282	892	3,071
Sankei	1933	2,025	1,156	4,072
Hokkaido	1942	763	762	1,977
Chunichi	1942	1,556	878	2,484
Tokyo	1922	463	317	1,365
Nishi Nippon	1877	651	276	1,686

Source: *Asahi Nenkan* (1972), p. 44.

[a] These newspapers publish both morning and evening editions. Most parts of the country receive both editions, but some rural areas receive only a morning edition. That is why the morning circulation is higher than the evening circulation.

[3] Promotional literature issued by the *Asahi Shinbun*.

The five nationals, the bloc newspapers, and the wire services constitute the mainstream of written journalism in Japan.[4] Table 1 gives other pertinent data concerning them. This article examines the national dailies. They dominate the field and I am most familiar with them. Yet most of my remarks will apply equally well to the other members of the mainstream. The regionals do not have the circulation problems of the nationals, but they are quite similar in structure.

THE ORGANIZATION OF A JAPANESE NEWSPAPER

Similarity among the newspapers starts with their office buildings. Though they may have been built at different times and reflect different architectural fancies, their layout is the same. The first and second floors, near the main entrance, are given over to sales, advertising, and in some newspapers cultural activities. The news-gathering section is in the heart of the building on the third floor. Also there, and on the second floor, are the composing rooms where tapes are punched from manuscripts for high-speed typesetters. Plates are sent to presses located in the basement or on the first floor. The newspapers are bundled and taken to trucks which are next door. Editorial writers and the executive officers occupy the upper floors of the building. Table 2 lists the various divisions of a daily national newspaper.

Table 2
Breakdown of the Divisions (*Kyoku*)
within a National Daily Newspaper

News-gathering	General administration
Printing	Accounting
Advertising	Cultural activities section[a]
Sales	Editorial writer's room
Publications	Other

[a] The national dailies promote cultural exchanges with other nations. In 1964, for example, the *Asahi* sponsored an exhibition of art from France which included the Venus de Milo. Such exchanges are the responsibility of the cultural activities section.

The newspapers break down much like the office building. Each story has its accepted place. For example, important news lands on the front page. Radio and television news is on the back page. The second page has political news. Pages 22 and 23 carry accounts of accidents and incidents.

[4] I do not wish to denigrate local newspapers. They fulfill an important but different role in Japanese society. A good study of their problems and responsibilities is Tamura Norio, *Nihon no rokaru shinbun* [Japanese local newspapers] (Tokyo: Gendai janarizumu shuppan kai, 1968).

Sports gets a page in the middle of the paper if it has been raining; two pages if it is a Monday. All articles are complete on their pages (Table 3 gives the page breakdown of a national daily).

Table 3
Page Breakdown of the Morning Edition
of a National Daily

Page	Description
1	important news
2	political news
3	important social news
4	special features or documents
5	editorials and letters to the editor
6, 7	international news
8, 9	economic news
10	advertisements
11	stock market news
12, 13, 14	advertisements
15	home section
16	advertisements
17	art, drama, movie reviews (book reviews once a week)
18, 19	sports
20	classified ads
21	local news
22, 23	lesser social news
24	radio and television

The two principal sources of revenue for the newspapers are advertising and subscriptions. Until 1963, subscriptions were the dominant source. Now advertising has assumed the lead. But the ratio is still close. In the *Asahi* case, advertising accounts for 54.9 percent of the revenues; subscriptions account for 45.1 percent.[5] The ratios for the other newspapers are not much different. Both advertising rates and the subscriptions depend on the number of readers and constitute the ultimate measure of success. Readership has been carefully studied. Each newspaper has a slightly different audience: the *Nihon Keizai* has a slightly higher percentage of readers in the professions than the other papers; the *Asahi*'s largest block of readers is office workers; and the *Sankei* attracts the greatest percentage of manual workers.

Geographical differences also exist. The *Yomiuri* is weak in Nagoya, because it has not been in that market very long, but it is strong in downtown Tokyo, probably because of its baseball team there. The *Asahi* is strong in suburban Tokyo. The *Sankei* does well in Osaka. But the differences are less important than the similarities. All newspapers are trying to appeal to the same audience throughout the country.[6]

---

[5] *Asahi* promotional literature.

[6] Research has also been directed at finding new markets. Is there a group in Japan that

The home-delivery practice in Japan means that the newspapers do not have to resort to sensationalism, a tendency of newspapers that rely on street sales. Editors can establish news policies more studied than a flaming headline over a wild lead. Since subscriptions are by month, however, the newspapers do not have an entirely captive audience, although most readers are constant in their loyalties. Editors continuously review their policies, and their efforts are evaluated quarterly by the Audit Bureau of Circulation. Successes get copied quickly. Failures get dropped abruptly. Editors innovate, but most cautiously. Nobody gets too far away from the others. A circulation increase is welcome, but a circulation decrease is to be avoided. Circulation figures will not change much if all papers look the same. Stasis reigns.

Some observers have suggested that the Japanese social penchant for unanimity is as much a cause for similarity among newspapers as the imperatives of a large circulation. They may have a point. But Japan is not the only country where the elements of a mass medium are peas in a pod. Americans rate individuality high on their social scale, yet American television network news programs differ only in their commentators, not their comment. Evening talk shows hew to a common format. A successful dramatic formula on one channel is soon emulated on the other channels.

Circulation is not the only reason why Japanese newspapers look alike. Structure is another. Table 4 presents a model of the news-gathering part of a newspaper. The names of the sections may differ. Recipes may be

Table 4
Model Layout of News-Gathering Structure

	Managing Editor			
	Sections			
		Content Analysis		Administration
Press Clubs	Political Economic			
	Foreign			Printing
Regional Section	Sports	Layout		
	Photo			Proofreaders
	Cultural			
Materials Section	Women		Telegraphic Section	
	Social			
	Writer's			
Overseas Services	Room			
		Internal Communications		
	Radio & Television Section			
	Broadcasting Centers	Other Printing Centers		

does not read the newspapers? The answer so far is negative. Sales, however, have increased with the breakup of the extended family into nuclear families.

found in the women's section in one paper and in the household section in
another, but all sections are present in all national newspapers. The basic
structure was created about forty years ago and has not changed much
since.

The political section is responsible for domestic and national politics. Its
reporters cover the activities of the ministries, the embassies, the political
parties, the Diet, the prime minister, and the cabinet. The economic
section covers the banks, business, the stock market, industry, and the
economic activities of the government. The foreign news section handles
the reports from the overseas correspondents and translates the reports of
foreign wire services or articles from foreign newspapers. These three
bureaus are collectively known as the "hard group." In the *Mainichi* and
the *Asahi*, the managing editor will often have been a reporter in one of
these sections.

The sports section, the science section, and the photographic section
need no explanation. The women's section covers activities that center on
the home—women's lib has hit Japan but not the Japanese newspapers.
The cultural section is responsible for education, theater, movies, and
other forms of entertainment. On one paper, the cultural and women's
section are one; on another, they are separate; and on a third, they are
combined with the science section and occupy a part of the managing
editor's office.

The social section is roughly equivalent to the city desk on an American
newspaper. It covers the police, courts, accidents, incidents, and just about
anything not assigned to another section. The social section has the largest
group of reporters. The managing editor of the *Yomiuri*, which has the
reputation of being the most easily read newspaper, usually has been a
reporter in the social section. These sections comprise the "soft group."

National newspapers require special facilities. The regional section is in
charge of receiving reports from the branch offices. The telegraphic section
is responsible for transmitting reports written in Tokyo to the other
publishing centers. Most nationals have four publishing centers; the *Asahi*,
for example, has centers in Tokyo, Nagoya, Osaka, and Kita Kyushu. The
internal communications section receives requests from the other publishing centers and writes stories with a Tokyo slant but of local interest for
them.

The radio and television section prepares and transmits news to the
radio and television stations belonging to the newspaper. The materials
section fulfills the same responsibilities as the morgue on an American
newspaper. The proofreaders on a Japanese newspaper differ from the
proofreaders on an American newspaper in that they are sharp-eyed and
accurate. Typographical errors are a rarity.

The content analysis section compares the stories that appear in its own
newspaper with the articles in the competitive newspapers. Every morning, the section chiefs assemble to hear its verdict. Some men do not
fit easily into any of the sections; they may have an unusual specialty

or a particular felicity of phrase. They are assigned to the writers' room.

The layout section takes stories from the other sections, evaluates their importance, decides space and placement, and writes the subheads and heads. Administration takes care of household matters. Overseeing this entire operation is the managing editor. He meets with the newspaper's directors, owners and advisers, and represents the newspaper to other newspapers and the outside world. He has three or four deputies, one of whom is always on duty.

A REPORTER'S CAREER

A reporter's career follows an established course. He enters the newspaper by examination after graduation, usually from one of the nation's better universities. He is first sent to a branch office in the countryside, where he will spend from three to five years learning his trade, developing his interests, and demonstrating his ability. If promising, he will be brought back to Tokyo and assigned to one of the sections. In all likelihood, he will remain in this section throughout his reporting career.

The first Tokyo assignment, then, is a key assignment. How is it made? Few descriptive statements can be made with certainty. If the young reporter was an outstanding athlete in his university, he will probably end up in the sports section. If he majored in science, particularly a natural science, he is likely to end up in the science section. But all other assignments are haphazard. Sometimes literature majors end up in the economic section and economic majors in the social section.

Formally, the head of the telegraphic section is supposed to satisfy the demand for personnel from each Tokyo section chief with the supply offered by the managers in the regional offices. But often the Tokyo section chief will avoid the telegraphic section open market and talk directly with one of the regional office managers, particularly if that chief and that manager have been reporters together. The young reporter will be consulted. He may have views, but generally he is happy to accept any assignment that means going to Tokyo. The young reporter is not given a veto even though the decision is fundamental to his future.

The region in which the young reporter serves initially may also influence the decision on which section he will be assigned to later. Many reporters who were first assigned to the branch offices in Nagano or Iwate end up in the political section. Since both those branch offices have only one daily edition and few crimes to report, the reporter does not have to get up early and chase the police all day. He can give his time to study and long, analytical articles. Reporters assigned to the Yokohama branch office, on the other hand, often end up on the social desk. Yokohama is served with both a morning and evening edition and, as a big city, has lots of incidents. Nowadays, new reporters are expected to serve in both a one-delivery and a two-delivery area.

Each section has its stereotype. The political reporter is supposed to be like the politicians he covers. The economic reporter is supposed to be well dressed and gentlemanly. The social reporter is supposed to be rude, but with a highly developed sense of justice. The foreign news reporter is supposed to be scholarly.

Each section, however, is organized along the same lines. It is headed by an editor or section chief. Beneath him are four or five deputy editors, at least one of whom is always present. The deputy editors, who are called by the English word "desk," run the section. Beneath the desk are the reporters, some of whom serve within the newspaper office and some of whom serve outside, either in one of the clubs attached to a ministry or as "roving troops." Some ministry clubs have more than one reporter from a newspaper. In that instance one of the reporters will be chosen to serve as captain (*kyappu*). The number of reporters varies from a handful (in the case of the science section) to over a hundred (in the case of the social section). Table 5 shows the breakdown and deployment of reporters in the *Asahi* political section.

The first assignment for a new reporter in the political section will probably be with the eight-man team covering the prime minister. The reporter will arrive at this official's residence early in the morning to watch for morning callers. He will follow the prime minister through the day until he, the prime minister, retires for the evening. After two years, the political editor will shuffle the reporters around. At this time, the reporter may get to cover one of the political parties, probably the ruling conservative party, since it has a four-man team. On the next shuffle, the reporter may get assigned to the Foreign Ministry or an opposition party. For the next twelve years or so, the reporter will gradually revolve through the various posts his section is supposed to cover. As he nears the end of this period, he will be serving as a captain on one of the larger teams or as desk.

Some teams are more desirable than others. The captain for the cabinet team is *primus inter pares*. He usually has the rank of desk. The second most desirable team covers the Liberal Democratic Party (LDP), the ruling party. Newsmen differ over which are the third- and fourth-ranking teams. Some rank covering the Foreign Ministry over covering the opposition parties; others reverse the order. They all rank assignment to the Diet team fifth and do not bother to rank the rest of the assignments.

The reporter faces change after he reaches age forty. If he is very fortunate, he will be promoted to section chief. This path may lead to a deputy editor's chair in the managing editor's office, and a possible chance at selection as the managing editor. If he is less fortunate, he may be assigned as a section chief to one of the other publishing centers. He may come back from that assignment to serve as a deputy managing editor and still have a chance at becoming the managing editor. If he has no luck, he will leave the desk and take up administrative duties in other parts of the newspaper. He might find himself handling labor problems with the

Table 5
Internal Structure of the Political Section of the *Asahi Shimbun* (Tokyo)

Title	Number	Locus	Comment
Political editor	1	newspaper office	
Deputy political editors	5	newspaper office	
Reporter	8	Prime Minister's Office	Captain often has rank of deputy editor
Reporter	4	Liberal Democratic Party	
Reporter	1	Japanese Socialist Party	Each party has a club to which the reporter belongs. The reporter's assignment, however, is to cover all opposition parties. Thus, these four reporters work as a team
Reporter	1	Democratic Socialist Party	
Reporter	1	Clean Government Party	
Reporter	1	Japanese Communist Party	
Reporter	3	National Diet	
Reporter	4	Foreign Ministry	Plus 1 reporter from the economic section
Reporter	1	Finance Ministry	Plus 3 reporters from the economic section
Reporter	2	Defense Agency	Plus 1 reporter from the social section
Reporter	1	Ministry of International Trade and Industry	Plus 3 reporters from the economic section
Reporter	1	Ministry of Justice	Plus 3 reporters from the social section
Reporter	1	Ministry of Local Autonomy	Plus 2 reporters from the regional section
Reporter	1	Ministry of Education	Plus 1 reporter from the social section
Reporter	1	Ministry of Labor; labor unions	Plus 2 reporters from the social section
Reporter	1	Ministry of Transportation	Plus 1 reporter from the social section
Reporter	1	Business (*zaikai*)	Plus 3 reporters from the economic section

printers or trying to recruit newspaper distributors. He may end up in book publishing. He probably will not write again. He will stay with his administrative duties until he retires at age fifty-five.

It would take many pages to outline all the career possibilities for reporters, but one pattern is clear. Before age forty, he faces only light competition, at least within his section. After forty, he faces fierce competition for a limited number of important posts.

FROM EVENT TO ARTICLE

Reporters are expected to be able to gather information, compose an acceptable sentence, and work well within a group. The third talent may be the most important. The political section is small—about forty men. Each man knows every other man quite intimately. Each year, two or three men will move out at the top and an equal number will move in at the bottom. Faces change but only gradually. For many years the same men will live and work together. Competition would bring social friction, which has no place here.

Reporting techniques require cooperation. The observant reader will notice that the only signed articles are written by overseas correspondents. Domestic articles are not signed since they are usually the product of group reporting. Space in a Japanese newspaper is scarce; reporters are many. Several reporters, therefore, are supposed to work on each story. One reporter, sometimes the captain, is the writer. If the captain is not known for his felicity of phrase, or if the team has several stories to produce, the writer will be the captain's immediate subordinate. The other reporters are charged with supplying him with information.

Group reporting results in stories that an individual reporter would not be able to write by himself. The stories on the cabinet meetings are an example. Originally, the Japanese ministers followed the British pattern. Cabinet decisions were announced, but no record was kept of the debate. This policy, its originators believed, would discourage posturing and encourage free discussion among the cabinet officers. In England, this policy has worked. In Japan, it has not. The English press accords its politicians rights of privacy. The Japanese press regards its politicians as fair game at any hour on any day.

The night attack (*yo-uchi*) is an accepted journalistic tactic. When a politician returns home after an important day, he will find reporters in his sitting room, drinking his whiskey, and eating his supper. He is expected to talk with them. Every few minutes a reporter will leave the sitting room and phone the writer, both to pass on the politician's remarks and to receive reports on other politicians' statements. A hydra-headed press conference is in progress. It ends when the writer is satisfied he has a full account of the cabinet discussions.[7] Politicians recognize the efficacy of this style of news-gathering. Nowadays, each minister holds a press conference in his ministry after the conclusion of a cabinet meeting. Even so, his evenings are rarely his own.

Not all stories are the result of group reporting. A reporter may spend years developing a promising politician so that when the politician reaches a position of authority, the reporter may tap him. Another reporter may

---

[7] Most conservative politicians, certainly politicians of cabinet rank, carry on an active evening schedule. The hour of such a politician's return home varies. Reporters usually arrive early. Who takes care of the reporters until the politician arrives? Political households divide into two groups. In the first group the responsibility falls to the wife. The Sato, Ikeda, Fukuda, Miki, Ohira, and Shiina households fall in this category. In the second group, the wife never appears. The Ishibashi, Kishi, Tanaka, Ono, and Kono households fall in that category. Mrs. Nakasone has just moved from the latter to the former category.

spend long hours analyzing a political problem and come up with an insight no one else has realized. A third reporter may stumble over a scoop while wandering through the corridors of the Diet. Such stories are individually written. And if the story is outstanding, the managing editor will hand out a cash reward. But the reward will be given to the section, not the man. The section chief usually turns the money over to a Ginza madame, and the section drinks it up.

The passage of a story from reporter's manuscript to placement in the paper is also a group endeavor. The reporter turns his story over to the desk. The desk makes the first evaluation of its news value. If the story is too long, he will cut it. If the story is too short, he will flesh it out with other stories, or with analysis. One copy of the story goes to the radio and television section, another to the telegraphic section for transmission to the other publishing centers, and a third to layout.

Layout makes the next evaluation. Is the story important enough to go on the front page, and if so, where? Are pictures part of the story? How much space should be given to them? Finally, heads and subheads: how big, how long, how many? If a desk cannot live with the decisions of the layout editor, he may appeal to the deputy editor on duty in the managing editor's office. But appeals are rare.

Each of the other publishing centers of the newspaper has received a copy of the Tokyo story. Each layout section goes through the same process as the Tokyo layout section. Within each section liaison men keep the other publishing centers informed on what its layout section is doing, but each publishing center makes independent decisions. In effect, the paper is being put together in quadruplicate. Each publishing center's judgment is being tested against the others.

Other newspapers get into the act. During the day, editions close about every thirty minutes. As each edition is published and distributed, other newspapers acquire copies. One paper may have news that another paper lacks. If so, a reporter is dispatched to fill the gap. One paper may interpret the facts differently than another. If so, the reporter will be called upon to justify his observations. One paper may play a story big, and another paper may play a story small. Layout sections in both papers will probably make adjustments. Big cities get the last editions. Publishing centers are there, and time does not have to be allocated for transportation. By the time these city editions are published, all national dailies look much the same.

What about competition? It is present. The scoop is a hallowed institution, even though it may only last an hour, and monthly subscriptions preclude the papers from making any money off it. But competition is not limited to rivalries among newspapers. Competition also exists between the sections in the same newspaper. An example is an incident that occurred in the spring of 1966.

A general election was in the offing. Rumors began to percolate that a sugar company had close financial ties to conservative politicians. The transportation minister was discovered to have ordered express trains to stop at local stations in his election district. His secretaries were found to be soliciting transportation businesses to join the minister's fan club at high initiation fees. The Defense Agency chief was found to be using generals, bands, and airplanes in his campaigning.

The economic reporters looked into the sugar company. They found nothing unprecedented and so did not write articles. The political reporters said the activities of the transportation minister and defense chief were harmless. They did not want to waste big newspaper bullets on such small game. The social reporters did not agree. They argued that any corruption, be it minor or long-standing, requires exposure. They investigated independently and wrote articles for their part of the papers. What the social reporters had started, the economic and political reporters were obliged to continue. Before long, the papers were filled with little else. Scandal became the major issue in the campaign.

The election tally suggests that voters agreed with the economic and political reporters. All the politicians involved in the scandals were returned to office, the transportation minister with the highest plurality he had ever obtained. But the important point for us is that the squabble was between the sections, not the reporters. Alliances were between newspapers and opponents were within the same newspaper.

THE PRESS CLUB

An institution that has contributed to breaking down the loyalty of a newsman to his newspaper has been the press club. All nations have press clubs, but Japanese press clubs are unique.

Press clubs are attached to each government agency and other important offices. The largest is the Nagata Club. It has two hundred and seventy members from seventy news companies. It is responsible for covering the prime minister and his cabinet. The smallest press club might be made up of the ten newsmen covering the mayor of a small city. Although no one has yet counted all the clubs, estimates run to at least a thousand. They constitute the principal vehicle for bringing news to the newspaper.

No one is sure how the press clubs started. The story is that newsmen used to gather under a tree in the Marunouchi section of Tokyo to eat lunch and exchange stories. If no one is alive who can substantiate that story, neither is there anyone to deny it. Extant records show the presence of a newsmen's club in the Imperial Diet of 1890 and in some of the ministries of 1902. Today's clubs have grown in number and become much more elaborate. But the functions of the original club—pleasure (lunch) and business (exchanging stories)—still seem to be in evidence.[8]

The most important clubs are in the national ministries in Tokyo. I will describe the Kasumi Club, which is attached to the Foreign Ministry, but the description will fit most other clubs.

At the end of the corridor on the third floor, right over the main entrance to the Foreign Ministry, and just beneath the office of the Foreign Minister, are a set of double doors. Pasted to one of them is a sign restricting admission to members. Inside is a large L-shaped room. Desks fill the space under the windows. The *Asahi* men sit directly in front of the double doors. There are five of them and they have four desks. The *Yomiuri* men occupy a similar cluster of desks on the north exposure. *Mainichi* has the corner. Smaller newspapers have fewer men and occupy less space. Some local papers, whose men do not show up very often, are obliged to share a single desk but with individual drawers.

Around the corner, on the leg of the L are the common facilities: a couch, usually decorated with a sleeping newsman; a blackboard listing the time and the subject of the various briefings offered by officials that day; a television set, a mahjong set, a *go* board and stones, and a Japanese chess set. Telephones are on all desks and a few other places besides. A young man is charged with keeping the room neat, but he is not too efficient. The furniture is shabby. Dust and papers cover everything.

The clubs limit their membership. Generally, reporters whose newspapers belong to the Japan Newspaper Association are admitted. Reporters who work for party, religious, company, union, and foreign media are excluded. The foreign media have been protesting their exclusion for years. Recently the Nagata Club relaxed restrictions. Foreign newsmen may now attend prime minister's public press conferences and ask questions through the club spokesman after the club members' questions are exhausted. Other clubs have not dropped their barriers. Table 6 shows the composition of the Kasumi Club.

Each club has formal written rules.[9] Violations of these rules can lead to discipline, which may involve expulsion from the club. The bureaucrats will usually honor a club decision, and a newspaper can find itself without access to information from a ministry if it or its reporters do not follow the club regulations.

Fights have occurred between the clubs and the newspapers over who speaks for the reporters. The issue usually involves the handling of news where the club has reached an agreement with which a newspaper has refused to comply.[10] These incidents have occurred often enough to have

---

[8] A brief history of the Japanese press clubs has been written by Fujii Tsuguo in *Shinbun no shuzai*, II, 266–290.

[9] Nagata Club rules can be found in *Shinbun no shuzai*, I, 118–120.

[10] Handling of the news means management of the news. Management may sound offensive, but some regulation is necessary. For example, if a ministry issues a long study, the reporters must agree when articles based on the study are to be published. If there is no

Table 6
Composition of the Kasumi Club[a]

Newspaper	Number of Reporters
Asahi	5
Mainichi	5
Yomiuri	5
Nihon Keizai	4
Sankei	3
Kyodo	4
Jiji	4
NHK[b]	4
Chūnichi	2
Tokyo	2
Hokkaido	1
Nishi Nippon	1
TOTAL	40

[a] This list is limited to those members who attend daily press briefings. Many local newspapers have pro forma membership which they do not exercise. Figures may vary from time to time.

[b] NHK stands for the Japanese Broadcasting Corporation, a government subsidized national television and radio network. It is one of the most powerful members of the mass media. It has a reportorial staff equivalent to the national newspapers, though it is organized differently.

Commercial radio and television networks have tie-ins with the mainstream newspapers and rely on them for news, although a separate club, the Minpō Club, has been set up for them in the Foreign Ministry.

the Japan Newspaper Association attempt to resolve the differences between the club and the newspaper. It has suggested, and the parties have adopted, the rule that no club can make an agreement without the concurrence of all the newspapers. In principle, this rule sounds good. In practice, it is unwieldy.

---

agreement, the reporters must write for the next edition. Justice is done neither to the reporters nor to the document.

This problem of news management has received a great deal of attention within the newspapers and within the Japanese Newspaper Association. The conclusion seems to be that agreements made among the newsmen are acceptable, but agreements made between newsmen and officials are not. The assumption underlying this conclusion is that newsmen are interested in publishing information, whereas officials are interested in suppressing information.

As a former official and news manager, I should like to suggest that officials are not interested solely in news suppression. I hope this paper gives some intimation that reporters are not concerned solely with the publishing of information.

In the Foreign Ministry, for example, the administrative vice-minister, the highest-ranking professional diplomat, talks every evening for an hour with the Kasumi Club members. His guidance is necessary if the reporters are to understand the intentions of the Japanese government. The vice-minister should speak bluntly. Yet bluntness is not a diplomatic virtue. If the vice-minister wants to spend the following day doing something other than defending his position to other nations' ambassadors, he will request the reporters to attribute his views to some generalized authority rather than to him directly. On some occasions, he may speak completely off-the-record. In theory, each of these requests should be referred to the newspapers for decision. In practice, the newsmen do not bother.

The occasional spats with the newspapers heightens the solidarity of the club. To my knowledge, only one major club—the Metropolitan Police Club—has partitioned off the desks of the various newspapers, and that was the officials' not the reporters' idea. In the other clubs, the desks are together; there are no walls except the exterior walls. The clubs are cooperative bodies.

They have to be. Reporters almost live in the clubs. They arrive in mid-morning and remain until early evening. Some reporters go directly from their home to the club and back. They show up in the newspaper offices only on payday.

Reporters are supposed to be available at all times, although if a reporter wanders away for the afternoon, other reporters will cover for him. If his desk calls, they will say he is off for an interview and, if news is announced, they will inform him of it when he returns.

What do the reporters do all day? Japan has wire services that report all the news, but only the local papers rely on them. Mainstream papers expect their reporters to call in each item themselves. During the day, reporters have to be on hand to update stories as successive editions close. They listen to the lectures held for them by officials, and they wander around the building. But most of the time, they talk among themselves. Hours are spent trying to decide what is important and what is not, analyzing interest, and puzzling out motive. It is not unusual that these discussions have a conclusion or that the conclusion shows up in all the newspapers. The clubs, then, often reach news judgments collectively. The system encourages the practice. The reporters have long ago learned that if all stories carry the same interpretation the desk will not question them. Phone calls come only when one story differs from another.

The clubs were started by the newsmen as a way of compelling attention from the bureaucrats. The bureaucrats may have initially opposed the clubs, but they soon learned that the clubs were in their interest as well. It is easier to handle a club's single request than to handle all the reporters' requests individually. Since the club is always leveling demands, it is easy for the officials to determine what the reporters are thinking and how they will be reporting. Since a reporter never wants to take the responsibility of failing to report what the government thinks important, the club proves to be a valuable vehicle for the ministry's public relations efforts. A bureaucrat soon learns that if he hands out sufficient news, the reporters will search no further. The skillful bureaucrat, then, through the judicious handling of briefings, lectures, and comment, can greatly influence what the reporter will write.

Clubs also exist among Japanese overseas correspondents. These clubs are slightly different. No one sits in a special room all day waiting for news to be given him. But in some respects, ties in the overseas press clubs are stronger than in the domestic clubs. Language barriers, inability to move freely through a foreign capital, lack of deep understanding of the foreign country, all encourage the reporters to make news-gathering a collective effort. The foreign news desk compares his correspondent's story with that of his competitor. So long as both stories look the same, the desk is satisfied that he is reading the truth.

VIEWS ON CONFORMITY

I have described the system enough now so that the reader is aware that all parts of the system urge conformity. What about the reporters? Are they willing to withstand these pressures? Or do they go along with them?

The Japan Recruit Center surveyed college graduates to discover which company they wished to join. The *Asahi* rated eighth on the list; most other national newspapers were not far behind. This popularity has meant that the papers can choose from among the top graduates of the land for their reporters. These circumstances are considerably different than before the war when journalism was not quite a respectable profession and the reporters were not always top drawer. But the old reporters regarded journalism as a calling; the new reporters seem to regard journalism as a job.

Support for this view comes from Ozaki Morimitsu, chairman of the literature department of Tokyo University, who has written a book describing the employment patterns of graduates from his department. He divides the years after the war into three periods. The first is from the end of the war until 1956 when almost all graduates became schoolteachers. The second period is from 1956 to 1960 when graduates mostly entered publishing, broadcasting, and newspapers. The third period runs to the present. While most of the graduates continue to join mass media, significant numbers were also beginning to enter manufacturing concerns, trading firms, and government agencies. These data suggest that working for a newspaper has become just another job,[11] though a damned good one.

---

[11] Morimitsu Ozaki, *Shūshoku* [Employment] (Tokyo: Chūko Shinso, 1969). See also *Shinbun no shuzai*, I, 9–10.

Finally, is it disadvantageous that all the newspapers look and sound the same? A Japanese would not pose that question. His society regards the unanimous decision as the correct decision. If all the newspapers have come around to saying the same thing, then what they are saying is correct.

Only an American would ask that question. His society believes that the truth is elusive, that the best way to apprehend it is to surround it with diverse views. It is easy, then, to dismiss the question by saying that the American will see disadvantages, the Japanese will not.

Yet even an American can see some advantage in having the newspapers speak with a single voice. If the role of the newspapers is to serve as a transmission belt of government ideas to the people, then the Japanese newspapers are most efficient. The five o'clock musings of the vice-minister of foreign affairs are laid on twenty-five million breakfast tables the next morning. When I worked in public affairs in the State Department, we used to regard six months as a fair interval for informing the American public of a change in policy.

If the role of the press is to oppose the government, then a single-voiced press is good. If the government has the power to speak with one tongue, so should the newspapers.

But there are dangers. A Japanese news story is as much a product of the internal pressures in the newspaper world as it is of external event. There is a delicate balance here, and if that balance is upset, the reader's interest is not served.

Not much danger is done in the domestic sphere. The Japanese reader innately knows his society and possesses common sense. He may even have news sources independent of the newspaper. He was not overwhelmed when all the newspapers urged that the rascals be thrown out of office in 1966.

But the Japanese reader does not have an innate understanding of foreign countries. Common sense in one country is not common sense in another. The Japanese reader does not have independent sources of news. I find Japanese reporting of international affairs factitious and thus dangerous, particularly in a world of growing interdependence in which the businessman, the scholar, and the professional are as important to international goodwill as the diplomat. The diplomats have their own sources of information. The others do not. Japan does not have a good record of either understanding or projecting other nations' behavior. Perhaps the reason lies with the newspapers.

The most frightening aspect of Japanese journalism is, for me, its conformity. Nowhere has this conformity been more apparent than in the newspapers' dealings with the People's Republic of China.[12] In order to

---

[12] A former reporter, now critic, Miyoshi Osamu, first described relations between the Japanese newspapers and the People's Republic of China in *Keizai Ōrai*, April 1972. Foreign

dispatch news correspondents to the mainland, the Japanese newspapers have been willing to accept three political principles imposed by the Chinese government. These principles were formalized in an agreement in 1968 but had been tacitly accepted as early as 1964. The Japanese newsmen abjure: (1) pursuing a hostile policy towards China; (2) participating in any plot to create "two Chinas"; and (3) obstructing the restoration of normal relations between Japan and China.

The Chinese authorities have interpreted these principles unusually and applied their interpretations harshly. They expelled the *Mainichi, Sankei,* and *Nishi-Nippon* correspondents because their newspapers had carried "anti-Chinese cartoons and reports." They expelled the *Yomiuri* correspondent because that newspaper had underwritten the exhibition of Tibetan treasures in Tokyo. They arrested the *Nihon Keizai* correspondent, charging that "he stole a great deal of Chinese political, economic, and military information and handed it to American and Japanese reactionaries." The correspondent was incarcerated for a year and a half.

The correspondent for NHK, the government radio and television network, had his reentry permit refused twice: the first time because NHK carried a program about Taiwan, and the second because NHK maintained membership in the Asian Broadcasters' Union, of which Taiwan was a member country. The *Asahi*'s correspondent had his permit held up because his newspaper reported on the NHK Taiwan program. The *Kyodo* correspondent was expelled from China because his wire agency had sponsored a meeting of the Organization of Asian News Agencies, which also included Taiwan.

No Japanese newspaper protested these Chinese acts. To the contrary, more than one editor sent a letter to the Chinese authorities apologizing for his newspaper's behavior. (Some letters were demanded by the Chinese; other letters were unsolicited.) The Japanese public was not informed of what was going on.

To the credit of the Japanese press, the editors spent long hours debating whether they were responding correctly. Often the question was raised whether the freedom of the press was in jeopardy. At one stage in the proceedings, the editors were on the verge of protesting the Chinese actions and stating publicly that they had done so. One newspaper was obdurately opposed. Its concern with keeping its correspondent in Peking was overriding. It threatened to walk out if such a protest were sent. A wire agency also felt much the same way. Rather than split the group, the editors went along with the Chinese demands.

The Japanese have a press code. Its first article reads in part: "The press have complete freedom of information and comment. . . . This freedom

correspondent Sam Jameson further elaborated this description in the *Los Angeles Times,* April 14, 1972. Professor Etō Shinkichi has analyzed both content and bias of the China stories published by the Japanese newspapers in *Bungei Shunjū,* April 1972.

must be protected by all means as a fundamental human right." All Japanese reporters and editors whom I have ever met subscribe whole-heartedly to this provision. They are utterly serious when they quote it to you. But if the Chinese case is any criterion, there is something more fundamental than the freedom to inform and comment. That is the urge to conform.

George Orwell has written about conformity. He has found it a greater threat to freedom of speech than outright government censorship. I quote from his introduction to *Animal Farm*, an introduction which, ironically, was suppressed:

At any given moment, there is an orthodoxy, a body of ideas which it is assumed that all right-thinking people will accept without question. It is not exactly forbidden to say this, that, or the other, but it is "not done" to say it, just as in mid-Victorian times it was not done to mention trousers in the presence of a lady. Any one who challenges the prevailing orthodoxy finds himself silenced with surprising effectiveness. A genuinely unfashionable opinion is almost never given a fair hearing, either in the popular press or in the highbrow periodicals.[13]

George Orwell was writing about England during the war years, but I believe that his words have pertinence in Japan today.

---

[13] George Orwell, "The Freedom of the Press," *New York Times Magazine*, October 8, 1972, p. 8.

Organizational Paralysis: The Case of Todai

IVAN P. HALL

Among the various subsystems of Japanese society today, the university must rate rather close to the bottom of the scale in terms of organizational adequacy and effectiveness in decision-making. The violent campus upheaval of 1968–1969 and the calls for drastic reform emanating from the government as well as the general public reflect the fact that the universities have adjusted far more slowly than have other subsystems to the requirements of Japan's emerging postindustrial society. Meanwhile, the inability of the universities to initiate meaningful reforms by themselves underscores serious flaws in their decision-making processes.

Nowhere have these problems surfaced more dramatically than in the case of Tokyo University (ab: Todai, pron: Tōdai). As Japan's first (and until 1898, only) modern university, as the model for the other national (formerly imperial) universities, as the bellwether of Japanese higher education as a whole, and as the training ground for Japan's bureaucratic, political, intellectual, and social elite, Todai for all its special features provides important clues to the ailments of Japanese universities in general.

This paper will discuss organization (primarily structure) and decision-making at Todai today. In order to place patterns and problems in a broader evolutionary perspective, each of these two themes will be introduced by a brief historical account. The final section will mention some of the proposals for the future.

I should like to make it clear here that by contrasting Todai to a somewhat abstracted American pattern, I do not mean to imply any value judgments. The yardstick I aim to use is functional performance. If much of my language about Todai is negative, this simply reflects my impression, as an outsider, of considerable organizational dysfunction—an impression fortified by loudly voiced Japanese frustrations with an institution which seems to be operating less than adequately in its own terms and in its own context.

ORGANIZATION: STRUCTURAL CHARACTERISTICS

Japanese universities today are prisoners of their past. At Todai, too, inherited structure has created not only the specific problems that urgently require decisions for reform, but also many of the obstacles that lie in the way of reaching those decisions effectively. The case of Todai serves as an eloquent reminder that behavior in a modernizing society is a product not only of traditional cultural conditioning but also of objective structural realities—whether imported or homespun—which have been arbitrarily created and imposed at specific historical points.

The most basic structural characteristic at Todai—with far-reaching implications for the decision-making process—is its organization into the highly distinct and quasi-independent Faculties or *Gakubu* (these are administrative units; this usage will be capitalized throughout to avoid confusion with "faculty" in the sense of teaching staff). There are nine Faculties—Law, Medicine, Engineering, Literature, Science, Agriculture, Economics, Education, and Pharmacology, all located on or near the main campus in the Hongō district. The College of General Education, which enrolls all undergraduates during their first two years, is located apart from the main campus in the Komaba district, but organizationally it is the equivalent of a tenth Faculty.

These Faculties are far more comprehensive and powerful than the typical department on an American campus, and they are considerably more independent of the university's central administration than even the graduate professional schools attached to American universities (such as law, medical, and business schools), which they resemble in some respects. Since general or liberal education at Todai has its own plant, faculty, and curriculum outside the main Faculty structure in the College of General Education, the Todai Faculties concentrate on undergraduate teaching at the professionalized third- and fourth-year levels, and on postgraduate teaching and research. The Faculty staffs, however, are burdened primarily with undergraduate teaching, which is Todai's main mission. With the best and most lavishly funded graduate and research facilities in Japan, Todai still has only four thousand of its sixteen thousand students in the graduate school (*daigakuin*). The graduate school is little more than a loose association of research divisions (*kenkyūka*), which are in effect extensions of the respective Faculties. Todai's fourteen research institutes (*kenkyūjo*) have independent staffs, but their members retain strong personal ties with their former Faculties. In many cases, the best research and graduate training in Japan today is found outside the university system, in the government and business sectors.

The overall result has been an articulation between general education, specialized education, and research quite different from the pattern in the United States. If the typical American university may be viewed as an upright T—with a smooth vertical articulation between general and specialized courses in its four-year college, crossed at the top by the robust horizontal of its professional and research-oriented graduate schools, then perhaps Todai may best be described as an upside-down T—with the massive vertical components of its ten Faculties resting uneasily on the detached freshman-sophomore course and petering out at the top in impoverished, inadequately organized, and clique-ridden research facilities.

This paradigm, for all its clumsiness, pinpoints the three major structural problems facing Todai today: (1) its division into rigid vertical units that often paralyze university-wide decision-making in the name of Faculty autonomy; (2) the orphaning of general education; and (3) the weakness of research.

The Historical Background

The autonomous spirit of Todai's Faculties derives in part from their initial constitution as separate colleges (*bunka daigaku*, literally "branch universities") under the Imperial University Ordinance (Teikoku Daigakurei) of 1886. While the 1886 ordinance is responsible for the basic physiognomy of the school, there are two other watershed dates that are important in the university's historical evolution: 1918, when the University Ordinance (Daigakurei) officially divided the graduate school into Faculty-related research divisions; and the late 1940s, when an expanded and in some respects debased preparatory course at the former First High School (Daiichi Kōtōgakkō) at Komaba was telescoped from three into two years and tacked onto the prewar course at Hongō in an attempt to realize general education.

In 1877, Tokyo University was established on the "amalgamated college" pattern then popular in the United States, with four departments but no graduate school. Its Department of Medicine was the direct descendant of the medical school of the Shogunate government (Igakushō), while the three other departments (law, science, and literature) were the collective heirs of the government's School for Western Studies (Kaiseijo). The old Confucian Shōheikō (Samurai School), which had formed the "Main Campus" (Honkō) of the 1869–1871 Daigakkō (university) and supported traditionalism during those years, disappeared without a trace after the establishment of a modern Ministry of Education

(Monbushō) in 1872, and left the new university with a Western-oriented, strongly utilitarian spirit.

In 1886, Education Minister Mori Arinori gave Todai its "imperial" sobriquet, placed it firmly under the control of the Ministry of Education, provided it with an independent and comprehensive graduate school, and reorganized it into the five colleges of law, medicine, engineering, literature, and science—incidentally taking a lead on Germany, France, and England with the engineering college. The colleges were to "teach the theory and application of the arts and sciences," while the graduate school was entrusted with "mastering their secrets," i.e., basic research.

Mori's aim was to raise up as rapidly as possible the bureaucratic, technocratic, and academic elite, as well as the fund of modern scientific and technological knowledge needed to bring Japan abreast with the Western powers. His frame of reference, often criticized for having been too "statist," was not all that different from the policy of present-day developing countries, which have to allocate resources rather narrowly for maximum impact. Likewise, his importation of the German graduate-school and research ethos was simply in line with a modern trend that was beginning to infect the Anglo-Saxon countries at about the same time. The imperatives of forced modernization, however, were not congenial (then as now) to the cultivation of humanistic, general educational, interdisciplinary approaches.

The vertical configuration of Japanese higher education owes much to this initial scramble for expertise—the effort to push each field ahead as fast as it would go. The concern for the totality and interrelatedness of knowledge—which the Western universities had inherited from their early nurture at the hands of medieval philosophy and Renaissance humanism—was lost by the Japanese when they found their own Confucian tradition wanting and abandoned it.

The colleges of 1886 operated with little concern for each other. Each college had its own faculty, regulated its own curriculum and examinations, and issued its own diplomas—subject to ministerial approval and standards. From an early date the teaching staff of each college began to meet informally in a Faculty council (kyōjūkai) to discuss the practical running of their school. Coordination of the university as a whole was accomplished through a president (sōchō) who was the direct appointee and representative—the proconsul, in effect—of the Ministry of Education and who kept tight control over the several college principals (gakuchō) who in turn, although professors in their respective colleges, were also selected by the education minister. The principal dealt with the university authorities and concerned himself with matters on the intercollege level. Intracollege affairs were in the hands of a vice-principal (kyōtō), who was likewise appointed from the professorial corps by the minister and who was responsible for "maintaining order in the classroom," and for "supervising the work" of the professors (*kyōju*), assistant professors (*jokyōju*), dormitory masters, and clerks attached to his school. Each college had several departments (*gakka*—for instance, English law, French law, and politics in the Law College), and in 1893, Education Minister Inoue Kowashi introduced the *kōza* (*Lehrstuhl*, or "chair") system in order that every major subject might be covered by an eminent scholar with sufficient funds, assistants, and prestige to devote himself wholeheartedly to his specialty. The need of the times, Inoue explained, was for the expert, not the amateur or jack-of-all-trades.

The central role of Todai in the development of Japan's higher education is underscored by the fact that, until the establishment of the second imperial university at Kyoto in 1898, it was the only recognized university in Japan. The ordinance of 1918, which finally granted university status to the private colleges and government higher technical schools in order to accommodate the swelling demand for higher education, also transformed Todai into a more unified, "comprehensive university" (*sōgō daigaku*), with the former colleges now becoming Faculties and their principals transformed into deans (*gakubuchō*). The University gradually won autonomy from the ministry, which gave it a greater cohesiveness than it had enjoyed in 1886, but to this day the Faculties have retained the basic identity and independence of the original colleges.

The graduate school, in Mori Arinori's original concept, was to stand above and apart from the colleges, and to coordinate research at the higher levels of all branches of learning. The idea of sharply differentiating teaching and research while maximizing the horizontal flow between various research facilities is one that has found favor with reformers again today. Inevitably, however, the vertical affinities within each discipline came to the fore. The research divisions, informally established in 1887, enabled the graduate student to spend two more years in his college before entering the graduate school proper, but after 1918 the graduate school became primarily a mechanism for administrative liaison. The postwar reforms revised the content and methods of graduate education in the direction of greater breadth of learning and more formal requirements (such as the accumulation of credits) but did not alter its structural grounding in the Faculty system.

The continuing hiatus at Todai between general and specialized education has deep historical roots in the fact that before the war the Japanese, like the major European nations, considered the university a place for professional (or at least academically specialized) training, with liberal or general education something to be fully mastered in the rigorous secondary courses of the *kōtōgakkō*—the Japanese counterpart to the lycée, Gymnasium, or English public school. Both types of education before the war in Europe and Japan were for a limited elite. The introduction of general education into the university under the American occupation was redolent of an alien social system (if not of the dilatoriness of American secondary education) and overlooked the fact that the prewar higher schools, while catering to the few, had provided imperial university students with an excellent general education.

In today's Japan, with the expansion and democratization of higher education, there is a general acceptance of the need for some sort of general education at the university level and for its meaningful integration with the specialized programs. At the time of the postwar reforms, however, Todai had no other choice than to accept a rather mechanical fusion with the general education program offered at Komaba, which, for all its changes, remains in many respects a *yobimon*, or preparatory department. For this there has been ample precedent. The Ministry of Education's Tōkyō Eigo Gakkō (English School) had been attached to the university and was officially known as the *yobimon* from 1877 to 1886. The state-operated higher schools established by Mori (and supplanting the *yobimon*) were intended to serve as terminal secondary schools as well as to provide preparation for the university; but they soon confined themselves to the second function. The seven top-ranking higher schools before the war prepared exclusively for the neighboring imperial university, and the curriculum at the old First Higher School at Komaba dovetailed smoothly into the several Faculties at Todai.

Todai Today: Patterns and Problems

The main structural components of Todai today are its ten Faculties, fourteen research institutes, the graduate school, and the administrative office (*jimukyoku*) that serves the university as a whole. There are also six research facilities for joint interfaculty or interuniversity use, including the Joint Nuclear Energy Research Center and two computer centers.

Both in the breakdown and arrangement of fields of learning and in the relative importance of successive levels of administration, there are significant departures from the usual American pattern. In the United States, at the larger Ivy League schools and at most state universities, there are traditionally several fields such as law, medicine, or business that are strictly professional and reserved for the graduate level. They are organized as separate schools, which possess their own full set of administrative organs, are subject in the final instance to control by the president and board of trustees, and are generally closed to undergraduates. Even where undergraduates may attend lectures, they are enrolled in their own undergraduate college, where the full roster of humanities and social and natural sciences is organized under a Faculty (or School) of Arts and Sciences, divided into departments of roughly equal standing (though not size), which offer a variety of courses—the menu shifting with the availability and preferences of the staff or with student demand. These departments also offer graduate training in fields not represented by the professional schools and cooperate in a variety of interdisciplinary programs at the graduate, undergraduate, and general-education levels. Each department, under its chairman, exercises general control over the development of its own program and has the primary say in appointments, but matters of a campus-wide nature are taken up at meetings of the entire arts and sciences faculty, in which professors more often act as individuals rather than as representatives of their own departments. The structure here is flexible and permits a high degree of lateral exchange and contact between specialized fields.

At Todai the articulation of fields is very different. What would be professional graduate schools in America—the Faculties of Law, Medicine, Education, Pharmacology (and in many cases Engineering and Agriculture)—at Todai enroll primarily third- and fourth-year undergraduates. Students are now earmarked for their Faculties upon joining the university and begin preparing for them actively during their second year at Komaba. A premedical student (as he would be called in America) studies not in the biology or biochemistry department of the Science Faculty (which trains only pure scientists) but in the medical department of the Faculty of Medicine. And the education major, although entitled to attend lectures in other Faculties, will rarely do so and will be deep into his specialty of educational psychology or school administration by his third year.

The other familiar departments of the typical American arts and sciences faculty are scattered throughout the remaining three Todai Faculties of Economics, Science, and Literature (the *bungakubu*, perhaps best translated as humanities or liberal arts), in various shapes and sizes. Economics rates an entire Faculty, albeit a small one. Politics (or government) crops up as one of the three courses (*kōsu*) that constitute the Law Faculty, reflecting the traditional role of the Law Faculty since 1887 as the seedbed of Japan's higher civil service. The former departments of sociology, anthropology, and psychology within the Literature Faculty simply appear as course offerings or as seminars (*kenkyūshitsu*) under one of the four broad areas (*rui*) into which the Literature Faculty recently has been divided: cultural studies (primarily philosophy), history, language and literature, and psychology and sociology. The social sciences have been cited here because their mutual isolation at Todai is particularly striking.

Neither do the various administrative levels at Todai necessarily correspond to those at most American institutions, despite the similarity of names. The Faculties are the main administrative entities, but in terms of scope the three we have just mentioned obviously fall somewhere between an American faculty of arts and sciences and an ordinary American department. The Faculties at Todai are further subdivided into departments (*gakka*), but these too are highly variable units: the Engineering Faculty, for instance, has twenty; the Medical Faculty only two, although it enrolls nearly one-third as many students as engineering. In the Science

Faculty, the departments represent familiar fields such as mathematics, physics, and chemistry, but in the Economics Faculty (as in Pharmacology and Medicine) they are virtually synonymous with the Faculty itself. Economics has only the two departments of economics and business management.

Below the department, finally, come two smaller structural units. The basic element for budgeting and staffing at Todai is the chair (*kōza*). Engineering, for instance, has 163 chairs, law 51, literature 54, and science 76. In several faculties two or more chairs are grouped together in a number of seminars (called either *kenkyūshitsu* in literature, for instance, or *kyōshitsu* in science and medicine—both terms are best translated as "research room" or "Seminar" in the German usage). The effective operating unit varies greatly from one Faculty to another. Where the Faculty has no departments, as in the Law Faculty, or where the departments are of a nonfunctional, catch-all nature, as in economics, the individual chair must be reckoned with in intrafaculty deliberations. Where there are many chairs but few departments, as in the Medical or Science Faculties (with respective ratios of 49:2 and 76:8), the seminar seems to gain operational weight. The department, however, is more important than the seminar in Faculties where there are few chairs, and where the departments themselves correspond closely to well-defined, traditional disciplines. This holds for the Education Faculty (with a 15:5 chair-to-department ratio) and the Literature Faculty (where the ratio is 54:18). In the latter, the present-day seminars are in effect the former eighteen departments in a new guise, and so they remain the effective subdivision of the Faculty.

The new postwar national universities have been established on the more familiar departmental model, without the chairs, which remain a distinctive feature of the eight former imperial universities—a distinction that helps perpetuate the gap in prestige and budgeting largesse between the older and the newer schools. More aptly (if somewhat facetiously) described as a "sofa" than a "chair," the *kōza* is a unit for instruction in a given subject up through the doctoral level. It is staffed by a prescribed and uniform complement of one full professor, one associate professor, and one research assistant (*joshu*)—or two of the latter in subjects involving experimental laboratory work. The research assistant functions variously as a laboratory teaching assistant in science, engineering and medicine; as a prestigious, full-time research fellow in law; and as an instructor and often as not as a personal aide to his professor in literature.

The budgetary allocation from the Ministry of Education is identical for all chairs within each of three categories: those with laboratory work (*jikken kōza*), those without laboratory work (*hijikken kōza*), and those with clinical work (*rinshō kōza*). Since the funding for experimental chairs is approximately four times that for nonexperimental chairs, great efforts are made to get new chairs identified as experimental chairs, especially in borderline cases. In any event, the allocation is for the chair as a unit, and in Faculties where the chairs are especially strong, the funds are placed entirely in the hands of the senior professor to use at his own discretion for research and teaching purposes. This money, commonly called research expenses (*kenkyūhi*), comes from the budgetary category known as "integrated school expenses for teachers" (*kyōkan atari sekisan kōhi*) and is in addition to the professor's own salary as a civil servant, which derives from "personnel expenses" (*jinkenhi*) in the budget.

Although there are minor variations (chairs that stop at the masters' level, or the undergraduate course—*kamoku*—structure at Komaba), the doctoral chair remains the basic building block at Todai and contributes to the rigidities and lack of horizontal mobility in Todai's structure—what Professor Etō Shinkichi has called the "petrification" and "octopus" effects. The chair, once it has been established, is permanent, and its creation and abolition is an elaborate process involving the consent of the Faculty, the university, the Ministry of Education, and ultimately the Ministry of Finance. The vested interest in established chairs is enormous. The chair allocation, however, prescribes fixed and uniform amounts for closely defined academic fields, without regard to the varying competence of teachers, the shifting demands of the students, the needs of society, or advances in human learning. The only way to get the money to keep abreast of new developments or strike out into new areas is to create new chairs for them.

Once established in his chair, the chief tends, in the words of two Todai professors (Nakamura Takafusa and Kumon Shunpei) to become "the absolute monarch of his little universe." He retains a free hand regarding standards, the content of lecture courses and research, and the duties of his subordinates. As a civil servant, he cannot be fired for incompetence and holds his position—blocking the advancement of lower staff—until he retires (at age sixty), dies, or resigns. His subordinates are beholden to him for their appointments, his ordinary pupils are beholden for proper introductions and placement in the outside world after graduation, and his graduate students generally fit their own research into that of the chair. Accordingly, the chairs (or the multiple-chair seminars, or small-scale departments in certain faculties) tend to become closed, highly specialized baronies competing with one another for money, space, and equipment— but there is little intellectual competition.

Graduate training at Todai gets short shrift. The student's own interests often do not coincide with the research priorities of the chair, and there is the almost universal necessity for part-time employment (*arubaito*). Graduate fellowships from the government or university are few, salaries for the young research assistants are niggardly, and there are no university scholarships for study abroad. Professors teaching at the graduate level belong either to the Faculties or to the research centers, and devote their primary energies to undergraduate teaching or center work. The graduate school has no plant, library, faculty, administrative staff, or budget of its own. It is, in fact, no more than a framework for sorting out graduate students into appropriate degree programs.

The graduate school consists of ten research divisions which correspond to the ten Faculties except for the College of General Education, which is not represented, and the excision of sociology from the Humanities Research Division (the graduate extension of the literature Faculty) to make the tenth division. Each research division offers several specialized courses of study (*senmon katei*), which correspond to departmental or other subdivisions in the appropriate "servicing" Faculty (*sewa gakubu*), and are taught by senior professors from the *sewa gakubu* with occasional assistance from members of other Faculties or research institutes. The funding of graduate training depends entirely on how the senior professor chooses to divide his chair money between his Faculty and graduate-school activities. The Graduate School Council (Daigakuin Iinkai), convened and presided over by the president, includes the chairman and two elected members of each research division committee (*kenkyūka iinkai*). These chairmen are without exception the deans of the corresponding Faculties, with the result that the Graduate School Council simply repeats the existing faculty rivalries and has virtually no role in university-wide decisions.

Another, and very basic, weakness of the graduate divisions is that they train exclusively for academic careers—in effect for the replenishment of the Faculties—and therefore lack the leaven that comes with training students for careers in the outside world. The graduate school is viewed as an extension of the undergraduate course—an extension preferably avoided by those anxious to get ahead in their careers. Many government bureaus and large private companies now provide better graduate-level training for their own researchers and other staff than the universities—including Todai in some fields—and there is a peculiar shunning of advanced academic degrees as a handicap to career advancement by young men headed for business or government work.

Not only in graduate-type training but in research as well much of the best work in Japan today is being performed at government- and business-operated research centers outside the university system. This is part of the price now being paid for decades of emphasis on practical application and immediate technological return at the expense of basic research. The funding of all research at Japan's universities today amounts to less than that of the business-supported centers. Todai has the finest facilities in the country taken as a whole (its fourteen research centers include the Institutes for Medical Science, Earthquake Research, Oceanography, Far Eastern Culture, Social Science, Newspaper Research, Historical Compilation, Industrial Technology, Applied Microbiology, Solid State Physics, Aeronautics and Space, Cosmic Ray Observation, Research on the Atomic Nucleus, and the Tokyo Astronomical Observatory). The funding is better than for the chairs but is spotty in important areas such as the humanities, social sciences, and basic science. Research at Todai suffers from the lack of a powerful graduate-school structure. The institute directors are not represented on the influential inner conclave known as the Deans' Conference (Gakubuchōkai) and the centers have often complained of their exclusion from the mainstream of Todai's decision-making process.

There is no reason why research activities should be confined to or even primarily conducted at university centers, and many of Japan's research needs promise to be adequately filled off-campus, subject of course to government and business priorities. What will increasingly suffer, however, from the skimping on university-centered graduate training and advanced research is the academic profession itself—that is, scholarship in the broader sense. The future quality of Japan's premier university is at stake when Todai professors can no longer compete with industry and bureaucracy for their own top students.

This disjunction between general and specialized education at Todai is not only curricular but physical as well. With half of the university's population crammed into its modestly expanded facilities at Komaba, halfway across the sprawling metropolis from Hongō, the College of General Education has found itself on the short end of money, space, facilities, library books, prestige, and general appeal ever since its establishment in 1949. Although some teachers from the main Hongō campus occasionally give "outside lectures" (*mochidashi kōgi*) at Komaba, the college has its own separate staff and resembles an American arts and sciences faculty, but caters only to the first two years. Many of the original college staff were carried over from the old higher school, where they had learned to teach from a broad, humanistic viewpoint but found themselves overwhelmed by numbers and by the inevitable debasement of standards. Professors in the Faculties at Hongō—like the students at Komaba—tend to view the two years in the college as a period of exile, which cuts into precious time needed for specialization and provides no more than an accumulation of fragmentary knowledge, much of which the student already has learned in high school.

There are, of course, sequential breaks between general and specialized education in the typical American pattern, but the sharpest disjunction (involving different administrative and curricular structures, and often a separate plant) falls between the undergraduate college and the professional graduate school rather than midway through the undergraduate course as at Todai. The American undergraduate enjoys far more flexibility in formulating his total program both forward and backward between introductory and advanced courses, and sideways among the various disciplines. A freshman or sophomore in good standing can often mix work toward a prospective major (which involves quasi-professional training in such fields as premedicine, engineering, education) with required "Gen-Ed" courses, while a senior is permitted to dip back into elementary courses outside his chosen field in order to cultivate late-blooming interests. During all four years, electives provide lateral mobility throughout the college, and the procedures for switching majors or degrees are relatively simple, with no more backtracking than is needed to make up the prerequisite courses.

At Todai, the applicant sits for only one of six possible entrance examinations covering six general areas: "Literature 1 (for law); "Lit. 2" (for economics); "Lit. 3" (for literature, education); "Science 1" (for physical, chemical and engineering sciences); "Sci. 2" (for biological and agricultural sciences); and "Sci. 3" (for medicine). If successful, he is already slotted for one or possibly two Faculties at Hongō before he even starts his studies at Komaba. Final Faculty assignment depends on his performance at the College of General Education. It is theoretically possible for the student to switch his area up to the middle of his second year, but barring an outstanding scholastic record, it is extremely difficult to shift targets, particularly from a less prestigious or popular Faculty to a more popular one or, for that matter, to get out of a slot for a prestigious Faculty (such as law) into one for a highly popular department of a less prestigious Faculty (such as sociology or psychology in the Literature Faculty). While at Komaba, the underclassman has no access to the regular departments or "star" professors at Hongō, while the upperclassman at Hongo has little practical leeway in his heavily specialized Faculty major for courses nominally available in other Faculties. In the extremely intensive scientific fields, it is simply a matter of time; in the humanities, more a matter of inclination, specifically of group feeling. As one Todai scholar has put it, "A student would feel lonely taking courses outside his own Faculty, away from his closest friends." If the would-be degree-switcher cannot effect his switch during his sophomore year, he has no other choice than to drop out altogether and sit for a new entrance examination in his preferred area, or graduate in his originally assigned Faculty and then take a special examination (*gakushi nyūgaku*) for admission to another Faculty at the third-year level. There is no switching of Faculties (which grant the degrees) once the student is at Hongō.

One exception to this pattern is the highly limited, prestigious four-year course at Komaba. The College now retains over two hundred honors students through their third and fourth years, awarding the bachelor's degree in its two departments of liberal arts and basic sciences. Any student is eligible on the basis of his first- and second-year record. The production of graduates has given the College a taxonomical equality with the other Faculties, and the tiny minority of undergraduates who do remain for the flexible but well-integrated four-year course experience something roughly similar to an undergraduate education on an American campus. As a new and less prestigious Faculty, however, the College of General Education is more malleable to the wishes of the administration and suffers from a very weak voice in university decision-making.

The College at Komaba was established in response to the greatly felt need after World War II for an infusion of general education into Japan's university curriculum, and under the vision and strong leadership of President Yanaibara Tadao, Tokyo University went further than any of its sister institutions in implementing the general education concept. The Komaba "experiment" remains a distinctive feature of Todai, but what successes it has achieved have been bought at the price of sundering the undergraduate experience, both social and intellectual, at the midriff.

DECISION-MAKING: AUTONOMY VERSUS ADMINISTRATIVE EFFICIENCY

The inability of Todai to take practical measures for reform from within is simply the latest symptom of the increasing paralysis of the university's decision-making processes. These processes display in a more extreme form features often found in Japanese decision-making, such as the preponderant weight of lower strata, the existence of figurehead entities toward the top, the osmosis of consensus from the bottom upwards, the principle of unanimity rather than majority rule, and the long strung-out *shingikai hōshiki* (deliberative consultation method). When it comes to consensus and decisions, Todai is a bowl full of jelly.

This state of affairs derives primarily from a weak university administration caught between the autonomy of a powerful faculty, with their own chairs, and a powerful Ministry of Education, which controls the budget and to a significant degree runs the university. The potential leverage of the Japanese state through finances has evoked a strong defensive reaction under the banner of university and Faculty autonomy, and in recent years the requirements of university administrative efficiency have been sacrificed to this pressure for autonomy.

For the modernizing Meiji state of 1886, national administrative efficiency came first, under the tight control of the Ministry of Education and of its proconsul, the president. By 1918 Todai had achieved a large measure of autonomy from the state, with the president now representing the university to the ministry as *primus inter pares* of the academic staff. Before World War II the major points at issue concerned the relation of Todai to the world outside, and the president generally enjoyed strong and cohesive support in his efforts to guard the university's autonomy against the pretensions of an increasingly totalitarian state. Since the war, with a fresh measure of independence from the ministry, the focus of attention at Todai has shifted inward toward the internal adjustments required first by Occupation policy and more recently by the momentous changes in Japanese society. The system, which had worked reasonably well before the war, broke down as the effective locus of autonomy itself shifted from the university to its component parts.

Complicating the decision-making process, meanwhile, is the fact that it remains a clumsily joined composite of two very different systems, which neither singly nor together are equal to today's needs. One is the typically authoritarian pattern (largely Western in inspiration) of direct ministerial control, dating from 1886. There are important residual elements of this, particularly in the area of budget-making and in the operation of the university's administrative services. The other is the typically Japanese pattern, with the features we have mentioned, which governs the relations among the various component units of the university itself. The aspect of upward osmosis is especially evident in the selection of new chairs in the annual budget requests, while deliberative consultation and unanimity figured heavily in the recent discussions of the Reform Chamber (Kaikakushitsu). The Central Council for Education (Chūō Kyōiku Shingikai), finally, has made proposals that attempt to improve internal cohesion and administrative efficiency while securing the independence of the university from political control or intervention by the state.

The Historical Background

A high degree of Faculty autonomy over matters such as curriculum, staff appointments, and the selection of university officials has been a traditional feature of university systems operated by the state, as in Germany and other continental countries. With money and basic policy both controlled by the government, academic affairs represented the only area in which the community of scholars could exercise independence, and they have claimed it to the hilt. In this area, as a matter of fact, they enjoy more freedom from their own founding or administrative authorities than the teaching staffs of the private or locally operated universities of the American tradition—where boards of trustees, churches, regents, and governing corporations retain considerable power of intervention in matters of instruction and personnel.

Japan's opting in mid-Meiji for a state-run university system on the German-French model was perhaps inevitable given the limited resources of the central treasury, the need for strong national leadership, and the precedent of placing the nation's leading schools of Western learning under direct control of the Shogunate government in Edo. The trend among the Western democracies, however, has been to approximate the ideal already realized by Britain and many of the American state universities of "support without control," whereby funds from the treasury are turned over to an autonomous body such as the University Grants Committee in Britain, which includes university-related members, makes the allocations entirely as it sees fit, and is not even required to report to Parliament. Japan has been slow to follow this trend, and there has been a tenacious resistance to the idea—now, as right after the war, when the Occupation promoted it—of an independent body including nonacademic members standing between the government and the universities themselves. There is the underlying fear that, given the lack of a strong liberal tradition in Japan, such a body would rapidly become the handmaiden of the state and prove responsive to various political forces. And at Todai there is a more subtle reason for resistance: the reluctance to forfeit the patronage and prestige it enjoys as the capstone of the state educational system.

In 1886, decision-making worked downwards from the ministry through the president, a man who was chosen for his administrative talents (in 1886 it was Watanabe Kyōki, ex-governor of Tokyo; from 1905 to 1912 Hamao Arata, who had been a ministry bureaucrat since 1872). The man was dispatched from the Ministry of Education, not elected by Todai, and held a tight rein over the principals (in effect deans) of the several colleges. The principals, although professors, were also appointed by the minister and exercised real authority in their respective colleges. The arrangements in 1886 also provided for a senate (Hyōgikai)—composed of the principals and two professors (selected, again by the ministry) from each college, and presided over by the president—to be the highest deliberative council in the university.

Mori Arinori's system met with resistance and calls for greater independence from the very start—beginning with Katō Hiroyuki's refusal to continue his services as president—and in 1893 the seeds of autonomy were firmly planted. In that year, under Inoue Kowashi, the senate was given fresh powers which gradually enabled Todai to have its own way in curriculum and personnel matters, and which made the senate in effect the university's supreme decision-making as well as deliberative organ. The president was no longer required to report the senate's deliberations to the minister, nor permitted to convene the senate on the ministry's premises; and he was ordered to drop his ex officio function as principal of the Law College with its powerful ties to the government bureaucracy. The professorial representatives in the senate were now elected by their colleagues, and the senate was empowered to create and abolish departments within the several colleges; to recommend the fields of Inoue's new chair system; to make university regulations on its own initiative or present proposals to the ministry where special ministerial decrees were required; and to grant degrees.

The Faculty councils officially established in each of the colleges in 1893 also weakened the ministry's grip on the university. Regular membership was restricted to full professors, but assistant professors and lecturers (kōshi) could also attend at the discretion of the principal, who chaired the meeting. The Faculty councils were empowered to discuss curriculum, examinations, and degree requirements, and by 1914 had won primary say in the teaching appointments in their own colleges.

In 1907, the Imperial Universities Special Account Law (Teikoku daigaku tokubetsu kaikeihō) set aside certain amounts of money for the imperial universities each year and gave them full responsibility for making budgetary allocations from this source—which included income from capital investments, tuition fees, gifts, and treasury grants. The final step toward prewar autonomy was taken in 1915, when Kyoto Imperial University elected one of its own professors as president—strictly speaking, a nomination requiring the minister's approval. By 1920, the precedent had become the rule at the state universities, and the ministry has never vetoed a Todai nomination. Deans, too, were now similarly chosen by their own Faculties, with pro forma approval of the ministry.

After 1918, decision-making at Todai worked upwards from the former colleges—now the Faculties—to the president, who now represented the university to the ministry as the spokesman for his own peers. The effort to protect the autonomy of the campus in an era of rampant thought control was conducive to intramural cooperation and effective leadership from the president. The ministry, however, retained important powers of inspection and the specifically stated right of control (kantoku).

The Occupation reforms reduced the powers of the ministry without, however, supplying clear-cut procedures to govern the relations between the universities and the government or spell out the lines of authority and formalize relations between the divisions within a single university. The basic legislation needed to fill this gap has been shelved by the Diet ever since the early 1950s. The LDP, from the Ikeda administration onward, has tended to link its calls for tighter university control with attacks on the leftist bias of the professors; and the academic profession has responded by opposing almost any sort of effective management as the thin edge of a totalitarian revival. The complete paralysis of the normal decision-making procedure in the violent upheaval of 1968–1969 was met with the Temporary Universities Control Law of August 1969, which only postponed real reform. In the meantime, it has become virtually an article of faith that university autonomy from the government is best preserved by the autonomy of the individual Faculty—which is borne out neither by logic nor by the historical record.

Residual Powers of the Ministry

The Ministry of Education Establishment Law of 1949 confined the ministry's function to counseling, coordinating, and assisting universities. At Todai and the other state universities, the ministry retains the right to approve promotions of staff and the appointments of teachers, deans, and presidents, but in practice follows the university's own recommendations. It also has the right to determine staff qualifications, pay schedules, student fees, and the budget; to establish new Faculties, institutes, and chairs; to set standards for graduate training and degrees; to fix staff-student and graduate-undergraduate ratios and specify the budgetary allocation per student (thereby influencing the size of enrollments); and has the ultimate right to establish or abolish the institutions themselves.

The possibilities for direct intervention or policy control by the ministry since the war have been severely limited, although the new national universities established after the war bend more easily to the ministry's will than the proudly independent former imperial schools. The powers that are not nominal are passive and serve a limiting function. The only way, for instance, that the ministry could pressure Todai and other state schools to bring order to the campuses in 1969 was to have the Diet pass the Temporary Control Law, which threatened the universities with closure or, if that failed, dissolution.

The ministry, nevertheless, retains considerable leverage at Todai through negotiations over the budget and the running of the university's administrative office. The fact that money from the central treasury is released today directly through the Ministry of Education rather than through an independent body as in Britain, and the fact that officials from the ministry still run the university's administrative services, go a long way to explain the teaching staff's lingering fear of political control and its tenacious clinging to the doctrine of autonomy. The academic staff remains highly sensitive to anything reminiscent of the thought control of the 1930s, and views the ministry's effective control of money and other residual powers as the loosely hinged door to a Pandora's box of totalitarian repression. The government bureaucracy, for its part, remains reluctant to relinquish control over funds and policy to the institutions, which it considers not only administratively incompetent but also ideologically given to leftist, antigovernment postures.

The financing of Japan's national universities is a murky business for anyone unfamiliar with the chair structure, or untutored in the backstage negotiations during the budget-making process. It is one of the great ironies of the postwar reform that the Special Account Law was rescinded in 1947, depriving the national universities of their independent budget management and throwing them back on the annual approval of the Ministries of Education and Finance for their allocations.

Since salaries and research expenses are geared to the chair system, the only way a university can get more money for either new or existing fields is to petition the ministry in its annual budget request for the creation of new chairs. Each level, from the departments through the faculty councils and the university president, in consultation with the heads of the administrative office (*jimukyokuchō*) and its accounting bureau (*keiribuchō*), annually discusses and sets priorities for new chairs. When the Ministry of Education receives the university's priorities in the form of its annual budget request, it sets them in line with its own policy and submits the list to the Ministry of Finance (*Ōkurashō*).

This annual scramble for more chairs represents the only occasion for anything resembling the consideration of a university-wide policy on education and research. The processing of the individual chair application may take as long as five years, with the liveliest point of contention usually being whether the chair should be designated as experimental or nonexperimental—since the research expenses for the former are so much greater than for the latter. Once a label is applied at one school, it sticks for any similar chairs in the national university system.

Certain budgetary allocations are fixed. The chair structure determines the number of salaries, and the appropriate civil service grades set salary levels. The minor category of "integrated school expenses for students" (*gakusei atari sekisan kōhi*) is likewise not open to negotiation, since it is predetermined by the number of students.

Apart, therefore, from requests for major expansion of physical plant, most of the annual budget-bargaining concerns the actual disposition of research expenses, which nominally should go in full amount to the heads of chairs for their research and teaching needs. As a matter of fact, a certain proportion of the research expenses (I have heard estimates ranging from 5 to 10 percent) are siphoned off at each succeeding administrative level—ministry, university, Faculty, department—for plant maintenance and other administrative expenses, leaving the chair professor at the end of the line with considerably less than his original allocation. The portion withheld by the Ministry of Education from the MOF appropriation is a point of negotiation between the Ministry of Education and the universities, and provides the former with important leverage. The apparent reason for this practice is the inadequate provision for property expenses (*bukkenhi*) and administrative expenses (*jimukyoku keihi*) in the annual budgets. Property expenses, including maintenance and operation of the existing plant, are pegged to a table of expenditures that is uniform for all government bureaus—and that overlooks, for instance, the whopping electricity bills run up by some of Todai's experimental laboratories. Therefore, there is pilfering from research expenses as the money is passed down through the administrative channels to pay for lighting, heating, repairs, and the ordinary running of administrative offices. There is nothing the academic staff can do about it except bargain for the least injurious settlement. This places a high premium on choosing deans and presidents who can "get the budget" within the rigid and unresponsive financing system.

Since the administrative staff members are employed directly by the Ministry of Education and few of them are specialists in the administration of higher education, the teaching staff must assume much of the actual administrative work. The situation further confuses functions already badly scrambled by administrative office leverage—through budget-making—on academic programs and planning. The director of the administrative office is a powerful figure, who serves under the president but is responsible to the minister. He takes charge of business, financial, and to some extent student affairs, and he sits in Todai's two highest councils—the senate and the deans' conference. The administrative staffs at the Faculty and departmental levels also tend to side with the ministry against the university, and to be jealous of their own bureaucratic prerogatives.

The Intramural Decision-Making Process

What the academic staff at Todai has lost in budgetary powers, it has perhaps more than recouped by its firm grip on teaching and appointments. A typical American university would respond more rapidly and flexibly to reasonable budgetary requests from the teaching side, but there would also be a greater chance for the administration and faculty as a whole to impose a chosen and coordinated educational policy on the university's various subdivisions.

At Todai the downward flow of the ministry's budgetary powers and the upward filtering of educational and other campus policies are not only poorly meshed. The latter also tends to fall apart in a decision-making process where authority is fragmented and has gravitated steadily toward the bottom; where individual Faculties retain an effective veto over university-wide decisions; and where consensus within the Faculty itself is little more than an amorphous confluence of the wills of individual professors, or of small, tightly-knit, intra-Faculty groups. Although the relative importance of the departments, seminars, and chairs varies considerably from one Faculty to the next, the effective decision-making (or blocking) power tends to lie with one or the other of the sub-Faculty groups.

The chair has become the most basic unit of autonomy within Todai today. The senior chair professor, with his subordinates roped in by a web of personal obligations and unremovable himself, exercises the preponderant power in intra-Faculty deliberations. He is also eligible for the position of subdivision chief, which is either assigned on a seniority basis or rotated among the heads of the constituent chairs. If temperamentally so inclined, the department or seminar head can be a formidable figure in Faculty deliberations. Although not formally binding, decisions at the department or seminar level are generally respected when the formal decisions are taken by the Faculty council.

In Faculties where the departments are powerful, for example, all important questions are first hammered out in departmental meetings; and especially in the selection of teaching staff, other departments will never veto the choice of the department that has the vacancy. A retiring senior professor is consulted about his possible successor, but as a rule he is excluded from the Faculty committee that makes the final decision.

To be precise, the Faculty council is the faculty meeting in each Faculty—since there is no regular meeting of the entire professorial staff at Todai. Each Faculty has its own rules of procedure, but at Todai all Faculty councils include both senior and junior professors, and in most the lecturers as well. In addition to electing their own deans, the Faculty councils make the official nominations for staff positions, formulate the Faculty's budget request, and lay down rules affecting admission, gradua-tion and credits. In the larger Faculties, the councils operate of necessity on a subcommittee basis, but in the smaller Faculties, or where the issue is of unusual importance, individual professors are reluctant to delegate their personal powers, throwing the council into time-consuming plenary sessions without the benefit of subcommittee work or referral to purely administrative echelons. The need to discuss many (and often trivial) issues in great (and often personal) detail immobilizes Faculty-wide decisions, widens existing divisions by inflaming latent jealousies, and drives the sub-Faculty groups into a conspiratorial, secretive frame of mind through this constant threat of exposure. Decision-making, accordingly, starts off badly hobbled at the Faculty level. And even when the respective Faculties do reach an internal consensus, "Faculty autonomy" often blocks the way to university-wide decisions.

Nominally, it is the senate that formulates university policy and functions as the supreme decision-making organ. Todai's senate today consists of the president (as chairman), the deans and two professors elected from each of the ten Faculties, the directors of the research institutes, the chairmen of the ten divisional research committees of the graduate school, and the head of the administrative office. The preroga-tives of the senate look impressive on paper, and include the creation, amendment, and abolition of university regulations; approval of the budget; the establishment of Faculties, departments, and other facilities; the determination of personnel standards and student numbers; the setting of policy on student affairs; the coordination of Faculties and institutes; and the discussion of matters affecting the administration of the university as a whole. Decisions must be carried unanimously and any Faculty or institute can exercise an effective veto simply by absenting itself from the meeting.

The senate, however, is a purely ornamental assemblage that does little more than rubber-stamp decisions taken by the deans' conference, an informal conclave with no basis in formal laws or regulations which exercises the only effective campus-wide authority at Todai. Since the deans act strictly as the spokesmen for their own Faculties, however, any decisions of the deans' conference reflect no more than an adjustment of individual Faculty positions, which leaves the ten Faculty councils as the most powerful voices in Todai's decision-making process. Here, as within each individual Faculty council, the lack of clear-cut statutory location of responsibility (as with a company president or a ministerial chief in the bureaucracy, whatever the informal consultation procedures of the business or government sectors) leaves decision-making at Todai at the mercy of unadulterated, consensus-style democracy: anybody can veto, nobody can decide.

The deans' conference (which dates from 1918) meets once every week and includes the president, the ten Faculty deans, and frequently the administrative chief, who does not, however, join as a full-fledged member. The deans' conference functions as an advisory body to the president and as his channel of liaison with the Faculties, but in fact discusses and holds a veto over all major administrative decisions. The president cannot move without the support of his deans, yet the deans must constantly refer matters back to the Faculties that elected them to represent their interests. The inability of the university to go against a single Faculty in the larger interest was dramatically exposed when former President Ōkōchi Kazuo in March 1968, respecting the autonomy of the Medical Faculty, passed on to the Senate for approval without emendation that Faculty's prescription for punishing some of its own students in the fast-spreading dispute over a new internship system. Ōkōchi himself considered the formula unfair and unwise, and inasmuch as the controversy had kindled violent student passions all over the campus it was clearly no longer a simple, one-Faculty affair. When the Senate backed up the Medical School, student militancy burst out in all the other Faculties. A solution was finally reached for ending the confrontation with most of the students, but this was achieved through the strong initiatives of the new president, Katō Ichirō, backed up against his deans and other faculty opposition by the new President's Office (Sōchōshitsu) set up in 1969.

The President's Office is a genuinely advisory staff of capable and trusted lieutenants, who help prepare policy options. It was able to move most effectively during the extreme crisis mood of 1969, and it has been able to speed up decisions in areas that do not pit it directly against important Faculty interests—such as a highly adroit mediation of an intramural dispute at the Microbiology Institute. But its creation has been resented by the traditional seats of power, and it cannot go against real opposition from the Faculties. Moreover, it operates mainly in areas that the deans' conference has left to others.

Under the present system the most important factor in moving matters toward a decision is the personal effectiveness of the president in dealing with his deans, and, to a lesser degree, of the deans in dealing with their professors. Any professor may be elected dean, and the deans—who serve only two years as a rule—are almost always glad to be rid of a chore that deprives them of nearly all time for their own study and research.

By contrast, until 1972 the president was elected for four years and if reelected served another two years. Today he is restricted to one four-year term. Chosen by his own peers, the president of Todai needs special talents and qualifications in order to succeed as a prophet in his own country. Traditionally these have included an outstanding reputation as a scholar; the ability to move with ease among and command the respect of Japan's bureaucratic, political, and social elite; and of course, managerial and negotiating skills for dealing with the ministry as well as his own teaching staff. In the past the presidents of Todai have been men of national stature and fairly advanced in years. According to some sources, President Katō was handicapped by his youth (he was the first president ever to be referred to in the familiar mode, as "Katō-kun"), while his predecessor, Ōkōchi, reportedly suffered from being insufficiently well known.

Todai has its own unique and traditional formula for electing presidents. It is the only occasion where the teaching staff participate in a university-wide, majority-type decision free of the usual Faculty barriers. All senior and junior professors participate in the vote, and lecturers may possibly be admitted in the near future. As the first step, seven delegates from each Faculty, and three from each institute, meet to put up names for nomination. The names are submitted anonymously on slips of paper and are written on an enormous horizontal banner. Any Japanese citizen is eligible—but the first round invariably produces a few tongue-in-cheek nominations which have included Eisenhower, Stalin, and the popular singer Miss Misora Hibari. The delegates then vote on the list and report the top five without tallies. Finally, the entire professorial body votes but is not restricted to this slate of five. Since no candidate has ever secured a majority on the first vote, there is inevitably a run-off between the top two.

One final element in the university's decision-making process are the commissions (*iinkai*), which have been established from time to time both before and after the war to deal with problems of unusual magnitude, such as university reform. They operate under the president in a purely advisory capacity, however, and cannot execute their recommendations without the approval of the senate, which in the end means the approval of the individual Faculties. Their procedure often follows the deliberative consultation method, where great numbers of people explore and discuss a problem in great detail only to create proposals which are less decisions, really, than a summary of the elements that went into the final, vaguely worded consensus.

Good examples of the commissions in operation were provided by the faculty study groups for university reform set up in response to the violent campus disturbances of 1968–1970. The Preparatory Investigation Commission for Reform (Kaikaku Junbi Chōsakai), established in January 1969 while police battled radical students for control of the Hongō campus, produced a flurry of literature and proposals in record time in response to the crisis of the moment. As the sense of crisis waned, however, so did the interest in reform and the capacity to develop strong, broadly supported proposals. The Reform Commission (Kaikaku Iinkai), established in April 1970 to work out reforms in staff discipline, presidential elections, university structure, and student participation, originally suggested, for instance, a drastic reduction in the number of Faculties. The Reform Chamber set up in May 1971 to develop the recommendations of the Reform Commission, however, changed its mind by October 1972. Having obviously met determined opposition from vested Faculty interests, the chamber concluded that a few mammoth Faculties were perhaps not such a good idea; that mammoth-, medium-, and mini-sized Faculties all had their merits and could be considered, but that it probably was best to work on a medium-sized model—all of which left no one badly bruised but brought the whole matter right back to square one. By 1973, with the crisis mood gone, talk of reform at Todai ground to a virtual halt. In the words of one Todai professor, "No fundamental changes can be expected short of another violent campus dispute, which we may get in another five years' time, but even then there probably will be many reports, but no serious action."

THE FUTURE OF TODAI

"The university will carry on as is, gradually disintegrating as good researchers abandon it for business and government institutes," says another Todai professor. "Eventually it will simply collapse—in about thirty years' time." There is an emphatic consensus that the government's sweeping proposals will fail at Todai.

Unlikely scenarios for Todai's future are contained in the recommendations of the university's own Reform Chamber—what Todai would do if it were able to move itself; and in the section on higher education in the final report (June 11, 1971) of the Central Council for Education—what would happen to Todai if a massive nationwide educational reform ever did get underway. These recommendations are summarized here, not as predictions for the future, but as present perceptions of the problems at hand.

With regard to the three basic structural problems of the Faculty-chair system, general education, and research, the consensus was reflected as follows in the May 1971 and October 1972 issues of Todai's reform newsletter, *Kaikaku fōramu*:

1. There is a strong preference for making the department (with a staff of approximately twenty to forty) the fundamental unit of teaching and administration. The later report hedged earlier recommendations for abolishing the chairs, but there is agreement that the Faculties should be reduced in number and serve primarily to facilitate liaison between related departmental fields.

2. There is unanimous agreement that the horizontal rift between Komaba and Hongō should be eliminated; general education should not be abolished, but it must be integrated with the specialized courses by transferring responsibility for it to the several Faculties.

3. There are suggestions for subdividing the research institutes along quasi-departmental lines for closer articulation with the graduate school, and a pronounced aversion to seeing research facilities slip out from under university control.

The most difficult deliberations on reform have been those concerning structural renovation. Above all, no one at Hongō wishes to move to

Komaba, which will have to receive some of the restructured units if the General Education College is abolished and its courses are integrated vertically into the Faculty structure. The Reform Chamber has postponed a decision on the ostensible grounds that it cannot decide between a new highrise campus at Hongō, retaining the two old campuses, or rebuilding Todai from scratch in the country; but by 1973 the deliberations actually were stalled over the question of how to rescramble the various academic divisions.

The proposals of the Central Council for Education for the restructuring of Japan's higher education are far more drastic. The basic suggestion—to create five new types of mutually independent institutions, sharply differentiated in function—would largely do away with Todai as we know it today. In addition to junior colleges and technical colleges much on the present pattern, there would be new universities offering three parallel three-year programs (nonspecialized, academically specialized, and professional-occupational). New graduate schools would offer a two-to-three year master's-level program as well as mid-career training for the public in general. Research centers would provide training in advanced research and guidance for the doctoral degree.

The Central Council further proposes a rigid separation of teaching and research facilities and of their organizational structures in the interest of greater functional efficiency. One presumed benefit would be better teaching at both graduate and undergraduate levels. It emphasizes, however, that individual scholars should be allowed to engage in both teaching and research activities, and that there should be free movement of students, faculty members, and administrators (and where feasible, coordinated management) both vertically between different levels in close physical proximity and horizontally with other institutions of the same type. The formal distinction between general and specialized education would be abolished and the university would offer maximum flexibility in structuring multidepartmental programs to fit the individual student's need. The plan for new universities, which passed the Diet in September 1973, is aimed at correcting many of the problems cited here. Beginning with the new Tsukuba University, other national universities are to have more powerful central administrations, less rigid faculty procedures, and more flexibility in creating and disbanding research teams.

The new graduate school would aim to make advanced academic training attractive once again to the general public and to bring young scholars into greater contact with the nonacademic world. The research centers, finally, would have teaching staffs of their own, either independently or in affiliation with a graduate school, one of the existing on-campus research institutes, or even appropriate facilities in the business or government sector. Doctoral and advanced research would at last receive the guidance and funding it deserves, and the maximum interflow of personnel and ideas between the research centers and other institutes would be encouraged without regard to the individual researcher's formal academic qualifications.

Structural reform would not of itself, of course, bring about any improvement in the decision-making process. Improved decision-making would require fundamental and clear-cut redefinitions of the lines of responsibility and authority, both between the Ministry of Education and the national universities, and within Todai itself. The new framework would have to provide concrete assurances of academic freedom while managing somehow to keep the normal Japanese propensities for factionalism within practical working bounds.

Todai's several reform study groups have not dealt with these fundamental questions of ministerial and intramural authority. The Central Council for Education, on the other hand, has presented two alternative plans for more effective administration free of both ministerial dictation and the trammels of a hypertrophic Faculty autonomy. One is to free the national universities entirely from the Ministry of Education by transforming them into public corporations, depending on the government only for a regular supply of funds—the British model, in short, but with a vague rider to the effect that the government would retain the right to decide whether each university corporation was "worthy of being granted public funds." The second choice would be to remain an agency of the government, with a new administrative organ within each university, which would include persons from outside the university community and would be given a greater range of authority over campus administration than is now the case, but would not carry the principle of autonomy from the government "beyond what it originally means."

Todai faculty are not happy with either proposal. Much depends on one's reading of the government's actual intentions. Many Todai professors fear that the government is not prepared to grant genuine financial autonomy on the British model and is, in fact, determined to maintain ultimate political control under one guise or another. There are also fears that, given the historical weakness of Japan's private sector in the face of government pressures, any laymen appointed to the governing board from outside the university would bend easily to bureaucratic and party-political pressures. Of course, what immediately skews any comparison with the British system is the extent to which the Japanese universities themselves have been politicized, and the depth of the ideological confrontation that divides government and academe in Japan. Of the two proposed alternatives, Todai probably would prefer the latter, inasmuch as it preserves a comfortable old dependency along with the strong likelihood that, whatever the new administrative devices, they will eventually succumb to the irresistible tug of autonomy.

Decision-making at Todai breaks down, in summary, at several levels and for several reasons. Basic is the pitting of the university's traditional claims to autonomy against the financial prerogatives (and fear of political intervention) of the central government—a struggle played out against the extremely fuzzy postwar backdrop of minimal statutory guidance. The confrontation over prerogatives and ideology is carried onto the campus itself, where a jealous teaching staff hesitates to delegate business to the ministry's local administrative staff, who often are poorly trained in academic affairs. The lack also of legislation establishing a clear-cut chain of command within the university itself has left decision-making at this complex modern-day institution to find its natural level—which turns out to be something oddly reminiscent of the quasi-egalitarian consensus politics of the traditional Japanese village. We have traced the independence of the individual Faculties to various historical and structural circumstances. The heavy weight of even the lower echelons would seem to be the result, in part, of (1) the effective control of teaching appointments at very low, sub-Faculty levels; (2) the overload of nondelegated business that hamstrings the Faculty councils; and (3) the Japanese social and psychological structure. The chairs, seminars, and departments at Todai are examples of primary, face-to-face social groupings that have never been galvanized to common effort by the profit motives of Japanese industry, or by the effective regulatory framework or national-interest achievement orientation of the Japanese bureaucracy, and have been left by special historical circumstance to cultivate their lush sectionalistic egos in the hothouse of "university autonomy."

Despite all the organizational problems, where good teachers and students are gathered together good learning tends to override material or political obstacles. Organizational efficiency per se is no guarantee of good education. Todai continues to possess the best faculty and the most talented and highly motivated students in Japan. Public complaints about faculty diversions in writing and commenting on public affairs, and about the students' lack of interest in attending classes, apply far more to other, especially the private, universities than they do to Todai, where attendance rates remain relatively high, and where the faculty speaks and writes for the public less for the money than to enhance prestige, or because of a sense of cultural or political mission.

Todai's controversial role at the apex of Japan's academic and social pecking order is a problem that transcends mere organizational dysfunction. Pride and a sense of history do, of course, embolden Todai professors in their claims to autonomy. But some proponents of university reform seem to forget that it will take not only the universities alone but the efforts also of government, industry, and society at large to make any real dent in the hierarchical social patterns that have favored Todai—such basic changes start with the pattern for hiring university graduates.

During the late 1960s, Todai as a symbol of Japan's elitist establishment became the lightning rod for a bewildering complex of political, academic, and personal grievances among the younger generation, and it was only natural that student protest should have turned its fury against an institution that was familiar, highly symbolic, and eminently vulnerable. The pressures of the campus upheaval would have placed the most efficient university administration under considerable strain, and at Todai, they penetrated like an x-ray to bring all of the organizational weaknesses into glaring relief.

Bibliography

Interviews: I should like to express my deep gratitude to the several members of the Tokyo University staff, both past and present, who generously provided the confidential discussions and interviews on which this paper has for the most part been based. The following works also proved useful in illuminating the historical background:

Burn, Barbara B. *Higher Education in Nine Countries* (New York: McGraw-Hill, 1971).

Journal of Social and Political Ideas in Japan, 1.2 (August 1963): part 4 (University reform), articles by Okada Yuzuru, Sagara Iichi, Kimura Takeyasu, Munakata Seiya, and Nagai Michio.

Kaigo Tokiomi and Terasaki Masao. *Daigaku kyōiku* [University education], vol. 9 of *Sengo Nihon no kyōiku kaikaku* [Educational reform in postwar Japan] (Tokyo: Daigaku shuppankai, 1969).

Ministry of Education, Japan. *Basic Guidelines for the Reform of Education* (Report of the Central Council for Education), 1972.

Monbushō. *Gakusei gojūnenshi* [Fifty-year history of the educational system], 1923.

———. *Daigaku shiryō* [Data on the universities], no. 39, September 1971.

Nagai Michio, tr. Jerry Dusenberry. *Higher Education in Japan* (Tokyo: University of Tokyo Press, 1971).

Nakajima Tarō. *Kindai Nihon kyōiku seidoshi* [History of the educational system in modern Japan]. Tokyo: Iwasaki Shoten, 1966), chaps. 1, 8, 11, 23, and 33.

Nakamura Takafusa and Kumon Shunpei. "Daigaku no kanri" [University administration], in Etō Shinkichi, Uchida Tadao, et al., *Atarashii daigakuzō o motomete* [In search of a new concept of the university] (Tokyo: Nihon Hyōronsha, 1969).

Tōkyō Daigaku. "Tōkyō daigaku no kaikaku no tame" [For the reform of Tokyo University], April 1972.

———. "Tōkyō daigaku no gaiyō" [General prospectus of Tokyo University], 1972.

———. *Kaikaku fōramu* [Reform forum] nos. 1–26 (December 1969–October 1972).

Participants
Conference on Japanese Organization and Decision-Making
Hawaii, January 1973

JAPANESE PARTICIPANTS

Professor Yoshinori Ide
Institute of Social Sciences
Tokyo University

Professor Nagamasa Ito
Department of Economics
Sophia University

Mr. Nobuo Kanayama
Japan Research Institute

Professor Hideichiro Nakamura
Department of Economics
Senshu University

Professor Kazuo Noda
Rikkyo University
Director, Japan Research Institute

Mr. Yoshihisa Ojimi
Former Administrative Vice-Minister
Ministry of International Trade and Industry

Professor Taishiro Shirai
Faculty of Business Administration, Hosei University
Member, Central Labor Relations Commission

Mr. Yukio Suzuki
Nihon Keizai Shinbun Sha

Professor Kenichi Tominaga
Department of Sociology
Tokyo University

Professor Joji Watanuki
Faculty of Foreign Languages
Sophia University

AMERICAN PARTICIPANTS

Professor John C. Campbell
Department of Political Science
University of Michigan

Professor Albert M. Craig
Department of History, Harvard University
Assoc. Director, Japan Institute Harvard University

Professor Gerald Curtis
Department of Political Science, Columbia University
Director, Columbia East Asian Institute

Professor George De Vos
Department of Anthropology
University of California at Berkeley

Professor Peter Drucker
Claremont Graduate School, California
Graduate Business School, New York University

Mr. Rick Dyck
Department of Sociology
Harvard University

Dr. Ivan P. Hall
Harvard-Yenching Institute
Tokyo

Professor Solomon B. Levine
Chairman, East Asian Studies Program
University of Wisconsin at Madison

Professor Herbert Passin
Chairman, Department of Sociology, Columbia University
Columbia East Asian Institute

Professor Hugh Patrick
Department of Economics, Yale University
Chairman, Yale Council on East Asian Studies

Professor Edwin O. Reischauer
Department of Government
Harvard University

Professor Thomas Rohlen
Department of Anthropology, Cowell College
University of California, Santa Cruz

Professor Bernard Silberman
Department of History
Duke University

Professor Nathaniel B. Thayer
Director, Asian Studies, School of Advanced International
Studies, Johns Hopkins University

Professor Ezra F. Vogel
Department of Sociology, Harvard University
Director, Harvard East Asian Research Center

Professor Robert Ward
Chairman, Commission on International Studies
Director, Center for Research on International Studies
Stanford University

Professor M. Y. Yoshino
Graduate School of Business Administration
Harvard University

Index